Art of Java
Web Development

STRUTS, TAPESTRY, COMMONS, VELOCITY, JUNIT,
AXIS, COCOON, INTERNETBEANS, WEBWORK

NEAL FORD

MANNING

Greenwich
(74° w. long.)

For online information and ordering of this and other Manning books, go to
www.manning.com. The publisher offers discounts on this book when ordered in
quantity. For more information, please contact:

> Special Sales Department
> Manning Publications Co.
> 209 Bruce Park Avenue   Fax: (203) 661-9018
> Greenwich, CT 06830   email: orders@manning.com

Manning Publications Co.   Copyeditor: Liz Welch
209 Bruce Park Avenue   Typesetter: Dottie Marsico
Greenwich, CT 06830   Cover designer: Leslie Haimes

ISBN: 1-932394-06-0
Printed in the United States of America
1 2 3 4 5 6 7 8 9 10 – VHG – 08 07 06 05 04 03

To Chuck,
who still teaches me stuff daily

brief contents

contents

preface

In ancient China (approximately 500 B.C.), Sun Tzu wrote *The Art of War*. In it, he described the state of the art in warfare. The book took a universal approach, describing wide-ranging topics that related to one another only through how they applied to warfare. In 1961, Julia Child published the classic *Mastering the Art of French Cooking*. In her book, she described the essentials of mastering French cooking. Her book covered an extensive array of topics, including both kitchen techniques and recipes.

Both of these influential books offered a comprehensive look at the current thinking in their fields. Each covered a variety of topics, discussing specific techniques and underlying theories. They included concrete, practical advice, and they talked about the tools available to make the job of warfare (or cooking) easier. *Art of Java Web Development* strives for the same breadth and depth of coverage for web development in Java. It is not a random selection of topics. Rather, it encompasses topics that web developers must master to deliver state-of-the-art software. It also examines the evolution of the cutting edge in web development architecture and design, describes the best tools (or weapons) available to developers, and explains specific, practical techniques for improving your web applications.

Most development books today fall into one of two categories: API or best practices. The API books focus on a single API, either from J2EE and Java or, for example, an open-source project. A perfect example is Manning's excellent *Struts in Action*, by Ted Husted et al. It takes you through everything you need to know about how to use Struts. The best (or worst) practices books focus on individual topics, examining design patterns and coding samples that represent the best (or worst) ways to perform a certain task. *Art of Java Web Development* overlaps some of the topics from these other types of books, but it does so in a synergistic manner, discussing how all these pieces (and others) combine to create real-world web applications.

acknowledgments

Writing any book is a daunting task, and the nature of this book made it even more so. This means that my supporting structure (i.e., my family and friends) suffered with and supported me even more than usual. For that, they have my undying gratitude. First, to all my immediate and extended family, thanks for all your support, especially my mother, Hazel, who bears the most responsibility for who I am today. Also, thanks to my dad, Geary, along with Sherrie, Elisha, and the whole menagerie for their support. I would also like to thank Lloyd, Michelle, John, Madison, and Max (a force of nature) for all their fun and companionship, along with Mechelle, Mark, Wyatt, and Wade. The whole Shephard clan deserves a nod, because they care a lot more about me learning to cook the secret family recipe for Death by Candied Yams than what I put to paper.

I would also like to thank my surrogate family here in Atlanta, as fine a bunch of people as you will ever meet: Margie, Wright, Melissa, Julie, Walker, Jim, Randy, and Karen. They have taken Candy and me into their family and made us feel like one of them.

There are several instructors whom I feel I should acknowledge as well. Being an instructor myself, I have insight into what it takes to do it right, and these people showed me all I know about it. I would like to thank K. N. King at Georgia State for excellence in computer science, Robert Goetzman for teaching me to appreciate literature at a finer level, and James Head for being the finest instructor whose classes I've had the pleasure to attend. Dr. Head and the others are shining examples of how quality instructors make fundamental changes to people's lives every day.

The entire crew at DSW deserves thanks and acknowledgment. I cannot imagine working with a finer group of people, who keep me technically sharp and firmly planted: Allan, Brooks, David, Emerson, Jamie, Mike, Noah, Shanna, Steve, and Tim. As long as I'm acknowledging technical folks, the most insane person I know, Glenn (but he's from Australia, so that's OK), belongs here, along with my good friends from Vancouver, Michael and Maggie. From the other side of the world, Masoud, Frank, and Stepan in Frankfurt are also friends whom I see too little and too briefly. Among technically inclined friends, I should include a thanks and acknowledgment to Chris (and his Evil Twin, Dallas), who is currently lost in Louisiana. I should also thank Steve Mikel, whom I admire because he shows that it is possible to have an interesting and diverse life.

I would also like to thank everyone at Manning, the best publisher I've ever encountered. Everyone there from the publisher down embodies what a book company should be. A special thanks goes out to my technical editor, Luigi Viggiano, for keeping me honest, along with the rest of the Manning cast, including (but not limited to) Marjan Bace, Liz Welch, Mary Piergies, Susan Capparelle, Ann Navarro, and Dottie Marsico. I would also like to thank all the technical reviewers who spent a great deal of time to make this book better: Jason Carreira, Erik Hatcher, Shahram Khorsand, Howard Lewis Ship, Steve Loughran, Ted Neward, Eitan Suez, and Luigi Viggiano. I appreciate their insights, comments, criticisms, and feedback.

It is virtually impossible to exist in this field if you don't have activities that fall completely outside the technical realm. For that I have other circles of friends, who are vaguely aware of what I do for a living, but frankly could care less. These include my neighbors, Jamie, Diane, Kitty, and Gail. Another large support group consists of all my triathlete buddies, who only know me as the slow guy behind them: Jon, Joan, Jane, and Robert all fall into that group of people who help keep me sane.

There aren't many people who span all the above groups (plus some other groups that I didn't even mention). In fact, there is really only one: Terry, who deserves special thanks for support and friendship, who is a good travel partner, geek, and Tri-geek. And thanks to Stacy for letting him do all that stuff.

Last but certainly not least is the person who both likes and dislikes this book the most. My beautiful and wonderful wife, Candy, whom I love more than anything, has spent far too long in the company of only Winston and Parker and deserves more of my time. Honey, this book is finally done, and I'm all yours again.

about the book

This book is for every Java web developer, regardless of his or her level of expertise. It is designed primarily for intermediate to advanced developers, who understand the specifics of the various web APIs in Java but haven't yet mastered the best way to apply them. It is perfect for developers who have heard terms like Model-View-Controller and Model 2, but weren't present for the series of events that led to the widespread adoption of these best practices. It is also perfect for designers and architects of web applications because it discusses the implications of architecture and design at every opportunity.

This book is also well suited to developers who have looked at (and possibly struggled with) one of the many web frameworks on the market. It is unique in its coverage of web frameworks, giving equal weight to six different frameworks and comparing them on equal ground. Whether you are planning to use a framework or you want to write your own, understanding the similarities and differences between the existing frameworks will save you a great deal of time. *Art of Java Web Development* also illustrates new possibilities for those who are using a framework but aren't happy with it.

In addition, this book is aimed at developers who must create applications in the real world. Many of the best practices books treat each tip as the sole focus of a chapter, with no discussion of integrating it into a real application. Real applications are messy, requiring lots of moving parts working together seamlessly. The best practices in this book are presented in the context of a working e-commerce application, with all the places that the real world intersects with the academia of the pattern discussed.

How this book is organized

Art of Java Web Development consists of three parts. It begins with coverage of the history of the architecture of web applications, highlighting the uses of the standard web API to create applications with increasingly sophisticated architectures. The discussion leads to the development of industry-accepted best practices for architecture. Instead of simply pronouncing one architecture as the best, *Art of Java Web Development* shows the history and evolution of each architecture.

The second part of the book provides a unique overview of the most popular web application frameworks. Trying to evaluate a framework is difficult because its documentation typically stresses its advantages but hides its deficiencies. This book builds the same application in six different frameworks, encouraging you to perform an "apples to apples" comparison. The last chapter of part 2 provides a candid evaluation of the pros and cons of each framework to assist you in making a decision or in evaluating a framework on your own.

The selection of the correct framework is only the beginning of the life cycle of an application. Part 3 examines best practices, including sophisticated user interface techniques, intelligent caching and resource management, performance tuning, debugging, testing, and web services.

Part 1

Chapter 1 serves as the jumping-off point for the book. It highlights all the topics to come in the subsequent chapters and explains my primary motivation for writing the book.

Chapter 2 begins our discussion of the evolution of web applications. The idea behind this chapter is to present an application built by a developer who is very good with Java and understands the web APIs but hasn't yet applied best practices and architecture. The first pass at the application uses only servlets (which was the only tool available when the web APIs first debuted). Then we build the same application using just JSP. In both cases, we highlight the strengths and weaknesses of the resulting applications.

Chapter 3 carries the evolution a step further with custom tags. It takes the JSP application built in the second chapter and improves it using custom JSP tags.

Chapter 4 represents the culmination of the evolution of architecture and design. Here, we rewrite our sample application as a Model 2 application. You'll also learn how to leverage design patterns to improve the Model 2 application.

Part 2

Part 2 covers six web frameworks. In *chapter 5*, you'll learn about Struts. We introduce this framework in chapter 1, but here we "deconstruct" it and describe all the important moving parts. *Chapter 6* examines Tapestry, another Model 2–based open-source framework. We show you how the Tapestry API completely encapsulates the web APIs in Java. *Chapter 7* takes a look at WebWork, another open-source Model 2 framework. It includes some innovative ideas for passing just-in-time information between the layers of Model 2.

Chapter 8 covers the only commercial framework in the book, InternetBeans Express, which is the framework included with Borland's JBuilder. It is a rapid application development environment that lets you create web applications in record time.

Chapter 9 examines Velocity, which can act as a replacement for JSP and other visual representation languages. Velocity is a popular open-source framework that is very cohesive and single-purpose. In *chapter 10*, you'll learn about Cocoon, an open-source publishing framework that also includes capabilities as a Model 2 web framework.

Chapter 11 offers an evaluation of all six frameworks. It lays out the criteria we used to judge them, and gives you the information you need to evaluate frameworks on your own.

Part 3

Part 3 looks at best practices and helpful techniques for building web applications in the real world. The topic coverage is very broad, but we focus on various techniques and tools for building web applications.

Chapter 12 discusses techniques for separating concerns between the tiers of the application. *Chapter 13* describes user interface techniques for managing the flow of information in web applications. It shows you how to build page-at-a-time displays and sortable columns without sacrificing clean Model 2 architecture. We also discuss building "undo" operations in web applications, using either transaction processing or the Memento design pattern. *Chapter 14* focuses on performance. You'll learn how to profile web applications to determine whether performance bottlenecks exist, using both SDK-supplied and commercial tools. Next, we look at performance pitfalls and common mistakes and offer solutions. Then we delve into object pooling and explain how to implement it using either Java references or Jakarta Commons pooling.

Chapter 15 complements the previous chapter by showing you how to conserve resources. We examine several sophisticated caching techniques using both the

Flyweight and Façade design patterns. In this chapter, we build caching into the sample eMotherEarth application.

Chapter 16 moves away from specific design techniques and focuses on debugging and logging. You'll learn how to debug web applications using nothing but the tools supplied with the SDK (i.e., the command-line debugger). We also show you how to use commercial and open-source debuggers, including JBuilder and NetBeans. The last part of the chapter examines the Java 1.4 SDK logging package and log4j, a popular open-source logging package.

In *chapter 17*, you'll learn about unit testing, an often-neglected part of application development, especially in web applications. We show you how to build tests for your web applications and discuss JUnit and JWebUnit, both very popular open-source testing frameworks.

Chapter 18 wraps up the best practices portion of the book by examining web services and explaining how to incorporate them into your existing web applications. Finally, *chapter 19* highlights some important topics that are simply beyond the scope of this book. The bibliography at the end of this book includes references to the books cited throughout the chapters.

Notes about the samples

Art of Java Web Development contains many samples, mostly based around two main web applications. The samples also embody some of my ideas about the structure of source code. The samples illustrate the techniques covered in the chapter, but the coding technique may look a little unusual if you aren't used to the style. However, once you see my rationale for writing code like this, you may well adopt it yourself.

The samples

Two primary samples appear throughout the chapters. The use of only two samples is intentional, but the reasons are different for each instance. The samples are designed to illustrate the topics in the chapters, including the architecture, design, and specific techniques.

The eMotherEarth.com sample

The architecture and technique samples revolve around the fictitious eMotherEarth e-commerce site. This site sells earth products, like dirt, leaves, mountains.... Fortunately, we don't have to worry about delivering the products; we're just presenting a catalog. The application is a simple four-page web application that allows logon, catalog display, checkout, and confirmation. Even though it's small, this site is sufficient for us to highlight navigation, techniques, and architecture.

We use the eMotherEarth application in the early chapters to illustrate the architecture of web applications and how it has evolved from servlets, to JSP and custom tags, to the currently accepted industry standards. In later chapters, we use the same sample application to illustrate various techniques for creating user interfaces, implementing caching, managing resources, and other advanced topics.

The schedule sample

The other primary sample in *Art of Java Web Development* is the schedule application. It is a simple two-page application that manages scheduling information, and it appears in all the framework chapters. One of the goals of our book is to show the various web frameworks in a manner that permits direct, head-to-head comparison of features. Evaluating the frameworks based on their samples and documentation doesn't allow you to perform this "apples to apples" comparison because there is no ANSI standard web application sample.

The framework chapters all build the same schedule application, each using the framework discussed in that chapter. Unless otherwise noted, all the samples use the same infrastructure for database access and representation of entities. The difference in each case is the framework itself. It is remarkable how different the versions of this sample end up, given the similarities of the basic architecture of most of the frameworks and the common elements used to build them. However, as you will see, the framework makes a tremendous difference in the implementation of a web application.

Sample setup

Art of Java Web Development is an intermediate to advanced book on web frameworks and best practices. As such, we do not cover the basics of setting up a development environment for the samples. You must handle that yourself. However, it is exhaustively covered in other books and on the Internet. Two infrastructure pieces are needed for the samples: a database server and a servlet engine. Each sample does include an Ant file to build the sample using the Ant build utility. Ant is available at ant.apache.org and is covered extensively in Manning's book *Java Development with Ant*, by Erik Hatcher and Steve Loughran.

The database

Virtually all the samples in this book connect to a database because most real-world applications also have to retrieve data from a database. We use the MySQL database (available at www.mysql.com) because it is open source (and therefore free for developer use) and because it is a great database server. However, you aren't forced to use it to run the samples. With each of the samples, we include a generic SQL setup script that builds the database for the application. The setup script is designed around MySQL but can be easily modified to work in any ANSI standard database server. To run the samples with MySQL, you must download it and set it up yourself. You'll find a hyperlink on the book's web site (www.manning.com/ford) that leads you to the MySQL site.

The servlet engine

The web applications in this book utilize standard Java web development code, so they all run in any Java 2 Enterprise Edition (J2EE)-compliant servlet engine. Unless otherwise noted, we generally use Tomcat for the samples because it is open source and is the reference implementation of the servlet API. Because the samples are J2EE compliant, they will run in any servlet engine.

The exceptions to the previous rule of thumb are applications that illustrate particular J2EE features not found in Tomcat. For example, chapter 12 features Enterprise JavaBeans and uses the JBoss application server instead of Tomcat. In any case, the samples all run in any servlet engine or application server that matches the standard J2EE architecture.

The frameworks

Part 2 of *Art of Java Web Development* covers various web development frameworks. These chapters include links where you can download the framework. We also include links to the frameworks on the book's web site (www.manning.com/ford). Because of the nature of open-source frameworks and the Internet in general, it is possible that the frameworks will have moved. For example, during the development of the book, the Tapestry framework moved from SourceForge to Jakarta. Don't be discouraged if you can't find the framework using the link provided in the chapter. Most of the frameworks featured in this book are well established, meaning that they shouldn't go away anytime soon. If you can't find a framework, either search using your favorite search engine or go to the book's resources web pages (www.dswgroup.com/art and www.nealford.com/art), which will have updated links.

The code structure

As you read the code in this book, you will notice some unusual characteristics about the structure of the code itself. For the structure of the code, I rely on a combination of the Template Method and Composed Method design patterns. The first is from the classic *Design Patterns: Elements of Reusable Object-oriented Software* by Gamma, Helm, Johnson, and Vlissides, (the "Gang of Four"), and the second appears in Kent Beck's *Smalltalk Best Practice Patterns*.

The Template Method design pattern mandates extremely small, cohesive methods so that common behavior may be pushed up higher in the class hierarchy. It encourages extremely granular, single-purpose methods that perform only one task. The Composed Method design pattern encourages the same structure with extremely cohesive methods, but also adds the characteristic of very readable method names.

The problem we attack with these patterns is the tendency for embedded comments (i.e., the comments inside the method definition) to "lie." They don't mean to lie—and they generally don't when first written. However, over time as the code changes, the comments fail to stay in sync. The solution to the less-than-truthful comments is to get rid of them. The method names themselves should indicate what the method does without the need for comments. Note that I'm not referring to method- and class-level comments (captured with JavaDoc). Those comments should remain in your code. The embedded comments should go.

To help enforce this coding style, we have a rule of thumb at our office that no method exceed 20 lines of code. If it is longer than that, it should be refactored into smaller, more cohesive (i.e., more composed) methods. Once you have this level of granularity, it is much easier to identify the methods that should move up in the class hierarchy (because they are generic) and apply the Template Method design pattern.

Using these coding techniques, the public methods of your class read like outlines of the intended actions of the method, which are in turn the private methods that perform the actual work. If the method names are clear enough, embedded comments (the ones that lie) aren't needed—the code "speaks" to you. For example, here is the doPost() method from one of the more complex samples:

```
public void doPost(HttpServletRequest request,
                   HttpServletResponse response) throws
     ServletException, IOException {

  HttpSession session = request.getSession(true);
  ensureThatUserIsInSession(request, session);
  ProductDb productDb = getProductBoundary(session);
  int start = getStartingPage(request);
  int recsPerPage = Integer.parseInt(
         getServletConfig().getInitParameter("recsPerPage"));
  int totalPagesToShow = calculateNumberOfPagesToShow(
         productDb.getProductList().size(), recsPerPage);
  String[] pageList = buildListOfPagesToShow(recsPerPage,
         totalPagesToShow);
  List outputList = productDb.getProductListSlice(
         start, recsPerPage);
  sortPagesForDisplay(request, productDb, outputList);
```

```
    bundleInformationForView(request, start, pageList,
                             outputList);
    forwardToView(request, response);
}
```

The intent of the `doPost()` method relies on the internal composed method names, each of which performs one atomic unit of work. If this method isn't working, it is a fault in one of the private methods, which are each small and thus easy to trace into.

All the code in our book uses this coding technique. I have used it for years, and I firmly believe that it leads to higher quality code. With the tools available in the Java world for refactoring, it is easier than ever to either create code like this or modify existing code to take advantage of this technique.

The other semi-controversial coding artifact seen in my code is the absence of unnecessary braces, particularly around decisions and loops. While this is a common defensive coding technique, I find that I don't like to code defensively. If you understand how the language works, defensive coding isn't necessary. However, I understand that many of my colleagues really like the extra braces. If you have trouble reading code that doesn't contain the extraneous braces, I recommend that you download the code and apply one of the source code beautifiers (like Jalopy, at sourceforge.net/projects/jalopy/) to "fix" the code.

Source code

All the code generated for *Art of Java Web Development* is available online, either at www.manning.com/ford or from my web site, www.nealford.com. My site has a page devoted specifically to this book at www.nealford.com/art. There is also a link to the samples on my company's site, www.dswgroup.com/art.

Typographic conventions

Italic typeface is used to introduce new terms.
`Courier` typeface is used to denote code samples as well as program elements.

Author Online

The purchase of *Art of Java Web Development* includes free access to a private web forum run by Manning Publications, where you can make comments about the book, ask technical questions, and receive help from the author and from other users. To access the forum and subscribe to it, point your web browser to www.manning.com/ford. This page provides information on how to get on the forum once you are registered, what kind of help is available, and the rules of conduct on the forum.

Manning's commitment to our readers is to provide a venue where a meaningful dialogue between individual readers and between readers and the author can take place. It is not a commitment to any specific amount of participation on the part of the author, whose contribution to the AO remains voluntary (and unpaid). We suggest you try asking the author some challenging questions lest his interest stray!

The Author Online forum and the archives of previous discussions will be accessible from the publisher's web site as long as the book is in print.

About the author

NEAL FORD is the chief technology officer at The DSW Group Ltd. in Atlanta, GA. He is an architect, designer, and developer of applications, instructional materials, magazine articles, and video presentations. Neal is also the author of *Developing with Delphi: Object-Oriented Techniques* (Prentice Hall PTR, 1996) and *JBuilder 3 Unleashed* (SAMS Publishing, 1999). His language proficiencies include Java, C#/.NET, Ruby, Object Pascal, C++, and C. Neal's primary consulting focus is the building of large-scale enterprise applications. He has taught on-site classes nationally and internationally to all phases of the military and many Fortune 500 companies. He is also an internationally acclaimed speaker, having spoken at numerous developers' conferences worldwide.

Neal is also an avid (but slow) Ironman triathlete, competing in several races a year of varying distance. He is also a voracious reader, loves to listen to very eclectic music, watch high-quality movies, travel to exotic locales, and eat at fine restaurants (sometimes enjoying combinations of the above). He has also been known to sit in front of a computer for vast amounts of time. When at home, Neal enjoys the company of his wife, Candy, and two cats, Winston and Parker.

about the cover illustration

The figure on the cover of *Art of Java Web Development* is a "Nukahiviens avec un Tatouage Tout Different," a resident of Nukahiva Island in the Marquesas in French Polynesia. Marquesans were known for their elaborate tatoos which, over a lifetime, would cover almost all of their bodies. Marquesan craftsmen also developed great skill in carving and decorating wood, stone and bone, and developed a rich repertory of surface designs and patterns, some of a type to be found throughout Polynesia, others distinctively Marquesan in origin and concept.

The illustration is taken from a French travel book, *Encyclopedie des Voyages* by J. G. St. Saveur, published in 1796. Travel for pleasure was a relatively new phenomenon at the time and travel guides such as this one were popular, introducing both the tourist as well as the armchair traveler to the inhabitants of other regions of France and abroad.

The diversity of the drawings in the *Encyclopedie des Voyages* speaks vividly of the uniqueness and individuality of the world's towns and provinces just 200 years ago. This was a time when the dress codes of two regions separated by a few dozen miles identified people uniquely as belonging to one or the other. The travel guide brings to life a sense of isolation and distance of that period and of every other historic period except our own hyperkinetic present.

Dress codes have changed since then and the diversity by region, so rich at the time, has faded away. It is now often hard to tell the inhabitant of one continent from another. Perhaps, trying to view it optimistically, we have traded a cultural and visual diversity for a more varied personal life. Or a more varied and interesting intellectual and technical life.

We at Manning celebrate the inventiveness, the initiative, and the fun of the computer business with book covers based on the rich diversity of regional life two centuries ago brought back to life by the pictures from this travel guide.

Part I

The evolution
of web architecture
and design

Look at the computer sitting in front of you, and you see the culmination of architecture and design going all the way back to Charles Babbage's steam-powered analytical engine. You can use a computer without knowing anything at all about the workings of the underlying mechanism. However, if you know *how* it evolved to the point where it is now, you have a much richer understanding of *why* it works the way it does. For the same reason, understanding how the design and architecture of web applications has evolved provides valuable insight into how and why the architecture is sound.

Part 1 covers the evolution of the architecture and design of state-of-the-art web applications. It does not discuss servlets, JSP, and custom tag development from an API standpoint because plenty of other texts are available that focus on those topics. Instead, we examine these APIs from a design and architecture perspective, describing how to build web applications that are scalable, maintainable, and robust. Chapter 1 provides an overview of the topics for the entire book. Chapter 2 covers the evolution of web development in Java; chapter 3 explores that evolution through custom JSP tags. Chapter 4 discusses the preferred design and architecture option, Model 2, along with some architectural options.

State-of-the-art web design

1

This chapter covers

- A brief history of Java web development
- The importance of design patterns
- An introduction to the Struts and Turbine frameworks
- A working definition of business rules

The World Wide Web is a perfect example of how a simple idea (pages linked via hypertext) can lead to extraordinary richness. Originally envisioned as a way to provide static pages (now affectionately known as "brochure-ware"), the medium quickly grew to embrace dynamic content. These original efforts were written in languages like C and Perl. As time and technology progressed, new application programming interfaces (APIs) sprang into existence, each building and improving on the preceding technologies. New APIs appear because developers discover limitations in existing languages and tools. Limitations in existing APIs led to the repurposing of Java for building dynamic web content, first as servlets, then as JavaServer Pages (JSP). The history leading from Perl, Common Gateway Interface (CGI), and C is well documented in just about every book on the servlet and JSP core APIs.

Developers coming from more traditional application development (for example, client/server applications) discover that building web applications is fundamentally different in many ways. Even if you are fluent in Java, the architecture and design of web applications doesn't necessarily come naturally. Just as the switch from console applications to event-driven applications required a major shift in thinking, the switch from event-driven applications to the stateless world of web development requires a paradigm shift as well. Even an understanding of the basic infrastructure of web applications won't immediately reveal the most effective architecture and design. Many decisions made early in the design and development process have unforeseen repercussions later in the process. Because of the oft-quoted and well-documented cost of architectural and design changes late in the application lifecycle, it behooves you to get it right from the outset.

This chapter provides an overview of the topics we cover in this book. First, we discuss the evolution of Java web development and the importance of design patterns. Next, we examine web application frameworks (which are the topic of part 2 of this book). Finally, we examine best practices (the focus of part 3), along with a hot-button issue that falls under that heading. The main goal of this book is to show you how to apply best software-engineering practices to the development of web applications in Java.

1.1 *A brief history of Java web development*

Java began life as a programming language designed for building traditional applications and applets. But as developers realized the benefits of Java, it quickly expanded into other realms of development, including distributed and web development.

When Java took its first baby steps into the world of distributed web applications, it was with *servlets*. The benefits of the servlet architecture have been covered extensively in other books, and we won't rehash them here. We are more interested in *why* servlets were being used.

In the beginning, developers used servlets to create dynamic web content. Managers quickly realized that the talents that make a good Java developer do not necessarily overlap with the talents needed to create an attractive user interface (UI) in HTML. (This isn't unique to Java developers—Perl, C, and other developers are similarly disadvantaged.) The person you wanted designing the UI for your web application tended to be more of a layout expert, usually with a penchant for Macintosh computers. So, to utilize the right people for the right jobs, managers had the art school folks crafting the UI while the Java developers worked on the functionality. At some point the UI gurus passed their carefully crafted HTML to the Java developers to incorporate into the dynamic content. This created a challenge for the Java developers: merging the HTML from the art majors into the servlets that generated dynamic content.

However, once this was done, the pain still wasn't over. Invariably, the president of the company would get a new online service disc in the mail over the weekend, stumble his way over to some web site he had never seen before, and come in on Monday morning with the mandate, "We're changing the look and feel of our company web site." The HTML coders had to implement the new Grand Vision. Meanwhile, the Java developers realized that their job had just gotten worse. Now, not only did they have to merge the HTML into the servlets, they also had to selectively replace the existing HTML without breaking anything. The verdict on servlets was *too much HTML mixed in with the Java code.*

Clever developers quickly cooked up their own template strategies. Special markers in the HTML were parsed and replaced as needed. In other words, the developers sprinkled special HTML comments into the UI, such as:

```
Customer Name: <!-- $customerName -->
```

As the page displayed, the servlet would search through the code, looking for these "magic markers" to replace with dynamic content. To render a page, the servlet was forced to parse and process the HTML before it was output to the browser. Each development team created its own tags, so no level of standardization existed for the syntax and use of these custom tags. Some companies created standard tags across development teams, but that was the extent of tag reusability.

Using templates is a big improvement because it separates dynamic content from the UI. However, the approach suffers from a scalability problem. Parsing HTML to render content is an expensive operation in terms of machine resources, including central processing unit (CPU) and input/output (I/O) subsystems. For very busy web sites with lots of concurrent users, the I/O burden of parsing alone could grind the servlet engine to a virtual standstill. Nonetheless, from a design standpoint, this was still better than mixing the HTML and Java together. In fact, several template designers developed clever workarounds to this problem that still exist. One such template system, Velocity, is discussed in chapter 9.

This situation led to the development of JavaServer Pages. JSPs validated the template concept and implemented a clever way around the expensive parsing operation. JSPs are parsed only once, converted to a servlet, and then executed. The template language for JSP consists of JavaBean components, scriptlets, and custom tags. Developers discovered that they could now mix the logic and content more gracefully. The idea was for the HTML developers to create the initial JSPs and then pass them to the Java developers to add the dynamic aspects. Unfortunately, this led to another serious problem. Because this process encouraged the mixing of UI and functional code, JSPs quickly degenerated into a maintenance nightmare. I have seen too many JSPs that mortified and depressed me because of this coupling. It is possible to create the worst possible type of coding horrors in JSP because it relies so much on "magic" symbols and encourages the unwholesome mixture of code and UI. The verdict on JSP is *too much Java in the HTML.*

Fortunately, a solution to this problem already exists. To get to the elegant answer to this issue, a diversion into design issues is called for.

1.2 The importance of design patterns

In the mid-twentieth century, an architect named Christopher Alexander noticed in his travels that architects tended to solve the same problems in more or less the same ways. This realization led him to the creation of a book of *design patterns* for architects. A design pattern "describes a problem which occurs over and over again in our environment, and then describes the core of the solution to that problem, in such a way that you can use this solution a million times over, without ever doing it the same way twice." Alexander was talking about architecture in the traditional sense, but in 1994 the book *Design Patterns: Elements of Reusable Object-Oriented Software*, by Erich Gamma, Richard Helm, Ralph Johnson, and John Vlissides (the "Gang of Four," or "GoF"), applied Alexander's ideas to software design. A pattern is a template that solves a particular problem that may appear in difference contexts. In the GoF book, a pattern has the following characteristics:

1   The *pattern name* is a succinct, easy-to-remember moniker for the pattern. The name is considered important because it becomes a part of the vocabulary of general design. It should be one or two words and describe the essence of the pattern.

2   The *problem* is a statement describing the difficulty and its context. This description includes all the details needed to understand the problem and the implications surrounding it, such as the class structure and a list of conditions where this problem arises.

3   The *solution* describes the software artifacts that solve this problem—design elements, class and object relationships, aggregations, and collaborations.

4   The *consequences* are the results and trade-offs of applying the pattern. A classic example of a trade-off is speed versus space. The pattern should list all known consequences to allow developers to make an informed decision as to whether they should use it.

The GoF book was influential in the software community, and numerous books have appeared to carry on the identification of more patterns. Design patterns are widely regarded as an evolutionary step beyond object-oriented programming (OOP) because they combine the atomic classes and objects defined by OOP into patterns that solve specific problems.

1.2.1 *The Model-View-Controller design pattern*

If you are familiar with design patterns, you have probably heard of the Model-View-Controller (MVC) pattern. MVC is the poster child for design patterns. In the GoF book, MVC appeared in the introductory chapters as the example pattern. MVC has its origins in Smalltalk, where it was used in the graphical user interface (GUI) for "traditional" (non-web) applications. It is a design pattern for separating data from its representation. The developers of Smalltalk realized that it is a Bad Thing to have the data and the view of a system coupled together too closely. Any change in either the data or the view requires changes to the other. MVC mitigates this problem by separating the parts of the system based on their function. Figure 1.1 shows a graphical view of the artifacts that make up MVC.

The *model* is responsible for the data and rules in the system. It coordinates business logic, database access, and all the other critical nonvisual parts of the system. In a spreadsheet, the model represents the numbers and formulas that

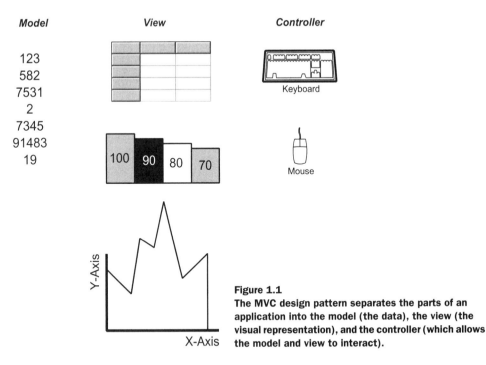

Figure 1.1
The MVC design pattern separates the parts of an application into the model (the data), the view (the visual representation), and the controller (which allows the model and view to interact).

make up the data. The *view* in MVC renders the display of the data. In the spreadsheet example, you can look at the numbers in a grid, a chart, or a graph. The numbers are the same; only the visual representation differs. The grid can become a chart (or vice versa) without you touching the underlying values of the numbers. The *controller* is the mechanism by which the view and the model communicate. In a spreadsheet, the controller can be the keyboard, the mouse, or some pen-based input device. In any case, the controller changes the value shown by the view and in turn changes the underlying model value. The controller acts as a conduit between the model and the view.

A good example of MVC in action is the Swing UI controls in Java. In Swing, each control (even components like JButton) has an underlying model that controls its content. This is why it is so easy to change the look and feel of a Java application—you are changing the view without touching the model. If you have written code for the more complex controls (like the JTable or JTree), you have ample experience in writing models. In Java, models are most frequently implemented as interfaces. You can think of the interface as a list of questions you must answer about the data being modeled. If you can answer the questions, the controller can take care of rendering the correct view.

MVC was created to handle the GUI portion of Smalltalk applications. The underlying idea is a good one. However, MVC as it is stated in the GoF book and elsewhere doesn't seem to mesh well with the web application world. It wasn't until recently that this pattern was extended to make it suitable for the distributed web world.

1.2.2 The emergence of Model 2

Let's return to the problems we mentioned earlier regarding the shortcomings of servlet-centric and JSP-centric application development. Managers and beleaguered developers both reached the same conclusion: There had to be a better way to build web applications. This dilemma is the same one that spawned MVC in the first place: the desire to separate business logic from the user interface. MVC was designed with traditional applications in mind; the UI portion has rich capabilities and is closely tied to the rest of the application. Web applications are different. The UI is rendered as HTML, which is then interpreted by the browser. This UI model is more "decoupled" than in traditional development environments like Smalltalk or desktop Java applications. In other words, the code that generates the content is not directly tied to the UI code. It must go through a translation layer to HTML, which is in turn rendered by a browser.

Designers looked at MVC and modified it to work within this new development paradigm. This work led to what is now popularly called "Model 2" (to distinguish it from the desktop-centric MVC). Model 2 doesn't change the definition of MVC; it just casts it in terms of web development. In Model 2 for Java web applications, JavaBeans represent the model. Notice that this may include simple JavaBeans, Enterprise JavaBeans (EJBs), or JavaBeans that act as proxies for EJBs. The view is rendered with JSP, which makes sense because JSP is closely tied to HTML. The controller is a servlet, well suited to executing Java code. This plays to the strengths of servlets, utilizing the services of the servlet container for lifecycle and invocation without forcing servlets to generate mixed Java code and HTML.

The typical Model 2 scenario is shown in figure 1.2. The user invokes a controller servlet (more about this design later). The servlet instantiates one or more JavaBeans that perform work. The servlet then adds the bean(s) to one of the JSP collections and forwards control to a JSP. The JSP extracts the JavaBeans and displays the results.

One of the key concepts in this design mandates that no real logic be performed by the JSP. The JSP is just the view and shouldn't be involved in any code that could be better implemented in the model. The model beans in this design should not be aware that they are being used in a web application. If you ever find

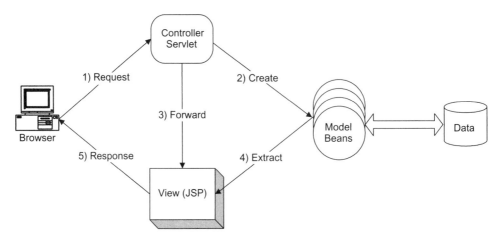

Figure 1.2 **The Model 2 design pattern separates the working parts of the application into specialized parts.**

yourself importing any of the web development packages (such as `javax.servlet.*`), you have erred. The model beans should be useful in non-web applications. Just as in traditional MVC, the controller servlet acts as a facilitator between the model and the view.

In contrast to more haphazard design, Model 2 features a clean separation of responsibilities between the parts of an application.

1.2.3 Evolution

Talking about design and partitioning of the UI from business rules is a necessary first step. However, it doesn't really hit home until you see for yourself both the problem and the solution. To that end, chapter 2 presents web applications written the "traditional" way, without the use of design patterns or other refined techniques. Our goal is to create a web application in the way a Java developer would—a developer who is familiar with how the web APIs work, but who hasn't been exposed to design patterns and other state-of-the-art design techniques. Chapter 3 expands on the samples written in chapter 2; it improves the design by showing you how to create custom JSP tags to clean up the JSP code. Chapter 4 takes the same applications and changes them into Model 2 applications. Our intent is to show the *evolution* of web development.

1.3 Using frameworks

Model 2 is a perfectly good design foundation for building web applications. As developers build applications and become more experienced, they start discovering common parts that can be used over and over. They quickly learn that many of these parts are generic and can be combined to form larger generic parts. For example, the controller servlets that are generated in Model 2 applications have many identical features. These generic parts can be built in such a way as to foster reusability. Design patterns facilitate building these types of reusable artifacts. Chapter 4 contains an example of using design patterns to create a reusable generic component of web applications.

Once you have a collection of prebuilt, generic parts, you have the beginnings of a *framework*. A framework is a set of related classes and other supporting elements that make application development easier by supplying prebuilt parts. Building application-specific parts from generic parts is an example of using a framework. In essence, frameworks provide infrastructure for application development. Similar to the foundation that exists when you construct a building, a framework provides the skeleton on which you can hang the specifics of the application.

Just as builders can choose among numerous kinds of frameworks when constructing a house, you can choose among many web application frameworks. Some offer specific, limited infrastructure, whereas others provide everything but the kitchen sink. Table 1.1 lists a few of the available frameworks. This list is far from exhaustive; dozens of frameworks are available.

Table 1.1   Web application frameworks

Framework	Download from	Description
Struts	http://jakarta.apache.org/struts	A lightweight, open–source framework primarily designed for building Model 2 applications.
Velocity	http://jakarta.apache.org/velocity	A Java-based template engine. Velocity permits anyone to use the simple yet powerful template language to reference objects defined in Java code.
Tapestry	http://jakarta.apache.org/tapestry	A framework that is positioned primarily as an alternative to JavaServer Pages. It replaces the scripting and code generation of JSPs with a full-fledged component object model.

continued on next page

Table 1.1 Web application frameworks *(continued)*

Framework	Download from	Description
WebWork	http://sourceforge.net/projects/opensymphony	A community project conducted using the open-source process, aimed at providing tools and a framework for building complex web sites in a short amount of time that are easy to understand and maintain.
Turbine	http://jakarta.apache.org/turbine	A large, open-source, services-based framework for building extensive web applications such as e-commerce sites.

Because so many are available, you can find a framework to fit virtually any project. Most are free or open source. The only expensive frameworks are those that incorporate some type of proprietary technology. For example, BEA sells a framework called Jolt for incorporating its Tuxedo messaging service with its application server.

Given the wealth of availability, which framework should you choose? Should you use one at all? The rate of turnover in the technology world frequently generates questions like this. Before choosing a framework, you should be careful to understand the distinction between a design pattern and a framework. Model 2 is a design pattern; Struts is a framework that utilizes the Model 2 design pattern. Turbine is also a framework that uses the Model 2 design pattern. Part 2 of this book discusses both these and other frameworks. In the construction world, the framework to create a doghouse is different from a skyscraper framework. Now matter how sexy a framework is, choosing the wrong one can impede your progress rather than enhancing it.

To give you an idea of how a framework fits together and how you might use it, the following sections provide an overview of the architecture and capabilities of two of the more popular frameworks: Struts and Turbine.

1.3.1 *A flavor of the Struts framework*

Struts is an open-source framework for building Model 2 web applications. It is part of the Jakarta project hosted by Apache. You can download Struts (including the documentation) at the Struts home page (http://jakarta.apache.org/struts). The primary areas of functionality in Struts are:

- A controller servlet that dispatches requests to appropriate action classes provided by the application developer

- JSP custom tag libraries and associated support in the controller servlet that assists developers in creating interactive form-based applications

- Utility classes that support XML parsing, automatic population of JavaBeans properties based on the Java reflection APIs, and internationalization of prompts and messages

The information flow of an application based on the Struts framework is shown in figure 1.3.

In Struts, the information flow is similar to that of plain Model 2 applications. All requests are dispatched through a single controller servlet that is part of the framework. This controller provides numerous application-wide services, such as database connection pooling and automatic request dispatching. The controller creates action classes, which are built by the developer to perform the work of the application. These action classes extend the Struts `Action` class. This is a perfect example of a reusable framework part—the controller is designed to create `Action` subclasses to perform work. This aspect of Struts is based on the Command design pattern, which allows for parameterizing activities. Chapter 4 examines the Command design pattern and describes how it is used in web applications (with or without Struts).

The action instances create model beans that perform domain-specific activities. Examples of these activities include executing business logic, connecting to

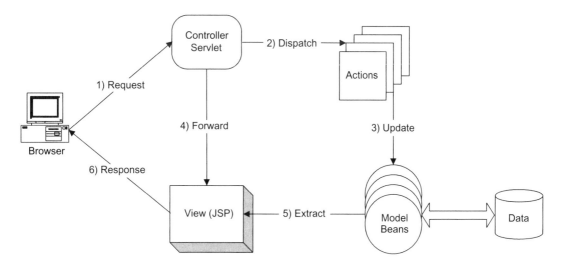

Figure 1.3 Struts provides a framework consisting of a generic controller servlet, classes (to encapsulate actions), and infrastructure (to pass information within the web application).

databases, and calling other bean methods. The model beans encapsulate the real work of the application, just as in Model 2. Once the action instance has utilized the model beans to perform work, it forwards the models that contribute to the display via the controller to a view component, generally a JSP (although other view options are possible; see the discussion on Velocity in chapter 9). The view extracts the model beans and presents the visual results to the user. As you can see, this is the same general information flow described in Model 2. Struts provides a great deal of the infrastructure to make it easy to accommodate this information flow.

Struts handles other details of application development as well. The framework includes numerous custom JSP tags to help you construct the view. It also provides classes that aid in internationalization, database connection pooling, and flexible resource mapping. Chapter 5 covers Struts in great detail and includes a sample application.

Struts is a fairly lightweight framework whose primary job is to facilitate building web applications using Model 2. I estimate that Struts saves from 35 to 40 percent of the typical amount of effort to build a Model 2 application. One of Struts' strengths is its cohesiveness—it doesn't supply services outside those needed for building Model 2 applications. Other frameworks are much more extensive; the Turbine framework is one of them.

1.3.2 *A flavor of the Turbine framework*

Turbine is a much broader web application framework than Struts. It is an open-source project available from the Jakarta web site hosted by Apache. (You can download the framework at http://jakarta.apache.org/turbine.) Turbine is a large, services-based framework. It is similar to the hardware bus on a computer, where you can plug in parts to provide capabilities. Figure 1.4 shows this concept. Turbine acts as a foundation for services covering a wide variety of capabilities. You can use as many or as few as you need to implement your application. The classes that define the services are registered with Turbine through a configuration properties file.

The Turbine framework consists of numerous classes (over 200) to handle a wide variety of pluggable services. A list of the base services provided by or supported by Turbine appears in table 1.2.

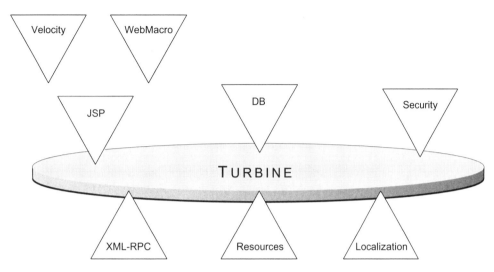

Figure 1.4 Turbine acts as a loose framework where services can be "plugged in" to build up the behavior of the web application.

Table 1.2 Turbine services

Service	Description	Use
Assembler Broker	The service that allows assemblers such as Screens, Actions, Layout, and Scheduled Jobs to be loaded.	Facilitates building Model 2 applications within Turbine.
Cache	Provides a persistent object storage mechanism within your application.	Allows you to cache object references (for example, serialized beans).
Castor	Provides support for the Castor object-relational database-mapping tool and Java-to-XML binding. Castor is a well-known open-source project that is supported by Turbine.	Used to model relational database tables and rows as objects and to model Java to XML. See www.castor.org.
DB	A common front end to all database systems, it handles database connectivity within Turbine. This service also provides the brokers for Connection Pooling and Database Map Objects.	Handles database management and interaction within the framework.
Factory	A service for the instantiation of objects with either the specified loaders or default class loaders.	Acts as an object factory to abstract the creation of objects.

continued on next page

Table 1.2   Turbine services *(continued)*

Service	Description	Use
FreeMarker	An alternative to JSP for rendering HTML output. This service processes FreeMarker files inside the Turbine Layout/Navigations and Screen structure.	Use FreeMarker instead of JSP or Velocity for the user interface part of your web application.
Intake	Provides input validation along with a standard parameter-naming framework.	Executes validation code for web applications (such as range checking, formatting, etc.).
JSP	A set of classes that process JSP files inside the Turbine Layout/Navigations and Screen structure.	Supports the use of JSP as the user interface for the web application.
Localization	A single point of access to all localization resources.	Used for building internationalized and localized applications.
Logging	The default Logging implementation for Turbine.	Allows custom logging for errors and application events.
Mime Type	Maintains the mappings between MIME types and corresponding filename extensions as well as between locales and character encoding.	Handles the valid document types for the web application as well as character set definitions.
Naming	Provides Java Naming and Directory Interface (JNDI) naming contexts.	Provides support for JNDI, which allows resources such as Enterprise JavaBeans to be referenced.
Pool	A service for the pooling of instantiated Objects, allowing for the recycling and disposal of Objects in the pool.	Provides support for generic object pooling. It provides the same kind of pooling mechanism that the Servlet engine uses for servlets but exposes it to the application developer.
Pull	Manages the creation of application tools that are available to all templates in a Turbine application.	Enables the developer to create tools (such as image processors) and makes them available to the web application via the standard attribute collections.
Resources	The set of classes and the functionality that allows for the reading and accessing of data from within properties files.	Supports accessing configuration information from properties files.
RunData	The service that manages the higher-level operations surrounding requests and responses.	Provides an infrastructure around the standard request and response mechanism of the Servlet engine.

continued on next page

Table 1.2 Turbine services *(continued)*

Service	Description	Use
Scheduler	Manages the schedule queue giving cron-like functionality.	Allows the application to configure and run scheduled tasks.
Security	A service for the management of Users, Groups, Roles, and Permissions in the system, allowing for those Objects to interact with either Database or LDAP back ends.	Handles authentication and authorization via this centralized service. This is similar to how most application servers handle security.
Servlet	Encapsulates the information provided by the ServletContext API and makes it available from anywhere in the code.	Provides infrastructure to make information from the Servlet engine available to the web application.
Template	A service for the mapping of templates to their screens and actions.	Supports user interfaces built from template languages (like Velocity).
Unique ID	Allows for the creation of Context unique and pseudo random identifiers.	Provides a generic mechanism for generating unique and random identifiers; useful for database keys or random number generation.
Upload	Manages multipart/form-data POST requests, storing them temporarily in memory or locally.	Provides the infrastructure to handle complex information passed to the web application from an HTML form tag, such as images or video.
Velocity	The service for the processing of Velocity templates from within the Turbine Layout/Navigations and Screen structure.	Used as the UI generator of the web application. Velocity is an open-source template engine for generating web output (i.e., HTML).
WebMacro	The service for the processing of Web-Macro templates from within Turbine Layout/Navigations and Screen structure.	Used as the UI generator. WebMacro is an open-source template engine for generating web output (i.e., HTML).
XML-RPC	Manages XML-RPC calls to a remote server.	Allows the application to handle remote procedure calls, such as Simple Object Access Protocol (SOAP) requests. This is an important component of service-oriented programming.
XSLT	Used to transform XML with an XSLT stylesheet.	Allows XML output of the web application that is transformed into suitable output (i.e., HTML) via Extensible Stylesheet Language Transformations (XSLT).

Many of the services listed in table 1.2 are not a part of Turbine per se. Rather, they are external APIs that are supported by the Turbine framework. For example, you can easily use Castor (which is an independent, open-source project) without using Turbine. Turbine is designed to be a loose framework with pluggable services.

Building Model 2 web applications with Turbine is only a small part of the overall framework. It is designed to offer one-stop shopping for just about any kind of service you might need when building

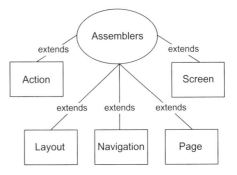

Figure 1.5 To produce Model 2 applications using Turbine, these Assembler types cooperate to encapsulate both business logic and visual layout.

a web application. As you can see in table 1.2, it covers a vast range of capabilities via its services. When building Model 2 applications with Turbine, several services interact to produce results. You can see the general relationship of these services in figure 1.5.

Assemblers in Turbine are classes that build (or *assemble*) things and are part of the Assembler Broker service. For example, the Screen assembler is responsible for building the body of a response page, whereas the Navigation assembler builds

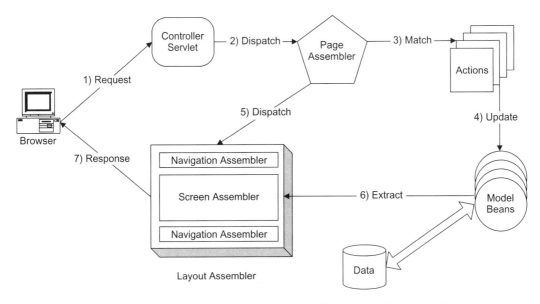

Figure 1.6 Turbine uses granular assemblers to build the appropriate response to a request.

the navigation header or footer for the page. Each of the assemblers is responsible for a small part of the overall handling of the request. This granular approach is good because the assemblers can be easily mixed and matched to customize the required behavior.

When you're building Model 2 applications in Turbine, the flow of information is similar to Struts. This flow appears in figure 1.6.

The page assembler is the outer-level container for the other modules in a Model 2 application. It processes a request, which is analogous to the controller servlet in Struts. When a request is received, the page matches an action class to the request and executes it. The Action module in Turbine is very much like the Action implementation in Struts. After the action has executed, the Page assembler uses the Screen, Layout, and Navigation assemblers to generate output. The Layout assembler is responsible for the general layout of the output. The Navigation assemblers provide an easy mechanism for header- and footer-style navigation on the page. The Screen assembler is the interior of the generated page. The relationship between these assemblers is shown in figure 1.7.

As you can see, more "moving parts" are involved when you're building a Model 2 application in Turbine. This is because Turbine is a more general framework. Each aspect of the web application is handled by a specific service, and the services can be changed in a modular fashion without affecting other services. The advantage of a framework like Turbine lies in the flexibility and options it provides developers. For example, the Screen and Navigation assemblers may be written in JSP (as in Struts). However, other services can be "plugged into" Turbine to handle the UI rendering. The Turbine developers themselves prefer the Velocity template engine (see chapter 9) to JSP for generating UIs in web applications.

The disadvantage of Turbine is its complexity. Because of its service-based architecture, building Model 2 applications in Turbine is more complex than with Struts.

I have only touched on the Model 2 aspects of Turbine in this chapter. As you can see, Turbine is a more extensive framework, providing numerous services beyond those needed to build Model 2 applications. Because it is so extensive (certainly a book's worth), we

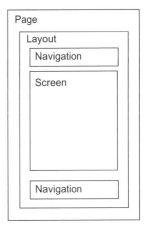

Figure 1.7 The Page assembler encapsulates the other assemblers to construct a complete page. The Layout assembler handles the general layout of the page, which consists of one or more Navigation assemblers and a Screen assembler.

don't cover Turbine any further in this book. However, in part 2 we do examine numerous other frameworks, some similar to Turbine (Tapestry, for example). We discussed it here to illustrate a services-based framework and to compare it to a lightweight framework like Struts.

1.3.3   Objectively choosing a framework

With so many available, how can you choose a suitable framework? Part 2 of this book attempts to answer that question. It compares frameworks by building the same application in a variety of frameworks, comparing and contrasting along the way. Our goal is to allow you to see how various frameworks handle the same issues and solve the same problems. By building the same (or as close to the same as possible) application, you can objectively weigh the relative merits of each. Chapter 11 sums up the similarities and differences between the frameworks and provides a checklist to help you choose the one most suitable for your project.

1.4   Best practices

Developers build up a repertoire of solutions to common problems over time. Whereas design patterns deal primarily with design issues (thus the name), another category of solutions exist that are generally lumped under the term "best practices." How they are implemented vary broadly, but the intent is always the same: solve some common problem in a generic and (it is hoped) graceful way. An example of a best practice follows from the Model-View-Controller discussion earlier. MVC forces the developer to partition the concerns of the application into their own tiers, which is a design issue. However, deciding what to separate lies more in the realm of best practices. Let's look at an example of a best practice for determining business rules.

1.4.1   Business rules

"Business rules" is one of the most used, yet least understood, concepts in all application development (not just web applications). Both managers and developers use this term, and frequently each has his or her own definition. Of course, no standard definition exists. It is not a technical term in the sense that it has an objective meaning. It is a useful concept because it affects the design of your applications, including web applications. So that we can discuss the design issues around this concept, let's first provide a working definition.

Defining "business rules"

As much as I would like to provide the ultimate, end-all definition of this term, I'm afraid it is impossible to do that. The problem with a comprehensive definition for a subjective term lies with the fact that different business domains have different criteria to define what constitutes a business rule. The rules that describe one business don't apply to other businesses. Even the common rules may have different levels of importance. For example, if you are selling sensitive, classified documents, you must meet stringent rules as to where items can be shipped. If you are selling a novel, the only thing you care about is how cheaply you can ship it. Both businesses are selling written works, but they have different rules that determine what it means to sell their product.

The only way to create a working definition of "business rules" is to find common ground that every business would agree on. Choosing the overlapping region in each business's domain where the unambiguous business rules reside is the only way to create a generic definition (see figure 1.8).

A working definition

With the realization that only a fool would attempt to define something as nebulous as "business rules," I proceed. Here is a simple working definition for this vague subjective concept:

> *Business rules relate to* why *you write the application, not* how.

How you write the application is all about the technology used, the architecture, the design, the tools, how the application is hosted, and many other details. ***Why*** you write the application has nothing to do with the technology or design, but

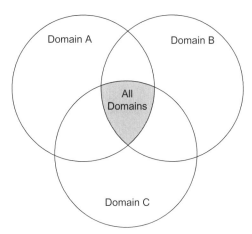

Figure 1.8
The only way to create even a working definition of "business rules" is to encompass the unambiguous areas that every business would agree constitutes a business rule.

concerns the business problem you are trying to solve. Typically, business rules change more frequently than other parts of the application, making them good candidates for partitioning.

A common business rule is a validation, in which user input is checked against rules established to ensure that the input is legal. Validations are a classic *why* because the business domain determines the rules enforced by the validations. Even criteria such as a phone number format (Where do the parentheses go? Is the area code required?) are examples of business rules. Questions like "How should we calculate raises for employees?" and "What is the chemical formula for our soda?" are also examples of business rules.

Only the people for whom the application is written can determine the business rules. This role is typically filled by a business analyst but can certainly be filled in a less formal way. Business rules come directly from the requirements documents for the application. They determine why you are writing the application in the first place. You may have the most wonderful, elaborate, scalable, maintainable application in the world, but if it doesn't implement the business rules correctly, it is not successful.

1.4.2   Where should the rules reside?

The most important question for web developers is not the definition of the rules (that definition is someone else's job) but rather *where* the rules should reside. Should the rules be coded so that they are a part of the server or the client? If on the server, should they be coded as part of the database (in the form of triggers and stored procedures) or in Java code? This question is of paramount importance because it affects important design decisions of the application and has a direct effect on scalability, maintainability, and extensibility.

Placing the rules in the database server

Fortunately, the Model 2 design pattern helps. JavaBeans designed to handle business rules and database connectivity are part of the Model 2 design. These beans are the perfect place for business rules to reside. If all your logic resides in Java-Beans, it is easy to change it because you won't have to hunt throughout the application for the code. You can also use the object-oriented nature of JavaBeans to model the real-world objects in your application. This allows your application to grow along with what you are modeling.

Another option for server-based rules is to place them into a relational database in the form of *triggers* and *stored procedures*. Here are a couple of reasons why I think that this is a bad idea. First, if you place your rules in triggers and stored procedures, you must write them in Structured Query Language (SQL). This is a bad choice for implementing your business rules because SQL is a set-based language, not procedural or object-oriented. SQL is highly optimized to return result sets from relational databases, but it lacks most of the facilities of Java for string processing, numerical analysis, and all the other rich support classes found in the Java libraries. SQL is also not really a standard language. Although an ANSI standard exists for SQL, it is a weak standard, so database vendors implement their own proprietary extensions. From a practical standpoint, SQL is not portable across databases. Some database servers now allow stored procedures to be written in Java, but they rely on a specific infrastructure and aren't portable across database vendors.

Second, the model part of the application is designed for business rules. Your application in Model 2 is really a three-tier application, with the presentation handled by JSP and the browser, the business rules handled by the model beans, and the persistence handled by the database server. You can take advantage of this inherent design by building the business logic in this middle tier. Using this approach lets you avoid having the rules split between the database and model beans. This is important because you may need to eventually scale the application into a larger distributed application using EJBs. In that case, your JavaBeans become proxies, calling the methods of the EJBs to handle business logic. (You'll learn more about this design option in chapter 12.) If you have rules in the database, you cannot easily migrate your application logic to EJBs.

Rules that do belong in the database server

The exception to the previous rule concerns data integrity and key generation. Database servers are optimized to handle such issues as referential integrity, ensuring that your data doesn't accidentally become corrupted because of errant code. Data integrity lies in the gray area of our business rules definition because it is an infrastructure issue and thus belongs more in the *how* category than the *why*. However, all the *whys* in the world won't help if your data isn't properly stored.

The same exception exists for key generation. Like it or not, most of today's applications must handle the messy business of reconciling an object-oriented language (Java) with set-based relational databases. A part of this relationship is the keys that define the relationships between the data in your tables. Most database servers have a mechanism for handling key generation, and it would be a lot of extra work to try to implement it yourself. Again, this is more in the realm of architecture and doesn't concern our definition of the *why* of business rules.

Placing rules in the client

The option of placing your rules in the client is easier in traditional applications because you have "real" code executing the client portion, not just a browser. To place the rules here in a web application means that you must write the rules in a scripting language (normally JavaScript) that the browser can interpret. This design is desirable because it allows you to perform instant validations and execute other code without having to call back to the web server. This is a big advantage because trips to the server can be expensive in terms of time and server resources. Placing rules in the client becomes a tempting option. Developers frequently want to mimic the behavior of desktop applications, where responses to input (such as validations) are instantaneous. This approach makes for a more responsive application. You also have greater control over the UI through client-side code for such behaviors as disabling controls based in input, creating dynamic dropdown lists, and other niceties. You should not succumb to temptation!

However, if you must place some business rules in the form of a scripting language in the UI, you can still do so without harming the architecture of your application. Chapter 12 shows you how to achieve the best of both worlds by generating the scripting business rules from the server.

1.4.3 *Leveraging best practices*

Like design patterns and frameworks, best practices ultimately lead you to better-performing web applications. Part 3 of this book catalogs a variety of best practices harvested from web development projects. Chapter 12 expands on the discussion started here on separating concerns and shows examples of how to accomplish this separation, including an example of porting a well-designed web application (developed in an earlier chapter) to use EJBs. Chapter 13 demonstrates how to handle workflow situations, including transaction processing and advanced UI techniques. Chapter 14 discusses performance tuning and examines how your web application can best utilize its resources. Chapter 15 covers resource management, including such topics as caching. Chapter 16 covers debugging, and chapter 17 covers testing—required reading for those of us who don't produce perfect code the first time. Chapter 18 covers web services, which fundamentally change distributed computing; Axis, an open-source web services engine; how to create new applications that rely on web services; and how to retrofit existing web applications. Finally, chapter 19 covers topics important to state-of-the-art web development that are too broad or complex to include in this book.

1.5 Summary

Designing web applications is not like designing any other type of application. It represents a serious paradigm shift from traditional application development. Understanding the base technology and APIs is the first step to writing that work well. However, an understanding of the design problems and solutions that are available is also critical. Choosing to build web applications with Model 2 greatly reduces your development and maintenance headaches. Once you've written several Model 2 applications, the common pieces start coming into focus, and you have the beginnings of a framework. Or you may decide to use one of the existing frameworks to speed up your development and cut down on the amount of hand-crafted code. As your design becomes more refined, you can start looking to other avenues (such as best practices) to improve your web applications.

Unfortunately, none of the design paradigms discussed here will guarantee a well-designed application. You must police the design and architecture at every opportunity (especially early in the development cycle) to ensure that you don't end up with an application that looks partitioned but that is, in reality, a mess of misplaced code.

In chapter 2, we look at creating web applications through the eyes of a developer who understands the web APIs but has no experience building well-architected applications. It covers design and architecture when you're using servlets and JSP without the benefits of design patterns or other best practices.

Building web applications

Java 2 Enterprise Edition (J2EE) contains a rich application programming interface (API) for building web applications. Starting with the foundation of servlets, this API has grown into a state-of-the-art interface. Understanding the details of the servlet and JavaServer Pages (JSP) APIs is an important first step in becoming an effective web developer. However, being familiar with the APIs will not make you an experienced distributed web application developer. Web applications are *distributed* applications, placing them in the family of the most difficult type of application development. Distributed applications require careful attention to resource allocation, cross-process communication, and a host of other complexities not faced in desktop applications.

Two aspects of building web applications arise from their distributed nature. The first is the interaction of the application with the API. A good example is the way threading is handled in web applications. Knowing how to protect your servlets (and, because they are a type of servlet, your JSPs) from multithreaded access is essential. However, the second part of the equation, and one often ignored elsewhere, is the design of the application—that is, the way in which you organize the artifacts in the application (classes, user interface elements, etc.) to fulfill the goals of the application development. Design and architecture are as critical to the long-term success of your application as recognizing how the APIs work—maybe more so. This book focuses primarily on that aspect of web development.

To realize why improving design is so important, you must start with something that is *not* well designed. This may be an application that appears to work but perhaps the elements that make up the application don't work well together. You have to consider architecture, coding decisions, how the user interface works, and a host of other issues. The intent here is not to create a "straw man argument," building something that any competent developer would recognize as inferior. Rather, our goal is to build an application from the perspective of someone who understands all the moving parts of the APIs but has no advanced experience. Ideally, the applications we build in this chapter should resemble the first attempt by most developers to build web applications in Java.

In this chapter, we build a minimal e-commerce site using only servlets, and then we build the same site using only JSP. Along the way, we talk about what is good and bad in each approach. Subsequent chapters improve the design, keeping the good and discarding the bad.

2.1 *Building web applications with servlets*

You are reading this book, which means you have already chosen Java as your web development platform and don't need to be convinced of its capabilities. This section walks you through a simple web application built with the "default" servlet API.

This application uses several classes, including servlets and helpers. Figure 2.1 illustrates the relationship between the classes. We discuss the source for these classes as we examine each aspect of the application.

2.1.1 *The eMotherEarth servlet application*

Our sample application built with servlets is a four-page e-commerce application called *eMotherEarth*. It allows you to buy products such as leaves, dirt, oceans, and other "earthy" wares. This application is concerned only with the technology and not with the logistics of delivery! The source code for this application appears in the source code archive as art_emotherearth_servlet.

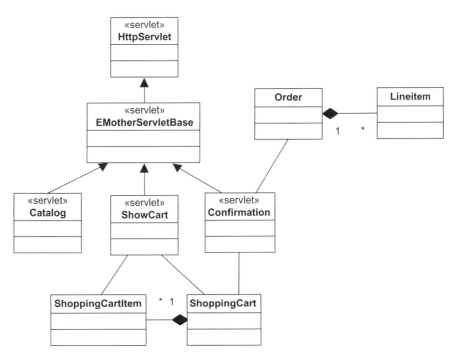

Figure 2.1   The eMotherEarth application consists of a variety of classes, including servlets and helper classes.

The first page: Welcome

The first page of the site is a simple login page, written in HTML (because at this point there is no need for dynamic content). The first page of the site appears in figure 2.2; the source for this page is shown in listing 2.1.

Listing 2.1   The simple login form for Welcome.html

```
<html>
<head><title>Welcome to eMotherEarth.com</title></head>
<body>
<h1>Welcome to eMotherEarth.com</h1>
<p><h3>Your 1-Stop Shop for Earth Products</h3><p>
Please enter your login info:<p>
<form action="catalog" method="post">
<p>Name: <input type="text" name="username"></p>
<p><input type="submit" name="Submit" value="Login">
</form>
</body>
</html>
```

The second page: Catalog

The Welcome page posts to a servlet called `Catalog`, which shows a catalog of products. The Catalog page appears in figure 2.3.

The servlet that generates the Catalog page has multiple duties to perform. It must:

1   Create a database connection pool for all servlets to share.

2   Validate the user and either:

- Welcome the user back.
- Add the user to the user database.

3   Display the catalog.

**Figure 2.2
The login page for eMotherEarth
is a simple HTML form.**

Figure 2.3
The Catalog page shows all the wares available from eMotherEarth.com.

The first portion of the catalog servlet appears in listing 2.2.

Listing 2.2   The declaration and init() sections of the Catalog servlet

```
package com.nealford.art.history.servletemotherearth;

import com.nealford.art.history.servletemotherearth.lib.*;
import java.io.*;
import java.sql.*;
import java.util.*;
import javax.servlet.*;
import javax.servlet.http.*;

public class Catalog extends EMotherServletBase {
    static final private String SQL_INS_USERS =
            "insert into users (name) values (?)";
    static final private String SQL_SEL_USERS =
            "select name from users where name = ?";
    static final private String SQL_SEL_PRODS =
            "select * from products";
    private String dbUrl;
    private String driverClass;
    private String user;
    private String password;

    public void init() throws ServletException {
        getPropertiesFromServletContext();
        addPoolToApplication(createConnectionPool());
    }

    private void getPropertiesFromServletContext() {
```

> Initializes global resources

```
        ServletContext sc = getServletContext();
        dbUrl = sc.getInitParameter("dbUrl");
        driverClass = sc.getInitParameter("driverClass");
        user = sc.getInitParameter("user");
        password = sc.getInitParameter("password");
    }

    private void addPoolToApplication(DbPool dbPool) {
        getServletContext().setAttribute(CONN_POOL_ID, dbPool);
    }

    private DbPool createConnectionPool() {
        DbPool p = null;
        try {
            p = new DbPool(driverClass, dbUrl, user, password);
        } catch (SQLException sqlx) {
            getServletContext().log("Connection Pool Error", sqlx);
        }
        return p;
    }
```

The `Catalog` class starts by declaring constants for SQL access and for member variables. The first of the servlet-specific declarations is for the `init()` method. Because it is the first servlet called in the application, it is responsible for creating the database connection pool used by the rest of the application. It is a common practice to use connection pools in web applications, and most application servers and frameworks include connection pool classes. Our sample uses a homegrown connection pool class called `DbPool`, which offers rudimentary database connection pooling. The source for it is trivial and is available as part of the source code archive, but won't be shown here for space considerations.

The `init()` method handles two jobs: getting the init parameters from the servlet context and adding the connection pool to the application context. The database connection definitions appear in the web.xml file as global init parameters. This is a common practice because it allows the developer to change such characteristics as the driver class and login information without having to recompile the application. The `getPropertiesFromServletContext()` method retrieves the pertinent values from the configuration file and populates the servlet's member variables.

The second chore handled by the `init()` method is to create the connection pool and place it in a location where all the other servlets can access it. The `createConnectionPool()` method builds the connection pool from the supplied parameters and returns it. If an error occurs, the cause of the exception is logged via the servlet context's `log()` method. The pool is then placed in the servlet context for the application. This is the global context, meaning that the pool will be accessible to the other servlets.

The next method of interest in the `Catalog` servlet is the `doPost()` method. It appears in listing 2.3.

Listing 2.3   The doPost() method of the Catalog servlet

```
public void doPost(HttpServletRequest request,
                   HttpServletResponse response)
         throws ServletException, IOException {
    PrintWriter out = generatePagePrelude(response, "Catalog");
    String userName = validateUser(request, out);
    DbPool pool = getConnectionPool();
    Connection con = null;
    try {
        con = pool.getConnection();
        handleReturnOrNewUser(out, userName, con);
        out.println("</h3><p>");
        addUserToSession(request, userName);
        displayCatalog(out, con);
        generatePagePostlude(out);
    } catch (SQLException sqle) {
        getServletContext().log("SQL error", sqlx);
    } finally {
        pool.release(con);
    }
}
```

The general rule of thumb in high-quality applications (and indeed for the rest of the code in the book) is to create very granular, cohesive methods. Cohesive methods perform a single task and no more. Making your methods cohesive leads to granularity, meaning the methods are very small (like grains of sand) and numerous. If successful, the public methods in a class should read like an outline of what the method does, with the details submerged in private methods. Applications using this coding pattern also generate more readable stack traces when you're debugging. The `doPost()` method in the `Catalog` servlet is an example of this technique.

The first job of this method concerns the generation of the page prelude. This code must appear at the top of the HTML document generated by this servlet. To handle this job, the `doPost()` method calls the `generatePagePrelude()` method (see listing 2.4).

Listing 2.4   The generatePagePrelude() method

```
private PrintWriter generatePagePrelude(HttpServletResponse response)
        throws IOException {
    response.setContentType(CONTENT_TYPE);
    PrintWriter out = response.getWriter();
    out.println("<html>");
    out.println("<head><title>Logon</title></head>");
    out.println("<body>");
    return out;
}
```

This method creates a print writer object (which it returns) and uses it to create the standard HTML elements for the top of the page. This method does not appear in the Catalog servlet. It appears instead in a base class servlet named EMotherServletBase. As with any application, common tasks exist that every servlet must perform. For example, every servlet in this application must get a reference to the connection pool and generate headers and footers for the HTML document. One of the side benefits of creating granular, cohesive methods is the ability to float them up in the hierarchy to the base class. In other words, it helps you identify the methods that may be generalized into a parent class, making the code easier to reuse. The more single-purposed the methods are, the more likely that they can be reused. The common methods for this application have been promoted to the base class servlet, which appears in listing 2.5.

Listing 2.5   EMotherServletBase consolidates common servlet methods.

```
package com.nealford.art.history.servletemotherearth;

import javax.servlet.*;
import javax.servlet.http.*;
import java.io.*;
import java.util.*;
import com.nealford.art.history.servletemotherearth.lib.DbPool;
import java.sql.SQLException;

public class EMotherServletBase extends HttpServlet {
    static final protected String CONN_POOL_ID = "DbPool";
    static final protected String CONTENT_TYPE = "text/html";

    protected DbPool getConnectionPool() {
        DbPool pool = (DbPool) getServletContext().
                    getAttribute(CONN_POOL_ID);
        if (pool == null)
            getServletContext().log("Pool cannot be loaded");
        return pool;
    }
```

```
protected PrintWriter generatePagePrelude(
        HttpServletResponse response, String title)
    throws IOException {
response.setContentType(CONTENT_TYPE);
PrintWriter out = response.getWriter();
out.println("<html>");
out.println("<head><title>" + title + "</title></head>");
out.println("<body>");
return out;
}

protected void generatePagePostlude(PrintWriter out) {
out.println("</body></html>");
}

protected HttpSession getSession(HttpServletRequest request,
                            HttpServletResponse response)
                throws IOException {
HttpSession session = request.getSession(false);
if (session == null)
    response.sendRedirect("Welcome.html");
return session;
}
}
```

Creating a base class servlet to consolidate common methods is a common practice, made more effective by cohesive methods.

The next task that `Catalog`'s `doPost()` method handles is to validate the user. Validation is handled in the method `validateUser()`, which returns the username. Listing 2.6 shows this method.

Listing 2.6 The validateUser() method ensures that the user entered a value.

```
private String validateUser(HttpServletRequest request,
                        PrintWriter out) {
String userName = request.getParameter("username");
if (userName.equals(""))
    out.println("<h1>Error! You must enter a user name!");
out.println("<h3>Hello, " + userName + ".");
return userName;
}
```

The `doPost()` method next sets up the servlet to handle database access. To do so, it calls the `getConnectionPool()` method from the base class (see listing 2.5).

Note the disassociation of the `init()` method from the remainder of the servlet. This servlet is the one that placed the pool in the application context in the beginning, so it could avoid going back to the servlet context to get a reference to the pool. Instead, it could hold onto the reference generated at the top. However, we chose to go ahead and get the connection in this servlet exactly as the others would: by using the common method. This approach adds consistency to the application and ensures that nothing will break if you need to add code to the base class later to enhance its functionality.

The doPost() method next establishes a database connection within a try ... finally block to ensure that the connection always closes. This resource-protection requirement drives the structure of the interior of this method, because the connection must be established and freed within this context. Next, doPost() generates a different message for existing or new users, which is handled by the handleReturnOrNewUser() method (see listing 2.7).

Listing 2.7   This method decides what message to present and whether to add a new user to the database.

```
private void handleReturnOrNewUser(PrintWriter out,
                                   String userName,
                                   Connection con)
    throws SQLException {
    if (isNewUser(con, userName))
        out.println("Welcome back to the store!");
    else {
        addUser(con, userName);
        out.println("Welcome to the store! We'll add " +
                    "you to the user database");
    }
    out.println("</h3><p>");
}
```

This method is itself composed of other helper methods, with the goal of creating the most granular code possible. The isNewUser() method (listing 2.8) checks to see whether the user is already present in the database.

Listing 2.8   The isNewUser() method

```
private boolean isNewUser(Connection c, String userName)
                throws SQLException {
    PreparedStatement ps = c.prepareStatement(SQL_SEL_USERS);
    ps.setString(1, userName);
    ResultSet rs = ps.executeQuery();
    return rs.next();
}
```

If the ResultSet contains a record, then that means the user is already present in the database and the next() method returns true. Otherwise, the user does not currently exist, so the application automatically adds that user. This is not typical behavior for most e-commerce sites, which go through a vetting process to add new users. Our vendor doesn't care, and will gladly add new users (even if they typed in the wrong username by accident). Of course, we could write more code to expand this behavior.

If a user must be added, the addUser() method handles the task. This method is shown in listing 2.9.

Listing 2.9 This method adds new users to the database.

```
private void addUser(Connection c, String userName)
            throws SQLException {
    PreparedStatement psi = c.prepareStatement(SQL_INS_USERS);
    psi.setString(1, userName);
    psi.executeUpdate();
}
```

The next task performed by the doPost() method is to create a session and add the user to it. This task is handled by a very short method:

```
private void addUserToSession(HttpServletRequest request,
                              String userName) {
    HttpSession session = request.getSession(true);
    session.setAttribute("user", userName);
}
```

It is worth creating separate methods even for two lines of code (in fact, it is sometimes worthwhile for a single line of code). The entries in the public methods should be consistent and perform the same level of work. It is undesirable to intersperse utility code like this among other high-level method calls. The high-level method calls should be descriptive enough to eliminate the need for additional comments. Maintaining comment synchronization is error-prone, so let the code speak for itself. Use method, variable, class, and interface names that don't need comments to convey their purpose. It is also likely that more code will accrue over time, making the public method longer. Any candidate for a nice cohesive method should be extracted. The code is consequently much more readable.

The display of the catalog occurs next. It is handled by the aptly named displayCatalog() method, which appears in listing 2.10.

Listing 2.10 displayCatalog() shows the entire catalog of products.

```java
private void displayCatalog(PrintWriter out, Connection con) {
    HtmlSQLResult output = new HtmlSQLResult(SQL_SEL_PRODS, con);
    output.setShoppingForm(true);
    out.println("<h1>Products</h1><p>");
    out.println(output.toString());
}
```

At first glance, it would seem that this method would be much more complex. It offloads much of the complexity to a helper class named `HtmlSQLResult`. This utility class takes a database connection and a SQL statement and renders the results into an HTML table. It also has an option for creating another column with a text field and a button that allows the user to purchase items. This class appears in listing 2.11.

Listing 2.11 The HtmlSQLResult class

```java
package com.nealford.art.history.servletemotherearth.lib;

import java.sql.*;
import java.text.NumberFormat;

public class HtmlSQLResult {
    private String sql;
    private Connection con;
    private boolean shoppingForm;

    public HtmlSQLResult(String sql, Connection con) {
        this.sql = sql;
        this.con = con;
    }
    /**
     * The <code>toString()</code> method returns a
     * <code>java.sql.ResultSet</code> formatted as an HTML table.
     *
     * NB: This should be called at most once for a given set of
     * output!
     * @return <code>String</code> formatted as an HTML table
     * containing all the elements of the result set
     */
    public String toString() {
        StringBuffer out = new StringBuffer();            // Generates the
        try {                                             // table from the
            Statement stmt = con.createStatement();        // ResultSet
            stmt.execute(sql);
            ResultSet rs = stmt.getResultSet();
            ResultSetMetaData rsmd = rs.getMetaData();
```

```
        int numCols = rsmd.getColumnCount();

        setupTable(out);
        generateHeaders(out, rsmd, numCols);

        while (rs.next()) {
            generateStandardRow(rs, rsmd, numCols, out);
            generateShoppingForm(out, rs.getInt("id"));
            endRow(out);
        }
        endTable(out);
    } catch (SQLException e) {
        out.append("</TABLE><H1>ERROR:</H1> " +e.getMessage());
    }

    return out.toString();
}

private void endTable(StringBuffer out) {
    out.append("</TABLE>\n");
}

private void endRow(StringBuffer out) {
    out.append("</TR>\n");
}

private void generateShoppingForm(StringBuffer b,
                                  int currentId) {
    if (shoppingForm) {
        b.append("<TD>");
        b.append("<form action='ShowCart' method='post'>");
        b.append("Qty: <input type='text' size='3' " +
                "name='quantity'>");
        b.append("<input type='hidden' name='id' " + "value='"+
                currentId + "'>");
        b.append("<input type='submit' name='submit' " +
                "value='Add to cart'>");
        b.append("</form>");
    }
}

private void generateStandardRow(ResultSet rs,
                                 ResultSetMetaData rsmd,
                                 int numCols, StringBuffer out)
                          throws SQLException {
    NumberFormat formatter = NumberFormat.getCurrencyInstance();
    out.append("<TR>");
    for (int i = 1; i <= numCols; i++) {
        Object obj = rs.getObject(i);
        if ((obj != null) &&
            (rsmd.getColumnType(i) == java.sql.Types.DOUBLE))
            out.append("<TD align='right'> " +
```

Iterates over the ResultSet and generates rows

Builds a form element for each row

```
                        formatter.format(rs.getDouble(i)));
            else if (obj == null)
                out.append("<TD> ");
            else
                out.append("<TD>" + obj.toString());
        }
    }

    private void generateHeaders(StringBuffer out,
                                 ResultSetMetaData rsmd,
                                 int numcols)
                      throws SQLException {
        for (int i = 1; i <= numcols; i++) {
            out.append("<TH>");
            out.append(rsmd.getColumnLabel(i));
        }

        if (shoppingForm)
            out.append("<TH>" + "Buy");

        out.append("</TR>\n");
    }
    private void setupTable(StringBuffer out) {
        out.append("<TABLE border=1>\n");
        out.append("<TR>");
    }
    public boolean isShoppingForm() {
        return shoppingForm;
    }
    public void setShoppingForm(boolean value) {
        shoppingForm = value;
    }
}
```

We included listing 2.11 primarily to make a point about developing with servlets. Anytime you need to generate a large HTML data structure like a table, you are always better off building it generically because the complexity of the mixed Java and HTML generation is overwhelming. This code is best developed once and reused rather than generated anew for ad hoc situations. In the next section, you'll see how JSP offers an alternative for this problem.

With the help of the utility class in listing 2.11, the remainder of `Catalog`'s `doPost()` method, the `generatePagePostlude()` method, comes free of charge from the base class (listing 2.5). This method generates the required footer information for the page.

Figure 2.4
The Shopping Cart page of the application shows the current contents of the shopping cart and allows the user to specify credit card information to make the purchase.

The third page: ShowCart

The third page (and corresponding servlet) in the application shows the contents of the user's shopping cart thus far, with an option at the bottom for completing the purchase. This page is shown in figure 2.4. The source for the ShowCart servlet appears in its entirety in listing 2.12.

Listing 2.12 This servlet shows the contents of the shopping cart.

```
package com.nealford.art.history.servletemotherearth;

import com.nealford.art.history.servletemotherearth.lib.*;
import java.io.*;
import java.sql.*;
import java.util.*;
import javax.servlet.*;
import javax.servlet.http.*;

public class ShowCart extends EMotherServletBase {
    static final private String SQL_GET_PRODUCT =
            "select * from products where id = ?";

    public void doPost(HttpServletRequest request,
                    HttpServletResponse response)
                throws ServletException, IOException {
        PrintWriter out = generatePagePrelude(response, "Cart");        <───┐
        HttpSession session = getSession(request, response);
        String userName = (String) session.getAttribute("user");
        ShoppingCart sc = getShoppingCart(session);    Isolates HTML generation
        out.println("<h3>" + userName +
                    ", here is your shopping cart:</h3>");
        int itemId = Integer.parseInt(request.getParameter("id"));
```

```
        int quantity =
                Integer.parseInt(request.getParameter("quantity"));
        Connection con = null;
        DbPool pool = getConnectionPool();
        try {
            con = pool.getConnection();
            if (!addItemToCart(con, itemId, quantity, sc))
                out.println("Error: Failed to add item to cart");
        } catch (SQLException sqlx) {
            getServletContext().log("SQL error adding item:",sqlx);
        } finally {
            pool.release(con);
        }
        out.println(sc.toHtmlTable());
        session.setAttribute("cart", sc);
        outputCheckoutForm(userName, out);
        generatePagePostlude(out);
    }

    private ShoppingCart getShoppingCart(HttpSession session) {
        ShoppingCart sc =
                (ShoppingCart) session.getAttribute("cart");
        if (sc == null)
            sc = new ShoppingCart();
        return sc;
    }

    private boolean addItemToCart(Connection c, int itemId,
                                  int quantity, ShoppingCart sc)
                        throws SQLException {
        PreparedStatement ps = c.prepareStatement(SQL_GET_PRODUCT);
        ps.setInt(1, itemId);
        ResultSet rs = ps.executeQuery();
        boolean status;
        if (status = rs.next()) {
            int id = rs.getInt("id");
            String name = rs.getString("name");
            double price = rs.getDouble("price");
            ShoppingCartItem sci = new ShoppingCartItem(id, name,
                    quantity, price);
            sc.addItem(sci);
        }
        return status;
    }

    private void outputCheckoutForm(String user, PrintWriter out) {
        out.println("<p><p><a href=\"catalog?username=" + user +
                "\"> Click here to return to catalog</a>");
        out.println("<p>");
        out.println("<h3>Check out</h3>");
        out.println("<form action='confirmation' method='post'>");
        out.println("Credit Card # <input type='text' " +
```

Manages database connection and records insertion

Outputs the shopping cart as an HTML table

Adds item to the database

Outputs an HTML form for checkout

```
                                  "name='ccNum'><br>");
            out.println("Credit Card Type <select name='ccType'>");
            out.println("<option value='Visa'>Visa</option>");
            out.println("<option value='MC'>MC</option>");
            out.println("<option value='Amex'>Amex</option>");
            out.println("</select>");
            out.println("Credit Card Exp Date <input type='text' " +
                        "name='ccExp'><br>");
            out.println("<input type='submit' value='Check out'>");
            out.println("</form>");
        }
    }
}
```

Like the previous servlet, this one extends EMotherServletBase, taking advantage
of the generic methods declared there. The first item of note in the doPost()
method of this servlet is the call to getShoppingCart(), one of the helper methods
in this servlet. The servlet must handle two cases; the first time the user hits this
page, the shopping cart does not yet exist, so it must be created. In every subsequent visit to this page, the shopping cart comes from this user's session. This
method handles both cases.

The ShoppingCart class is a helper class in this application. It encapsulates a
collection of ShoppingCartItem objects. The ShoppingCartItem class is a simple
value class (an entity in Unified Modeling Language [UML] terms), with fields for
all the pertinent information about an item, such as the item ID, quantity, and so
forth. This class is so simple that we won't include it here for space considerations.
However, the ShoppingCart class contains some methods of interest and appears
in listing 2.13.

Listing 2.13 The ShoppingCart holds ShoppingCartItems.

```
package com.nealford.art.history.servletmotherearth.lib;

import java.text.NumberFormat;
import java.util.*;

public class ShoppingCart {
    private List items = new Vector(5);

    public String toHtmlTable() {
        NumberFormat formatter = NumberFormat.getCurrencyInstance();
        StringBuffer out = new StringBuffer();
        out.append("<TABLE border=1>\n");
        out.append("<TR>");
        out.append("<TH> ID");
        out.append("<TH> Name");
        out.append("<TH> Quantity");
```

```
        out.append("<TH> Price");
        out.append("<TH> Total");
        out.append("</TR>\n");

        Iterator it = items.iterator();
        while (it.hasNext()) {
            ShoppingCartItem item = (ShoppingCartItem) it.next();
            out.append("<TR>");
            out.append("<TD> " + item.getItemId());
            out.append("<TD> " + item.getItemName());
            out.append("<TD> " + item.getQuantity());
            out.append("<TD align='right'> " +
                    formatter.format(item.getItemPrice()));
            out.append("<TD align='right'> " +
                    formatter.format(item.getTotal()));
            out.append("</TR>\n");
        }
        out.append("</TABLE>\n");
        return out.toString();
    }

    public void addItem(ShoppingCartItem sci) {
        items.add(sci);
    }

    public double getCartTotal() {
        Iterator it = items.iterator();
        double sum = 0;
        while (it.hasNext())
            sum += ((ShoppingCartItem)it.next()).getExtendedPrice();
        return sum;
    }

    public List getItemList() {
        return items;
    }

    public String getTotalAsCurrency() {
    •   return NumberFormat.getCurrencyInstance().
                format(getCartTotal());
    }
}
```

This class includes a method that outputs the contents of the shopping cart as an HTML table. While this is certainly handy in our example, it violates one of the rules we encounter later concerning the separation of logic and presentation. However, in this case, it is an expedient way to output the shopping cart. This class also contains methods to both calculate the cart total and show it as currency.

Let's turn our attention back to the `doPost()` method in listing 2.12. The method retrieves the parameters passed from the catalog, establishes a connection to the database, and adds a new record to the shopping cart. The catalog servlet passes only the item ID and quantity, so the `addItemToCart()` method must use that to build up all the information about an item in the cart. It returns success or failure, which is acted on by the servlet. Next, the servlet calls the helper method `outputCheckoutForm()` to generate the HTML that appears at the bottom to accept payment information. This method is simply a series of HTML generation lines. Finally, the servlet adds the updated cart back to the session and generates the footer.

The fourth page: confirmation

The fourth and final page of the application adds a new order (with corresponding line items) and provides a confirmation number to the user. The page output appears in figure 2.5. The source for the `Confirmation` servlet appears in listing 2.14.

Listing 2.14 The Confirmation servlet inserts the new order and provides a confirmation number.

```
package com.nealford.art.history.servletemotherearth;

import com.nealford.art.history.servletemotherearth.lib.*;
import java.io.*;
import java.sql.*;
import java.util.*;
import javax.servlet.*;
import javax.servlet.http.*;

public class Confirmation extends EMotherServletBase {

    public void doPost(HttpServletRequest request,
                       HttpServletResponse response)
             throws ServletException, IOException {
```

Figure 2.5
The Confirmation page indicates that the order was placed successfully, implying a series of behind-the-scenes activities.

```
        response.setContentType(CONTENT_TYPE);
        PrintWriter out = generatePagePrelude(response,
                "Confirmation");
        HttpSession session = getSession(request, response);
        String user = (String) session.getAttribute("user");
        ShoppingCart sc =
                (ShoppingCart) session.getAttribute("cart");
        DbPool dbPool = getConnectionPool();
        Order order = insertOrder(request, session, response, out,
                            user, sc, dbPool);
        if (order == null) {
            getServletContext().log("Failed inserting order");
            out.println("<h1>Error processing order</h1>");
            generatePagePostlude(out);
            return;
        }
        generateConfirmation(out, user, order.getOrderKey());
        generatePagePostlude(out);
        session.invalidate();
    }

    private Order insertOrder(HttpServletRequest request,
                            HttpSession session,
                            HttpServletResponse response,
                            PrintWriter out, String user,
                            ShoppingCart sc, DbPool pool)
                    throws IOException {
        Order order = new Order();
        order.setDbPool(pool);
        String ccNum = request.getParameter("ccNum");
        String ccType = request.getParameter("ccType");
        String ccExp = request.getParameter("ccExp");
        try {
            order.addOrder(sc, user, ccNum, ccType, ccExp);
        } catch (SQLException sqlx) {
            getServletContext().log("Order insert error", sqlx);
        }
        return order;
    }

    private void generateConfirmation(PrintWriter out, String user,
                                    int orderKey) {
        out.println("<h1>");
        out.println(user + ", thank you for shopping at " +
                "eMotherEarth.com");
        out.println("</h1>");
        out.println("<h3>");
        out.println("Your confirmation number is " + orderKey);
        out.println("</h3>");
        out.println("<p>");
        out.println("<P>");
        out.println("<a href='Welcome.html'> " +
```

Gathers artifacts needed to complete the order

Inserts the order into the database

```
                        "Click here to return to the store</a>");
            out.println("</P>");
            out.println("</P>");
        }
    }
```

Even though the output is minimal, the `Confirmation` servlet has one of the most complex tasks to perform. It must accept both the shopping cart and payment information and generate an order (which consists of order and line item information) in the database. Fortunately, the `Order` and `Lineitem` classes handle most of the work. The `Lineitem` class is very simple, containing accessors and mutators for each of the fields of the object. The only method of interest posts a line item to the database using a `PreparedStatement`. We omit the `Lineitem` class code here for space considerations. The `Order` class must do the lion's share of the work because it has to enter orders within a transaction. The `Order` class consists of a large number of accessors and mutators, along with the methods that perform unique work. Portions of the `Order` class (minus the accessors and mutators) appear in listing 2.15.

Listing 2.15 The Order class encapsulates order information and adds orders to the database.

```
private static final String SQL_GET_USER_KEY =
    "SELECT ID FROM USERS WHERE NAME = ?";
private static final String SQL_INSERT_ORDER =
    "INSERT INTO ORDERS (USER_KEY, CC_TYPE, CC_NUM, CC_EXP) " +
    "VALUES (?, ?, ?, ?)";
private static final String SQL_GET_GENERATED_KEY =
        "SELECT LAST_INSERT_ID()";

public void addOrder(ShoppingCart cart, String userName,
        String ccNum, String ccType, String ccExp)
        throws SQLException {
    Connection c = null;
    try {
        c = dbPool.getConnection();
        c.setAutoCommit(false);
        int userKey = getUserKey(userName, c);
        addTheOrder(c);                          Inserts order and
        orderKey = getOrderKey(c);               line items within a
        insertLineItems(cart, c);                transaction
        c.commit();

    } catch (SQLException sqlx) {
        c.rollback();       Rolls back transaction
        throw sqlx;         upon failure
```

```
        } finally {
            dbPool.release(c);
        }
    }

    private void insertLineItems(ShoppingCart cart, Connection c)
            throws SQLException {
        Iterator it = cart.getItemList().iterator();
        Lineitem li = new Lineitem();
        while (it.hasNext()) {
            ShoppingCartItem ci = (ShoppingCartItem) it.next();
            li.addLineItem(c, orderKey, ci.getItemId(),
                            ci.getQuantity());
        }
    }

    private int getOrderKey(Connection c) throws SQLException {
        ResultSet rs = null;
        Statement s = null;
        int orderKey = -1;
        try {
            s = c.createStatement();
            rs = s.executeQuery(SQL_GET_GENERATED_KEY);
            if (rs.next())
                orderKey = rs.getInt(1);
            else {
                throw new SQLException(
                        "Order.addOrder(): no generated key");
            }
        } finally {
            rs.close();
            s.close();
        }
        return orderKey;
    }

    private void addTheOrder(Connection c) throws SQLException {
        int result = -1;
        PreparedStatement ps = c.prepareStatement(SQL_INSERT_ORDER);
        try {
            ps.setInt(1, userKey);
            ps.setString(2, ccType);
            ps.setString(3, ccNum);
            ps.setString(4, ccExp);
            result = ps.executeUpdate();
            if (result != 1)
                throw new SQLException(
                        "Order.addOrder(): order insert failed");
        } finally {
            ps.close();
        }
    }
```

> Iterates over a collection of line items and inserts each

```
private int getUserKey(String userName, Connection c)
        throws SQLException {
    PreparedStatement ps = null;
    ResultSet rs = null;
    int userKey = -1;
    try {
        ps = c.prepareStatement(SQL_GET_USER_KEY);
        ps.setString(1, userName);
        rs = ps.executeQuery();
        if (!rs.next()) {
            throw new SQLException(
                    "Order.addOrder(): user not found");
        }
        userKey = rs.getInt(1);
    } finally {
        rs.close();
        ps.close();
    }
    return userKey;
}
```

The addOrder() method first gets a connection from the pool, and then sets the autoCommit property of the connection to false. In the database, orders consist of both order information (such as credit card, status, etc.) and order line items, which reside in another table. To enter an order in the database, records must atomically post to both the Order and Lineitem tables. Therefore, transaction processing is required.

The next task performed by addOrder() is the retrieval of the user's ID from the user table. The name is the only piece of information about that user passed from servlet to servlet, so the name is used to retrieve the user's key (which is one of the foreign keys in the Order table). Next, the addTheOrder() method executes a PreparedStatement to add the new order to the database.

The database used for this example is MySQL, an open-source database server. One of the characteristics of MySQL (shared by almost all database servers) is the automatic generation of key values. The table column for the primary key is defined as a certain type, and the database takes care of generating the unique keys. This is an obvious benefit for the developer, because key-generation code can become quite complex. However, the developer must consider how keys are generated when dealing with master/detail relationships like the one represented by orders and line items in this database. For MySQL, a special stored procedure exists that returns to the database the last key generated for a particular table for this connection. Database servers handle this in this different ways—there is no standard SQL way of dealing with this issue. The `getOrderKey()` method, called from `addOrder()`, calls the MySQL specific stored procedure to get the newly generated order key, which is then used to add line item records via the call to the `insertLineItems()` method.

The last order of business for the `addOrder()` method is to commit the changes to both tables via the `commit()` method of the connection. The `catch` block ensures that the entire transaction is rolled back upon failure via the call to `rollback()`. The `Confirmation` servlet in turn displays the ID number of the order as the confirmation number for the user. This completes the servlet version of the eMotherEarth application.

2.1.2 Evaluating the servlet approach

While the eMotherEarth site is certainly a functioning application, it is also clearly flawed. Its flaws lie not with its application of the servlet API or its visual design (which is sparse on purpose). Instead, it is flawed in the design of the application. If you look over the code for the servlets, you'll see that the visual and logic aspects of this application are hopelessly coupled. Any change to either aspect requires careful consideration to make sure that the other aspect isn't broken. Even splitting the methods of the servlet into small, cohesive chunks doesn't decouple the user interface from the logic. Creating helper classes and methods to handle generic HTML generation, such as the `ShoppingCart` class in this application, helps create reusable building blocks at the expense of embedding presentation code deep within library routines.

To address this problem, developers of complex sites introduced workarounds, which for the most part improved the situation. However, the workarounds became unnecessary as the servlet and JSP APIs evolved, so I won't investigate them here. One of the main changes in the servlet API that helped the presentation layer was the development of JavaServer Pages.

2.2 Building web applications with JSP

JSP aided the development of the presentation layer immensely by helping to eliminate embedded HTML in servlet code without losing the benefits of compiled code (JSPs end up as binary servlets). JSP applications are generally easier to write than servlet-only applications because the JSP API automatically handles much of the infrastructure. You simply build the pages and let the servlet engine handle compilation and deployment. Of course, JSP introduces its own shortcomings. The next example illustrates both the benefits and shortcomings of the JSP approach to application development.

2.2.1 The JSP eMotherEarth application

Our next example is the eMotherEarth application rewritten in JSP. Keep in mind that this is not a port from the servlet version but rather the application as written by a developer who understands JSP. As before, the intent is to present the type of application that a traditional application developer might create as the first pass at a web project. This application appears in the source code archive as art_emotherearth_jsp.

The first page: Welcome

The Welcome page of this application is the same as the Welcome page for the servlet application. Both are rendered as simple HTML documents. This Welcome page is identical to the one shown in figure 2.2 and listing 2.1.

The second page: Catalog

The Catalog page, a JSP, appears in figure 2.6. The source for the catalog JSP must perform the same kinds of tasks that the servlet version had to perform: it must establish the connection pool, validate the user, and show a list of catalog items. The top of the page includes imports and declarations of methods that will

Figure 2.6
The Catalog page of the JSP application is designed to meet the same requirements as the servlet version, so they look virtually identical.

appear outside the scope of the service() method of the JSP. Listing 2.16 shows this code.

Listing 2.16 The top portion of the catalog JSP

```
<%@ page import="com.nealford.art.history.emotherearthjsp.*" %>
<%@ page import="java.util.*" %>
<%@ page import="java.sql.*"%>
<%@ page import="java.text.NumberFormat"%>

<%!
private static final String SQL_PRODUCTS = "SELECT * FROM PRODUCTS";

public void jspInit() {
    String driverClass =
            getServletContext().getInitParameter("driverClass");
    String dbUrl = getServletContext().getInitParameter("dbUrl");
    String user = getServletContext().getInitParameter("user");
    String password =
            getServletContext().getInitParameter("password");
    DbPool dbPool = null;
    try {
        dbPool = new DbPool(driverClass, dbUrl, user, password);
        getServletContext().setAttribute("DbPool", dbPool);
    } catch (SQLException sqlx) {
        getServletContext().log("Connection exception", sqlx);
    }
}

private ResultSet getResultSet(Connection c) throws SQLException {
    Statement s = null;
    ResultSet rs = null;
    s = c.createStatement();
    rs = s.executeQuery(SQL_PRODUCTS);
    return rs;
}

%>
```

The first task performed by the JSP is the establishment of the connection pool. Because this is the first dynamic page of the application the user accesses, the jspInit() method of this page is overridden to handle the job. It pulls init parameters from the web.xml file and builds the same type of connection pool used in our first example. The other declared method at the top of the page returns a result set containing all products. This is a helper method used later in the page.

The next portion of the code for this page appears before the first content but outside the jspInit() method, so it appears within the service() method of the generated servlet rather than the `init()` method. A regular JSP scriptlet block rather than a declaration block contains this code (see listing 2.17).

Listing 2.17   The setup code for the Catalog page

```
<%
    String userName = request.getParameter("username");
    if (userName == null || userName.equals(""))
        userName = (String) session.getAttribute("user");
    NumberFormat formatter = NumberFormat.getCurrencyInstance();
    DbPool dbPool = null;
    Connection connection = null;
    try {
        dbPool = (DbPool)getServletContext().getAttribute("DbPool");
        connection = dbPool.getConnection();
        ResultSet resultSet = getResultSet(connection);
        ResultSetMetaData metaData = resultSet.getMetaData();

%>
```

This code retrieves the username, creates a result set and the result set metadata, and establishes the connection from the connection pool. The block ends with an open try clause, which must be closed before the bottom of the page. This block is designed to protect the connection and ensure that it is eventually released.

The next code on the Catalog page handles the user interface. This file contains mixed HTML, scriptlet, and expression code (see listing 2.18).

Listing 2.18   The main body of the Catalog page

```
<%@ page contentType="text/html; charset=iso-8859-1" language="java"
        errorPage="GeneralErrorPage.jsp" %>
<head>
<title>Catalog</title>
</head>
<body>
<h3>Hello, <%= userName %>. Welcome back to the store!</h3>

<h1>Products </h1>
<table border="1">
    <tr>
    <%
        for (int i = 1; i <= metaData.getColumnCount(); i++) {
    %>
            <td><%= metaData.getColumnName(i) %></td>
    <%
        }
    %>
```

Prints out
column headers

```
<td> </td>
</tr>
<%
    while (resultSet.next()) {
%>
    <tr>
  <%
        for (int i = 1; i <= metaData.getColumnCount(); i++) {
            if (metaData.getColumnType(i) == Types.DOUBLE) {
            %>
            <td align='right'>
            <%= formatter.format(resultSet.getDouble(i)) %>
            </td>
            <%
        } else {
        %>
            <td>
            <%= resultSet.getObject(i).toString() %>
            </td>
        <%
        }
    %>
        }
    %>

    <td><form method="post" action="ShowCart.jsp">
        Qty:
        <input type="text" size='3' name="quantity" />
        <input type="hidden" name="id"
                value='<%= resultSet.getInt("id") %>' />
        <input type="submit" name="Submit" value="Add to Cart"/>
    </form></td>
</tr>
<%
    }
%>
</table>
<p> </p>
<%
    session.setAttribute("user", userName);
%>
</body>
</html>
<%
    } finally {
      dbPool.release(connection);
    }
%>
```

Handles the special case for currency

Prints out rows

The messy code on this page uses the result set and metadata to build the table view of the catalog. Some of the cells must be formatted as currency, so multiple decisions are made in-line to accommodate the correct presentation. At the end of the page, the user's name is added to the session and the `try` block started in the initial scriptlet code is finished off with a resource protection block to release the database connection.

The body of this page illustrates the main disadvantage of JSP. To generate output, you end up with lots of mixed scriptlets, expressions, and HTML. Because JSP relies on specific delimiters, it is very unforgiving of syntax errors. These pages are consequently difficult to maintain because they become fragile. Necessary changes to this page may accidentally break another part of the page because of the heavy mixture of presentation and code elements. It is also difficult for more than one developer to work on the pages at the same time. Many large organizations have dedicated user interface designers, whose job is the generation of the presentation layer. When the code and presentation are mixed, it is difficult to separate responsibilities.

The third page: ShowCart

The third page (figure 2.7) shows the contents of the user's shopping cart. Listing 2.19 contains the code for the Shopping Cart page.

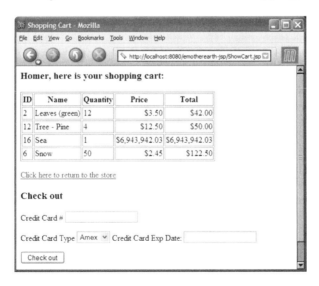

Figure 2.7
The JSP Shopping Cart page shows the contents of the cart and allows the user to add purchasing information.

Listing 2.19   The Shopping Cart JSP

```jsp
<%@ page import="com.nealford.art.history.emotherearthjsp.*" %>
<%@ page import="java.util.*" %>
<%@ page import="java.sql.*"%>
<%@ page import="java.text.NumberFormat"%>

<%!
    static final private String SQL_GET_PRODUCT =
            "select * from products where id = ?";

    private ShoppingCart getCart(HttpSession session) {
        ShoppingCart cart =
                (ShoppingCart) session.getAttribute("shoppingCart");
        if (cart == null)
            cart = new ShoppingCart();
        return cart;
    }

    private boolean addItemToCart(Connection c,
                                  int itemId,
                                  int quantity,
                                  ShoppingCart sc)
            throws SQLException {
        PreparedStatement ps = c.prepareStatement(SQL_GET_PRODUCT);
        ps.setInt(1, itemId);
        ResultSet rs = ps.executeQuery();
        boolean status;
        if (status = rs.next()) {
            int id = rs.getInt("id");
            String name = rs.getString("name");
            double price = rs.getDouble("price");
            ShoppingCartItem sci = new ShoppingCartItem(id, name,
                    quantity, price);
            sc.addItem(sci);
        }
        return status;
    }
%>
<%
    DbPool dbPool = null;
    Connection connection = null;
    ShoppingCart cart = getCart(session);
    String userName = (String) session.getAttribute("user");
    int itemId = Integer.parseInt(request.getParameter("id"));
    int quantity = Integer.parseInt(
            request.getParameter("quantity"));
    try {
        dbPool =(DbPool)getServletContext().getAttribute("DbPool");
        connection = dbPool.getConnection();
```

The top scriptlet, which
contains most of the code

```
%>
<%@ page contentType="text/html; charset=iso-8859-1" language="java"
        errorPage="GeneralErrorPage.jsp" %>
<html>
<head>
<title>Shopping Cart</title>
</head>

<body>
<%
    if (! addItemToCart(connection, itemId, quantity, cart)) {
%>
        Error! Could not add item to cart!
<%
    }
%>
<h3><%= userName %>, here is your shopping cart:</h3>

<%= cart.toHtmlTable() %>

<p><a href="Catalog.jsp">Click here to return to the store</a> </p>

<h3>Check out</h3>
<form method="post" action="Confirmation.jsp">
  <p>Credit Card #
    <input type="text" name="ccNum">
  </p>
  <p>Credit Card Type
    <select name="ccType">
      <option value="Amex">Amex</option>
      <option value="Visa">Visa</option>
      <option value="MC">MC</option>
    </select>
    Credit Card Exp Date:
    <input type="text" name="ccExp">
  </p>
  <p>
    <input type="submit" name="Submit" value="Check out">
  </p>
</form>
<p> </p>
</body>
</html>
<%
    session.setAttribute("shoppingCart", cart);
    } finally {
      dbPool.release(connection);
    }
%>
```

This page is structured much like the previous example. At the beginning, we have helper methods used in the body, followed by the beginning of the code that will make up the `service()` method, and then the mixed presentation and logic. The same helper classes (`ShoppingCart` and `ShoppingCartItem`) are used, including the `toHtmlTable()` method of `ShoppingCart` that creates an HTML table representing the cart. For better presentation flexibility, the table should be generated by hand (as in the Catalog page) or relegated to a JSP custom tag.

The fourth page: Confirmation

The fourth and final page of our application (see figure 2.8) resembles the corresponding page in the servlet sample. The code for this page is shown in listing 2.20.

Listing 2.20 The Confirmation JSP source

```
<%@ page import="com.nealford.art.history.emotherearthjsp.*" %>
<%@ page import="java.sql.*"%>

<%@ page contentType="text/html; charset=iso-8859-1" language="java"
    errorPage="GeneralErrorPage.jsp" %>

<%!
    private Order insertOrder(HttpServletRequest request,
                              HttpSession session,
                              String user,
                              ShoppingCart sc,
                              DbPool pool) {
        Order order = new Order();
        order.setDbPool(pool);
        order.setCcNum(request.getParameter("ccNum"));
        order.setCcType(request.getParameter("ccType"));;
        order.setCcExp(request.getParameter("ccExp"));
        try {
            order.addOrder(sc, user);
        } catch (SQLException sqlx) {
```

Figure 2.8
The Confirmation page inserts the order and presents the user with a confirmation number.

```
                        getServletContext().log("Order insert error", sqlx);
            }
            return order;
        }
%>
<%
        DbPool dbPool = null;
        Connection connection = null;
        ShoppingCart cart =
                (ShoppingCart) session.getAttribute("shoppingCart");
        if (cart == null)
            throw new Exception("Nothing in shopping cart!");
        String userName = (String) session.getAttribute("user");
        try {
            dbPool = (DbPool)getServletContext().getAttribute("DbPool");
            connection = dbPool.getConnection();
            Order newOrder = insertOrder(request, session, userName,
                                    cart, dbPool);
%>
<html>
<head>
<title>Confirmation</title>
</head>

<body>
<h1><%= userName %>, thank you for shopping at eMotherEarth.com</h1>
<h3>Your confirmation number is <%= newOrder.getOrderKey() %></h3>
<p><a href="Welcome.html">Click here to return to the store</a></p>
</body>
</html>
<%
        } finally {
            dbPool.release(connection);
        }
%>
```

This page also makes heavy use of the helper class Order to post the order and line items to the database. The presentation part of this page is trivial and appears at the bottom.

2.2.2 *Evaluating the JSP approach*

The JSP version of this application solves many of the presentation problems of the servlet version but adds some of its own. Although much of the business logic is encapsulated into helper classes (both utility classes such as ShoppingCart and business classes like Order), the pages still quickly become a mess of mixed presentation and logic.

As in the servlet example, there is nothing inherently wrong with the function of a web application built like this one. However, the faults appear when it comes time to maintain or enhance the application. JSP by its nature encourages the mixing of code and presentation logic, which makes the pages fragile. It also hinders parallel development by a specialized development team. In addition, JSP makes it more difficult to create granular, reusable methods. An intimate knowledge of the inner workings of the JSP API is required before you can leverage common behavior from a base class. For example, the kind of code reuse achieved in the servlet example is more difficult in the JSP case.

2.3 Summary

While the servlet and JSP APIs are powerful, they don't force developers to use them in the most effective way. Servlets become very labor intensive when presentation code must be emitted from Java source code. You can employ template strategies and other techniques to mitigate this problem, but they introduce their own problems, such as the high processor cost of parsing every page to replace templates. Servlets are certainly the best option when it comes to writing code to perform work. Because they are standard classes, you can use good coding practices, such as granular methods and inheritance, to improve the structure of the code. However, melding the functional code with the presentation layer becomes a problem, especially in cases where the presentation layer requires major updates but the function has to remain the same.

When writing JSPs, you are spending your time in the presentation layer, which makes it easy to build the visual aspect of your application, which is the most difficult part of using servlets. At the same time, though, good coding practices are either more difficult or impossible in JSP. It seems a shame to discard your hard-earned knowledge of code structure for the benefit of easier-to-use user interfaces. JSP works extremely well for simple sites, where development time is short and maintenance is not a big concern. Yet, as the size of the application grows, JSP becomes harder to manage.

We designed the examples in this chapter to give you a baseline reference of how web applications are too often created. Subsequent chapters show you how to move away from this starting point and truly leverage the potential of web development in Java. In chapter 3, we solve some of the shortcomings of servlets and JSP by using JSP custom tags.

Creating custom JSP tags

This chapter covers
- Building custom JSP tags
- Using the Java Standard Tag Library
- Using other third-party JSP tags

In chapter 2, we used the building blocks of web applications to create a simple program. While our web application was fully functional, it suffered in the design department. In both the servlet and JSP versions of the application, a clear separation of presentation and logic was missing. Custom tags offer one way to solve that problem.

While JSP is excellent for handling presentation, the amount of code embedded within scriptlets poses maintenance problems. A good way to get rid of some of that code is to encapsulate it with custom JSP tags. We will be doing so throughout this chapter. Our goal is to solve the problems inherent in the design and architecture of the applications from chapter 2 by utilizing custom tags. We'll cover handwritten, standard, and third-party tags.

This chapter presents a brief overview of the custom tag facilities in Java. This is a large topic, and entire books are available that delve into the finer details of tag creation. An excellent example is *JSP Tag Libraries*, by Gal Shachor, Adam Chace, and Magnus Rydin (Manning Publications, 2001). This chapter focuses on creating custom tags to improve the code we used in chapter 2. We also discuss using tags developed by others, including the standard set of tag libraries introduced with JSP 1.2.

3.1 *The case for custom tags*

The developers of the JSP technology included capabilities for expanding and customizing the API by creating a custom tag facility. Custom tags appear in the Extensible Markup Language (XML) syntax for tags, similar to the JSP tags for manipulating JavaBeans:

```
<jsp:setPropertry name="emp" property="salary" value="120.00" />
```

Custom JSP tags may be used for a variety of purposes, including encapsulating complex snippets of code away from the page developer. Because of their reusable nature, custom tags are also used to build frameworks, displacing standard HTML controls; to build logic into pages; and any other behavior a web developer can imagine.

Tag development appears here as a design option for reducing the complexity of too busy JSP pages. We do not mean to suggest that this is the primary or even the best use of tags. Tag development is a broad topic, and it appears in other guises later in the book. This chapter concerns the evolution of web development in Java, and tag development is the next step.

3.2 *The tag interfaces*

To create a custom tag, you must implement one of several interfaces defined in the servlet API. The tag API consists of a series of interfaces. Depending on the type of tag you are creating, you implement either the `Tag` or `BodyTag` interface. The `Tag` interface supports the building of tags that do not include a body; `BodyTag` includes additional helper method signatures for supporting a tag with a body (which is a tag with code between the `begin` and `end` elements).

The custom tag API defines a hierarchy of interfaces and supporting objects utilized by tag developers. While it is beyond the scope of this book to delve deeply into the details of this API, a look at the base classes helps set the foundation for building tags. The remainder of this section highlights the key interfaces and classes in the custom tag API. You must be familiar with the methods of these interfaces to write custom tags.

3.2.1 *The Tag interface*

The `Tag` interface includes the callback methods and other infrastructure that support JSP. You must implement this interface to create a custom tag. An abbreviated version (minus the JavaDoc comments) appears in listing 3.1.

Listing 3.1 The Tag interface from the servlet API

```
package javax.servlet.jsp.tagext;

import javax.servlet.jsp.*;

public interface Tag {
    public final static int SKIP_BODY = 0;          ① Control
    public final static int EVAL_BODY_INCLUDE = 1;     flow flags
    public final static int SKIP_PAGE = 5;
    public final static int EVAL_PAGE = 6;

    void setPageContext(PageContext pc);   ② Infrastructure
    void setParent(Tag t);                    support methods
    Tag getParent();
    int doStartTag() throws JspException;   ③ Tag-processing methods
    int doEndTag() throws JspException;
    void release();  ② Infrastructure support methods
}
```

① This interface includes constants that are returned from the callback methods `doStartTag()` and `doEndTag()`, which determine the control flow of the tag.

❷ The first three methods provide infrastructure support (setting the page context and the parent). The parent in this case is another tag, which supports building nested tags. It is sometimes necessary to get information provided in the parent tag from the child tag. For example, a `Database` tag might propagate connection information to all the statement tags enclosed within its body. The last method, `release()`, provides support for cleaning up any resources allocated by the tag (such as database connections and file streams). This method is guaranteed to be called by the JSP when the processing of this tag is complete. The method provides good encapsulation of your tag code so that you don't have to force the user to worry about resource allocation done by the custom tag.

❸ The workhorse methods defined in this interface are `doStartTag()` and `doEnd-Tag()`. These methods are the ones the developer overrides to perform tasks within the custom tag. As their names imply, the `doStartTag()` method executes at the start of tag processing and `doEndTag()` executes at the end. Both methods return integers, with the intention of returning one of the constants defined in this interface to inform the JSP about the control-flow intention.

Frequently, you may need to implement the `Tag` interface but don't have to supply method definitions for all the methods declared in the interface. Instead of writing stub method bodies, you can create adaptor classes instead. An adaptor class implements an interface and provides either default or stub (i.e., no code) implementations for all the methods. This allows the user of the interface to extend the adaptor rather than implementing the interface directly. This is a common pattern in event handlers in Java, and it appears in this API as well (see Swing/AWT Event Listeners, for example). Instead of implementing `Tag` directly, you have the option of extending `TagSupport`, a base class with default implementations for the methods defined in `Tag`. From a practical standpoint, you always extend `TagSupport` instead of implementing `Tag` directly, which frees you from writing empty method bodies for methods you don't need for your tag.

3.2.2 *The IterationTag interface*

The `IterationTag` interface extends `Tag` and adds support for tags that must iterate over some collection. The interface includes only one constant and one method signature (see listing 3.2; we omitted the JavaDoc comments).

Listing 3.2 IterationTag adds support for iterating over a collection.

```
package javax.servlet.jsp.tagext;

import javax.servlet.jsp.*;

public interface IterationTag extends Tag {
```

```
    public final static int EVAL_BODY_AGAIN = 2;

    int doAfterBody() throws JspException;
}
```

This interface adds the `EVAL_BODY_AGAIN` constant as a legal return value from the status methods of a tag. It also defines a `doAfterBody()` method that supports body tags.

This interface was added in the JSP 1.2 specification to incrementally add support for tags with a body. The method and constant formerly appeared (in slightly different form) in the `BodyTag` interface. Splitting it out into its own interface lets you take a more granular approach to building tags. This interface is the stepping-stone to building a tag that includes body elements, which we look at next.

3.2.3 *The BodyTag interface*

The other primary interface for tag development is `BodyTag`, which supports building tags that include body elements. A body element is content (either other tags or output elements such as HTML) encapsulated between the beginning and end of the tag. An example of this type of tag from the standard tag API is the `use-Bean` tag, which may include body elements that initialize a bean when the JSP must create it rather than pull it from a collection:

```
<jsp:useBean id="item"
    scope="session"
    class="com.nealford.art.history.customtags.ShoppingCartItem">
        <jsp:setProperty name="item" property="itemId" value="0" />
        <jsp:setProperty name="item" property="quantity" value="0"/>
        <jsp:setProperty name="item" property="itemName"
            value="None" />
        <jsp:setProperty name="item" property="itemPrice"
            value="0.0" />
</jsp:useBean>
```

The `BodyTag` interface (minus JavaDoc comments) appears in listing 3.3.

Listing 3.3 The BodyTag interface provides callback methods for body tags.

```
package javax.servlet.jsp.tagext;

import javax.servlet.jsp.*;

public interface BodyTag extends IterationTag {
    public final static int EVAL_BODY_TAG = 2;
    public final static int EVAL_BODY_BUFFERED = 2;

    void setBodyContent(BodyContent b);
```

```
      void doInitBody() throws JspException;

}
```

The `BodyTag` interface builds on the `doAfterBody()` method defined in its interface (`IterationTag`) by adding constants and a couple of methods. The constants defined here are status codes returned by the various "do" methods of a tag. The `setBodyContent()` method is called by the JSP runtime to supply you with a `BodyContent` object, which encapsulates information about the tag body and the implicit "out" object. The `doInitBody()` method is called at the start of the body processing for the tag. The `doAfterBody()` method, defined in `IterationTag` and therefore in this interface by virtue of inheritance, is called at the end of body processing.

3.3 *Building simple tags*

The best way to understand custom tag development is to build a custom tag one step at a time, including both the code and the registration process to utilize the tag.

3.3.1 *The HtmlSqlResult tag*

The `HtmlSqlResult` custom tag generates an HTML table for a ResultSet, making it easy to output the results from a SQL statement. For this example, we don't need a body, so we will implement the `Tag` interface through the `TagSupport` adaptor. This custom tag is related to code that originally appeared in listing 2.11. It is a modified version of the class named `HtmlSqlResult`. The original class accepted a SQL string and a Connection object and generated an HTML table based on the ResultSet. It also contained code that generated a shopping form via a flag set on the instance of the class. This class eliminated the task of handwriting a table based on a query.

This class is a perfect candidate for conversion into a custom tag and a good example of utility code that has potential for reuse across multiple applications. One of the principle governing criteria of the usefulness of writing a custom tag should hinge on the reusability of the code. Because it requires more effort to create a custom tag than to create the code in the first place, it is a waste of time to build a tag for a single use. However, most applications have this kind of code lurking around, waiting for the chance to be abstracted into a more generic place.

When you find code like this, placing it in a custom tag saves development and debugging time for later projects.

Following the coding style we'll use in the rest of the book, the methods in our custom tag are as granular as possible, with public methods acting as the driving force for private methods. Some of the methods of the custom tag appear virtually unchanged from the original class. The top of the class and some of the private methods appear in listing 3.4.

Listing 3.4   The prelude to the HtmlSqlResult custom tag

```
package com.nealford.art.history.customtags;

import java.io.IOException;
import java.sql.Connection;
import java.sql.ResultSet;
import java.sql.ResultSetMetaData;
import java.sql.SQLException;
import java.sql.Statement;
import java.text.NumberFormat;
import javax.servlet.jsp.JspException;
import javax.servlet.jsp.JspWriter;
import javax.servlet.jsp.tagext.TagSupport;

public class HtmlSqlResult extends TagSupport {
    private String sql;
    private String dbPool;
    private String formActionDestination;
    private String shoppingForm;

    private Connection getConnection()
            throws SQLException, JspException {
        DbPool dbPool = (DbPool) pageContext.getServletContext().
                    getAttribute(this.dbPool);
        Connection c = dbPool.getConnection();
        if (c == null)
            throw new JspException("Couldn't get connection");
        return c;
    }

    private void releaseConnection(Connection con) {
        DbPool dbPool = (DbPool) pageContext.getServletContext().
                    getAttribute(this.dbPool);
        dbPool.release(con);
    }
```

The `HtmlSqlResult` class extends `TagSupport` only because it isn't necessary for this tag to implement all the methods mandated by the `Tag` interface—this class doesn't need to override the infrastructure support methods because the implementation supplied by TagSupport is sufficient. The HtmlSqlResult class includes some standard member variables and helper methods for getting and releasing a database connection from a pool. A change in this code from the previous incarnation is the presence of the JspException in the method signature of the get-Connection() method. JspException appears so that problems getting the database connection can propagate up through the JSP runtime, allowing for consistent error handling in the JSP. Both the getConnection() and releaseConnection() methods rely on the application context containing an instance of the connection pool class.

The next private methods of this class deal with the generation of HTML and appear in listing 3.5.

Listing 3.5   The private HTML generation methods

```
private void setupTable(StringBuffer out) {          Generates the prefix
    out.append("<table border=1>\n");                 for the table
    out.append("<tr>");
}
                                                       Uses ResultSetMetaData
private void generateHeaders(StringBuffer out,         to generate headers
                    ResultSetMetaData rsmd,
                    int numcols)
        throws SQLException {
    for (int i = 1; i <= numcols; i++) {
        out.append("<th>");
        out.append(rsmd.getColumnLabel(i));
    }

    if (shoppingForm.equalsIgnoreCase("true"))
        out.append("<th>" + "Buy");

    out.append("</TR>\n");                             Outputs a row of
}                                                      the table based on
private void generateStandardRow(ResultSet rs,        the result set
                    ResultSetMetaData rsmd,
                    int numCols, StringBuffer out)
        throws SQLException {
    NumberFormat formatter = NumberFormat.getCurrencyInstance();
    out.append("<tr>");
    for (int i = 1; i <= numCols; i++) {
        Object obj = rs.getObject(i);
        if ((obj != null) &&
            (rsmd.getColumnType(i) == java.sql.Types.DOUBLE))
            out.append("<td align='right'> " +
            formatter.format(rs.getDouble(i)));
            else if (obj == null)
```

```
                    out.append("<td> ");
                else
                    out.append("<td>" + obj.toString());
                out.append("</td>");
        }
    }
    private void endRow(StringBuffer out) {         ⟵   Cleans up the
                                                         end of the row
        out.append("</tr>\n");                           definition
    }
    private void generateShoppingForm(StringBuffer b,  ⟵   Generates a column
                                                             to select items for
                            int currentId) {                 purchase
        if (shoppingForm.equalsIgnoreCase("true")) {
            b.append("<td>");
            b.append("<form action='" + formActionDestination +
                    "' method='post'>");
            b.append("Qty: <input type='text' size='3' " +
                    "name='quantity'>");
            b.append("<input type='hidden' name='id' " + "value='" +
                    currentId + "'>");
            b.append("<input type='submit' name='submit' " +
                    "value='Add to cart'>");
            b.append("</form>");
        }
    }
    private void endTable(StringBuffer out) {        ⟵   Cleans up the end
                                                          of the table
        out.append("</table>\n");
    }
```

All of these private methods are building blocks, used by the public methods of the class to build a single piece of the resulting table. This separation of responsibilities is desirable because it makes the code more readable and exposes previously unseen opportunities for code reuse.

The remainder of the custom tag consists of public accessors and mutators (omitted here for brevity's sake) and the vitally important doStartTag() method, shown in listing 3.6.

Listing 3.6   The doStartTag() method

```
public int doStartTag() throws javax.servlet.jsp.JspException {
    StringBuffer out = new StringBuffer();
    Connection con = null;
    try {
        con = getConnection();
        Statement stmt = con.createStatement();
        stmt.execute(sql);
```

```
        ResultSet rs = stmt.getResultSet();
        ResultSetMetaData rsmd = rs.getMetaData();
        int numCols = rsmd.getColumnCount();

        setupTable(out);
        generateHeaders(out, rsmd, numCols);

        while (rs.next()) {
            generateStandardRow(rs, rsmd, numCols, out);
            generateShoppingForm(out, rs.getInt("id"));
            endRow(out);
        }

        endTable(out);
        pageContext.getOut().write(out.toString());
    } catch (SQLException e) {
        out.append("</table><h1>ERROR:</h1> " + e.getMessage());
    } catch (IOException ex) {
        pageContext.getServletContext().log(
                "Error generating output", ex);
    } finally {
        releaseConnection(con);
    }

    return SKIP_BODY;
}
```

The `doStartTag()` method is the callback method invoked by the JSP runtime when the beginning of the custom tag is encountered. Because this tag doesn't include a body, this method solely defines what the tag is going to do. It consolidates the private methods and puts them to work. As in the previous version, all the HTML is generated into a `StringBuffer` for efficiency before output. This method creates a connection, builds the table, optionally generates the shopping form, and ends the table. The details appear in the private methods.

The next order of business is to output the generated HTML to the JSP runtime, which occurs at the line

```
    pageContext.getOut().write(out.toString());
```

This method attaches the output buffer used by the JSP runtime to the tag. The `getOut()` method of the page context gives the developer access to the buffered output stream, and the `write()` method outputs the `StringBuffer` containing the table.

After the tag handles the potential exceptions and releases the database connection back to the pool, its final task is to return an integer value to the JSP runtime to inform it of the intended control flow. In this case, any body that exists for this tag is irrelevant to the tag, so we inform the runtime to skip the body and continue processing the rest of the page. Tags without a body usually return the `SKIP_BODY` constant.

3.3.2 *Registering the tag*

The next step is to create the tag library descriptor for your custom tag. This information is kept in a file with a .tld extension. It is an XML document (validated by a document type definition [DTD] specified by Sun Microsystems) that is part of the custom tag API. This DTD and the documentation for it reside in the JSP specification document, created and maintained by Sun (see http://java.sun.com/products/jsp/download.html#specs). The specification is a PDF file that contains a well-documented version of the DTD. The descriptor specifies name, parameters, and other characteristics of a group of custom tags. Listing 3.7 shows our TLD file, emotherearth.tld.

Listing 3.7   emotherearth.tld

```xml
<?xml version="1.0" encoding="ISO-8859-1" ?>
<!DOCTYPE taglib
    PUBLIC "-//Sun Microsystems, Inc.//DTD JSP Tag Library 1.1//EN"
    "http://java.sun.com/j2ee/dtds/web-jsptaglibrary_1_1.dtd">

<taglib>

  <tlibversion>1.0</tlibversion>
  <jspversion>1.1</jspversion>
  <shortname>emotherearth</shortname>
  <uri>http://com.nealford.art.emotherearth</uri>

  <tag>
    <name>htmlSqlResult</name>
    <tagclass>
        com.nealford.art.history.customtags.HtmlSqlResult
    </tagclass>
    <bodycontent>empty</bodycontent>
    <attribute>
      <name>sql</name>
      <required>true</required>
      <rtexprvalue>true</rtexprvalue>
    </attribute>
    <attribute>
      <name>dbPool</name>
      <required>true</required>
      <rtexprvalue>false</rtexprvalue>
    </attribute>
    <attribute>
      <name>formActionDestination</name>
```

```
      <required>true</required>
      <rtexprvalue>false</rtexprvalue>
    </attribute>
    <attribute>
      <name>shoppingForm</name>
      <required>true</required>
      <rtexprvalue>false</rtexprvalue>
    </attribute>
  </tag>

</taglib>
```

The information at the top of the descriptor applies to all the tags declared in this file. The information starting with `tag` specifies the characteristics specific to this tag. It includes the short name, fully qualified class name, the presence of a tag body, and the collection of attributes available for this tag. Each attribute allows you to mandate that the tag is required and that a runtime expression may be included as content. Including a runtime expression allows the user to use JSP markup (for example, a JSP expression) for the contents of the tag. It tells the JSP engine to process the content before passing it to the attribute.

It is possible to automate the generation of the TLD file using an open-source tool called XDoclet, available from http://xdoclet.sourceforge.net/. You place JavaDoc comments directly in the source code for your custom tag, and XDoclet generates the TLD for you. XDoclet is a general-purpose tool for generating XML descriptors (it was actually created to create Enterprise JavaBeans [EJB] deployment descriptors) and works in the same way as the standard JavaDoc mechanism.

Once you have written the TLD for the tag, you still must tell the web application where to find the file. You do this in the application's web.xml document. One of the legal entries is a reference to a location for tag libraries available for this application:

```
<taglib>
  <taglib-uri>http://com.nealford.art.emotherearth</taglib-uri>
  <taglib-location>/WEB-INF/emotherearth.tld</taglib-location>
</taglib>
```

The last step you need to complete before you can use your custom tag is to place a directive in the JSP that uses the tag. Generally at the top of the page (although it is legal anywhere on the page), the `taglib` page directive points to the URI specified in the web.xml file and provides a short, friendly name for use on the page:

```
<%@ taglib uri="http://com.nealford.art.emotherearth"
    prefix="emotherearth" %>
```

Figure 3.1
The Catalog page of the application looks the same to the user, but the markup is greatly improved by the use of a custom tag.

The tag can now be used on the page, using the `emotherearth` prefix:

```
<emotherearth:addDbPoolToApplication  initUser="user"
    initPassword="password" initUrl="dbUrl"
    initDriverClass="driverClass" />
```

You aren't forced to use the short name defined in the descriptor—it is a page-specific shortcut to the custom tag. The result of using this tag appears in figure 3.1. The code underlying the page is much cleaner, as you can see in listing 3.8. Compare that to listing 2.18. We've eliminated the large group of mixed scriptlet and presentation code by using the custom tag.

Listing 3.8 The Catalog page featuring the custom tag

```
<%@ taglib uri="http://com.nealford.art.emotherearth"
    prefix="emotherearth" %>

<%@ page import="com.nealford.art.history.customtags.*" %>
<%@ page import="java.util.*" %>
<%@ page import="java.sql.*"%>
<%@ page import="java.text.NumberFormat"%>

<%!
private static final String SQL_PRODUCTS = "SELECT * FROM PRODUCTS";

private ResultSet getResultSet(Connection c) throws SQLException {
    Statement s = null;
    ResultSet rs = null;
```

```
    s = c.createStatement();
    rs = s.executeQuery(SQL_PRODUCTS);
    return rs;
}
%>
<emotherearth:addDbPoolToApplication  initUser="user"
    initPassword="password" initUrl="dbUrl"
    initDriverClass="driverClass" />
<%
    String userName = request.getParameter("username");
    if (userName == null || userName.equals(""))
        userName = (String) session.getAttribute("user");
%>

<%@ page contentType="text/html; charset=iso-8859-1" language="java"
        errorPage="GeneralErrorPage.jsp" %>
<head>

<title>Catalog</title>
</head>
<body>
<h3>Hello, <%= userName %>. Welcome back to the store!</h3>

<h1>Products </h1>
<emotherearth:htmlSqlResult dbPool="DbPool"        Replaces the
    sql="<%= SQL_PRODUCTS %>"                       original
    formActionDestination="ShowCart.jsp"            scriptlet code
    shoppingForm="true" />
<p> </p>
<%
    session.setAttribute("user", userName);
%>
</body>
</html>
```

Using tags in this manner greatly reduces the complexity of the page. The tag code still includes a great deal of mixed Java and HTML code (emitted by the tag), but the code in the tag is written only once and can be reused in numerous applications. In general, better ways exist to handle the functionality shown here, using the techniques we describe in subsequent chapters. For example, embedding HTML directly into a tag avoids the use of Cascading Style Sheets (CSS) to control the visual aspects of the page where this tag resides. This does not itself represent a best practice, but rather a step in the evolution of web development that leads to the best practices and designs starting in chapter 4.

3.4 *Validating tag attributes*

The custom tag API provides a facility for validating the correctness of the tag attributes. This facility allows for compile-time checking of the correctness of the tags. You should exploit every opportunity to get the compiler and framework to perform more work on your behalf. By validating the attributes of the tag, you can ensure that a developer uses the tag correctly and guards your tag code against invalid or missing attributes. Thus, validating the attributes as part of the tag eliminates the need for extra error-handling code.

3.4.1 *Adding DbPool to the application tag*

Our next example builds a custom tag that encapsulates the code necessary to add a database connection pool to the application context as the application initializes. Every page must use this database connection pool to retrieve a connection to the database, and the first page accessed pulls init parameters from the application to build the pool. Recall from the example in listing 2.16 that the first JSP page in the application included scriptlet code at the top of the page that added a connection pool instance to the servlet context collection. This scriptlet code appears in listing 3.9.

Listing 3.9 Scriptlet code for adding a connection pool to the application

```
<%!
private Connection connection = null;
private static final String SQL_PRODUCTS = "SELECT * FROM PRODUCTS";

public void jspInit() {
    String driverClass =
            getServletContext().getInitParameter("driverClass");
    String dbUrl = getServletContext().getInitParameter("dbUrl");
    String user = getServletContext().getInitParameter("user");
    String password =
            getServletContext().getInitParameter("password");
    DbPool dbPool = null;
    try {
        dbPool = new DbPool(driverClass, dbUrl, user, password);
        getServletContext().setAttribute("DbPool", dbPool);
        connection = dbPool.getConnection();
    } catch (SQLException sqlx) {
        getServletContext().log("Connection exception", sqlx);
    }
}
%>
```

The code in `jspInit()` pulls init parameters from the application scope (Servlet-Context), constructs a database connection pool, and adds it to the application context. This listing exemplifies the type of code that clutters up the presentation aspects of a JSP.

Our example custom tag replaces the previous code with a single call to the `AddDbPoolToApplication` tag (see listing 3.10).

Listing 3.10 The custom JSP tag invocation that replaces the jspInit() code

```
<emotherearth:addDbPoolToApplication  initUserName="user"
    initPasswordName="password" initUrlName="dbUrl"
    initDriverClassName="driverClass" />
```

As you can see, the `addDbPoolToApplication` custom tag allows for much cleaner presentation. The properties of the tag specify the names of the attributes in the application configuration file used to create the `DbPool` object. These names are used to access the corresponding init parameters in the custom tag. The tag source is shown in listing 3.11.

Listing 3.11 The source for the custom tag addDbPoolToApplication

```
package com.nealford.art.history.customtags;

import java.sql.SQLException;
import javax.servlet.jsp.tagext.*;
                                                              Extends
public class AddDbPoolToApplication extends TagSupport {  ◁──┘ TagSupport
    private String initUrlName;
    private String initDriverClassName;
    private String initUserName;              Contains the callback
    private String initPasswordName;          method from the tag API

    public int doStartTag() {  ◁──────────────┘
        String driverClass = pageContext.getServletContext()
                        .getInitParameter(initDriverClassName);
        String dbUrl = pageContext.getServletContext()
                    .getInitParameter(initUrlName);
        String user = pageContext.getServletContext()
                    .getInitParameter(initUserName);
        String password = pageContext.getServletContext()
                        .getInitParameter(initPasswordName);
        DbPool dbPool = null;
        try {
            dbPool = new DbPool(driverClass, dbUrl, user, password);
            pageContext.getServletContext().setAttribute("DbPool",
                                                            dbPool);
        } catch (SQLException sqlx) {
```

```
            pageContext.getServletContext().log(
                "Connection exception", sqlx);
        }
        return SKIP_BODY;   <──┐ Defines
    }                          │ constants
    public void setInitUrlName(String initUrl) {
        this.initUrlName = initUrl;
    }

    public void setInitDriverClassName(String initDriverClass) {
        this.initDriverClassName = initDriverClass;
    }

    public void setInitUserName(String initUser) {
        this.initUserName = initUser;
    }

    public void setInitPasswordName(String initPassword) {
        this.initPasswordName = initPassword;
    }
}
```

The code in doStartTag() resembles the code that used to appear at the top of the page. The primary difference is the use of the pageContext object for getting a reference to the page's instance of the servlet context. Custom tags have access to all the same facilities of the underlying JSP (which in turn have access to all the facilities of the generated servlet) through the pageContext object. This code is called from the servlet generated by the JSP compiler, so you are free to access the servlet's collections (session, request, and servlet context), request, response, and other implicit objects.

The addDbPoolToApplication tag includes set methods for identifying the attributes of the tag. These strings correspond to the names of the init parameters, which in turn point to the objects in the application deployment descriptor file. The user of this tag must include all the attributes—the tag cannot possibly work without them because they are all required to successfully connect to the database. So, to force the user to include all the attributes, we create a TagExtraInfo class. This abstract class allows you to add validation and other metadata to the tags. TagExtraInfo appears (without the JavaDocs) in listing 3.12.

Listing 3.12 The TagExtraInfo class from the JSP API

```
package javax.servlet.jsp.tagext;

public abstract class TagExtraInfo {
```

```
    public VariableInfo[] getVariableInfo(TagData data) {
        return new VariableInfo[0];
    }

    public boolean isValid(TagData data) {
        return true;
    }
    public final void setTagInfo(TagInfo tagInfo) {
        this.tagInfo = tagInfo;
    }

    public final TagInfo getTagInfo() {
        return tagInfo;
    }

    private TagInfo tagInfo;
}
```

This class provides a method (getVariableInfo()) for retrieving tag metadata and a validation method (isValid()) for tag attributes. Even though the class includes no abstract methods, it is still designated as abstract to force developers to extend it and override some or all of the methods.

For the addDbPoolToApplication tag, validation is the only extra behavior needed. To that end, the isValid() method is overloaded to ensure that the user has supplied all the attributes necessary for the tag to work. Listing 3.13 shows the implementation of AddDbPoolTagExtraInfo.

Listing 3.13   The Tag Extra Info class for the custom tag validates the attributes.

```
package com.nealford.art.history.customtags;

import javax.servlet.jsp.tagext.TagData;
import javax.servlet.jsp.tagext.TagExtraInfo;

public class AddDbPoolTagExtraInfo extends TagExtraInfo {

    public boolean isValid(TagData data) {
        return checkData(data.getAttribute("initDriverClass")) &&
                checkData(data.getAttribute("initUrl")) &&
                checkData(data.getAttribute("initUser")) &&
                checkData(data.getAttribute("initPassword"));
    }

    private boolean checkData(Object toBeChecked) {
        return (toBeChecked != null) &&
                (((String) toBeChecked.trim()).length() > 0);
    }
}
```

The `AddDbPoolTagExtraInfo` class utilizes a helper method that verifies that the attribute isn't null and that it isn't a zero length string. The overridden `isValid()` method calls the helper on all the attributes defined by the tag.

To associate the `TagExtraInfo` class with the tag, an extra entry appears in the TLD file for registration purposes. The portion of the TLD file that registers this tag appears in listing 3.14.

Listing 3.14 The TLD entry for this tag includes the Extra Info class.

```
<tag>
  <name>addDbPoolToApplication</name>
  <tagclass>
      com.nealford.art.history.customtags.AddDbPoolToApplication
  </tagclass>
  <teiclass>
      com.nealford.art.history.customtags.AddDbPoolTagExtraInfo
  </teiclass>
  <bodycontent>empty</bodycontent>
  <attribute>
    <name>initUser</name>
    <required>true</required>
    <rtexprvalue>false</rtexprvalue>
  </attribute>
  <attribute>
    <name>initPassword</name>
    <required>true</required>
    <rtexprvalue>false</rtexprvalue>
  </attribute>
  <attribute>
    <name>initUrl</name>
    <required>true</required>
    <rtexprvalue>false</rtexprvalue>
  </attribute>
  <attribute>
    <name>initDriverClass</name>
    <required>true</required>
    <rtexprvalue>false</rtexprvalue>
  </attribute>
</tag>
```

Once the `Tag Extra Info` class is associated with the `addDbPoolToApplication` tag, the JSP runtime automatically calls the `isValid()` method for you, ensuring that all attributes have a valid value.

The `addDbPoolToApplication` custom tag replaces the messy code at the top of the JSP shown originally in listing 2.18 and cleans it up as shown in listing 3.8.

Like the `HtmlSqlResult` tag, it is used to encapsulate common code that is useful across multiple pages. Every database application will need this behavior, so it makes sense to build a tag to handle it cleanly.

3.5 *Using prebuilt tags*

You don't always have to write your own tags. As you would guess, JSP development includes many common tasks that are needed in every application. To serve this purpose, a wide variety of prebuilt custom tags is available. Sun realized the need for tag behavior outside the rudimentary facilities built into JSP, so it sponsored a Java Specification Request (JSR) through the Java Community Process to create a standard set of tag libraries that encapsulates common needs. JSR 52 specifies a Java Standard Tag Library (JSTL) for JavaServer Pages. You can find information about this JSR at http://www.jcp.org/en/jsr/detail?id=52. You can also download the complete specification from this location, which details all the tags included in the library and how to use them. In addition to the JSTL tags, a wide variety of custom tags are available for download. One excellent repository of custom tags is the Jakarta site at http://jakarta.apache.org/taglibs/doc/standard-doc/intro.html, and some of these tags appear in section 3.5.2.

Building the specification is an important first step, but in order for it to be useful, someone must write code that adheres to the specification. One of the first implementations of the JSTL specification is available from the Jakarta site, hosted by Apache. You can download an implementation of JSTL at http://jakarta.apache.org/taglibs. It is open source, so you are free to download the source as well.

The JSTL includes tags in a variety of categories, each providing tags for solving a particular problem or performing some task. Table 3.1 highlights JSTL categories, the URI, and the prefix used in code.

Table 3.1 The JSTL tags

Functional Area	URI	Prefix
Core	http://java.sun.com/jstl/core	c
XML processing	http://java.sun.com/jstl/xml	x
I18N capable formatting	http://java.sun.com/jstl/fmt	fmt
relational db access (SQL)	http://java.sun.com/jstl/sql	sql

Each of the functional areas in table 3.1 (especially core) is further subdivided into general common functionality groups. JSTL represents an extensive library of reusable tags. To provide a snapshot of the types of tags available, table 3.2 describes some of the tags.

Table 3.2   Selected JSTL categories and tags

Common Group	Tag	Description
General Purpose	<c:out>	Evaluates an expression and outputs the result of the evaluation to the current `JspWriter` object.
General Purpose	<c:set>	Sets the value of an attribute in any of the JSP scopes.
General Purpose	<c:remove>	Removes a scoped variable.
General Purpose	<c:catch>	Catches a `java.lang.Throwable` thrown by any of its nested actions.
Conditional	<c:if>	Evaluates its body content if the expression specified with the `test` attribute is true.
Conditional	<c:choose>	Provides the context for mutually exclusive conditional execution.
Conditional	<c:when>	Represents an alternative within a <c:choose> action.
Iteration	<c:forEach>	Repeats its nested body content over a collection of objects, or repeats it a fixed number of times.
Iteration	<c:forTokens>	Iterates over tokens, separated by the supplied delimiters.
SQL	<sql:query>	Queries a database.
SQL	<sql:update>	Executes an SQL `INSERT`, `UPDATE`, or `DELETE` statement and may also be used with Data Definition Language (DDL) statements.
SQL	<sql:transaction>	Establishes a transaction context for its <sql:query> and <sql:update> subtags.

3.5.1   Using JSTL

Our goal for this chapter has been to clean up the JSP in our sample application in an attempt to achieve better separation of functional areas. JSTL looks like an easy way to help remove some of the extraneous scriptlet code from the application. To use JSTL, you must download an implementation (like the one at the Jakarta site), add the library JAR file to your web application, and add the TLD to the web.xml configuration file:

```
<taglib>
  <taglib-uri>http://java.sun.com/jstl/core</taglib-uri>
  <taglib-location>/WEB-INF/c.tld</taglib-location>
</taglib>
```

Listing 3.15 shows the refactored portion of the ShowCart page from the eMotherEarth application. It still uses the custom tags developed earlier in the chapter, but it now also uses JSTL tags to iterate through the list of items, formatting when appropriate.

Listing 3.15   The refactored ShowCart page features the use of JSTL tags to handle iteration and formatting.

```
<%@ taglib prefix="c" uri="http://java.sun.com/jstl/core" %>
<%@ taglib uri='http://java.sun.com/jstl/fmt'  prefix='fmt'%>
<h3>
    <sess:attribute name="userName"/>, here is your shopping cart:
</h3>

<table border="1">
  <tr>
  <c:forEach var="column" items="ID,Name,Quantity,Price,Total">
    <th><c:out value="${column}"/></th>
  </c:forEach>
  </tr>

  <c:forEach var="cartItem" items="${items}">
  <tr>
    <td><c:out value="${cartItem.itemId}" /></td>
    <td><c:out value="${cartItem.itemName}" /></td>
    <td><c:out value="${cartItem.quantity}" /></td>
    <fmt:formatNumber type="currency" var="itemPriceAsCurrency"
            value="${cartItem.itemPrice}"/>
    <fmt:formatNumber type="currency" var="extendedPriceAsCurrency"
            value="${cartItem.extendedPrice}"/>
    <td align='right'>
        <c:out value="${itemPriceAsCurrency}" />
    </td>
    <td align='right'>
        <c:out value="${extendedPriceAsCurrency}" />
    </td>
  </tr>
  </c:forEach>
</table>
```

The code in listing 3.15 shows the table portion of the page. The previous version of this sample contained code that generated the table showing the items in the cart embedded in the ShoppingCart class. Generally, it is not a good idea to embed HTML directly into a class (unless you are building a custom tag) because it destroys the separation of code and presentation. If you have a presentation specialist working on the page, he or she has no control over the formatting emitted from code.

The `forEach` tag offers a couple of options for the items over which you iterate. In listing 3.15, the headers of the table are placed in a comma-delimited string, and the `forEach` tag takes care of separating them as it executes. The second use of the tag is more sophisticated. It will also iterate over a standard Java collection. However, in this case, `items` is a `pageContext` variable containing a `java.util.List` of `ShoppingCartItems`. JSTL used the `${…}` syntax to identify variables within tags, so the `${items}` reference retrieves a page-level variable, notices that it is a `List`, and makes it available under the name `cartItem` (another attribute of the tag) for the body of the tag. Within the body of the tag, you can use the standard dot notation to reference fields of an object. Just as in the other parts of the JSP API, the property `${cartItem.itemId}` actually calls the `cartItem.getItemId()` method of the object. This syntax is a little less cumbersome than the standard JSP expression syntax. The JSTL `out` tag allows you to output values embedded in page-level variables, so it is used to output the items from the list. This syntax will be added to JSP 2.0 Specification as "Expression Language" functionality—or just "EL"—to minimize the use of JSP expression `<%= … %>`. This leads to less Java code in HTML and therefore makes applications easier to maintain.

JSTL also includes tag libraries to make it easy for you to format numbers, both for localization and internationalization. For the table output in listing 3.15, two of the numbers should appear as currencies. The `formatNumber` tag lets you apply formatting to a number and place the result into another page-level variable:

```
<fmt:formatNumber type="currency" var="itemPriceAsCurrency"
        value="${cartItem.itemPrice}"/>
```

Here, instead of accessing `cartItem.itemPrice` directly in the table, we use the `itemPriceAsCurrency` value.

You can use JSTL to improve the readability of the page without resorting to encapsulating HTML into Java classes that have no business generating presentation code. The intent of JSTL is to build a standard set of generic tags to make common tasks easier. Almost every web application needs to iterate over a collection at some point. A great deal of reusable flexibility is embodied in the JSTL library. Because it is a standard, many implementations are possible, so it is less likely that a particular vendor or open-source taglib will disappear.

3.5.2 *Using other taglibs*

JSTL is not the only game in town. Java developers haven't waited around for Sun to create a specification for reusable tags. Tag libraries already exist, from various vendors, to address needs not handled in JSTL. Many of these tag libraries predate JSTL but have moved the JSTL behaviors into a library that supports the standard.

The Jakarta Taglibs project includes the categories listed in table 3.3.

Table 3.3   The Taglibs project

Taglib	Description
Application	Contains tags that can be used to access information contained in the `ServletContext` for a web application.
Benchmark	Aids in the performance testing of other taglibs and JSP pages in general.
BSF	An architecture for incorporating scripting into Java applications and applets.
Cache	Lets you cache fragments of your JSP pages.
DateTime	Contains tags that can be used to handle date- and time-related functions.
DBTags	Contains tags that can be used to read from and write to a SQL database.
I18N	Contains tags that help manage the complexity of creating internationalized web applications.
Input	Lets you present HTML `<form>` elements that are tied to the `ServletRequest` that caused the current JSP page to run.
IO	Contains tags that can be used to perform a variety of input- and output-related tasks from inside JSP.
JMS	Contains tags that can be used to perform a variety of Java Message Service-related operations, such as sending and receiving messages from inside JSP.
JNDI	Creates an instance of a `javax.naming.Context` based on the values of the attributes providing some of the standard values.
Log	Allows you to embed logging calls in your JSP that can be output to a variety of destinations thanks to the power of the log4j project.
Mailer	Used to send email.
Page	Contains tags that can be used to access all the information about the `PageContext` for a JSP page.
Random	Used to create random string and number generators.
Regexp	Contains tags that can be used to perform Perl syntax regular expressions.

continued on next page

Table 3.3 The Taglibs project *(continued)*

Taglib	Description
Request	Contains tags that can be used to access all the information about the HTTP request for a JSP page.
Response	Contains tags that can be used to set all the information for an HTTP response for a JSP page.
Scrape	Lets you scrape, or extract, content from web documents and display the content in your JSP.
Session	Provides tags for reading or modifying client `HttpSession` information.
String	Used to manipulate Strings.
XTags	Lets you use XML.

As you can see, some of these libraries (like XTags and SQL) overlap the capabilities already found in JSTL. In these cases, the Taglibs project does things a little differently than JSTL, so a parallel implementation is suitable, for both backward compatibility and developer preference.

You can download each of these libraries separately, and each has documentation and samples to show how they work. All the needed artifacts (the JAR files, TLDs, and web.xml entries) are part of the download. Use these libraries as you would as any other library.

Other taglibs

The custom taglibs from Jakarta allow more cleanup of the scriptlet code that resides on a JSP page. These tags encapsulate common functionality normally handled by scriptlets and reliance on implicit JSP objects. For this example, we have refactored the Catalog page of the eMotherEarth application. The custom tags created specifically for this application are still in use, but using the custom tags cleaned up some of the scriptlet and JSP expression code. Listing 3.16 shows the entire refactored Catalog page.

Listing 3.16 The Catalog page written with Taglib tags

```
<%@ taglib uri="http://jakarta.apache.org/taglibs/request-1.0"
    prefix="req" %>
<%@ taglib uri="http://jakarta.apache.org/taglibs/session-1.0"
    prefix="sess" %>
<%@ taglib prefix="c" uri="http://java.sun.com/jstl/core" %>
```

```
<%@ taglib uri="http://com.nealford.art.emotherearth"
    prefix="emotherearth" %>

<%@ page import="com.nealford.art.history.customtags.stl.*" %>
<%@ page import="java.util.*" %>
<%@ page import="java.sql.*"%>
<%@ page import="java.text.NumberFormat"%>

<emotherearth:addDbPoolToApplication  initUserName="user"
    initPasswordName="password" initUrlName="dbUrl"
    initDriverClassName="driverClass" />

<sess:existsAttribute name="userName" value="false">
  <sess:setAttribute name="userName"><req:parameter name="userName"/>
  </sess:setAttribute>
</sess:existsAttribute>

<%@ page contentType="text/html; charset=iso-8859-1" language="java"
        errorPage="GeneralErrorPage.jsp" %>
<head>

<title>Catalog</title>
</head>
<body>
<h3>Hello, <sess:attribute name="userName"/>
    . Welcome back to the store!</h3>

<h1>Products </h1>
<emotherearth:htmlSqlResult dbPool="DbPool"
  sql="SELECT * FROM PRODUCTS" formActionDestination="ShowCart.jsp"
  shoppingForm="true" />
<p> </p>
</body>
</html>
```

As you can see, the Catalog page is now free of all scriptlet and JSP expression code, leaving only HTML, custom tags, and tags from the Jakarta Taglibs project. In this page, the request parameter of userName is pulled from the request variable and placed in the session upon first invocation. The session tags from Taglibs allow you to check for the existence of a session attribute and conditionally add it. In the listing, the value of the session attribute comes from a request attribute.

3.6 *Custom tag considerations*

The samples in this chapter represent only the tip of the iceberg when it comes to custom tags. Only the simplest features of the API appear here. Yet these features are enough to improve the readability and maintainability of the pages of our web application and to give you a flavor of what can be done using JSP tag extension features. Any time you can separate responsibilities and encapsulate them into their own niche, you create code that is better organized and easier to manipulate. Adding custom tags (whether your own or third-party) changes the design of the application and introduces new concerns.

3.6.1 *Resource usage*

One downside to the JSPs implemented with custom tags in this chapter is the hidden resource cost. Web development features several finite pools of resources. The most obvious is memory—every computer has a limited amount of memory—but there are other resource pools as well. For example, most servlet engines pool threads so that pages are dispatched more quickly. Another finite resource is database connections.

These resource constraints highlight the problems with code resembling the `addDbPoolToApplication` tag presented in this chapter. The `addDbPoolToApplication` tag makes use of the application context to store information. In doing so, it stealthily uses some memory in the application context. Storing the database connection pool in the application collection is necessary within the context of the application and all applications like it. It's not as if you can stop storing needed objects and information in the global context. However, by encapsulating code that references global resources in a custom tag, you hide the fact that it is happening to the casual users of the tag. If the code appears on the page, everyone sees it (which is both good and bad). I don't mean to imply that encapsulating code in this manner is a bad practice, but you should be aware of the consequences. It is acceptable to handle common resources (like database connections, memory caches, etc.) with custom tags as long as the consequences are well documented for the users of the tags. It is less advisable to use tags to create ad hoc consumers of shared resources.

To manage the finite resource pools of web applications, many very scalable applications employ a "session cop." This is a member of the development team who looks after the shared memory collections in the web application to make sure that no one is abusing them by placing extraneous information there. If you allow anyone free access to shared resources, someone will inadvertently harm the scalability of the application by using that space as a "magic repository" for his or her stuff. The point here is that if you create a custom tag that uses global resources, it should be well documented so that the users of the tag are aware of the consequences of using it.

3.6.2 *Building a framework*

You should always think about how the custom tags you build are used, in both the current application and future ones. For example, the `addDbPoolToApplication` tag could have been written to place hard-coded values in the application context. Instead, it was written so that the user specifies the name of the values in the web.xml document, making it easier to use in other applications. The amount of work involved in creating the class wasn't significantly greater, but the reusability achieved is considerable. When you write custom tags to encapsulate behavior, think about other applications where the tag might be used and build for the future.

Building tags that are reusable across multiple applications is the start of building your own framework. A *framework* is a collection of interrelated classes that make it easier to build applications of a certain type (such as web applications). Building reusable assets is the first step in building a framework. As you will see in subsequent chapters, it isn't the only step, but it is the start.

3.7   *Now that we're here, where are we?*

One of the early goals of this chapter was to decrease the complexity and high coupling of the applications created in the previous chapter. The question is: have we achieved that goal? If you look at listing 3.16, you can see that we have certainly managed to remove Java code from the page. By using custom-built tags to handle database functionality and tags downloaded from Jakarta, we're down to just JSP code with no Java. Is this page more readable? That is debatable. It is certainly more homogeneous, without the unwholesome mixture of various types of elements.

The same could be said of the refactored ShowCart page in listing 3.15. By using JSTL and Jakarta tags, we made the page much more homogeneous. Some scriptlet code still appears at the top of the page (not shown in listing 3.15), but you could eventually chase away all the scriptlet code using a combination of handwritten and additional taglibs.

We've managed to clean up the syntax, but have we really attacked the fundamental problems of the design of the application? There is still a high degree of coupling between the logic and presentation of the application. This grows even more if we eliminate the SQL code currently embedded in the Java classes (like `Order`) and use the JSTL SQL tags instead. When you need to make a change to the application, how many places do you have to touch? If you want to build a large application, how easy is it to split the developer team into specialized areas and allow them to work more or less independently of one another? All these questions address the amount of coupling in the application.

Don't think for a moment that I am denigrating the custom tag facility. It is a very nice tool in the arsenal of web development. But it still hasn't gotten me to where I want to be. I want an application that offers good separation of responsibilities, with high cohesion and low coupling between the working parts of the application. I would like to be able to make major changes to one part of the application without affecting (or at least having a minor effect on) the other parts of the application. Custom tag libraries help, but aren't the end-all solution to these problems. In the evolution of web development we have another tool, but we don't have a good blueprint yet. Wait—it's coming.

3.8 *Summary*

The code for the examples in this chapter appears in the project directory art_emotherearth_customtags_stl. This chapter showed you how to use custom JSP tags to help mitigate some of the complexity and brittleness of typical JSP applications. We presented two custom tags. The first built an HTML table from a SQL statement, greatly reducing the amount of hand-coding required. It replaced a large chunk of mixed scriptlet and HTML code, and improved the readability and maintainability of our page. The second tag performed the typical web application task of placing a database connection pool into the global application context, making it available to all subsequent pages. This tag also featured validation of the attributes, which should always be included in custom tag development.

You also learned how to use custom tag libraries that are already available. These fall into two broad categories: the Java Standard Tag Library (JSTL) and other custom tag libraries. We incorporated both JSTL and Jakarta Taglibs into our application, making the syntax more homogeneous.

The most important point of this chapter is the architectural considerations implied by the use of tags to encapsulate messy code. Clearly, the pages produced using this technique are cleaner, and include less logic, than their predecessors. But it still doesn't diminish the core concerns for building truly state-of-the-art web applications. As a web developer who has evolved to this point in thinking about building web applications, you might be thinking that there should still be a better way. There is. In chapter 4, we look at how design patterns and best practices solve many of the problems highlighted in the first three chapters.

The Model 2
design pattern

This chapter covers

- Using the Model 2 design patterns as an architectural framework
- Improving web application design by separating concerns
- Parameterizing commands to create a generic controller servlet

All too often, web applications use the design path of least resistance. In other words, the design sort of "happens" while you are building the application. Generally, you are under severe deadline pressure, so you focus on getting the requirements of the application implemented correctly without giving much thought to the bigger design picture. This model works to a point. Just as you can construct a doghouse without blueprints, you can build small applications while designing on the fly. However, the larger the house (or application), the more critical the design becomes.

This chapter emphasizes the implementation of the design. Chapter 1 introduced the Model 2 design pattern and discussed its origins and theoretical underpinnings. However, we did not show a working application that applies the pattern. To understand abstract concepts, it helps to see them implemented. The examples in this chapter are small but working applications that illustrate proper design principles. When you build applications to illustrate a point, other interesting points pop up that are also important but not direct reflections on design per se. Because applications are the sum of parts, the interaction of the parts is always important. The focus of this chapter is the implementation of Model 2, but some interesting sideline topics crop up as well.

We'll look at two implementations of this design pattern. The first shows how to build a simple web application with Model 2. The next demonstrates how to take advantage of design patterns to make building Model 2 applications easier.

4.1 Using Model 2 as your framework

As you'll recall, in chapter 1 we discussed the use of Model 2 as a way to separate the parts of the application. In particular, it mandates that the model (i.e., the data access and business rules) be kept separate from the user interface (UI) and that the controller be the intermediary between them. To that end, the model is implemented as JavaBeans, the UI as JSP, and the controller as a servlet.

On a fundamental level, web applications are just collections of related request/response pairs. When looking at the pieces of the Java web API, JSP is the clear choice for the response because it is already a type of output document. Servlets are the clear choice for the request because the servlet API already handles much of the details of HTTP. Plain old Java classes are optimally suited for executing code that performs work, such as database access, business logic, and so forth. Model 2 web applications reflect the suitability of each building block by using the simple rule "use what is most naturally suited to solving the design problem of web applications."

Model 2's separation of responsibilities allows the various aspects of the application to be built concurrently. Thus, the Java developers can concentrate on building the models and controllers and the UI designers can build user interfaces. When you have several people working on an application at the same time, it is important that everyone agrees on the information flow before significant work begins. The JSPs rely on information pulled from model JavaBeans. Therefore, it is critical that the bean authors and UI designers agree on what information will be required. This avoids headaches later in the process when the UI cannot effectively pull information from the model without an inordinate amount of work. It is enough to agree on the accessors and mutator method names of the beans and define other required methods. This tells the UI designers what information is available (through the methods they may call) and the model writers what information to provide (through the methods they must write). You might also consider extracting all the methods needed by the UI designers into an interface implemented by the models. This creates a firmer contract between the two teams. The UI designers write to the interface and the model writers adhere to it.

If you are the sole author, you have a choice as to whether you want to write the models or the UI first. If the project is based on information from a database, it makes sense to create the models first. The flow of the application will depend on the structure of the database. The JSPs you create will rely on the model beans for dynamic information. Even if you plan to tackle the models first, you might want to develop a UI prototype to make sure you are creating models for the information you need to display. A UI prototype also allows the application's users to see the UI and make comments earlier, reducing the amount of change later in the application's lifecycle. Just as in the concurrent development case, it is important to think about this early on in the process. Essentially, the roles of model writer and UI designer collapse to one person (you). You will find it just as unrewarding yelling at yourself about a poor design as yelling at someone else. The prototype can be the beginnings of the full-fledged JSP, with static data in lieu of the "real" data. For the sample application for this chapter, the models are built first because the UI is simple.

4.1.1 *The Model 2 schedule application*

Our first implementation of this model is a web application that tracks a user's schedule. It will consist of two pages. The first page (figure 4.1) is a list of the currently scheduled events, and the second page allows the user to add more events. The complete source code for this application appears in the source code archive under the name art_sched_mvc.

Figure 4.1   The Model 2 Schedule application's first page shows the events scheduled for a busy person.

As you can see, the UI is very sparse. This is intentional so that the design and architecture of the application become the center of attention. The information flow in Model 2 applications can sometimes be hard to see from the code. Because each artifact that the user sees is the culmination of several classes and JSPs, it is useful to see a collaboration diagram of the interaction before the code. Figure 4.2 shows the interaction between the classes and JSPs discussed.

In the diagram in figure 4.2, the solid lines represent control flow and the dotted lines represent a user relationship. Views use the model to show information, and the controller uses the model to update it. The user invokes the ViewSchedule controller, which creates the appropriate model objects and forwards them to ScheduleView. The view allows the user to invoke the ScheduleEntry controller, which also uses the model. It forwards to the ScheduleEntryView, which posts to the SaveEntry controller. If there are validation errors, this controller returns the entry view. Otherwise, it forwards back to the main view to show the results of the addition. Let's take a look at the code that makes all this happen.

Building the schedule model

The ScheduleBean class is the main model of the application. It is responsible for pulling schedule information from the database. The database structure for this application is simple, as shown in figure 4.3.

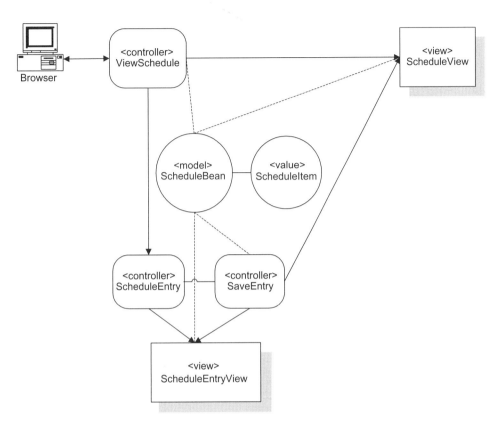

Figure 4.2   The controller servlets create and manipulate the model beans, eventually forwarding the ones with displayable characteristics to a view JSP.

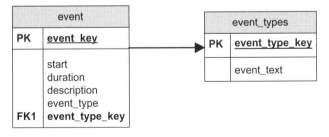

Figure 4.3   The database schema diagram for the schedule application shows that it is a simple database structure.

The first part of `ScheduleBean` establishes constants used throughout the class. It is important to isolate strings and numbers so that they can be changed easily without searching high and low through code. The first part of `ScheduleBean` is shown in listing 4.1.

Listing 4.1   The declarations and database connection portions of ScheduleBean

```java
package com.nealford.art.mvcsched;

import java.sql.*;
import java.util.ArrayList;
import java.util.List;

import javax.sql.DataSource;
import java.util.*;

public class ScheduleBean {
    private List list;
    private Map eventTypes;
    private Connection connection;
    private static final String COLS[] = {"EVENT_KEY", "START",
            "DURATION", "DESCRIPTION", "EVENT_TYPE"};
    private static final String DB_CLASS =
            "org.gjt.mm.mysql.Driver";
    private static final String DB_URL =
            "jdbc:mysql://localhost/schedule?user=root";
    private static final String SQL_SELECT = "SELECT * FROM event";
    private static final String SQL_INSERT =
            "INSERT INTO event (start, duration, description, " +
            "event_type) VALUES(?, ?, ?, ?)";
    private static final String SQL_EVENT_TYPES =
            "SELECT event_type_key, event_text FROM event_types";

    private Connection getConnection() {
        //-- naive, inefficient connection to the database
        //-- to be improved in subsequent chapter
        Connection c = null;
        try {
            Class.forName(DB_CLASS);
            c = DriverManager.getConnection(DB_URL);
        } catch (ClassNotFoundException cnfx) {
            cnfx.printStackTrace();
        } catch (SQLException sqlx) {
            sqlx.printStackTrace();
        }
        return c;
    }
```

The constants define every aspect of this class's interaction with the database, including driver name, URL, column names, and SQL text. Because these values are likely to change if the database type or definition changes, it is critical that they appear as constants. Many of these values could also appear in the deployment descriptor configuration file (and will in subsequent examples).

Note that the two collections used in this class are declared as the base interfaces for the corresponding collection classes. For example, the `List` interface is the basis for all the list-based collection classes, such as `Vector` and `ArrayList`. Obviously, you cannot instantiate the collection using the interface—a concrete class must be assigned to these variables. However, you should always use the most generic type of definition possible for things like lists. This gives you the flexibility to change the underlying concrete class at some point in time without changing much code. In fact, you should just be able to change the actual constructor call for the list, enabling more generic and flexible code. You can always declare an object as a parent, an abstract parent, or an interface as long as you instantiate it with a concrete subclass or implementing class.

List eventTypes = new ArrayList();`Vector` and `ArrayList` offer the same functionality. The key difference between them relates to thread safety: the `Vector` class is thread safe and the `ArrayList` class is not. A thread-safe collection allows multiple threads to access the collection without corrupting the internal data structures. In other words, all the critical methods are synchronized. Thread safety imposes a performance penalty because each operation is locked against multithreaded access. A non-thread-safe collection doesn't include these safeguards and is therefore more efficient. If you know that your collections are never accessed from multiple threads, then you don't need thread safety and you can use the more efficient `ArrayList` class. If in the future you need thread safety, you can change the declaration to create a `Vector` instead, enhancing your code to make it thread safe with a small change. `Vector` is left over from earlier versions of Java. If you need a thread-safe collection, you should use `Collections.synchronizedCollection(Collection c)`, which encapsulates any collection in a thread-safe wrapper. For more information about collections and thread safety, consult the `Collections` class in the SDK documentation.

The `getConnection()` method in listing 4.1 creates a simple connection to the database. This practice does not represent a good technique for creating connections. You generally shouldn't create direct connections to the database from model beans because of scalability and performance reasons. The preferred way to handle database connectivity through beans is either through Enterprise Java-Beans (EJBs) or database connection pools. This is a quick-and-dirty way to connect to the database for the purposes of this sample. We discuss better ways to manage database connectivity in chapter 12.

The next slice of code from ScheduleBean (listing 4.2) handles database connectivity for the bean.

Listing 4.2   The database population and addition code for ScheduleBean

```
public void populate() throws SQLException {
    //-- connection to database
    Connection con = null;
    Statement s = null;
    ResultSet rs = null;
    list = new ArrayList(10);
    Map eventTypes = getEventTypes();
    try {
        con = getConnection();
        s = con.createStatement();
        rs = s.executeQuery(SQL_SELECT);
        int i = 0;
        //-- build list of items
        while (rs.next()) {
            ScheduleItem si = new ScheduleItem();
            si.setStart(rs.getString(COLS[1]));
            si.setDuration(rs.getInt(COLS[2]));
            si.setText(rs.getString(COLS[3]));
            si.setEventTypeKey(rs.getInt(COLS[4]));
            si.setEventType((String) eventTypes.get(
                    new Integer(si.getEventTypeKey())));
            list.add(si);
        }
    } finally {
        try {
            rs.close();
            s.close();
            con.close();
        } catch (SQLException ignored) {
        }
    }
}

public void addRecord(ScheduleItem item) throws
        ScheduleAddException {
    Connection con = null;
    PreparedStatement ps = null;
    Statement s = null;
    ResultSet rs = null;
    try {
        con = getConnection();
        ps = con.prepareStatement(SQL_INSERT);
        ps.setString(1, item.getStart());
```

```
            ps.setInt(2, item.getDuration());
            ps.setString(3, item.getText());
            ps.setInt(4, item.getEventTypeKey());
            int rowsAffected = ps.executeUpdate();
            if (rowsAffected != 1) {
                throw new ScheduleAddException("Insert failed");
            }
            populate();
    } catch (SQLException sqlx) {
        throw new ScheduleAddException(sqlx.getMessage());
    } finally {
        try {
            rs.close();
            s.close();
            con.close();
        } catch (Exception ignored) {
        }
    }
}
```

The methods `populate()` and `addRecord()` are typical low-level Java Database Connectivity (JDBC) code. In both cases, the unit of work is the `ScheduleItem` class. The `populate()` method builds a list of `ScheduleItem` instances and the `addRecord()` method takes a `ScheduleItem` to insert. This is an example of using a *value object*. A value object is a simple class, consisting of member variables with accessors and mutators, that encapsulates a single row from a database table. If the value object has methods beyond accessors and mutators, they are utilitarian methods that interact with the simple values of the object. For example, it is common to include data-validation methods in value objects to ensure that the encapsulated data is correct.

When `populate()` connects to the database in the `ScheduleBean` class, it builds a list of `ScheduleItems`. A design alternative could be for the `populate()` method to return a `java.sql.ResultSet` instance, connected to a cursor in the database. While this would yield less code, it should be avoided. You don't want to tie the implementation of this class too tightly to JDBC code by using a ResultSet because it reduces the maintainability of the application. What if you wanted to port this application to use EJBs for your model instead of regular JavaBeans? In that case, the EJB would need to return a list of value objects and couldn't return a ResultSet because ResultSet isn't serializable and therefore cannot be passed from a server to a client. The design principle here is that it is preferable to return a collection of value objects from a model than to return a specific instance of a JDBC class.

The only disadvantage to using the collection is that it will occupy more memory than the ResultSet. Because a ResultSet encapsulates a database cursor, the data stays in the database and is streamed back to the ResultSet only as requested. This is much more efficient than storing the results in the servlet engine's memory—the records are stored in the database's memory instead. This should be a decision point in your application: do you want to enforce good design practices at the expense of memory usage, or is the memory issue more important? Fortunately, this isn't a binary decision. It is possible to write the populate() method more intelligently to return only a portion of the results as a list and retrieve more on demand. Generally, it is better to put a little more effort at the beginning into keeping the design correct than to try to "fix" it later once you have compromised it.

The populate() method includes a throws clause indicating that it might throw a SQLException. The throws clause appears because we don't want to handle the exception here in the model. Ultimately, we need to write the exception out to the log file of the servlet engine (and perhaps take other actions to warn the user). However, the model class doesn't have direct access to the ServletContext object, which is required to write to the error log. Therefore, our model class is deferring its error handling to the servlet that called it. The controller servlet can take the appropriate action based on the exception.

One incorrect solution to this problem is to pass the ServletContext object into the model object. The model should not be aware that it is participating in a web application (as opposed to a client/server application). The goal is reusability of the model object. Tying it too closely with a web implementation is a design error, going against the concept of clean separation of responsibilities underlying Model 2 implementations.

The addRecord() method takes a populated ScheduleItem and adds it to the database via typical JDBC calls, using a parameterized query. The executeUpdate() method of PreparedStatement returns the number of rows affected by the SQL statement. In this case, it should affect exactly one row (the newly inserted row). If not, an exception is thrown. In this case, a ScheduleAddException is thrown instead of a SQLException. The ScheduleAddException (listing 4.3) is a custom exception class created just for this web application.

Listing 4.3   The ScheduleAddException custom exception

```
package com.nealford.art.mvcsched;

public class ScheduleAddException extends Exception {

    public ScheduleAddException() {
```

```
        super();
    }

    public ScheduleAddException(String msg) {
        super(msg);
    }
}
```

This exception class allows an explicit message to be sent back from the model bean to the controller—namely, that a new record could not be added. This is preferable to throwing a generic exception because the catcher has no way of discerning what type of exception occurred. This technique demonstrates the use of a *lightweight exception*. A lightweight exception is a subclass of Exception (or RuntimeException) that permits a specific error condition to propagate. Chapter 14 discusses this technique in detail.

The last portion of ScheduleBean, shown in listing 4.4, returns the two important lists used by the other parts of the application: the list of event types and the list of schedule items.

Listing 4.4   The getEventTypes() and getList() methods of ScheduleBean

```
public Map getEventTypes() {
    if (eventTypes == null) {
        Connection con = null;
        Statement s = null;
        ResultSet rs = null;
        try {
            con = getConnection();
            s = con.createStatement();
            rs = s.executeQuery(SQL_EVENT_TYPES);
            eventTypes = new HashMap();
            while (rs.next())
                eventTypes.put(rs.getObject("event_type_key"),
                        rs.getString("event_text"));
        } catch (SQLException sqlx) {
            throw new RuntimeException(sqlx.getMessage());
        } finally {
            try {
                rs.close();
                s.close();
                con.close();
            } catch (Exception ignored) {
            }
        }
    }
    return eventTypes;
}
```

```
public List getList() {
    return list;
}
```

The getEventTypes() method retrieves the records in the event_types table shown in figure 4.2. Because this list is small and practically constant, it isn't efficient to execute a query every time we need a mapping from the foreign key event_type in the event table to get the corresponding name. To improve efficiency, this method caches the list upon the first request. Whenever this method is called, it checks to see whether the map has been created yet. If it has, it simply returns the map. If the table hasn't been created yet, the method connects to the database, retrieves the records, and places them in a HashMap. This is an example of "lazy loading," a caching technique in which information isn't gathered until it is needed, and is kept for any future invocation, avoiding having to reload the same data every time. Chapters 15 and 16 discuss this and other performance techniques.

The other item of note in both these methods is the use of the generic interface as the return type rather than a concrete class. Remember that the public methods of any class form the class's contract with the outside world. You should be free to change the internal workings of the class without breaking the contract, which requires other code that relies on this class to change.

Building the ScheduleItem value object

Applications that access rows from SQL tables commonly need an atomic unit of work. In other words, you need a class that encapsulates a single entity that forms a unit of work that cannot be subdivided. This unit of work is usually implemented as a value object. Methods in model classes, such as the model bean discussed earlier, can use the value object to operate on table rows. If the value object contains methods other than accessors and mutators, they are usually methods that interact with the internal values. Range checking and other validations are good examples of helper methods in a value object.

The schedule application uses a value object to encapsulate the event table. The ScheduleItem class is shown in listing 4.5.

Listing 4.5   The ScheduleItem value object

```
package com.nealford.art.mvcsched;

import java.io.Serializable;
import java.util.ArrayList;
import java.util.List;
```

```java
public class ScheduleItem implements Serializable {
    private String start;
    private int duration;
    private String text;
    private String eventType;
    private int eventTypeKey;

    public ScheduleItem(String start, int duration, String text,
            String eventType) {
        this.start = start;
        this.duration = duration;
        this.text = text;
        this.eventType = eventType;
    }

    public ScheduleItem() {
    }

    public void setStart(String newStart) {
        start = newStart;
    }

    public String getStart() {
        return start;
    }

    public void setDuration(int newDuration) {
        duration = newDuration;
    }

    public int getDuration() {
        return duration;
    }

    public void setText(String newText) {
        text = newText;
    }

    public String getText() {
        return text;
    }

    public void setEventType(String newEventType) {
        eventType = newEventType;
    }

    public String getEventType() {
        return eventType;
    }

    public void setEventTypeKey(int eventTypeKey) {
        this.eventTypeKey = eventTypeKey;
    }

    public int getEventTypeKey() {
        return eventTypeKey;
```

```
    }

    public List validate() {
        List validationMessages = new ArrayList(0); // never null!
        if (duration < 0 || duration > 31)
            validationMessages.add("Invalid duration");
        if (text == null || text.length() < 1)
            validationMessages.add("Event must have description");
        return validationMessages;
    }

}
```

Most of this class consists of the member declarations, the constructors, and the accessor/mutator pairs. The sole helper is the `validate()` method. This method checks the validity of the duration and text fields of the schedule item, and then returns a list of validation errors. The caller of this method checks to see if the list is empty (the result of this method will never be null). If not, then at least one error has returned. The list of errors returns as a generic `java.util.List` so that the implementation could change in the future to another list structure without breaking code that calls this method.

The `ScheduleBean` and the `ScheduleItem` classes make up the entire model for this application. Ideally, you could use these exact two classes in a client/server version of the same application. Because changes are required for either the web or client/server application, the changes to the model shouldn't break the other application. In fact, the `ScheduleItem` class doesn't use any of the `java.sql.*` classes—the `ScheduleBean` is responsible for "talking" to the database, and it is the only class in the application that needs to do so. It is good design to partition the functionality of the application into discrete elements as much as possible. Chapter 12 discusses model objects (including value objects) and the theory behind them.

Building the main controller

In Model 2 applications, the controller servlet is the first point of contact with the user. It is the resource the user invokes in the web application, and it is responsible for creating the models, making them perform work, and then forwarding the results to an appropriate view. In the schedule application, the first controller is the Welcome page (listing 4.6).

Listing 4.6   The ViewSchedule controller

```
package com.nealford.art.mvcsched;

import java.io.IOException;
import javax.servlet.RequestDispatcher;
import javax.servlet.ServletException;
import javax.servlet.http.HttpServlet;
import javax.servlet.http.HttpServletRequest;
import javax.servlet.http.HttpServletResponse;
import com.nealford.art.mvcsched.boundary.ScheduleBean;

public class ViewSchedule extends HttpServlet {

    public void doGet(HttpServletRequest request,
            HttpServletResponse response) throws
            ServletException, IOException {
        ScheduleBean scheduleBean = new ScheduleBean();
        try {
            scheduleBean.populate();
        } catch (Exception x) {
            getServletContext().log(
                "Error: ScheduleBean.populate()", x);
        }
        request.setAttribute("scheduleItems",
                        scheduleBean.getList());
        RequestDispatcher rd = request.getRequestDispatcher(
                "/ScheduleView.jsp");
        rd.forward(request, response);
    }
}
```

Controllers in Model 2 applications tend to be small, and this one is no exception. This servlet starts the application by creating a new ScheduleBean, populating it, and then adding it to the request attribute. A RequestDispatcher is created that points to the appropriate view, and the request is forwarded to that view. The model bean is already constructed and populated when it passes to the view. Notice that it would be a mistake to defer creating the model bean and populating it in the view. The view consists of UI code and nothing else. The relationship between the controller, model class, and view is illustrated in figure 4.4.

Building the main view

To complete this request, the view JSP named ScheduleView accepts the forwarded scheduleBean and displays the results. This JSP appears in listing 4.7.

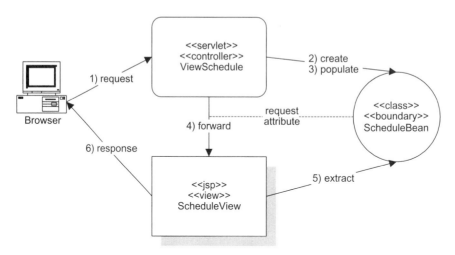

Figure 4.4 The controller servlet creates and populates the model class, then forwards it to the view via a request attribute. The view extracts the viewable information and generates the response for the user.

Listing 4.7 The introductory view page ScheduleView.jsp

```
<%@ taglib prefix="c" uri="http://java.sun.com/jstl/core" %>
<jsp:useBean id="scheduleItems" scope="request"        ❶ Passes a collection
        type="java.util.List" />                          as a generic List

<html>
<head>
<title>
Schedule Items
</title>
</head>
<body>

<p><h2>Schedule List</h2></p>
<table border="2">

    <tr bgcolor="yellow">
        <c:forEach var="column" items="Start,Duration,Text,Event">
          <th><c:out value="${column}"/></th>
      </c:forEach>                              Uses a JSTL iterator ❷
    </tr>
    <tr>
  <c:forEach var="item" items="${scheduleItems}">
  <tr>
    <td><c:out value="${item.start}" /></td>
    <td><c:out value="${item.duration}" /></td>
```

```
      <td><c:out value="${item.text}" /></td>
      <td><c:out value="${item.eventType}" /></td>
   </tr>
   </c:forEach>
</table>
<p>

<a href="scheduleentry">Add New Schedule Item</a>

</body>
</html>
```

❶ This JSP uses the list supplied by the `ScheduleBean` model from the controller in listing 4.6 via the request collection.

❷ The JSP uses a JSTL iterator to avoid placing scriptlet code on the page.

Depending on how often the user needs to see updated schedule information, this list of schedule items could have been added to the user's session instead. The advantage of that approach would be fewer database accesses for this user upon repeated viewing of this page. The controller could check for the presence of the list and pull it from the session on subsequent invocations. The disadvantage of adding it to the user session is threefold. First, because the `List` object exists for the lifetime of the user's session, it will occupy more server memory. Second, if changes are made and the `populate()` method isn't called to refresh the list, the user will see stale data. When building an application, you must consider tradeoffs between scalability for speed (adding model lists to the session) and speed for scalability (adding model lists to the request). (The topics of performance and scalability reappear in chapters 14 and 15.) Third, in a clustered system, either you need a router to redirect calls to the same server or you must have a way of sharing session data across all instances of the application on all machines, depending on how the session replication works for the servlet engine or application server you are using. If you don't handle caching via one of these two mechanisms, you end up with one cached copy per server.

When using Model 2 design methodology, the primary goal is to place as little scriptlet/expression code as possible in the JSP. In the view JSP in listing 4.7, all the scriptlet code that could be present for iterating over the collection has been replaced by core JSTL tags. As a rule of thumb, each occurrence of a scriptlet tag doubles the potential maintenance headaches. One way to mitigate this problem is to create custom JSP tags to replace this generic scriptlet code. Look back at chapter 3 for some examples of this technique.

This completes the first page of the application. The user invokes the controller, which creates the model and forwards the results to the view.

Building the entry controller

The main page of the application has a link at the bottom that allows the user to add new schedule items. This link leads the user to the entry portion of the application, shown in figure 4.5. Listing 4.8 contains the code for the entry controller, ScheduleEntry.

Listing 4.8   The entry controller

```
package com.nealford.art.mvcsched;

import javax.servlet.*;
import javax.servlet.http.*;
import java.io.*;
import java.util.*;

public class ScheduleEntry extends HttpServlet {

    public void doGet(HttpServletRequest request,
            HttpServletResponse response) throws
            ServletException, IOException {
        request.getRequestDispatcher("/ScheduleEntryView.jsp").
                forward(request, response);
    }
}
```

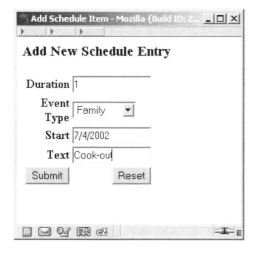

Figure 4.5
The entry part of the application allows the user to add new schedule entries.

The `ScheduleEntry` controller is extremely simple. In fact, this controller is technically not even necessary—the link on the previous page could simply point directly to the JSP dispatched by this controller. However, it is still a good idea to have a controller, for a couple of reasons. First, it makes the application consistent. You always link or post to a controller servlet but not a JSP. Second, chances are excellent that sometime in the future code will become necessary in this controller. If the controller is already present, you won't have to modify any of the code surrounding it; you can simply add the required functionality.

Building the entry view

The view page forwarded by `ScheduleEntry` in listing 4.8 is much more complex than the previous JSP. This page is responsible for two tasks: allowing the user to enter a new record and handling validation errors that are returned for an unsuccessful entry. The first portion of this JSP appears in listing 4.9.

Listing 4.9   The header of the entry view

```
<%@ page import="java.util.*" %>
<%@ taglib prefix="c" uri="http://java.sun.com/jstl/core" %>

<jsp:useBean id="scheduleItem" scope="request"                      ❶ Request scoped
    class="com.nealford.art.mvcsched.ScheduleItem" />                  schedule item
<jsp:useBean id="errors" scope="request"                           ❷ Request scoped
    class="java.util.ArrayList" type="java.util.List" />              generic error list
<jsp:useBean id="scheduleBean" scope="page"
    class="com.nealford.art.mvcsched.ScheduleBean" />              ❸ ScheduleBean
<jsp:setProperty name="scheduleItem" property="*" />  ❹             created with
                                        Automatic repopulation of      Page scope for
<HTML>                                     fields from request          combobox
<HEAD>
<TITLE>
Add Schedule Item
</TITLE>
</HEAD>
<BODY>
<H3>
Add New Schedule Entry
</H3>
```

❶ At the top of the page, there is a declaration for a `scheduleItem` reference. This declaration is scoped to the request, indicating that this object may have been passed to this JSP. The controller servlet in listing 4.8 passes nothing to this page. We'll see that the validation controller may pass an invalid record back via this variable.

❷ An errors bean is declared. Referring back to the `ScheduleItem.validate()` method in listing 4.5, a failed validation generates a `List` object, which is returned to this page so that the list of errors may appear. You can pass generic versions of concrete objects by using the `type` attribute of the `useBean` tag. The `type` attribute is designed for exactly this situation. Even though the class identifies it as an `ArrayList`, it can be passed as the more generic `List` class. However, notice that both the `class` and `type` attributes are included, which is unusual. Both are needed in this case because in the initial case, no errors list is passed to this JSP. If just the `type` attribute appears, an error will be generated when no list is passed to this JSP because it cannot automatically instantiate the bean. In this case, we include both, which allows the page to create an empty `ArrayList` when no list is passed and use the `List` when it is.

❸ `ScheduleBean` is declared with page scope on this page. It is required only to get the list of event types, so it can be instantiated locally.

❹ The last part of the prelude is a call to populate the `scheduleItem` instance with any parameter values passed in the request, which is also used in the validation case.

The next portion of the page, shown in listing 4.10, handles validation errors.

Listing 4.10   The validation display section of ScheduleEntryView.jsp

```
<c:if test="${! empty errors}">
    <hr/>
    <b><u>Validation Errors</u><///b3><br>
    <font color="red">
    <c:forEach var="error" items="${errors}">
        <c:out value="${error}" /><br>
    </c:forEach>
    </font>
    <hr/>
</c:if>
```

The section of the JSP shown in listing 4.10 determines whether any errors have been passed back by checking the errors collection for records. If the JSP was called in response to a validation error, the errors list will not be empty. The JSP runtime ensures that all beans have been instantiated, either as a result of being passed to the page or via automatic construction. Therefore, this errors object will never be null. If errors are present, the list is iterated over (using JSP Standard Tag Library, or JSTL, tags), printing out each error in turn before showing the rest of the page. Figure 4.6 shows the result when a user has entered invalid data.

Figure 4.6
When the user enters invalid data, the application redirects him or her back to the entry page and displays a list of errors for the user to repair.

The last portion of the page handles the data-entry chores (listing 4.11).

Listing 4.11 The data-entry portion of ScheduleEntryView.jsp

```
<!-- Data entry form -->
<form action="saveentry" method="post">
<table border="0" width="30%" align="left">
  <tr>
    <th align="right">
      Duration
    </th>
    <td align="left">
    <input name="duration" size="16"
        value="<jsp:getProperty name="scheduleItem"
                property="duration"/>">
    </td>
  </tr>
  <tr>
    <th align="right">
      Event Type
    </th>
    <td align="left">
      <select name="eventTypeKey">
<%
        //-- get the list of allowable event types from bean
          int currentValue = scheduleItem.getEventTypeKey();
          Map eventMap = scheduleBean.getEventTypes();
          Set keySet = eventMap.keySet();
          Iterator eti = keySet.iterator();
          while (eti.hasNext()) {
```

Generates items for <select> from the model

```
                    int key = ((Integer) eti.next()).intValue();
    %>
                    <option value='<%= key %>'<%= (currentValue == key ?
                        "selected" : "") + ">" +
                        eventMap.get(new Integer(key)) %>
    <%
              }
    %>
          </select>
        </td>
      </tr>
      <tr>
        <th align="right">
          Start
        </th>
        <td align="left">
          <input name="start" size="16" value="<jsp:getProperty
              name="scheduleItem" property="start"/>"/>
        </td>
      </tr>
      <tr>
        <th align="right">
          Text
        </th>
        <td align="left">
          <input name="text" size="16"    value="<jsp:getProperty
              name="scheduleItem"    property="text"/>"/>
        </td>
      </tr>

      <tr>
        <td align="right">
            <input type="submit" name="Submit" value="Submit">
        </td>
        <td align="right">
            <input type="reset" value="Reset">
        </td>
      </tr>
    </table>
    </form>

    </body>
    </html>
```

The portion of the ScheduleEntryView JSP shown in listing 4.11 has the requisite HTML elements for entry, including both inputs and a select tag. Notice that in each of the inputs the value appears as a call to the scheduleItem bean. This results in no value when the page is initially called but allows the values of the input form to be re-populated when a validation error occurs. Using this property tag syntax means that the user doesn't have to reenter the valid values.

The code for the HTML <select> tag is more convoluted. The <select> tag encapsulates a set of <option> tags, one of which may be flagged as selected. The list of items should *never* be hard-coded into the JSP. This information must come from the model because it is a business rule for this application. It is a serious mistake to sprinkle hard-coded values throughout the view portion of the application because it breaks Model 2's clean separation of responsibilities. It also becomes a maintenance nightmare when (not if) those values change. Even when using Model 2 for separation of concerns, complexity still manages to creep in because of the necessary interface between display and logic.

Building the Save controller

The last file in the Model 2 schedule application is the SaveEntry controller, which handles validation and updates. It appears in Listing 4.12.

Listing 4.12   The SaveEntry controller performs validation and updates.

```
package com.nealford.art.mvcsched.controller;

import java.io.IOException;
import java.util.List;
import javax.servlet.RequestDispatcher;
import javax.servlet.ServletException;
import javax.servlet.http.HttpServlet;
import javax.servlet.http.HttpServletRequest;
import javax.servlet.http.HttpServletResponse;
import com.nealford.art.mvcsched.boundary.ScheduleDb;
import com.nealford.art.mvcsched.entity.ScheduleItem;
import com.nealford.art.mvcsched.util.ScheduleAddException;

public class SaveEntry extends HttpServlet {               ❶ Provides a top-level
                                                              outline of the behavior
    public void doPost(HttpServletRequest request   ◁─┘
                       HttpServletResponse response) throws
        ServletException, IOException {
        ScheduleItem newItem = populateNewItemFromRequest(request);
        List validationErrors = newItem.validate();
        if (!validationErrors.isEmpty())
            returnToInput(request, response, newItem,
                       validationErrors);
        else {
            addNewItem(newItem);
            forwardToSchedule(request, response);
        }
    }
```

```
private void addNewItem(ScheduleItem newItem) throws
        ServletException, IOException {
    try {
        new ScheduleDb().addRecord(newItem);
    } catch (ScheduleAddException sax) {
        getServletContext().log("Add error", sax);
    }
}

private void forwardToSchedule(HttpServletRequest request,
        HttpServletResponse response)
        throws ServletException, IOException {
    RequestDispatcher dispatcher =
            request.getRequestDispatcher("/viewschedule");
    dispatcher.forward(request, response);
}

private void returnToInput(HttpServletRequest request,
                          HttpServletResponse response,
                          ScheduleItem newItem,
                          List validationErrors) throws
        ServletException, IOException {
    RequestDispatcher dispatcher =
            request.getRequestDispatcher(
            "/ScheduleEntryView.jsp");
    request.setAttribute("scheduleItem", newItem);
    request.setAttribute("errors", validationErrors);
    dispatcher.forward(request, response);
    return;
}

private ScheduleItem populateNewItemFromRequest(
        HttpServletRequest
        request) {
    ScheduleItem newItem = new ScheduleItem();
    populateDuration(request, newItem);
    populdateEventTypeKey(request, newItem);
    populateStart(request, newItem);
    populateText(request, newItem);
    return newItem;
}

private void populateText(HttpServletRequest request,
                          ScheduleItem newItem) {
    String text = request.getParameter("text");
    if (text != null)
        newItem.setText(text);
}

private void populateStart(HttpServletRequest request,
                          ScheduleItem newItem) {
    String start = request.getParameter("start");
    if (start != null)
```

② Adds a new item to the database

③ Forwards back to the Schedule page

④ Returns to the input page (with an error list)

⑤ Creates a new item from request parameters

⑥ Assigns values from the request to ScheduleItem

```
                newItem.setStart(start);
        }

        private void populdateEventTypeKey(HttpServletRequest request,
                                          ScheduleItem newItem) {
            String typeKey = request.getParameter("eventTypeKey");
            try {
                if (typeKey != null)
                    newItem.setEventTypeKey(Integer.parseInt(typeKey));
            } catch (NumberFormatException nfx) {
                getServletContext().log("Conversion error:eventTypeKey",
                                        nfx);
            }
        }

        private void populateDuration(HttpServletRequest
                                    request, ScheduleItem newItem) {
            String duration = request.getParameter("duration");
            try {
                if (duration != null)
                    newItem.setDuration(Integer.parseInt(duration));
            } catch (NumberFormatException nfx) {
                getServletContext().log("Conversion error:duration",
                                        nfx);
            }
        }
    }
```

❶ The top-level public method performs the step-by-step behavior of the controller servlet. It populates a new item from request parameters, performs a validation on the item, and either dispatches to the input page (if errors exist) or adds the item and forwards them to the main view.

❷ The addNewItem() method adds a new item to the database via the boundary object.

❸ The forwardToSchedule() method performs a request dispatcher forward back to the main page of the application.

❹ The returnToInput() method bundles the error list and newly created item into the request collection and forwards back to the input page. Because the errors collection is populated, the errors will appear at the top of the form and the values present in newItem will appear in the form fields.

❺ The populateNewItemFromRequest() method takes care of populating a new ScheduleItem object with the values passed in the request parameters. This method performs its work by calling additional helper methods to handle the validation and assignment of the individual fields.

❻ The `populateText()` method is representative of the other helper methods that
validate and assign values from request parameters to the new item.

4.1.2   Options in Model 2

The Model 2 schedule application demonstrates the servlet-centric approach to
Model 2 applications. Note that we could have used JSPs throughout, replacing
the controller servlets with JSP pages. In particular, much of the code that appears
in listing 4.12 could be replaced with a single line of code that populates the bean
from request parameters:

```
<jsp:setProperty name="scheduleItem" property="*"/>
```

However, this contradicts the idea that JSPs should be used only for display and
servlets for code. In general, placing non-UI code in a JSP is a mistake, no matter
how convenient it may be. That convenience comes at a price. First, this practice
dilutes the consistency of your architecture. If you follow Model 2 to the letter,
you can always be assured that every JSP is a UI element and that every servlet executes code with no UI. Not every servlet is a controller, and no servlet contains UI
code. Second, pitfalls exist in some of JSP's automatic behavior. The automatic
population of properties we discussed earlier can cause problems for fields of the
bean that you don't want overwritten. For example, the user can pass a parameter
on the URL and inadvertently replace a value by automatically calling the mutator
method. Like many scripting languages, JSP is powerful—but that power breeds
danger. Even though the servlet code is more verbose, you shouldn't relinquish
control for the sake of expediency. You might prefer to create a utility class that
automatically populates the fields from the request parameters. Several web
frameworks discussed in part 2 use this approach.

Disadvantages of Model 2

The advantages in Model 2 have been spelled out in the sample code of this chapter, but there are disadvantages as well. First, more source files are generated.
Generally, you have at least three files for every unit of work in the web application. However, these files are usually small and (more important) highly cohesive.
Each file is responsible for one task and never blurs its responsibility into other
facets of the application where it has no business. Many small, single-purpose files
are better than a few, highly coupled files.

Second, when using Model 2 you must be diligent not to violate the architecture. If you start allowing model code into the view, you end up with the worst of
all worlds—more source files, each of which is a tangle of spaghetti-like coupled
code. Instead of searching through one poorly designed file, you must search

through a set of them. A perfect example of this kind of diligence appears in the entry view of our sample application, and particularly in listing 4.11. It would be easy (and involve less code) to place the event types directly into the HTML <select> tag on the JSP. This embodies the kind of design that must be avoided. When the event types change, the model changes and propagates through the application. Model 2 requires close attention to architecture and design throughout the project. Especially for teams who are new to this practice, code reviews should be conducted early and often to make sure that no undesirable code is slipping into the wrong place.

Third, Model 2 appears more complex than ad hoc web applications. However, once the development team understands the architecture, it makes development (and particularly maintenance) so much easier. Sometimes it is hard to convince developers to buy into Model 2. However, they will quickly see the improved maintainability and lead happier lives!

4.2 *Parameterizing commands with controller servlets*

One of the problems with Model 2 applications is the explosion of virtually identical controller servlets. Because you tend to have a controller per type of user request, you end up with numerous servlets. To consolidate these controller servlets, the Command design pattern from the Gang of Four (GoF) book seems appropriate.

The Command design pattern states its intent as:

> *Encapsulate a request as an object, thereby letting you parameterize clients with different requests, queue, or log requests, and support undoable operations.*

The Command pattern includes the kind of structure we need: an abstract class that allows subclasses to substitute generically for the parent. The intent is to create a combination of classes (a controller servlet and an action class) that combine to create much of the infrastructure common to all controller servlets.

Every controller servlet has set responsibilities. It should receive requests, optionally create beans, call methods on them, and forward to another resource, frequently a JSP. It is desirable to automate as much of this behavior as possible. Command encapsulates the common elements into an abstract super class, in this case called Action. This class includes methods for receiving requests, responses, and a servletContext. It also includes an abstract execute() method. Concrete child classes inherit from Action and override the execute() method to perform work. A sample inheritance tree looks like figure 4.7.

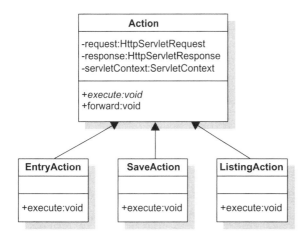

Figure 4.7
The Command design pattern abstracts commands into objects instead of switch statements, allowing for easy extendibility.

Once the Action class is in place, you can write a generic controller servlet that will have the job of creating action objects, which in turn do work and forward requests. The generic controller uses a reference list that matches requests to actions. This is often referred to as the Front Controller design pattern.

4.2.1 An example of parameterizing commands

The sample application that illustrates parameterizing commands is a simple web application that shows a list of all Java keywords and provides a link at the bottom for submitting requests for new keywords. Figure 4.8 shows the main page. This sample application appears in the source code archive as art_parameterizedcommands.

Figure 4.8
A sample application that shows Java's keywords and implements the Command design pattern to generically handle requests.

Building the model

Listing 4.13 shows most of the Model class.

Listing 4.13   The Model class for the parameterized requests sample

```
package com.nealford.art.parameterizedrequests;

import java.util.*;

public class TheModel {
    private List keywords = new Vector(10, 5);
    private List proposedKeywords = new Vector(5, 2);

    public TheModel() {
        keywords.add("abstract");
        keywords.add("default");
        keywords.add("if");

//-- lines ommitted for brevity's sake

        keywords.add("goto");
        keywords.add("package");
        keywords.add("synchronized");
    }

    public List getKeywords() {
        return keywords;
    }

    public List getProposedKeywords() {
        return proposedKeywords;
    }

    /**
     * Allows the user to add a new proposed keyword to the
     * langauge. Note that the new keywords aren't persisted
     * anywhere because a) This is a simple example and b) I
     * don't want people arbitrarily adding keywords to Java!
     */
    public void addKeyword(String newKeyword) {
        proposedKeywords.add(newKeyword);
    }
}
```

The model for this sample is simple. Most of the constructor doesn't appear due to space considerations. The deleted code is left to the reader's imagination. This model maintains two lists: one for existing keywords and the other for proposed keywords. The proposed keywords aren't persisted anywhere because this is a simple example.

The abstract Action class

Listing 4.14 shows the important portions of the abstract `Action` class.

Listing 4.14   The Action class declaration, execute(), and forward() methods

```
package com.nealford.art.parameterizedrequests;

import javax.servlet.http.HttpServletRequest;
import javax.servlet.http.HttpServletResponse;
import javax.servlet.*;
import java.io.IOException;

abstract public class Action {
    private HttpServletRequest request;
    private HttpServletResponse response;
    private ServletContext servletContext;

    abstract public void execute();

    public void forward(String forwardResource) {
        try {
            RequestDispatcher rd =
                getRequest().getRequestDispatcher(
                forwardResource);
            rd.forward(getRequest(), getResponse());
        } catch (IOException iox) {
            servletContext.log("Forward Error", iox);
        } catch (ServletException sx) {
            servletContext.log("Servlet Error", sx);
        }
    }
}
```

Annotations in listing:
- `abstract public void execute();` — **Overridden in each child action**
- `public void forward(String forwardResource) {` — **Generic forward() method for all actions**

The `Action` class is an abstract class with a few concrete methods. It is an abstract class and not an interface because there is some behavior that can be defined in this class. The private member variables are declared at the top, and their public accessors and mutators appear at the bottom of the class (we omitted them for space considerations). The key method of this class is the abstract `execute()` method. It is the sole abstract method in the class and the one that is overridden to perform real work by the child classes. The `forward()` method is a helper method that accepts a resource and handles the details of creating a `RequestDispatcher` and forwarding the request. The `forward()` method is forced to handle the checked exceptions generated by the `RequestDispatcher`. One of the reasons that the `Action` class contains the `ServletContext` member variable is to allow for graceful logging of errors via `servletContext.log()`. We cover graceful logging in depth in chapter 16.

Concrete actions

Three concrete subclasses of Action appear in the parameterized command application (the classes shown in figure 4.6). The first Action subclass is the entry point of the application, ListingAction (listing 4.15). The code in listing 4.15 looks very much like servlet code. However, instead of directly referencing a request variable, the getRequest() method, the accessor method from the parent Action class is called. When the controller creates the ListingAction object, it automatically populates the request, response, and servletContext.

Listing 4.15   The entry point of the application

```java
package com.nealford.art.parameterizedcommands;

import java.util.Collections;
import java.util.List;
import javax.servlet.http.HttpSession;

public class ListingAction extends Action {

    public void execute() {
        TheModel model = getOrCreateModel();
        List sortedKeywords = getSortedKeywords(model);
        bundleAttributesForView(model, sortedKeywords);
        forwardToView();
    }                                           ❶ Gets model from session
                                                    or creates new one
    private TheModel getOrCreateModel() {   ◁
        HttpSession session = getRequest().getSession(true);
        TheModel model = null;
        model = (TheModel) session.getAttribute("model");
        if (model == null) {
            model = new TheModel();
            session.setAttribute("model", model);
        }
        return model;
    }                                           ❷ Sorts the collection
                                                    of keywords
    private List getSortedKeywords(TheModel model) {   ◁
        List sortedKeywords = model.getKeywords();
        Collections.sort(sortedKeywords);
        return sortedKeywords;
    }                                    Places displayable
                                    attributes in the request ❸
    private void bundleAttributesForView(TheModel model,   ◁
            List sortedKeywords) {
        getRequest().setAttribute("keywords", sortedKeywords);
        getRequest().setAttribute("proposed",
                model.getProposedKeywords());
    }
```

```
    private void forwardToView() {
        forward("/Listing.jsp");
    }
}
```

**Uses the inherited
❹ forward()**

❶ ListingAction creates a session and checks to see if a model object is already there. If not, a new one is created and placed into the session. The getOrCreate-Model() method handles the situation where a user has added proposed keywords to the model and returned to this page. In fact, this builds a type of singleton access for the model—each user will have only one model object (until his or her session times out).

❷ Next, ListingAction gets the list of keywords and sorts them, using the standard Collections.sort() method.

❸ The keywords and proposed keywords are bundled into the request collection.

❹ The request is dispatched to the JSP for display.

The target JSP, shown in listing 4.16, is simple and straightforward.

Listing 4.16   The listing JSP that corresponds to the listing action

```
<%@ taglib prefix="c" uri="http://java.sun.com/jstl/core" %>
<%@ page import="java.util.*" %>
<jsp:useBean id="keywords"
            scope="request" class="java.util.List" />
<jsp:useBean id="proposed"
            scope="request" class="java.util.List" />
<html>
<head>
<title>Listing</title>
</head>
<body>
<hr><h1>Listing of Java Keywords</h1><hr>
<p><c:forEach var="keyword" items="${keywords}">
    <b><code><c:out value="${keyword}"/></code></b><br>
</c:forEach></p>
<hr><h2>Proposed New Keywords</h2><hr>
<p><c:forEach var="propKeyword" items="${proposed}">
    <b><code><c:out value="${propKeyword}"/></code></b><br>
</c:forEach></p>
<form method="post" action="controller?cmd=formEntry">
<input type="submit" name="Add Keyword" value="Add New Keyword">
</form>
<hr>
</body>
</html>
```

Near the bottom of listing 4.16, the HTML `<form>` tag that allows users to add new proposed keywords appears. The URL invokes the main servlet, passing a `cmd` parameter for `formEntry`. This servlet is the generic controller servlet. It accepts a parameter that indicates which action should be created to handle the request. The `formEntry` action is shown in listing 4.17.

Listing 4.17   The formEntry action

```
package com.nealford.art.parameterizedcommands;

public class EntryAction extends Action {

    public void execute() {
        forward("/EntryForm.jsp");
    }

}
```

The `EntryAction` class could hardly be simpler. It is similar to the controller servlet from listing 4.8 in that it could be eliminated—the dispatcher could map directly to the JSP. However, as we explained earlier, there are benefits to having trivial actions present to ensure consistency and maintainability. Eventually, it is likely that code will need to execute to set up the entry page. If the link from the previous view page points directly to the JSP, this action will have to be added. If it is already in place, only the new code has to be added. Thus, using a simple action (or controller) unifies the navigation in the application, making it consistent throughout the application.

The `EntryForm` JSP is also simple (listing 4.18).

Listing 4.18   The EntryForm JSP

```
<html>
<head>
<title>
EntryForm
</title>
</head>
<body>
<h1>
Add New Java Keyword
</h1>
<form method="post" action="controller?cmd=saveAction">
<br>Enter new keyword   :   <input name="keyword"><br>
<br><br>
<input type="SUBMIT" name="Update" value="Submit">
```

```
    </form>
  </body>
</html>
```

In fact, the entry page isn't technically a JSP at all, but a straight HTML document. In web applications, it is still a good idea to make any document that might ever contain code a JSP. In the future, code could easily be added to this page without changing any of the actions or servlets that reference it as a JSP. The entry page's form command maps to a save action, which appears in listing 4.19.

Listing 4.19 SaveAction saves changes to the model.

```
package com.nealford.art.parameterizedcommands;

public class SaveAction extends Action {

    public void execute() {
        TheModel model = (TheModel) getRequest().getSession().
                getAttribute("model");
        model.addKeyword(getRequest().getParameter("keyword"));
        forward("controller?cmd=listing");
    }
}
```

The SaveAction class retrieves the model from the user's session, adds the new keyword, and dispatches back to the main listing page. This action completes the circle for the web application, returning to the initial page via the main action class. The controller servlet is referenced by its short name, controller, and passed a parameter indicating which action it should invoke. The controller can be referenced by its short name because it has a servlet alias defined in the web.xml file for the project. The servlet mapping is shown in listing 4.20.

Listing 4.20 The servlet tag from the application's web.xml

```
<servlet>
  <servlet-name>controller</servlet-name>
  <servlet-class>
      com.nealford.art.parameterizedcommands.MainController
  </servlet-class>
  <init-param>
    <param-name>mapping</param-name>
    <param-value>/WEB-INF/mappings.properties</param-value>
  </init-param>
  <load-on-startup>1</load-on-startup>
</servlet>
```

The controller servlet mapping includes an init parameter that points to a properties file. The properties file is the cross-reference that maps the command parameters to the corresponding action classes. The mapping file is shown in listing 4.21.

Listing 4.21 The mapping file for this application

```
#Initial generation
#Thu Jan 24 17:11:27 CST 2002
formEntry=com.nealford.art.parameterizedcommands.EntryAction
listing=com.nealford.art.parameterizedcommands.ListingAction
saveAction=com.nealford.art.parameterizedcommands.SaveAction
```

Depending on the implementation of the controller servlet, the mapping might not be necessary. However, it would mean that every request would have to specify the formal action class name. As you can see from this example, the action class names can become quite long and cumbersome to type. The mapping document allows you to alias the commands and use a short name.

Building the generic controller

The generic controller servlet, shown in listing 4.22, is the last piece of this application. It is generic in that it isn't tied to this project at all. It will work equally well in any project with any set of actions. In fact, you should never need to change this controller.

Listing 4.22 The declaration and init() method of the MainController servlet

```
package com.nealford.art.parameterizedcommands;

import javax.servlet.*;
import javax.servlet.http.*;
import java.io.*;
import java.util.*;

public class MainController extends HttpServlet {
    private Properties mappings;

    public void init(ServletConfig config) throws      ❶ Loads mappings
            ServletException {
        super.init(config);
        InputStream is = null;
        try {
            String location =
                    config.getInitParameter("mapping");
            is = getServletContext().getResourceAsStream(
                    location);
            mappings = new Properties();      Loads properties via ❷
            mappings.load(is);                    init parameter
```

```
        } catch (IOException iox) {
           getServletContext().log("I/O Error", iox);
              iox.printStackTrace();
        } finally {
           try {
              is.close();
           } catch (IOException ignored) {
           }
        }
     }

    public void doGet(HttpServletRequest request,
           HttpServletResponse response) throws
           ServletException, IOException {
        String command = request.getParameter("cmd");
        String actionClass = (String) mappings.get(command);
        Action action = null;                    Translates request ❸
        try {                               parameter into class name
           action =
              (Action) Class.forName(actionClass).newInstance();
        } catch (ClassNotFoundException cnfx) {
           getServletContext().log("Class Not Found", cnfx);
           cnfx.printStackTrace();          Dynamically loads Action ❹
        } catch (IllegalAccessException iax) {
           getServletContext().log("Security Exception", iax);
        } catch (InstantiationException ix) {
           getServletContext().log("Instantiation Exception",
                  ix);
        }
        action.setRequest(request);
        action.setResponse(response);           ❺ Executes
        action.setServletContext(getServletContext());  the action
        action.execute();
     }

    public void doPost(HttpServletRequest request,
           HttpServletResponse response) throws
           ServletException, IOException {
        doGet(request, response);
     }
  }
```

❶ The `MainController` is a standard `HttpServlet`. It contains a single private member variable of type `java.util.Properties` that contains the mappings.

❷ The `init()` method of the servlet locates the mappings file via the init parameter from web.xml and loads it into memory. Note that thread safety isn't an issue because the `init()` method is called only once per servlet instance. Once `init()` has executed, the servlet "owns" a copy of the mappings. This means that this servlet doesn't support the dynamic modification of the mappings—it only reads them as it is instantiated by the servlet engine.

❸ The `doGet()` method retrieves the requested action parameter from the request. Next, it matches that command string with a class found in the mappings file. Note that because this is a global object in the servlet, thread safety is an issue. However, we don't have to worry about it in this case because mapping is a `Properties` object, a descendent of `Hashtable`, which is inherently thread safe. Additionally, the properties are only read, not modified, after the original access. If this mappings document changes in the future (for example, to an XML document) and becomes dynamic, you must ensure that this variable remains thread safe.

❹ The `Action` class is dynamically loaded into memory and instantiated. The feature of this design that makes this dynamic instantiation possible is the existence of the abstract `Action` class. All the actions are created as if they were just an `Action`, when in reality they are subclasses that have implemented `execute()` methods. If the mappings are misspelled in the properties file, an exception will be generated as the class attempts to load.

❺ Once the action has been created, the common properties are assigned and the `execute()` method is invoked.

4.2.2 *Advantages and disadvantages*

The advantage of parameterizing the commands and building a generic controller servlet lies in the fact that you never have to create any more controller servlets. The action classes are simpler than full-blown servlets and are tightly focused on their job. Part of the plumbing of the web application has been written generically and can thus be used whenever it is needed. A disadvantage of servlets in large Model 2 applications is that they stay in memory until evicted by the servlet engine. `Action` objects, on the other hand, are just regular Java objects and can be garbage-collected when they go out of scope. This can be an advantage on sites with several pages that are viewed infrequently. Using servlets for controllers means that you have a large number of quiescent servlets in memory.

The fact that `Action` objects don't stay in memory can be a disadvantage in applications that have a few very busy pages. In such an application, you can mitigate this problem in a couple of ways. You create the controllers for the busiest parts of the applications as "regular" controller servlets and leave the action infrastructure in place for the less busy parts. Nothing in the design using parameterized commands prevents you from mixing and matching actions and servlets. Another approach is to create your own caching scheme for `Action` objects, perhaps adding a flag in the properties file for the ones you want to cache. Then, when you create a cacheable action you can add it to a collection maintained by the controller servlet. When subsequent requests appear for that resource, you pull it from the collection instead of creating it anew.

Another advantage is that the displayed page in the browser's address bar will always be "controller" (you can use hidden fields to send the cmd parameter) so the user cannot bookmark pages embedded within the application. If users do create bookmarks, they will be taken to the main page when they use the bookmark, not to the bookmarked page. This gives the web developer more control over the access to the pages of the application.

The important aspect of the parameterized commands sample is the generic controller servlet. Everything else represents the simplest number of moving parts to demonstrate it. Nothing ties it specifically to this application. You can take the controller (with a different properties file) and use it in a variety of situations.

4.3 *Summary*

This chapter contained complete implementations of the design topics discussed in chapter 2. As you can see, the prime benefit of Model 2 is the clean separation between the responsibilities in the application. In practical applications, you must be diligent in policing this design. The worst problem facing Model 2 applications is the stealthy leaking of code outside its designated place. For example, it is all too easy to place items such as lists of values into JSPs rather than delivering them from a model bean. Once this has happened, you have crippled the main advantage of Model 2's clean separation and instead you now have a poorly designed application with more source files. It is critical to avoid this problem when you are new to Model 2. I recommend that a "design cop" be assigned to new projects to make sure everyone is implementing the pattern correctly.

The judicious use of design patterns can improve the efficiency and maintainability of your application while reducing the amount of code necessary. Using the Command design pattern, we were able to create a generic, reusable controller, which is an example of the benefits of good design. It is a fallacy that using design patterns leads to more code. Instead, frequently you end up with more classes but less code. In general, you should try to create more cohesive classes. Classes should be as single-purpose as possible. It is easier to reuse 10 single-purpose, highly cohesive classes than to reuse one class that does 10 separate things. Of course, while using design patterns isn't the only way to gain this benefit, it frequently results from their use.

The second example of this chapter showed you how to create code that is reusable in other web applications. It is, in fact, the beginnings of a web application framework. The next chapter expands on this idea.

Part II

Web frameworks

A framework is a set of related classes and other supporting elements that make application development easier by supplying prebuilt parts. Frameworks become popular because they solve common problems and do so without seriously compromising the intent of the application they support. As development becomes more intricate, we rely on frameworks to ease complexity, enabling us to write at a higher level of abstraction. Just as frameworks become more abstract and powerful, the applications we write become increasingly complex. To reap the full benefit of using a framework, you must evaluate it in the context of the problem you are trying to solve (i.e., for the application you are currently writing). If the framework makes your job easier without forcing you to compromise, it is a good match. If you constantly have to code around the framework and "kludge" together solutions to problems caused by it, you should discard it.

The chapters in part 2 highlight a variety of frameworks that make building web applications easier. Most of them adhere to the Model 2 design pattern covered in part 1. Even though the same application appears in each chapter, the number of viable frameworks that exist to solve the same problem is surprising.

5

Using Struts

This chapter covers

- Building Model 2 applications with Struts
- Using `ActionForms` as entities
- Validating user input using validators

In the previous chapter, you saw how the judicious use of design patterns can help you consolidate common code into reusable assets—the first step in constructing your own framework. If you extrapolate this behavior to multiple developers and multiple projects, you have a generic framework, built from parts that are common to most applications. For example, many web applications need a database connection pooling facility—which is a perfect candidate for a framework component. Fortunately, you don't have to build each framework for web development from scratch; they already exist in abundance. Chapter 1 provided an overview of some available frameworks without showing how they are used to build real applications. This chapter does just that: it shows an example application built with the open-source Model 2 framework we described in chapter 1: Jakarta Struts. As the example unfolds, notice how this project is similar (and how it is different) from the two projects that appear in chapter 4.

5.1 Building Model 2 Web applications with Struts

Refer back to chapter 1 (section 1.3.1) for download instructions and for an overview of Struts' capabilities. The application we'll build next is similar in behavior to the schedule application from chapter 4, allowing for easy comparison and contrast. In the Struts schedule application, most of the "plumbing" code is handled by Struts. This sample application is available from the source code archive under the name art_sched_struts and uses Struts version 1.1.

5.1.1 The Struts schedule application

The first page of our Struts application shows a list of the currently scheduled events, and the second page allows the user to add more events. The first page appears in figure 5.1.

The user interface is quite sparse because we wanted to avoid cluttering the functionality of the code underneath. As in the Model 2 schedule application, the first order of business is the creation of the model.

The data access in this application uses virtually the same model beans for database access developed in chapter 4. Because Struts is a Model 2 framework, its architecture is similar enough that we can utilize the same type of model objects. However, one change appears in the `ScheduleDb` boundary class that makes building the input JSP much easier. Instead of returning a `Map` of the associations between the event key and the event, the Struts version of `ScheduleDb` returns a Struts object named `LabelValueBean`. The updated `getEventTypeLabels()` method appears in listing 5.1.

Figure 5.1
The Struts schedule application displays a schedule of upcoming events.

Listing 5.1 LabelValueBean encapsulates an association between a label and value.

```
public List getEventTypeLabels() {
    if (eventTypeLabels == null) {
        Map eventTypes = getEventTypes();
        eventTypeLabels = new ArrayList(5);
        Iterator ei = eventTypes.keySet().iterator();
        while (ei.hasNext()) {
            Integer key = (Integer) ei.next();
            String value = (String) eventTypes.get(key);
            LabelValueBean lvb = new LabelValueBean(value,
                key.toString());
            eventTypeLabels.add(lvb);
        }
    }
    return eventTypeLabels;
}
```

The built-in `LabelValueBean` class creates a mapping between a label (typically a `String`) and a value (typically also a `String`, although other types are possible). This is useful in cases where you need to show the user one text content (the label) but map it to a type used internally in the application (the value). The HTML `<select>` tag contains nested `<option>` tags, which consist of label-value pairs. The user selects the label from the display, but the value is what the `<select>` returns. `LabelValueBeans` are classes that encapsulate this label-value relationship.

5.1.2 *Value objects as form beans*

Struts manages value objects for the developer, providing such services as automatic population of values and validation that fires automatically when performing an HTML form POST. We discuss the mechanics of validation in a moment. To utilize Struts' value object infrastructure, your form-based value objects extend the Struts `ActionForm` class, transforming them into `ActionForms`. The Schedule-Item `ActionForm` is shown in listing 5.2.

Listing 5.2   The ScheduleItem ActionForm class

```
package com.nealford.art.strutssched;

import java.io.Serializable;
import javax.servlet.http.HttpServletRequest;
import org.apache.struts.action.*;

public class ScheduleItem extends ActionForm
        implements Serializable {
    private String start;
    private int duration;
    private String text;
    private String eventType;
    private int eventTypeKey;

    public ScheduleItem(String start, int duration, String text,
            String eventType, int eventTypeKey) {
        this.start = start;
        this.duration = duration;
        this.text = text;
        this.eventType = eventType;
        this.eventTypeKey = eventTypeKey;
    }

    public ScheduleItem() {
    }

    public void setStart(String newStart) {
        start = newStart;
    }

    public String getStart() {
        return start;
    }

    public void setDuration(int newDuration) {
        duration = newDuration;
    }
```

```
        public int getDuration() {
            return duration;
        }

        public void setText(String newText) {
            text = newText;
        }

        public String getText() {
            return text;
        }

        public void setEventType(String newEventType) {
            eventType = newEventType;
        }

        public String getEventType() {
            return eventType;
        }

        public void setEventTypeKey(int eventTypeKey) {
            this.eventTypeKey = eventTypeKey;
        }

        public int getEventTypeKey() {
            return eventTypeKey;
        }
    }
```

This `ActionForm` is mostly a collection of properties with accessor and mutator methods and is identical to the similar value object from the Model 2 schedule application (also named `ScheduleItem`), except for the super class.

The `ScheduleDb` collection manager and the `ScheduleItem` `ActionForm` make up the model for this application. Directly extending the Struts `ActionForm` in `ScheduleItem` does tie this value object to the Struts framework, diminishing its usefulness in non-Struts applications. If this is a concern, you may implement the entity as a separate class and allow the `ActionForm` to encapsulate the entity. In this scenario, the `ActionForm` becomes a proxy for the methods on the entity object. In this application, the entity directly extends `ActionForm` for simplicity's sake.

5.1.3 *Objectifying commands with Struts' actions*

Chapter 4 (section 4.2) illustrated the use of the Command design pattern to parameterize commands. We used an abstract `Action` class and a master controller servlet written in terms of that generic Action. For new pages, the developer extended `Action` and wrote page-specific behavior. The Action and controller combination handled much of the basic infrastructure of dispatching requests, freeing the developer to concentrate on the real work of the application. Struts employs the same pattern. The Struts designers have already implemented the controller servlet that understands Struts `Action` classes, which are classes that extend the Struts `Action` class and encapsulates a great deal of behavior within the framework. These actions act as proxies for the controller servlet, so they are responsible for the interaction between the models and the views. The first action invoked is `ViewScheduleAction`, which appears in listing 5.3.

Listing 5.3   The ViewScheduleAction is the first action invoked.

```
package com.nealford.art.schedstruts.action;

import java.io.IOException;
import java.sql.SQLException;
import javax.servlet.http.HttpServletRequest;
import javax.servlet.http.HttpServletResponse;
import javax.sql.DataSource;

import org.apache.struts.action.*;
import com.nealford.art.schedstruts.boundary.*;
import javax.servlet.*;

public class ViewScheduleAction extends Action {
    private static final String ERR_POPULATE =
            "SQL error: can't populate dataset";

    public ActionForward execute(ActionMapping mapping,
                                 ActionForm form,
                                 HttpServletRequest request,
                                 HttpServletResponse response)
        throws IOException, ServletException {

        DataSource dataSource = getDataSource(request);    <--- DataSource retrieval from the Struts controller
        ScheduleDb sb = new ScheduleDb();
        sb.setDataSource(dataSource);

        try {
            sb.populate();
        } catch (SQLException x) {
            getServlet().getServletContext().log(ERR_POPULATE, x);
        }
        request.setAttribute("scheduleBean", sb);
        return mapping.findForward("success");
    }
}
```

The Struts developers have created helper classes that handle many of the details of building a Struts application. For example, notice that the `execute()` method returns an `ActionForward` instance via the `mapping` parameter. This is a class that facilitates forwarding a request. It encapsulates the behavior of a `RequestDispatcher` and adds more functionality. The `ViewScheduleAction` first retrieves the `DataSource` instance created by the controller servlet by calling the `getDataSource()` method, which it inherits from `Action`. It then creates a `ScheduleDb`, populates it, adds it to the request, and dispatches to the appropriate view. The controller servlet is responsible for two tasks in the `ViewScheduleAction` class. First, it creates the connection pool and adds it to the appropriate collection. Second, it manages the mapping between requests and the appropriate `Action` instances.

5.1.4 *Configuring Struts applications*

The connection pool, mappings, and other configuration information for Struts appear in the Struts configuration XML file, which is shown in listing 5.4. The Struts framework defines this document's format.

Listing 5.4   The Struts XML configuration file

```xml
<?xml version="1.0" encoding="UTF-8"?>
<!DOCTYPE struts-config PUBLIC
"-//Apache Software Foundation//DTD Struts Configuration 1.1//EN"
"http://jakarta.apache.org/struts/dtds/struts-config_1_1.dtd">

<struts-config>
  <data-sources>              ❶ DataSource
    <data-source    ◁──────      definition
            type="com.mysql.jdbc.jdbc2.optional.MysqlDataSource">
      <set-property property="url"
            value="jdbc:mysql://localhost/schedule"  />
      <set-property property="user" value="root"  />
      <set-property property="password" value="marathon" />
      <set-property property="maxCount" value="5"  />
      <set-property property="driverClass"
            value="com.mysql.jdbc.Driver"  />
      <set-property value="1" property="minCount" />
    </data-source>
  </data-sources>
  <form-beans>         ❷ Form bean definition
    <form-bean name="scheduleItem"
            type="com.nealford.art.schedstruts.entity.ScheduleItem"
            dynamic="no" />
  </form-beans>
  <action-mappings>        ❸ Action definitions
    <action
      type="com.nealford.art.schedstruts.action.ViewScheduleAction"
      path="/sched">
```

```
                <forward name="success" path="/ScheduleView.jsp" />
    </action>
    <action
      type="com.nealford.art.schedstruts.action.ScheduleEntryAction"
      path="/schedEntry">
                <forward name="success" path="/ScheduleEntryView.jsp" />
    </action>
    <action name="scheduleItem"
      type="com.nealford.art.schedstruts.action.AddToScheduleAction"
      validate="true" input="/ScheduleEntryView.jsp"
      scope="session" path="/add">
                <forward name="success" path="/sched.do" />
                <forward name="error" path="/ScheduleEntryView.jsp" />
    </action>
  </action-mappings>
  <plug-in className="org.apache.struts.validator.ValidatorPlugIn">
    <set-property
      property="pathnames"
      value="/WEB-INF/validator-rules.xml,/WEB-INF/validation.xml"/>
  </plug-in>
</struts-config>
```

❶ The top section defines a Java Database Connectivity (JDBC) data source that is delivered from the Struts connection pooling utility class. This configuration file allows you to define all the characteristics of your database connection.

❷ This section of the document allows you to define form beans. These are the `ActionForm` subclasses utilized by the framework. The `ScheduleItem` class defined in listing 5.2 is the example declared here.

❸ This section of the document lists the action mappings. Each action mapping may define local forwards, which are web resources the Action may reference. In the `ViewScheduleAction` in listing 5.3, the return value is the mapping for success, which maps to the local forward defined in the configuration document for the `/sched` action.

Struts allows you to define properties beyond the mapping for each action. The path definition in the configuration file becomes the resource you request in the servlet engine. Typically, either a prefix mapping or extension mapping exists in the web.xml file for the project that allows you to automatically map resources to the Struts controller servlet. In this sample, we are using extension mapping. In the web.xml deployment descriptor, the following entry maps all resources with the extension of .do to the Struts controller:

```
<servlet-mapping>
 <servlet-name>action</servlet-name>
```

```
      <url-pattern>*.do</url-pattern>
   </servlet-mapping>
```

When this application executes, you request the sched.do resource from the web site. The extension-mapping mechanism maps the extension to the Action servlet. The Action servlet consults the struts-config document and maps sched to the class com.nealford.art.schedstruts.action.ViewScheduleAction. Thus, you can freely reference resources in your web application with the .do extension and rely on them being handled by the Struts controller. We aren't forced to use Struts for every part of the application. Any resource that should not be under the control of Struts can be referenced normally.

Struts configuration for the web application

The Struts controller is automatically loaded in the web.xml configuration document for the web application. It is a regular servlet instance that is configurable via init parameters. The web.xml file for this sample is shown in listing 5.5.

Listing 5.5   The web.xml configuration document for the schedule application

```xml
<?xml version="1.0" encoding="UTF-8"?>
<!DOCTYPE web-app PUBLIC
"-//Sun Microsystems, Inc.//DTD Web Application 2.3//EN"
"http://java.sun.com/dtd/web-app_2_3.dtd">
<web-app>
  <servlet>                                         Struts controller
    <servlet-name>action</servlet-name>   <──┘     servlet configuration
    <servlet-class>
        org.apache.struts.action.ActionServlet
    </servlet-class>
    <init-param>
      <param-name>application</param-name>
      <param-value>
        com.nealford.art.strutssched.Schedule
      </param-value>
    </init-param>
    <init-param>
      <param-name>config</param-name>
      <param-value>/WEB-INF/struts-config.xml</param-value>
    </init-param>
    <init-param>
      <param-name>debug</param-name>
      <param-value>2</param-value>
    </init-param>
    <load-on-startup>2</load-on-startup>
  </servlet>                              Extension mapping
  <servlet-mapping>          <───────┘   for the Action servlet
    <servlet-name>action</servlet-name>
```

```
      <url-pattern>*.do</url-pattern>
    </servlet-mapping>
    <session-config>
      <session-timeout>30</session-timeout>
    </session-config>
    <taglib>              ◁———┘ Struts taglib definitions
      <taglib-uri>/WEB-INF/struts-bean.tld</taglib-uri>
      <taglib-location>/WEB-INF/struts-bean.tld</taglib-location>
    </taglib>
    <taglib>
      <taglib-uri>/WEB-INF/struts-html.tld</taglib-uri>
      <taglib-location>/WEB-INF/struts-html.tld</taglib-location>
    </taglib>
    <taglib>
      <taglib-uri>/WEB-INF/struts-logic.tld</taglib-uri>
      <taglib-location>/WEB-INF/struts-logic.tld</taglib-location>
    </taglib>
    <taglib>
      <taglib-uri>/WEB-INF/struts-template.tld</taglib-uri>
      <taglib-location>/WEB-INF/struts-template.tld</taglib-location>
    </taglib>
  </web-app>
```

The configuration document for the web application loads the Struts controller on startup so that it need not to be loaded on first invocation. The parameters for this servlet specify the locations of a couple of configuration documents. The first is the struts-config.xml document (shown in listing 5.4). The other is under the `application` parameter, which points to a properties file. We'll explore the usefulness of this properties file shortly. The rest of this document defines URL patterns and the custom Struts tag libraries that make building the view JSPs easier.

5.1.5 *Using Struts' custom tags to simplify JSP*

The `ViewScheduleAction` eventually forwards the request to ScheduleView.jsp, which is shown in listing 5.6.

Listing 5.6 The main display JSP for the Struts version of the schedule application

```
<%@ taglib uri="/WEB-INF/struts-logic.tld" prefix="logic" %>
<%@ taglib uri="/WEB-INF/struts-bean.tld" prefix="bean" %>
<%@ taglib uri="/WEB-INF/struts-html.tld" prefix="html" %>

<html>
<head>
<title>                                  ┌─── Pulls text labels
<bean:message key="title.view" />  ◁───┘    properties
</title>
```

```
</head>
<body>
<h2><bean:message key="prompt.listTitle" /></h2></p>
<table border="2">
    <tr bgcolor="yellow">
        <th><bean:message key="prompt.start" /></th>
        <th><bean:message key="prompt.duration" /></th>
        <th><bean:message key="prompt.text" /></th>
        <th><bean:message key="prompt.eventType" /></th>
    </tr>
<logic:iterate id="schedItem"         ⟵—┘  Iterates with Struts tag
        type="com.nealford.art.schedstruts.entity.ScheduleItem"
        name="scheduleBean" property="list" >
        <tr>
            <td><bean:write name="schedItem" property="start" />
            <td><bean:write name="schedItem"
                            property="duration" />
            <td><bean:write name="schedItem" property="text" />
            <td><bean:write name="schedItem"
                            property="eventType" />
        </tr>
</logic:iterate>
</table>
<p>
<a href="schedEntry.do"> Add New Schedule Item</a>
</body>
</html>
```

While the `Action` class is very similar to the controller from the Model 2 schedule application in chapter 4 (section 4.1.1), this JSP is significantly different. The first major difference is the declaration of a number of taglibs at the top of the file. Struts defines numerous custom tags, in four different categories, to aid you in building JSPs. The four categories are listed in table 5.1.

Table 5.1   Struts custom tags

Name	TLD File	Description
Bean tags	struts-bean.tld	The struts-bean tag library contains JSP custom tags useful in defining new beans (in any desired scope) from a variety of possible sources, as well as a tag that renders a particular bean (or bean property) to the output response.
HTML tags	struts-html.tld	The struts-html tag library contains JSP custom tags useful in creating dynamic HTML user interfaces, including input forms.

continued on next page

Table 5.1 **Struts custom tags** *(continued)*

Name	TLD File	Description
Logic tags	struts-logic.tld	The struts-logic tag library contains tags that are useful in managing conditional generation of output text, looping over object collections for repetitive generation of output text, and application flow management.
Template tags	struts-template.tld	The struts-template tag library contains tags that are useful in creating dynamic JSP templates for pages that share a common format. These templates are best used when it is likely that a layout shared by several pages in your application will change.

Continuing with the analysis of ScheduleView in listing 5.6, the next item of interest concerns the text labels. In the Model 2 schedule application, the title was placed directly inside the JSP page. However, Struts defines a mechanism whereby you can isolate the labels and other user interface (UI) elements into a separate resource file and reference those resources via a Struts tag. The external resource is a PropertyResourceBundle, which has the same format as a properties file, and the key attribute indicates the key value for the string resource. The resource properties file for this application is shown in listing 5.7.

Listing 5.7 The resource properties file for our application

```
prompt.duration=Duration
prompt.eventType=Event Type
prompt.start=Start Date
prompt.text=Text
prompt.listTitle=Schedule List
prompt.addEventTitle=Add New Schedule Entry

title.view=Schedule Items
title.add=Add Schedule Items

button.submit=Submit
button.reset=Reset

errors.header=Validation Error
errors.ioException=I/O exception rendering error messages: {0}
error.invalid.duration=
    Duration must be positive and less than 1 month
error.no.text=You must supply text for this schedule item

errors.required={0} is required.
errors.minlength={0} can not be less than {1} characters.
errors.maxlength={0} can not be greater than {1} characters.
errors.invalid={0} is invalid.
```

```
errors.byte={0} must be a byte.
errors.short={0} must be a short.
errors.integer={0} must be an integer.
errors.long={0} must be a long.
errors.float={0} must be a float.
errors.double={0} must be a double.

errors.date={0} is not a date.
errors.range={0} is not in the range {1} through {2}.
errors.creditcard={0} is an invalid credit card number.
errors.email={0} is an invalid e-mail address.
```

This mapping mechanism serves two purposes. First, it allows you to ensure common labels and titles throughout the application. If you have a specific label for a button that appears in multiple locations, you can reference the same resource and change it everywhere with a simple change to the resource. The other benefit involves internationalization, which we look at in the next section.

5.1.6 *Internationalization with Struts*

You can define the resource bundle keys used by Struts custom tags independently of the language of the labels and other resources. The location of this properties file is the `application` init parameter in the web.xml file in listing 5.5. Struts allows you to create a properties file in a particular language (in our case, American English) as the default resource file. You can then create additional resource files that have the same name with an additional locale code suffix. The internationalization characteristics provided by Struts supports the standard capabilities in the SDK using ResourceBundles. For example, to create a French version of the properties file, you would create schedule_fr.properties. When a request arrives from a browser, part of the request information indicates the user's locale, which is a predefined two- or four-digit identifier indicating the language of that user. If a user accesses the web application using a browser that identifies it as a French speaker, Struts automatically pulls the labels from the localized properties file named schedule_fr.properties. If the user is Canadian, Struts will look for a properties file with the fr_CA suffix. If it doesn't exit, the user gets the generic French localized properties. If a language is requested that doesn't have a specific properties file, the user gets the default one. A partial listing of some locales appears in table 5.2.

The next item of interest in listing 5.6 is the `iterate` tag. In the Model 2 schedule application in chapter 4 (in particular, listing 4.7), one of the few places in the JSP where we were forced to resort to scriptlet code and/or JSP Standard Tag

Table 5.2   Some character locales supported by Struts

Locale	Language	Country
da_DK	Danish	Denmark
DE_AT	German	Austria
DE_CH	German	Switzerland
DE_DE	German	Germany
el_GR	Greek	Greece
en_CA	English	Canada
en_GB	English	United Kingdom
en_IE	English	Ireland
en_US	English	United States
es_ES	Spanish	Spain
fi_FI	Finnish	Finland
fr_BE	French	Belgium
fr_CA	French	Canada
fr_CH	French	Switzerland
fr_FR	French	France
it_CH	Italian	Switzerland
it_IT	Italian	Italy
ja_JP	Japanese	Japan
ko_KR	Korean	Korea
nl_BE	Dutch	Belgium
nl_NL	Dutch	Netherlands
no_NO	Norwegian (Nynorsk)	Norway
no_NO_B	Norwegian (Bokmål)	Norway
pt_PT	Portuguese	Portugal
sv_SE	Swedish	Sweden
tr_TR	Turkish	Turkey
zh_CN	Chinese (Simplified)	China
zh_TW	Chinese (Traditional)	Taiwan

Library (JSTL) tags was when we needed to iterate over a list of items. Struts handles this situation with the `iterate` custom tag. This tag uses the attributes listed in table 5.3.

Table 5.3 The Struts iterate tag attributes

Attribute	Value	Description
id	schedItem	The local (i.e., within the tag body) name of the object pulled from the collection.
type	com.nealford.art.sched-struts.entity.ScheduleItem	The type of objects found in the collection. The tag automatically casts the items it pulls from the collection to this class.
name	scheduleBean	The name of the bean that you want to pull from a standard web collection (in this case, `schedule-Bean` from the request collection).
property	list	The name of the method on the bean that returns the collection.

The `iterate` tag works with a variety of collections of objects, including arrays. This is a powerful tag because it takes care of typecasting and assignment for you. Within the tag body, you can freely reference the properties and methods of the objects from the collection without worrying about typecasting. Also notice that there is no longer any scriptlet code in the JSP, not even a `useBean` declaration. The code on this page is much cleaner than the corresponding code in a typical Model 2 application.

At the bottom of the file, an HTML `<href>` tag appears that points to SchedEntry.do. Clicking on this link invokes another Action object (`ScheduleEntryAction`) through the Struts controller.

5.1.7 *Struts' support for data entry*

`ScheduleEntryAction` is the action invoked when the user clicks on the hyperlink at the bottom of the view page. It leads to the data-entry screen, shown in figure 5.2.

`ScheduleEntryAction` is responsible for setting up the edit conditions. The code appears in listing 5.8.

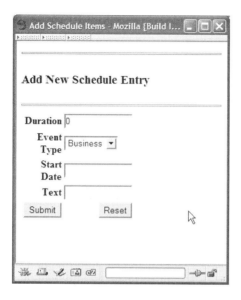

Figure 5.2
`ScheduleEntryAction` allows the user to enter new schedule items and performs automatic validation through the `ActionForm` associated with `AddToScheduleAction`.

Listing 5.8   The ScheduleEntryAction action subclass sets up editing.

```
package com.nealford.art.schedstruts.action;

import javax.servlet.http.*;
import javax.servlet.ServletException;
import java.io.IOException;
import org.apache.struts.action.*;
import javax.sql.DataSource;
import com.nealford.art.schedstruts.boundary.*;

public class ScheduleEntryAction extends Action {
    private static final String ERR_DATASOURCE_NOT_SET =
            "ScheduleEntryAction: DataSource not set";

    public ActionForward execute(ActionMapping mapping,
            ActionForm form, HttpServletRequest request,
            HttpServletResponse response) throws IOException,
            ServletException {

        ScheduleDb sb = new ScheduleDb();
        DataSource ds = getDataSource(request);
        if (ds == null)
            throw new ServletException(ERR_DATASOURCE_NOT_SET);
        sb.setDataSource(ds);
        //-- place the scheduleBean on the session in case the
        //-- update must redirect back to the JSP -- it must be
        //-- able to pull the scheduleBean from the session, not
        //-- the request
        HttpSession session = request.getSession(true);
```

```
        session.setAttribute("eventTypes", sb.getEventTypeLabels());
        return mapping.findForward("success");
    }
}
```

The view JSP for this page must be able to pull event types from the `ScheduleDb` to display in the HTML select control. Adding the `ScheduleDb` to the request and forwarding it to the JSP could normally accomplish this. However, the automatic validation functionality of Struts adds some complexity to this scenario. More about this issue appears in section 5.1.8. For now, trust that the session, not the request, must be used here. Before this mystery is unraveled, let's discuss the view portion of this request.

Building the entry view

The action in listing 5.8 forwards the schedule bean to the entry view JSP, which appears in listing 5.9.

Listing 5.9   ScheduleEntryView.jsp provides the insertion user interface.

```
<%@ taglib uri="/WEB-INF/struts-html.tld" prefix="html" %>
<%@ taglib uri="/WEB-INF/struts-bean.tld" prefix="bean" %>
<%@ taglib uri="/WEB-INF/struts-logic.tld" prefix="logic" %>

<html>
<head>
<title><bean:message key="title.add" /></title>
</head>
<body>
<h3><bean:message key="prompt.addEventTitle" /></h3>
<logic:messagesPresent>
    <h3><font color="red">
        <bean:message key="errors.header"/>
    </font></h3>
    <ul>
        <html:messages id="error">
            <li><bean:write name="error"/></li>
        </html:messages>
    </ul>
    <p/>
</logic:messagesPresent>

<html:form action="add.do">
<table border="0" width="30%" align="left">
  <tr>
    <th align="right">
      <bean:message key="prompt.duration"/>
    </th>
```

```
    <td align="left">
      <html:text property="duration" size="16"/>
    </td>
  </tr>
  <tr>
    <th align="right">
      <bean:message key="prompt.eventType"/>
    </th>
    <td align="left">
      <html:select property="eventTypeKey">        Struts' <select> tag
        <html:options collection="eventTypes" property="value"
                      labelProperty="label"/>
      </html:select>

    </td>
  </tr>
  <tr>
    <th align="right">
      <bean:message key="prompt.start"/>
    </th>
    <td align="left">
      <html:text property="start" size="16"/>
    </td>
  </tr>
  <tr>
    <th align="right">
      <bean:message key="prompt.text"/>
    </th>
    <td align="left">
      <html:text property="text" size="16"/>
    </td>
  </tr>

  <tr>
    <td align="right">
        <html:submit>
            <bean:message key="button.submit"/>
        </html:submit>
    </td>
    <td align="right">
        <html:reset>
            <bean:message key="button.reset"/>
        </html:reset>
    </td>
  </tr>
</table>
</html:form>

</body>
</html>
```

This JSP provides two fertile topics, and they are covered in reverse order. The first topic appears in the body of the page with the custom Struts JSP tags. Using Struts tags instead of standard HTML tags provides at least two benefits for this page. The first benefit is the ability to define the text labels in the application-wide properties file, discussed earlier. The second benefit is the immense simplification of some HTML constructs. If you refer back to the Model 2 schedule application in listing 4.11, you will find that 17 lines of mixed HTML and scriptlet code are required to generate the list of select options from the database. That code is ugly and hard to maintain. The annotation in listing 5.9 shows how the same behavior is accomplished with Struts.

5.1.8 *Declarative validations*

Another topic of interest on the `ScheduleEntryView` page is validation. One of the most common tasks in web applications is the validation of data entered by the user via an HTML POST. Generally, this is handled in the controller where the page posts. If the validations fail, the user is redirected back to the page to correct the errors. A friendly web application will replace all the values the user typed in so that the user only has to correct the errors, not type all the values back into the page. This behavior is coded by hand, frequently using the JSP * `setProperty` command to automatically repopulate the fields:

```
<jsp:setProperty name="beanName" property="*" />
```

However, this command presents some problems in that it isn't very discriminating.

Struts provides a graceful alternative. Referring back to the struts-config document in listing 5.8, one of the action entries (`AddToScheduleAction`) is associated with a `<form-bean>` tag. The tag associates a name (`addItem`) with a class that is in turn associated with the `add` action. Struts allows you to associate action forms with actions via the `<form-bean>` tag. In those cases, Struts performs some special handling of the action form classes. When a form bean is associated with an action and that action is invoked, Struts looks for an instance of the form bean in the user's session. If it doesn't find one, it automatically instantiates it and adds it to the session.

Struts is intelligent enough to pull data automatically from the form bean and populate the HTML fields with the values. So, for example, if you have a `getAddress()` method in your form bean and an HTML input called `address`, Struts automatically fills in the value of the field. This mechanism makes it easy to build wizard-style interfaces with Struts, where the user supplies information across a series of screens. This mechanism also assists in validation.

Declarative validations allow the developer to define rules in a configuration document that are automatically enforced by the framework. Many web applications have simple validation needs, usually falling into the categories of required fields, minimum and maximum values, and input masks. To configure declarative validations, you must first define the validation rules for your form in an XML document, whose format is mandated by Struts. The validation document for the Struts 1.1 schedule application is shown in listing 5.10.

Listing 5.10 The validation.xml rules file for the Struts schedule application

```
<?xml version="1.0" encoding="ISO-8859-1" ?>

<!-- DTD omitted for space considerations -->

<form-validation>
  <formset>
    <form     name="scheduleItem">
    <field    property="duration"
              depends="required,integer,intRange">
         <arg0 key="prompt.duration"/>

         <arg1 name="intRange"
               key="${var:min}" resource="false"/>

         <arg2 name="intRange"
               key="${var:max}" resource="false"/>

         <var>
             <var-name>min</var-name>
             <var-value>0</var-value>
         </var>
         <var>
             <var-name>max</var-name>
             <var-value>31</var-value>
         </var>
    </field>
    <field    property="text"
              depends="required,minlength">
         <arg0 key="prompt.text"/>
         <arg1 name="minlength"
               key="${var:minlength}" resource="false"/>
         <var>
             <var-name>minlength</var-name>
             <var-value>1</var-value>
         </var>
    </field>
    </form>
  </formset>
</form-validation>
```

Validation declaration for duration **❶**

Message resource key for validation message **❷**

Variable declarations defining validation criteria **❸**

Variable values for validation criteria **❹**

Validation declaration for the text field **❺**

❶ This mapping creates a validation for the `duration` property of the `scheduleItem` class, validating that a value for the field exists (`required`) and that it is an integer (`integer`), and defining a range (`intRange`).

❷ The first argument is a mapping into the application's resource file, pulling the same prompt value for the field used on the form.

❸ The fields may contain several arguments. In this case, the minimum and maximum arguments are supplied as replaceable variables, defined in the entry in the file. The syntax for referencing the variables is the now common $\{x\}$ syntax used by JSTL.

❹ The last part of the field definition includes the variable values used in the preceding arguments. In this example, the `min` and `max` values define the minimum and maximum duration values.

❺ The text field validation requires a value and it must be at least one character in length.

The next step in configuring declarative validations is the addition to the struts-config file of the validator plug-in. The Struts configuration file supports plug-ins to provide additional behavior (like validations); listing 5.11 shows the plug-in portion of the struts-config document.

Listing 5.11   The struts-config document's <plug-in> tag with the validator plug-in

```
<plug-in className="org.apache.struts.validator.ValidatorPlugIn">
  <set-property
    property="pathnames"
    value="/WEB-INF/validator-rules.xml,/WEB-INF/validation.xml"/>
</plug-in>
```

The validator plug-in specifies two XML configuration documents: the document particular to the application (validation.xml, shown in listing 5.10) and validator-rules.xml, which is generic across all Struts applications. The presence of the plug-in and the configuration documents enable declarative validations.

The results of the validation are shown in figure 5.3.

Declarative validation is ideal for situations like the schedule application, where the validation requirements fit into the scope of the validator plug-in (namely, required fields and minimum values). Struts also includes a more robust validation mechanism for more complex cases. The `ActionForm` class includes a `validate()` method, which may be overridden in child `ActionForms`. When posting to an action, Struts performs declarative validations and then checks to see if a

Figure 5.3   The validation in the Struts 1.1 version of the schedule application uses validations declared in the validations.xml configuration file.

form bean has a `validate()` method. This method returns a collection of `Action-Error` objects. If the collection is empty, Struts continues with the execution of the action. If there are items in the collection, Struts automatically redirects back to the input form that invoked the controller, passing the form bean back with it.

Struts tags placed on the page test for the presence of validation failures and display the results. For example, the top of the `ScheduleEntryView` page in listing 5.9 includes the following code:

```
<logic:messagesPresent>
    <h3><font color="red">
        <bean:message key="errors.header"/>
    </font></h3>
    <ul>
        <html:messages id="error">
            <li><bean:write name="error"/></li>
        </html:messages>
    </ul>
    <p/>
</logic:messagesPresent>
```

If validation error messages are present in the collection, the messages (pulled from the application's properties file) are displayed, yielding the result shown in figure 5.3.

Building the AddToScheduleAction

The last piece of the Struts schedule application is the action object that is posted from the entry JSP. AddToScheduleAction is shown in listing 5.12.

Listing 5.12   AddToScheduleAction inserts the record.

```
package com.nealford.art.schedstruts.action;

import java.io.IOException;

import javax.servlet.ServletException;
import javax.servlet.http.HttpServletRequest;
import javax.servlet.http.HttpServletResponse;
import javax.servlet.http.HttpSession;

import com.nealford.art.schedstruts.boundary.ScheduleDb;
import com.nealford.art.schedstruts.entity.ScheduleItem;
import com.nealford.art.schedstruts.util.ScheduleAddException;
import org.apache.struts.action.Action;
import org.apache.struts.action.ActionForm;
import org.apache.struts.action.ActionForward;
import org.apache.struts.action.ActionMapping;

public class AddToScheduleAction extends Action {
    private static final String ERR_INSERT =
            "AddToScheduleAction: SQL Insert error";

    public ActionForward execute(ActionMapping mapping,
            ActionForm actionForm, HttpServletRequest request,
            HttpServletResponse response) throws IOException,
            ServletException {
        ScheduleDb sb = new ScheduleDb();
        sb.setDataSource(getDataSource(request));
        ScheduleItem si = (ScheduleItem) actionForm;
        try {
            sb.addRecord(si);
        } catch (ScheduleAddException sax) {
            getServlet().getServletContext().log(ERR_INSERT, sax);
            sax.printStackTrace();
        }
        //-- clean up extraneous session reference to eventTypes
        HttpSession session = request.getSession(false);
        if (session != null)
            session.removeAttribute("eventTypes");
        return mapping.findForward("success");
    }
}
```

Notice that no code appears in the AddToScheduleAction class to handle the validation. When the action is invoked, Struts "notices" that the form bean is associated with it in the struts-config.xml document. Because the form bean was created on the page that posted to this action, Struts validates the form based on the declarative validations. Failure of the validation automatically redirects to the entry JSP and fills in the form values. If the validation was successful, this action is invoked normally. To get the values entered via the form bean, we need only cast the `actionForm` instance that is passed to the `execute()` method. Once we have retrieved the value object, we pass it to the `ScheduleDb` to add it to the database and forward back to the listing page.

Because of the automatic form validation, this action may not be executed immediately. The event type list must be present for the HTML `<select>` tag to access the event types. However, if the user is automatically redirected back to the JSP because of a validation error, the list will no longer be available on the request. Thus, the event type list must be added to the session before invoking the page the first time. While it is generally a bad idea to place long-lived objects on the session, this action is careful to remove it when it has completed its work.

The last order of business is the forward to the next resource via the mapping object. In this case, the target is another action object via Struts, not a JSP. The `ActionForward` (like a `RequestDispatcher`) can be directed to any web resource, not just a JSP.

5.2 *Evaluating Struts*

As frameworks go, Struts is not overbearing. Many times, frameworks are so extensive that you can't get anything done outside the context of the framework. Or, 80 percent of what you want to do is extremely easy to do in the framework, another 10 percent is possible but difficult, and the last 10 percent cannot be accomplished because, of or in spite of, the framework. Struts is a much more lightweight framework. It fits into standard Model 2 type applications but doesn't preclude your writing code that doesn't need or want to fit into Struts. I estimate that Struts saves developers from having to write between 30 and 40 percent of the plumbing code normally required for a typical web application.

Struts provides support for building Model 2 applications by supplying a large part of the code necessary for every web application. It includes a variety of powerful custom tags to simplify common operations. It offers a clean automatic validation mechanism, and it eases building internationalized applications. Its disadvantages chiefly lie in its complexity. Because there are numerous moving parts in Struts, it takes some time to get used to how everything fits together. It is still a new framework, so you may experience some performance issues with extremely busy sites. However, my company has used it for several moderately busy web applications and been pleased with its performance and scalability, and the lack of serious bugs. Struts is now in its second release (Struts 1.1) and has garnered considerable developer support.

One apparent disadvantage of Struts goes hand in hand with one of its advantages. To fully exploit Struts' custom tags, you must write your JSPs in terms of Struts elements, replacing the standard HTML elements like `<input>`, `<select>`, and so on. However, one of the stated goals of the Model 2 architecture is a separation of responsibilities, ideally allowing the graphics designers to work solely on the user interface. If they are forced to use Struts tags, they can no longer use their design tools.

The Jakarta web site contains links to resources for Struts. One of these is a plug-in that allows you to use custom JSP tags within Dreamweaver UltraDev, one of the more popular HTML development environments. By using this extension, your HTML developers can still drop what looks like standard HTML elements (like `inputs`, `selects`, etc.), and the tool generates Struts tags. The extension is nice enough to allow the HTML developer to fill in attribute values for tags and generally work seamlessly with the Struts tags. We have used this within our company, and HTML designers who know virtually nothing about Java quickly become accustomed to working in this environment. Now you can have the Model 2 advantages of separation of responsibilities and still use Struts. Check out http://jakarta.apache.org/taglibs/doc/ultradev4-doc/intro.html for information on this and other useful Struts extensions.

If you are using more recent versions of Dreamweaver, it already offers support for all custom JSP tags, which includes the Struts tags. Several Java development environments are adding support for Struts. Starting with version 8, Borland's JBuilder development environment has wizards and other designers to facilitate Struts development.

5.3 Summary

Struts has found the middle ground of being useful, powerful, but not too complex. Using Struts is easy to anyone familiar with Model 2, and it helps developers build highly effective web applications. This chapter covered the open-source Struts framework. We walked you through the development of the schedule application, building the parts that accommodate the framework along the way. Struts contains many elements and can be daunting because of the perceived complexity, but once you understand it, it fits together nicely.

This chapter covered the basic classes necessary for the application, including the boundary and entity classes. We then discussed Struts Actions, comparing them to the Parameterized Command example from chapter 4. The discussion of actions led to the description of the main Struts controller servlet; we explained how to configure it through both the web.xml and struts-config.xml files. We described how action mappings work and how the controller dispatches requests. You learned about the user interface elements of Struts, including several of the Struts custom tags. Our schedule application showed you how to create pages with little or no Java code, relying on the custom tags. You also learned about complex HTML elements like `<select>`, and the concept of internationalization.

Next, we turned to validations and the automatic validation built into the framework. Finally, we discussed the advantages and disadvantages of using Struts.

In the next chapter, we look at Tapestry, another framework for building Model 2 applications that has virtually nothing in common with Struts.

Tapestry

Up to this point, we've looked at frameworks that are closely tied to the web APIs available in Java. A close tie to the web APIs is a natural preference when you're creating a web application; however, it is not a strict requirement. As you'll see in this chapter, Tapestry moves away from strictly web-based APIs and allows you to create web applications that feel more like traditional applications. Instead of worrying about such web topics as session tracking, URLs, and other minutia of HTTP and the Web in general, Tapestry builds a framework that effectively hides all these details. It uses an object model similar to traditional graphical user interface (GUI) development. Tapestry doesn't prevent you from accessing the servlet API, but it encapsulates it to the point where you don't need to very often. This approach means that developers coming from a desktop development background can capitalize on their skills without getting too far into web-specific APIs.

The goal of the Tapestry developers is to create a highly productive framework, where you shouldn't have to write any unnecessary, repetitive, or mechanical code. This chapter, like the other chapters highlighting frameworks, creates the schedule application using the Tapestry framework. As you will see, even though the application looks the same to the user, the internals are vastly different from the "straight" Model 2 or Struts versions.

6.1 Overview

Tapestry is an open-source Java framework for creating web applications in Java. It was developed by Howard Lewis Ship and is part of the Jakarta project at Apache. You can download it at http://jakarta.apache.org/tapestry. The version we use for this chapter is 2.2; version 3 was in beta at the time this book was written.

Tapestry is a large framework, more like Turbine than Struts. It provides a wealth of prebuilt components for handling such details as object pooling, session management, and HTML components. Because of the nature of the framework, it provides a high level of reusability for commonly needed elements in a web application. Coding in Tapestry is in terms of objects, properties, and methods, not URLs and query parameters. The framework handles all the low-level web details of the application.

6.2 The architecture

For presentation, Tapestry uses an alternative to scripting languages, such as JSP and Velocity. It provides an all-encompassing framework using a combination of

Java reflection, the JavaBeans API, and HTML templates. Much of the interaction between components in Tapestry takes place through interfaces designed into the framework. The framework defines the flow of logic through the system with a collection of specifications (written as XML documents) and framework objects.

A Tapestry application starts when the user accesses the application through the browser by pointing to the Tapestry `ApplicationServlet`. The servlet acts as the universal controller. It creates the Application Engine, which is the framework object that handles a user's interaction with the application. An instance of the engine is created for each user and acts as a proxy for that user. The engine reads the application specification from a configuration file, which defines the pages. The engine then reads the page specification and template for the requested page to determine the contents of the page, and uses this information to render the page for the user. Most of the configuration documents are cached in memory, so this process isn't as resource intensive as it might appear. The overall architecture is shown in figure 6.1.

The specification documents (both application and page) are XML documents. The template is an HTML document with replaceable portions. It is not a JSP or template-based view like Velocity (covered in chapter 9). Instead, the HTML elements serve as placeholders, replaced by the controls and JavaBeans

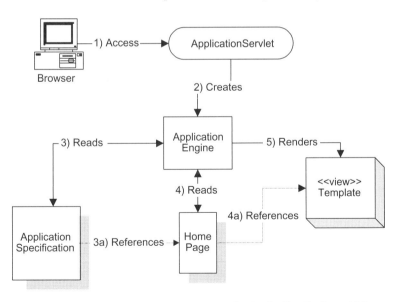

Figure 6.1   The application servlet bootstraps the Application Engine, which reads the specifications for the application and renders the results.

referenced in the specification document. The application servlet acts as the entry point into the framework. Once it has created the engine, there are no other parts of the "traditional" web API in a Tapestry application. Tapestry contains several "moving" parts. Because the framework handles so much of the application for you, it must perform a lot of work.

Tapestry's actions are driven by specification documents. The application, pages, components, and libraries are all referenced through these documents. Generally, the first access to a resource by Tapestry is through the specification document, which leads to the other resources Tapestry must load to fulfill the request. You must understand the specification documents to use Tapestry successfully.

This overview shows the basics of Tapestry's architecture and includes a working application. Rather than delve immediately into the schedule application, we think Tapestry is complex enough to warrant a "Hello, World" application to give you a flavor of its moving parts.

6.3   A simple Tapestry application

It is traditional when learning new language to create a "Hello, World" application to show the basic processes required to get an application up and running. We use this simple application because it includes the parts required for every Tapestry application.

6.3.1   Tapestry Hello, World

The Tapestry Hello, World application consists of the application servlet, the application and Home page specifications, and the Home page template.

The application servlet

The entry point for a Tapestry application is the application servlet. This is the bridge between the web world and the Tapestry world. In the web application configuration, it is the only registered servlet. That means that it is the only point where you can connect your application to the typical kinds of facilities from the web API, such as context parameters (as you will see, a Tapestry alternative exists for these). Fortunately, the ApplicationServlet class contains several protected methods you can override to plug in such information as the Locale, log file locations, and the application URL path. Listing 6.1 contains a typical web.xml file for a Tapestry application.

**Listing 6.1   The application servlet is the only registered servlet
                 in a Tapestry application.**

```xml
<?xml version="1.0" encoding="UTF-8"?>
<!DOCTYPE web-app PUBLIC
    "-//Sun Microsystems, Inc.//DTD Web Application 2.3//EN"
    "http://java.sun.com/dtd/web-app_2_3.dtd">
<web-app>
  <context-param>
    <param-name>log-file-location</param-name>
    <param-value>c:/logs/tapestry.log</param-value>
  </context-param>
  <servlet>
    <servlet-name>welcome</servlet-name>
    <servlet-class>hellotapestry.Welcome</servlet-class>
  </servlet>
  <servlet-mapping>
    <servlet-name>welcome</servlet-name>
    <url-pattern>/welcome</url-pattern>
  </servlet-mapping>
</web-app>
```

The first setting in this file is a context parameter for the location of the log file. Tapestry's treatment of logging is first rate. (For more information about logging for other frameworks, see chapter 16.) The logging configuration information can also appear in another location (discussed later in section 6.5.1), but it is traditional to place it here where it is easily accessible to the application servlet. The only other entries in this configuration file are the servlet registration and the URL pattern for the servlet. The `hellotapestry.Welcome` servlet (listing 6.2) in this application extends `ApplicationServlet`.

Listing 6.2   The ApplicationServlet subclass

```java
package hellotapestry;

import net.sf.tapestry.ApplicationServlet;
import net.sf.tapestry.RequestContext;
import org.apache.log4j.ConsoleAppender;
import org.apache.log4j.FileAppender;
import org.apache.log4j.Level;
import org.apache.log4j.Logger;
import org.apache.log4j.SimpleLayout;


public class Welcome extends ApplicationServlet {
```

```
protected String getApplicationSpecificationPath() {
    return "/tutorial/hello/HelloWorld.application";
}

protected void setupLogging()
        throws javax.servlet.ServletException {
    super.setupLogging();
    logger.getRootLogger().addAppender(
            new ConsoleAppender(new SimpleLayout()));
    String logFileLocation = getServletContext()
            .getInitParameter("log-file-location");
    try {
        logger.getRootLogger().addAppender(
                new FileAppender(new SimpleLayout(),
                logFileLocation));
    } catch (IOException ex) {
        logger.error(ex);
    }
    logger.setLevel(Level.INFO);
}
}
```

The only entry required in this servlet is the getApplicationSpecificationPath() method. The return from this method points to the application-specification document (which appears in listing 6.3). The other optional entry in the welcome servlet is an override of a protected method, setupLogging(), which is one of the protected methods you can override to customize the behavior of the framework. Tapestry uses the Jakarta log4j logging facility (discussed in chapter 16). The setupLogging() method allows you to add your own customized logging to the logging already present in Tapestry. In listing 6.2, we added both a console and a file log.

The welcome servlet is where the context parameter comes into play. The application servlet is the ideal place in Tapestry to read and respond to context parameters. If no configuration is required, you can directly reference the ApplicationServlet in web.xml without subclassing it.

The application specification

The next step in the Tapestry process is the processing of the application specification file. This is the document returned from the getApplicationSpecificationPath() method of the application servlet. This XML document specifies the page mappings and engine used by the application. The specification for the Hello World application appears in listing 6.3.

Listing 6.3 The application specification HelloWorld.application for the Hello World project

Listing 6.3   The application specification HelloWorld.application
for the Hello World project

```
<?xml version="1.0" encoding="UTF-8"?>
<!DOCTYPE application PUBLIC
  "-//Howard Lewis Ship//Tapestry Specification 1.3//EN"
  "http://tapestry.sf.net/dtd/Tapestry_1_3.dtd">
<application
  name="Hello World Tutorial"
  engine-class="net.sf.tapestry.engine.SimpleEngine">

    <page name="Home"
    specification-path="/tutorial/hello/Home.page"/>

</application>
```

The engine created for this application is an instance of the `SimpleEngine` class. For more complex applications, you might use a subclass of `SimpleEngine` to either override existing behavior or provide additional services. The other entries in the specification are the names of the pages in the application, which map to a specification path. The path in turn points to a .page file, which contains the definition of a Tapestry page. A mapping in this document may also point to a new component specification (an example of which appears later in the schedule application). In this simple application, only the Home page exists. Every Tapestry application must have a Home page; it is by definition the first page of the application and automatically launches when the Tapestry application starts.

The Home page specification

The *page specification* is a configuration document that binds together the HTML template and the components that appear on the page. Each visible page in Tapestry consists of a combination of a page specification and the corresponding user interface template. The page specification for the Hello World application is very simple and is shown in listing 6.4.

Listing 6.4   The Home page specification

```
<?xml version="1.0" encoding="UTF-8"?>
<!DOCTYPE page-specification PUBLIC
  "-//Howard Lewis Ship//Tapestry Specification 1.3//EN"
  "http://tapestry.sf.net/dtd/Tapestry_1_3.dtd">

<page-specification class="net.sf.tapestry.html.BasePage"/>
```

This very simple application has no Tapestry components on the page (i.e., no elements that will be replaced by components), so the page specification simply consists of the base class for the page. In more complex applications, you typically subclass `BasePage` to add your own dynamic behavior to the page.

The Home page template

The last piece of the application is the user interface template. In this case, it features no dynamic content, so it is a standard HTML document. When you're using dynamic Tapestry components, the HTML elements become placeholders for the dynamic elements, which is illustrated in the Tapestry schedule application in section 6.5. The Home page template appears in listing 6.5.

Listing 6.5　The Home page template Hello.html

```
<!DOCTYPE HTML PUBLIC "-//W3C//DTD HTML 4.0 Transitional//EN">

<html>
<head>
    <title>Hello World</title>
</head>

<body>

Welcome to your first <b>Tapestry Application</b>.

</body>
</html>
```

The Hello, World application is now complete. To deploy it, package all the files shown here into a Web archive (WAR) file along with the Tapestry libraries and deploy it to a servlet engine. The running application is shown in figure 6.2.

Figure 6.2
The running Tapestry
"Hello, World" application

6.4 *The Tapestry framework*

The sample application shown in the previous section utilizes many of the key classes in Tapestry. It shows the lifecycle of a typical (albeit simple) application. Because Tapestry encapsulates the entire web API, it is important to understand the key classes in Tapestry. When writing a Tapestry application, all of your time is spent on the framework and its classes rather than on the web API, so let's focus on some of the key classes in the framework and their responsibilities. Many of the classes covered here are represented as interfaces, which Tapestry identifies with an initial capital *I*. This is a good example of loose coupling, discussed at length in chapter 12.

6.4.1 *Framework classes and interfaces*

The Tapestry framework is loosely divided into support classes and interfaces and the components that make up visual elements.

IEngine

The `IEngine` interface in Tapestry defines the core, session-persistent object used to run the application. When a client invokes the application, that client owns an instance of the class that implements `IEngine`. The engine provides core services to the pages and components that make up the application. Because each user has his or her own instance of the engine, it is persisted in the user's session (although this is invisible to the developer). Almost every class and component in the framework has a `getEngine()` method that returns this user's instance of the engine.

Visit

Because Tapestry eschews the traditional web APIs, it must provide a mechanism for the developer to pass information from one page to another. That mechanism is the `Visit` object. This object is included in the application specification and is automatically maintained by the engine. Because it is part of the engine, which resides in the session, both the engine and the encapsulated `Visit` object may be serialized (thus, your `Visit` object should implement `Serializable`).

`Visit` is a concept that does not implement a particular interface or extend a base class. The `Visit` object is any object you create and register with the page specification. This means that it can include any information and behavior you want. Typically, it is implemented as a JavaBean, with standard accessors and mutators, but even that isn't required. It is more flexible than `HttpSession` because it isn't restricted to name-value pairs. Just as in `HttpSession`, you must be careful about how much information you encapsulate in Visit. Because each user owns an engine instance, each user owns the Visit object as well, which can lead to scalability problems if too much information is kept there. Pages can also store server-side state. An application stores global information in Visit but stores page-specific state as page properties. Tapestry uses object pooling and other techniques internally to make this efficient.

The engine includes getVisit() and setVisit() methods, both written in terms of the Object class. When retrieving the Visit from the engine, you must typecast it to the appropriate type. The Visit object is listed in the application specification as a property. Listing 6.6 shows the application specification for the Hangman tutorial supplied with Tapestry, which includes the property definition for the tutorial.hangman.Visit object. This specification also shows the syntax for declaring multiple pages.

Listing 6.6 The Visit object is created as a property of the application.

```xml
<?xml version="1.0" encoding="UTF-8"?>
<!DOCTYPE application PUBLIC
  "-//Howard Lewis Ship//Tapestry Specification 1.3//EN"
  "http://tapestry.sf.net/dtd/Tapestry_1_3.dtd">

<application name="Tapestry Hangman"
        engine-class="net.sf.tapestry.engine.SimpleEngine">

  <property name="net.sf.tapestry.visit-class">         Specified as a
        tutorial.hangman.Visit                          property
  </property>

  <page name="Home"
        specification-path="/tutorial/hangman/Home.page"/>

  <page name="Guess"
        specification-path="/tutorial/hangman/Guess.page"/>

  <page name="Failed"
        specification-path="/tutorial/hangman/Failed.page"/>

  <page name="Success"
        specification-path="/tutorial/hangman/Success.page"/>

</application>
```

The Visit object is automatically constructed upon first request (in other words, the first time it is retrieved from the engine), using the default constructor. If the class doesn't implement a default constructor, the engine method createVisit() is called instead. The developer must supply this method to create the Visit.

IRequestCycle

One of the goals of Tapestry is to encapsulate much of the stateless nature of web applications through its framework classes. However, the application must respond to requests because it is still a web application. This behavior is handled by the `IRequestCycle` interface. The implementing object (`RequestCycle`) handles a single request cycle, or an access by the client to a page in the web application. The request in Tapestry triggers the following sequence of events:

- Responds to the URL by finding the `IEngineService` object (provided by the `IEngine`) for this user
- Determines what the resulting page will be by consulting the configuration documents
- Renders the page, which includes creating the components and merging them with the user interface template
- Releases the temporary resources

While this sequence is occurring, the framework also handles the following jobs:

- Exception handling
- Loading of pages and templates from resources
- Tracking of changes to page properties and restoring of pages to prior states
- Pooling of page objects

The `RequestCycle` also handles some pooling and rendering of components. The request cycle is broken into two phases. The first phase is called the *rewind* phase. This phase exists primarily to support form submissions. Because of the loose coupling between components on a page and the page that contains them, it is necessary to "rediscover" some of those relationships when a form is submitted by re-rendering. This effectively discards the previous output back to a certain point. This facility provides the ability to undo previously generated output on the current page. For example, if a page encounters an exception during rendering, the request cycle can rewind the state of the components on the page back to a specified point. Once the rewind has completed, the `ActionListener` associated with this page is notified and can update the state of the page or select an entirely new output page.

The second phase of the request cycle is the *render* phase. During this phase, the page is rendered (in other words, the page is generated from the combination of components and the user interface template) and output to the browser.

The Tapestry framework provides as much desktop application functionality as possible. The components are developed much like user interface widgets for a desktop application. Tapestry also includes event handling, much like a desktop application. For example, you can register `ActionListener` objects with forms in Tapestry. Of course, the full complement of desktop behavior isn't available for a web application.

The `RequestCycle` encapsulates much of the functionality that makes Tapestry an effective framework. For example, it takes care of pooling page objects for reuse. In other frameworks, the developer must write code to handle this. Tapestry does a lot of work behind the scenes to make this process efficient and transparent to the developer. This behavior represents both the good and the bad in a framework that provides numerous services for you. If the code is well written and does exactly the job you want, it is a perfect match. On the other hand, if the code doesn't do exactly what you want, you must find a way to separate the behavior from the framework and do it yourself. This is one of the reasons that Tapestry is written largely in terms of interfaces. If there is a part (such as the request cycle) that you need to replace, you can write your own class that implements the interface and plug it into the framework seamlessly by subclassing `BaseEngine` and overriding the factory-like methods it implements. It is important in extensive frameworks that mechanisms exist to customize its behavior without major surgery.

6.4.2 Components

Tapestry components are built much like the user interface widgets for desktop applications, particularly Swing components. Tapestry components use the Model-View-Controller (MVC) design pattern, using the information represented by the component as a model class and the user interface as a template.

AbstractComponent and BaseComponent

The foundation for components in Tapestry is the `AbstractComponent` class, which encapsulates the key characteristics of all user interface elements. It implements the `IComponent` interface, which defines dynamic content in Tapestry by enforcing common semantics and properties. For example, every component must have an `Id` property, which is defined here as an accessor and mutator pair (and implemented with properties in `AbstractComponent`). In all, `IComponent` contains more than 25 methods.

The `IRender` interface contains only a single method signature: `render()`. This method is implemented by any component that must paint itself for a particular writer (identified by the `IMarkupWriter` interface) during a request cycle (identified by the `IRequestCycle` interface). This is the method overridden in each component that renders itself in the appropriate format. Currently, the Tapestry components render themselves as HTML. However, you could create a set of classes that render as XML (to be passed to a transformation engine) or even a user interface framework like Velocity (covered in chapter 9). Because all components must render themselves, `IComponent` implements the `IRender` interface.

`AbstractComponent` is an abstract class that implements the `IComponent` interface. This pattern is similar to the relationship in the Software Development Kit (SDK) between the `TableModel` interface and the `AbstractTableModel` class. `AbstractComponent` implements the interface and provides helper methods to keep subsequent inheritors from having to provide the entire infrastructure imposed by the interface. `BaseComponent` is one step beyond `AbstractComponent`. It is an instantiable class that serves as the direct ancestor to the user interface classes in Tapestry. Figure 6.3 shows the relationship between these classes and interfaces. We provide an example of building a new Tapestry component in section 6.5.

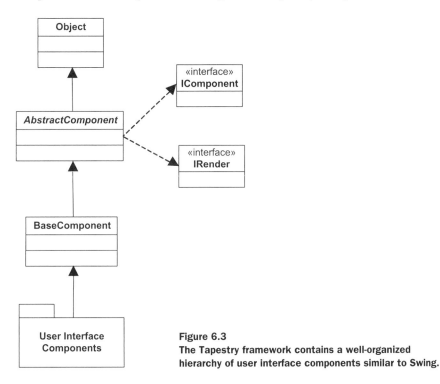

Figure 6.3
The Tapestry framework contains a well-organized hierarchy of user interface components similar to Swing.

ITableModel

The last of the infrastructure components we'll cover is the `ITableModel` and its related interfaces and classes. One of the common user interface elements used in both desktop and web applications is the table. Tapestry has created an elaborate structure for both displaying and accessing table data. Like the `JTable` and related classes and interfaces in Swing, Tapestry's table components create a well-organized (but complex) hierarchy.

Two important branches of this tree handle the data portions of the table. The `ITableModel` interface is similar to Swing's `JTable`. It includes methods for getting columns, current row, counts, and other information needed to render the control. The `ITableDataModel` interface handles concrete data requirements for the rows. This interface has two primary methods—`getRowCount()` and `getRows()`—which return an Iterator over the rows of data. Tapestry splits the responsibilities for the definition of the columns and the values in the rows into two separate interfaces.

The `SimpleTableModel` class is a concrete class that serves as a simple generic table model implementation. It encapsulates an `Object` array for row values and creates simple column structures. When creating your own table, you may either implement the `ITableModel` directly or subclass `SimpleTableModel` and selectively override methods.

The `ITableDataModel` hierarchy has more members. The immediate implementer of this interface is the `AbstractTableDataModel`. Like Swing's `AbstractTableModel`, it provides a simple `List`-based implementation for `ITableDataModel`. It is an abstract class, so the intent is for developers to subclass it and provide implementations for the `getRows()` and `getRowCounts()` methods. To make life easier for developers, Tapestry already provides two concrete subclasses: `SimpleListTableDataModel` and `SimpleSetTableDataModel`. These classes are `TableDataModels` backed by `Lists` and `Sets`, respectively.

You must understand a fair amount of framework hierarchy to implement tables in Tapestry. The relationship between these interfaces and classes is shown in figure 6.4.

To create a table component, you must supply a `TableModel`, a `TableDataModel`, and a user interface template. Creating a table in Tapestry is more complex than creating one in Swing. In Swing, you have a single table model that encapsulates both row and column information. In Tapestry, those responsibilities are split between two hierarchies.

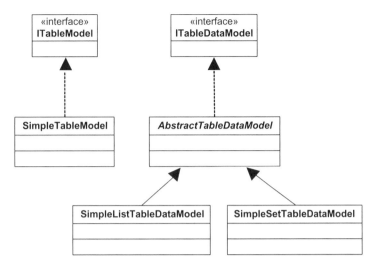

Figure 6.4   The Table hierarchy in Tapestry features separate branches for the user interface and data.

Fortunately, building a table isn't quite as overwhelming as it seems. In the next section, we show you a sample application that builds a simple table with a minimum amount of coding. Like all things in Tapestry, an attempt has been made to create a rich, robust hierarchy that doesn't force developers to create huge piles of code to perform simple tasks. On the other hand, the hierarchy is present that allows you to build highly complex artifacts with careful implementation and overriding.

6.5 *Scheduling in Tapestry*

As in the other framework chapters, we will build the two-page schedule application using Tapestry. The boundary and entity classes are exactly the same as in previous chapters, preserving our goal of keeping the framework separate from the model aspect of the application. The schedule application in this section represents a Model 2 web application built using the Tapestry framework. It is available in the source code archive as art_sched_tapestry.

6.5.1 *Bootstrapping the application*

The first two items in a Tapestry application are the application specification and the servlet that extends `ApplicationServlet` to bootstrap the application into the framework.

The application specification

The Tapestry application specification is an XML document that defines the application, global properties (Tapestry's equivalent of context parameters), the pages in the application, and the custom components. The application specification for the schedule application appears in listing 6.7.

Listing 6.7   Schedule application specification

```xml
<?xml version="1.0" encoding="UTF-8"?>
<!DOCTYPE application PUBLIC
        "-//Howard Lewis Ship//Tapestry Specification 1.3//EN"
        "http://tapestry.sf.net/dtd/Tapestry_1_3.dtd">

<application name="sched-tapestry"              Application definition  ❶
        engine-class="net.sf.tapestry.engine.SimpleEngine">
    <property name="driverClass">com.mysql.jdbc.Driver</property>
    <property name="dbUrl">
        jdbc:mysql://localhost/schedule              Database   ❷
    </property>                                   configuration
    <property name="user">root</property>          parameters
  <property name="password">marathon</property>

    <page name="Home" specification-path="/resources/Home.page"/>
    <page name="Add"  specification-path="/resources/Add.page" />
                                            Page path definitions  ❸
    <component-alias type="SchedTable"
            specification-path="/resources/SchedTable.jwc"/>
    <library id="contrib"
    specification-path="/net/sf/tapestry/contrib/Contrib.library"/>
                                   Custom component definitions  ❹
</application>
```

❶ The specification defines the application as using the Tapestry `SimpleEngine` class.

❷ This code defines properties for database connectivity, which are defined here rather than in the web.xml file.

❸ This code defines the two pages in the application along with the locations of the page specification files.

❹ This code defines the custom `SchedTable` component, pointing to its component specification file (with a .jwc extension) and the library on which is it based. The table controls in Tapestry reside in another library. The library is a Tapestry construct, which allows you to group and register classes logically within the framework. The library resides in another specification document, parsed by the framework, which defines the grouping of objects. It is not a requirement to group items together in libraries; it is strictly an organizational construct.

The application servlet

The second part of the bootstrapping process is the application servlet. It provides the connection between the web APIs and the Tapestry world. For this application, it is the welcome servlet (see listing 6.8).

Listing 6.8 The welcome servlet bootstraps the application by pointing to the application specification file.

```
package com.nealford.art.schedtapestry.util;

import java.io.IOException;
import net.sf.tapestry.ApplicationServlet;
import net.sf.tapestry.RequestContext;
import org.apache.log4j.ConsoleAppender;
import org.apache.log4j.FileAppender;
import org.apache.log4j.Level;
import org.apache.log4j.Logger;
import org.apache.log4j.SimpleLayout;

public class Welcome extends ApplicationServlet {
    private static Logger logger = Logger.getLogger(Welcome.class);

    protected String getApplicationSpecificationPath() {
        return "/resources/sched-tapestry.application";
    }

    protected void setupLogging()
            throws javax.servlet.ServletException {
        super.setupLogging();
        logger.getRootLogger().addAppender(
                new ConsoleAppender(new SimpleLayout()));
        String logFileLocation = getServletContext().
                getInitParameter("log-file-location");
        try {
            logger.getRootLogger().addAppender(
                    new FileAppender(new SimpleLayout(),
                                     logFileLocation));
        } catch (IOException ex) {
            logger.error(ex);
        }
        logger.setLevel(Level.INFO);
    }

}
```

The only method required by this servlet is `getApplicationSpecification-Path()`, which points to the application specification. Once this method has returned the path to the specification, you have left the traditional web world and are ensconced in Tapestry for the remainder of the application. The other method that appears here sets up logging for the application by overriding the `setupLogging()` method. This isn't strictly necessary; logging configuration may be handled by properties files, as we explain in chapter 16.

6.5.2 The Home page

The first page in every Tapestry application is the Home page. Each page consists of at least these elements: the page specification, the class, and the HTML template. The Home page for the schedule application is shown in figure 6.5.

The Home page specification

The specification shown in listing 6.9 defines the components and behavior for our Home page.

Listing 6.9 The Home page specification defines the components and behavior for the page.

```
<?xml version="1.0" encoding="UTF-8"?>
<!DOCTYPE page-specification PUBLIC
        "-//Howard Lewis Ship//Tapestry Specification 1.3//EN"
        "http://tapestry.sf.net/dtd/Tapestry_1_3.dtd">

<page-specification
        class="com.nealford.art.schedtapestry.page.Home">
    <component id="schedTable" type="SchedTable" />

    <component id="Add" type="PageLink">
        <static-binding name="page">Add</static-binding>
    </component>
</page-specification>
```

The `class` attribute points to the Java class that implements the components and properties for the page. This page includes two components: the table and the hyperlink at the bottom. The link at the bottom includes a `static-binding` property for the link. A static binding is one that won't be supplied by a property from the backing class for this page. In other words, it is a value that won't change. For this link, we supply the name of the page from the application specification document to which the link points.

The Home page template

The Home page user interface template for this page is very simple. It is shown in listing 6.10.

Figure 6.5
The Home page of the schedule application displays the first page of schedule items with navigation at the top.

Listing 6.10 The Home page template defines placeholders for the Tapestry components.

```
<html>
<head>
<title>Schedule</title>
</head>
<body>

<h2>Schedule</h2>

<span jwcid="schedTable">
</span>

<p><a jwcid="Add">Add a new Schedule Item</a>
</body>
</html>
```

The entries in the user interface template don't have to be the same type as the underlying component. If you want to supply some property values for them (for example, the width of the control), you can use the control as the template placeholder. However, Tapestry completely replaces whatever component resides in the template. Frequently, you can use the HTML span control as the placeholder. This is what we did for the table component in this page. The table component is a custom-built table (which appears in the next section). The only representative for the component needed on this page is an HTML element (like <span>) that includes the jwcid attribute identifying this control. This attribute is required for every control that Tapestry will replace on the page, and it maps to the component name registered in the page specification. When this page is rendered, the table replaces the <span> tag and the hyperlink replaces the <anchor> tag. Tapestry refers to the HTML document as a template, and that is really the extent of it. The actual controls that are ultimately rendered are Tapestry user interface components.

The Hello page class

The third piece of the Hello page is the underlying class. The name of the class appears in the page specification as the class attribute. This class supplies property values and lifecycle events for the page. The definition of this class is shown in listing 6.11.

Listing 6.11 The Home class provides the underlying infrastructure for the Home page.

```
package com.nealford.art.schedtapestry.page;

import com.nealford.art.schedtapestry.boundary.ScheduleDb;
import com.nealford.art.schedtapestry.util.ScheduleException;
import net.sf.tapestry.IEngine;
import net.sf.tapestry.html.BasePage;
import org.apache.log4j.ConsoleAppender;
import org.apache.log4j.Level;
import org.apache.log4j.Logger;
import org.apache.log4j.SimpleLayout;

public class Home extends BasePage {
    static Logger logger = Logger.getLogger(Home.class);
    private ScheduleDb scheduleDb;

    static {                              ← Sets up logging
        logger.addAppender(new ConsoleAppender(new SimpleLayout()));
        logger.setLevel(Level.DEBUG);
    }

    public Home() {
        logger.debug("Entering Home page constructor");
    }
                                          Returns a populated
    public ScheduleDb getScheduleDb() {  ←┘ boundary class
        if (scheduleDb == null)
            scheduleDb = createScheduleDb(getEngine());
        try {
            scheduleDb.populate();
        } catch (ScheduleException ex) {
            logger.error("Home.getScheduleDb", ex);
        }
        return scheduleDb;
```

```
    }
    private ScheduleDb createScheduleDb(IEngine engine) {
        String dbUrl = engine.getSpecification().
                    getProperty(
            "dbUrl");
        String driverClass = engine.getSpecification().
                        getProperty("driverClass");
        String user = engine.getSpecification().
                    getProperty(
            "user");
        String password = engine.getSpecification().
                        getProperty(
            "password");
        return new ScheduleDb(driverClass, dbUrl, user,
                            password);
    }
    protected void firePageBeginRender() {
        super.firePageBeginRender();
        try {
            scheduleDb.populate();
        } catch (ScheduleException ex) {
            logger.error("Home.beginResponse()", ex);
        }
    }
}
```

Creates the boundary class using init parameters

Is invoked when the page is drawn

The Home class extends BasePage, the base class for all underlying pages. You provide properties and override lifecycle methods to customize the behavior of the page. The first section of code sets up logging for this page, using the log4j logging built into Tapestry. Next, a couple of support classes for accessing the boundary class appear. The createScheduleDb() method is responsible for creating the boundary class. In previous applications, the configuration information for the connection appeared in the web.xml file. Here, however, that information appears in the application specification, and the engine.getSpecification() method accesses it. This method lazily instantiates a new instance of the schedule boundary if it doesn't already exist.

The other method on this page is a framework callback, overridden from the parent BasePage class. The overridden firePageBeginRender() method is an example of several callback methods that provide access to the rendering pipeline. In this method, we want to make sure that the page (and the table on it) responds to changes to the underlying database. The populate() method on the boundary class refreshes the list of items. By placing it in this method, we ensure that the information is updated every time the page is drawn for this user.

6.5.3 *The custom table component*

One notable omission from the Home page is any information about the table itself. The table is its own component and handles its own rendering and events. As with all artifacts in Tapestry, custom components consist of three parts: the specification, the template, and the backing class. Tables in Tapestry are split into two definitions: one for the data rows and another for the columns. Each of these definitions flows from different inheritance hierarchies (see section 6.4.2 for details).

The table specification

The first part of the custom table component is the specification, shown in listing 6.12.

Listing 6.12   The specification for the custom table component

```xml
<?xml version="1.0" encoding="UTF-8"?>
<!DOCTYPE component-specification PUBLIC
        "-//Howard Lewis Ship//Tapestry Specification 1.3//EN"
        "http://tapestry.sf.net/dtd/Tapestry_1_3.dtd">

<component-specification
        class="com.nealford.art.schedtapestry.component.SchedTable"
        allow-body="no" allow-informal-parameters="yes">

    <component id="table" type="contrib:Table">
        <binding name="tableModel" expression="tableModel"/>
    </component>

</component-specification>
```

The `SchedTable` specification indicates the backing class's fully qualified name, whether this component will have a body, and other properties. The body of the component is the encapsulated `Table` component from the contrib library, which is registered with this application via the application specification in listing 6.7. The lone property for this component is the table model used to populate the table. The expression `tableModel` maps to a `getTableModel()` method in the backing class file.

The table template

The user interface template for the custom table control is very simple because the default characteristics of the built-in table component are sufficient. The template consists of a single line, specifying the `jwcid` and `border` attributes:

```
<table border="1" jwcid="table" />
```

As do the user interface page templates, the table template contains placeholders for the actual Tapestry components that will replace them. In this case, the Tapestry table component will replace this one with the added characteristic of a single-width border. Note that the component definitions for both specifications and templates are the same. Once you understand how Tapestry handles artifacts, you'll see that it handles them consistently throughout.

The table class

The real purpose of creating the table component as a custom control is to control the columns and data that appear in it. Obviously, the template doesn't highly customize the appearance. Listing 6.13 shows the first part of the SchedTable class.

Listing 6.13 The declaration and table model portion of the custom table backing class

```
package com.nealford.art.schedtapestry.component;

import com.nealford.art.schedtapestry.boundary.ScheduleDb;
import com.nealford.art.schedtapestry.entity.ScheduleItem;
import com.nealford.art.schedtapestry.page.Home;
import net.sf.tapestry.BaseComponent;
import net.sf.tapestry.ComponentAddress;
import net.sf.tapestry.contrib.table.model.ITableColumn;
import net.sf.tapestry.contrib.table.model.ITableColumnModel;
import net.sf.tapestry.contrib.table.model.ITableModel;
import net.sf.tapestry.contrib.table.model.simple.
        SimpleListTableDataModel;
import net.sf.tapestry.contrib.table.model.simple.SimpleTableColumn;
import net.sf.tapestry.contrib.table.model.simple.
        SimpleTableColumnModel;
import net.sf.tapestry.contrib.table.model.simple.SimpleTableModel;
import org.apache.log4j.Logger;

public class SchedTable extends BaseComponent {
    private ScheduleDb scheduleDb;

    public ITableModel getTableModel() {
        scheduleDb = ((Home) getPage()).getScheduleDb();
        SimpleListTableDataModel listTableDataModel =
                new SimpleListTableDataModel(scheduleDb.getList());
        return new SimpleTableModel(listTableDataModel,
                                   createColumnModel());
    }
```

A huge number of classes collaborate to create the SchedTable control, mostly from the Tapestry framework. The component itself extends from BaseComponent, which defines all the common component elements. The getTableModel()

method returns the rows for the table. To do this, it must get a reference to the boundary class.

Tapestry provides a couple of ways to access the boundary class in this situation. If we were passing the information from one page to another, we would use a `Visit` object, discussed in section 6.4.1. In this case, we're passing the information via another mechanism. Because the table resides on the page that instantiates the boundary object, we can get to the underlying page directly and access the class. The `BaseComponent` class includes a `getPage()` method that returns the page definition for the page this component resides on. For the `SchedTable` component, we cast `getPage()` to our Home page and directly access the `getScheduleDb()` method.

The next order of business is to create the table model, which is similar in intent to the table models defined by Swing. Fortunately, Tapestry already includes a `SimpleListTableDataModel` class, which constructs a table model around an existing list. Because our boundary class returns a list of items, we can wrap it into the Tapestry helper with no additional work. It certainly pays to look around in the Tapestry classes to see if they already define something you need. Chances are good, especially if what you need is generic, that a helper class already exists.

The last line of the method returns the simple table model constructed around the `listTableDataModel` and the method call to `createColumnModel()`. Listing 6.14 contains the remainder of this class, which includes the classes and methods that build the column model.

Listing 6.14   The last part of the table definition creates the table column model.

```
private ITableColumnModel createColumnModel() {
    String[] col = ScheduleDb.getColumns();
    return new SimpleTableColumnModel(new ITableColumn[] {
            new StartColumn(col[1]),
            new DurationColumn(col[2]),
            new TextColumn(col[3]),
            new EventTypeColumn(col[4])});
}

private class StartColumn extends SimpleTableColumn {
    public StartColumn(String colName) {
        super(colName);
    }

    public Object getColumnValue(Object row) {
        return ((ScheduleItem) row).getStart();
    }
}
```

Method that returns an array of ITableColumn objects

Custom column for start

```
        }

        private class DurationColumn extends SimpleTableColumn {
            public DurationColumn(String colName) {
                super(colName);
            }

            public Object getColumnValue(Object row) {
                return new Integer(((ScheduleItem) row).getDuration());
            }
        }

        private class TextColumn extends SimpleTableColumn {
            public TextColumn(String colName) {
                super(colName);
            }

            public Object getColumnValue(Object row) {
                return ((ScheduleItem) row).getText();
            }
        }

        private class EventTypeColumn extends SimpleTableColumn {
            public EventTypeColumn(String colName) {
                super(colName);
            }

            public Object getColumnValue(Object row) {
                return ((ScheduleItem) row).getEventType();
            }
        }
    }
```

Custom column for duration

Custom column for text

Custom column for eventType

Each column in the column model requires definition. The Tapestry Simple-TableColumn class is sufficient for simple display columns. The primary method in all the private column subclasses is the getColumnValue() method. It is passed a row object, which is derived from the TableDataModel's underlying value. In this case, it is cast to the entity type (ScheduleItem) and returned as an object. It is typical to define the column classes as private nested classes inside the TableData-Model because they are typed to a particular entity (the one passed as the row). It is possible to create them as higher-level objects if there is an opportunity to reuse them.

The remaining method is createColumnModel(). This method obtains the list of columns from the boundary class and instantiates a SimpleTableColumnModel that wraps an array of instances of the column classes defined at the bottom of the class. This column model is ultimately returned to the constructor of the `Simple-TableModel` class.

The combination of the specification, template, and class completes the definition of the table component. This component resides on the Home page, which is defined in that page's specification. The component specification (with a .jwc extension), the template file, and the class that creates both the row and column models define the table.

You may have noticed that the table shown in figure 6.5 automatically handles multipage scrolling. This is a feature built into the Tapestry table component. We didn't write any code to make it work—it works "out of the box" that way.

The table component in Tapestry is very powerful. One of the examples that come with Tapestry shows off the capabilities of the table component when customized, and it appears in figure 6.6.

The customized table component example illustrates the ability to place nontext controls in cells (the first column), automatic paging (like the table used in the schedule application), and the ability to sort column headers. Notice that the right-hand column has a sorting direction indicator.

The elaborate capabilities of the customized table component illustrate our earlier point that Tapestry attempts to create a framework like Swing where the components are easily customizable. The fact that they are ultimately rendered as HTML is irrelevant. The component is written to the framework, which takes care of rendering it at the appropriate time. Building your own paging and sortable columns (without using Tapestry) is covered in chapter 13.

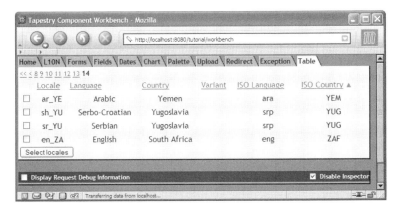

Figure 6.6 The Tapestry table component is quite powerful when customized. This example shows automatic paging, controls in columns, and sortable columns.

6.5.4 *The Add page*

The second page of the schedule application also illustrates how Tapestry handles the interaction between the user interface and the backing class. This is the page that is linked via the hyperlink on the Home page. It allows the user to add new schedule items (with validation). Figure 6.7 shows the Add page.

The Add page specification

As usual, the first order of business in Tapestry is the specification for the page. This specification is considerably longer than previous ones because this page contains more components. The specification consists of two logical sections. The first handles the controls and their relationships to the form (listing 6.15); the second handles the validations for the form.

Listing 6.15 The top of the Add page specification

```xml
<?xml version="1.0" encoding="UTF-8"?>
<!DOCTYPE page-specification PUBLIC
        "-//Howard Lewis Ship//Tapestry Specification 1.3//EN"
        "http://tapestry.sf.net/dtd/Tapestry_1_3.dtd">

<page-specification class="com.nealford.art.schedtapestry.page.Add">

  <component id="form" type="Form">
    <binding name="listener" expression="listeners.formSubmit"/>
    <field-binding name="stateful" field-name="Boolean.TRUE"/>
  </component>

  <component id="startDate" type="TextField">
      <binding name="value" expression="startDate"/>
  </component>
```

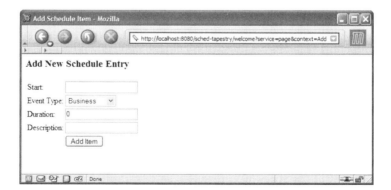

Figure 6.7   The Add page allows the user to add new schedule items.

```
<component id="eventType" type="PropertySelection">
    <binding name="model" expression="events"/>
    <binding name="value" expression="eventType"/>
</component>

<component id="duration" type="TextField">
    <binding name="value" expression="duration"/>
</component>

<component id="text" type="TextField">
    <binding name="value" expression="description"/>
</component>

<component id="addSubmit" type="Submit">
    <binding name="listener" expression="listeners.formSubmit"/>
</component>
```

The Add page specification defines the class that backs this page as an attribute of the page specification root. It also defines a form for this page. The form includes in its definition a property for a listener. As with Swing and other GUI frameworks, you may register listeners for form events. The backing class includes methods for the page. In this case, when the user submits the form, the framework invokes the Add class's formSubmit() method. The form is also defined as *stateful*, meaning that the framework will keep field values between invocations. Behind the scenes, the form checks to ensure that the HttpSession exists and displays an error message if the HttpSession has been lost (due to inactivity). This check has been improved (and is less intrusive) in Tapestry version 3.

Each of the components that appear on the form has definitions in this specification. The expressions bind them to properties of the backing page class. For example, the startDate expression maps to a getStartDate() method on the underlying page class. Any class property or method is legal here, but the properties (following the standard JavaBean naming conventions) on the page class are referenced as regular fields.

The Add page template

Like the Add page specification, the template has more elements than the previous example as well. It appears in listing 6.16.

Listing 6.16   The Add page template

```
<html>
<head>
<title>
Add Schedule Item
```

```
</title>
</head>
<body>
<h3>Add New Schedule Entry</h3>

<form jwcid="form">

<font color='red'>
<span jwcid="foreachError">
    <span jwcid="error" /><br>
</span>
</font>
<table>
    <tr>
        <td>Start:</td>
        <td><span jwcid="startDate"/></td>
    </tr>
    <tr>
        <td>Event Type:</td>
        <td><span jwcid="eventType"/></td>
    </tr>
    <tr>
        <td>Duration:</td>
        <td><span jwcid="duration"/></td>
    </tr>
    <tr>
        <td>Description:</td>
        <td><span jwcid="text"/></td>
    </tr>
    <tr><td> </td><td>
    <input type="submit" jwcid="addSubmit" value="Add Item"/>
    </td></tr>
</table>
</form>

</body>
</html>
```

The controls on the Add page are almost all represented by span placeholders. The key property is the jwcid field, which maps to the component definition in the page specification. The eventType field appears on the running form as an HTML <select> control. It is defined in the page specification as a PropertySelection with two fields. However, in the template it appears as just another span placeholder. To understand how the PropertySelection component works, you must first see the backing class file. We will return to it (and the validation errors at the top of the page) after discussing the Add class.

The Add class

The Add class includes the code for populating the fields of the template, handling errors, and saving new records. The first portion of this class is shown in listing 6.17.

Listing 6.17 The Add class handles the details of adding a new item.

```
package com.nealford.art.schedtapestry.page;

import com.nealford.art.schedtapestry.boundary.ScheduleDb;
import com.nealford.art.schedtapestry.entity.ScheduleItem;
import com.nealford.art.schedtapestry.util.ScheduleException;
import net.sf.tapestry.IMarkupWriter;
import net.sf.tapestry.IRequestCycle;
import net.sf.tapestry.form.IPropertySelectionModel;
import net.sf.tapestry.form.StringPropertySelectionModel;
import net.sf.tapestry.html.BasePage;
import org.apache.log4j.Logger;

public class Add extends BasePage {
    private String startDate;
    private int duration;
    private String eventType;
    private String description;
    private java.util.List errors;
    private String error;
    private ScheduleDb scheduleDb;
    private IPropertySelectionModel events;

    public void beginResponse(IMarkupWriter markupWriter,
                            IRequestCycle requestCycle) throws
          net.sf.tapestry.RequestCycleException {
        super.beginResponse(markupWriter, requestCycle);
        String dbUrl = getEngine().getSpecification().
                    getProperty("dbUrl");
        String driverClass = getEngine().getSpecification().
                            getProperty("driverClass");
        String user = getEngine().getSpecification().
                    getProperty("user");
        String password = getEngine().getSpecification().
                        getProperty("password");
        scheduleDb = new ScheduleDb(driverClass, dbUrl, user,
                            password);
        events = new StringPropertySelectionModel(scheduleDb.
            listEventTypes());
    }

    public IPropertySelectionModel getEvents() {
        return events;
    }
```

Like most of the classes built with Tapestry, the `Add` class includes a large number of framework references. It extends `BasePage` and declares a variety of private fields. They fall into several categories: logging, fields that back the components in the specification, error lists, the boundary class, and the `PropertySelection` component support.

The `beginResponse()` method performs two tasks: it creates a new boundary class and builds the selection model for the select control. The boundary class is re-created here for convenience. Rather than re-creating it, we could have placed it on a `Visit` object in the Home page and passed the instance to this page. However, we took the simple approach for expediency. For a more robust application, you would use Tapestry object pooling to handle both database connection pooling and object pooling.

The last part of the method creates the `PropertySelectionModel` interface, which defines the semantics for an HTML select control (i.e., a combobox). The interface (`IPropertySelectionModel`) includes methods for accessing the option, label, value, and number of options. As usual, you can implement this interface directly to provide customized behaviors. For simple cases (like the one for the schedule application), the `StringPropertySelectionModel` wraps a `PropertySelectionModel` around an existing list. Again, Tapestry provides a helper class for the common cases.

From the page specification in listing 6.15, the `PropertySelection` component accepts two binding properties instead of one:

```
<component id="eventType" type="PropertySelection">
    <binding name="model" expression="events"/>
    <binding name="value" expression="eventType"/>
</component>
```

The `model` property points to an instance of a class that implements `IPropertySelectionModel`, and the `value` property maps to the set method for the field whose value is selected by the control. The backing class includes a `getEvents()` method that returns the `PropertySelectionModel` and an accessor/mutator pair for `get/setEventType()`.

The remainder of the class handles updating and error handling; it appears in listing 6.18.

Listing 6.18 The remainder of the Add class includes event handling and error generation.

```
public void formSubmit(IRequestCycle cycle) {
    ScheduleItem item = new ScheduleItem(startDate, duration,
            description, eventType);
```

```
        errors = item.validate();
        if (errors.isEmpty()) {
            try {
                scheduleDb.addRecord(item);
            } catch (ScheduleException ex) {
                logger.error("AddPage.formSubmit()", ex);
            }
            cycle.setPage("Home");
        } else
            cycle.setPage("Add");
    }

    public java.util.List getErrors() {
        return errors;
    }

    public void setErrors(java.util.List errors) {
        this.errors = errors;
    }
```

The rest of the Add class consists of accessor and mutator pairs for the private fields of the class (we've omitted that here for space considerations). The form-Submit() method is called when a user clicks the form's Submit button. Notice how much Tapestry mimics desktop applications. The design decision in Tapestry to create the backing class with the specification and template becomes clearer. If you're using "normal" HTML forms, it is much harder to hide the HTTP GET/POST semantics. However, in Tapestry, the framework is only executing code on the backing class and the included components, which are written with this infrastructure in mind. By completely replacing the standard web API, Tapestry can mimic statefulness and other desktop application behavior.

This formSubmit() method creates a new ScheduleItem object from the fields on the form. The framework has already called the mutators for all the private fields as part of the POST operation. The mutators are mapped to the components in the specification document. The ScheduleItem class features a validate() method that returns a list of error messages. The list consists of simple strings, packaged in a List. The ScheduleItem entity object creates the list of errors in the validate() method, shown in listing 6.19.

Listing 6.19 ScheduleItem's validation method

```
public List validate() {
    List validationMessages = new ArrayList(0);
    if (duration < 0 || duration > 31)
        validationMessages.add("Invalid duration");
```

```
    if (text == null || text.length() < 1)
        validationMessages.add("Event must have description");
    return validationMessages;
}
```

If no errors return, the boundary class inserts the new schedule item and uses the request cycle to return to the Home page.

Validations

If the schedule item returns a list of errors in the `formSubmit()` method of the `Add` class, the request cycle returns to the Add page. The Add page includes code at the top of the template for outputting the list of validation errors. The results of a failed validation are shown in figure 6.8.

The error output is handled by entries in both the specification and the template. Listing 6.20 contains the last part of the page specification.

Listing 6.20 The Add page specification includes components that iterate over a list.

```
    <!-- handle errors -->
    <component id="foreachError" type="Foreach">
        <binding name="source" expression="errors"/>
        <binding name="value" expression="error"/>
    </component>

    <component id="error" type="Insert">
        <binding name="value" expression="error"/>
    </component>
</page-specification>
```

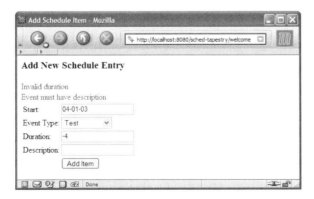

Figure 6.8
When an item validation fails, the application returns to the input page and displays a list of errors at the top.

This specification slice shows a different kind of Tapestry component. All the components we've covered thus far have been user interface widgets. Tapestry also includes programming constructs as components. The `Foreach` component iterates over a collection (either a `List`, `Array`, or `Map`) and makes each item available for processing. The `Insert` component provides a mechanism for outputting an HTML label on the form. The template includes the `Foreach` block at the top, represented as a `span`:

```
<font color='red'>
<span jwcid="foreachError">
    <span jwcid="error" /><br>
</span>
</font>
```

If the list of errors is empty, there is nothing to iterate over, so this code produces no output. If the errors list is not empty, the `Foreach` construct iterates over the list, printing out the error message. This completes the Tapestry version of the schedule application.

6.6   *Evaluating Tapestry*

As demonstrated by even the basic examples in this chapter, Tapestry is a complex framework. To create the simplest web application, you must understand a fair amount about the architecture and components. Because it is all-encompassing, you can't rely on your prior knowledge of the web APIs in Java. It is much like learning a completely new user interface framework from scratch. Fortunately, the authors did not reinvent the entire wheel. If you have used other GUI frameworks, you can see many familiar features in Tapestry. In particular, it leverages the JavaBeans component model for much of its automatic functionality (like matching accessor and mutator names to properties on a page).

6.6.1   *Documentation and samples*

When you're learning a completely new framework, two elements are critical: the documentation and the samples. Tapestry excels in both these areas; it supplies well-written documentation in two formats and good examples. Because Tapestry is complex, the success of the framework hinges on the quality of the documentation.

Documentation

The documentation in Tapestry is stellar, particularly for an open-source application. In fact, it is better than some commercial tools. The JavaDoc API reference is good, with most of the properties and methods documented. In particular, the JavaDoc for the components features two sets of pages. The first is a standard Java-Doc page describing the component and its fields and methods. A representative sample appears in figure 6.9.

However, the description of the fields and methods for a Tapestry component only tells part of the story. The other critical piece of information is the syntax for declaring it in the page specification. Each of the component JavaDoc pages also includes a Component Reference hyperlink (see the lower right-hand corner in figure 6.9). This leads to a detailed page that explains how to declare the component and includes numerous examples. A representative sample of one of these pages is shown in figure 6.10.

For additional documentation on Tapestry, check out *Tapestry in Action*, by Howard Lewis Ship (January, 2004.) Ship is the original author and primary contributor to the Tapestry project, so his book on the subject is authoritative.

Samples

Another key feature of a framework is the sample applications. Most developers want to see code before they read hundreds of pages of documentation. The samples are simple but good. The tutorial is well written and paced well, which is particularly important in an enveloping framework like Tapestry. No one could ever

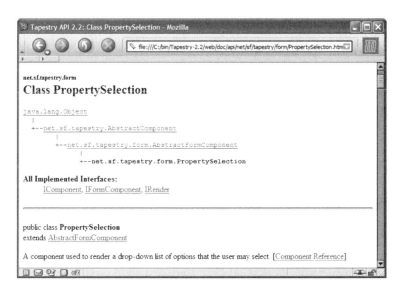

Figure 6.9 The JavaDoc pages for components feature good descriptions.

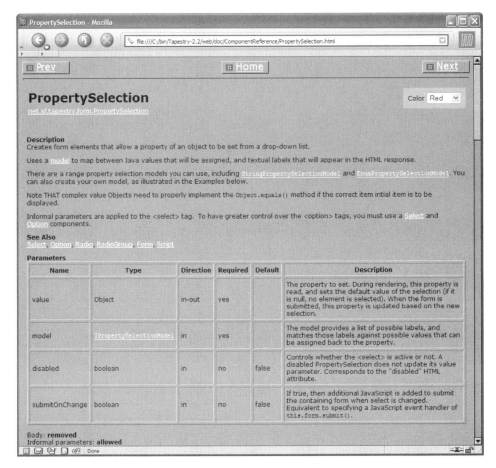

Figure 6.10   The additional Component Reference pages are critical for the page specifications and for using the full features of the components.

figure out how to start a Tapestry application without some assistance! The tutorial creates a trivial application to illustrate how the triad of artifacts works for each page: the specification, the template, and the backing class.

The tutorial continues with a Hangman game, which illustrates interaction and behaviors that are more complex. It then moves on into some more advanced Tapestry topics, like internationalization. Although the tutorial starts well and contains useful samples, it doesn't go very far into the real workings of Tapestry. However, it does introduce you to the framework so that you can start experimenting on your own.

Note that the tutorial can build and run itself with the Ant build tool. The `ant` run target builds the appropriate artifacts and starts its own web server (Jetty) to host the sample. This is a more comprehensive approach than I've seen before. Generally, frameworks give you a web archive (WAR) or Enterprise Archive (EAR) file to deploy in your servlet engine of choice. Tapestry even provides the servlet engine.

6.6.2 *Debugging support*

Another outstanding feature of Tapestry is the debugging support provided by the framework. The stack traces delivered to the browser are informative and contain both Tapestry internal messages and the full Java stack trace, which makes it easy to track down bugs.

Tapestry also includes a handy tool for helping you debug your running Tapestry applications. Because it handles so many details of the application for you, you want to find out what's going on within the framework from time to time. Tapestry includes a debugging aid called the "Inspector." You can enable it for your application while debugging. This tool shows up as an icon in the lower-right side of the browser page, as shown in figure 6.11.

Clicking on the Inspector icon launches a new window with statistics and details about the page you are looking at, along with some framework information. The results of clicking the Inspector icon on the page in figure 6.11 are shown in figure 6.12.

The exception pages are also first-rate in Tapestry. The standard exception page "unwinds" nested exceptions and displays all the servlet API and Java system

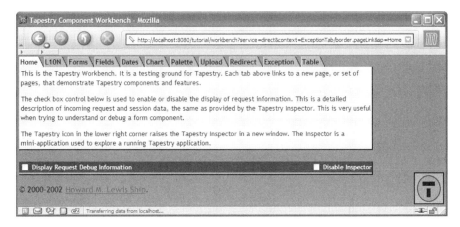

Figure 6.11 The Tapestry Inspector appears in the lower right.

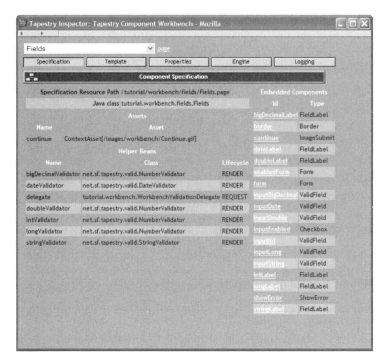

Figure 6.12   The Inspector shows information about the current page and the state of the components on it.

properties as well. Many developers move to Tapestry just for the debugging support alone. In version 3.0, the exception support has gotten even better, with precise line number reports for errors.

6.6.3   *Using Tapestry*

The Tapestry version of the schedule application is vastly different from the "straight" Model 2 or Struts versions. In fact, it is not like any other version of the schedule application in this book! This application touches only the tip of the iceberg of the Tapestry framework. It is a huge code base, covering a large number of topics. The authors of this framework have gone to great lengths both to hide the underlying web APIs and to provide a desktop look and feel to the code written within the framework. The `ApplicationServlet` is the jumping-off point for the framework, and virtually no standard web API code exists beyond that point.

Tapestry handles a great deal of complexity behind the scenes. Many of the objects created by the framework are pooled and cached for you. The framework handles the serialization and persistence of the engine instances it maintains for each user. The framework also creates pseudo-events that mimic desktop applications. The component model is also familiar in intent (if not in implementation) to Swing and other GUI frameworks. Once you understand the basic concepts behind how Tapestry wants you to work, you'll find it a productive environment.

Good debugging support is important in Tapestry. When developing applications using it, you might find the complexity of the framework to be overwhelming. If the debugging support wasn't so good, it would be a much more difficult framework in which to develop. Even so, the sheer volume of the framework is frequently daunting.

To make effective use of this framework, it helps to immerse yourself in it for a long period of time. More than any other framework mentioned in this book (with the possible exception of Turbine), Tapestry requires a great deal of effort to master. However, the trade-off may be worth it for some types of development. If you want to create web applications that look and feel more like desktop applications, Tapestry is built for you.

Tapestry is in version 2.2 as of this writing and seems very stable. It "feels" like a mature framework. The hierarchies are well defined and laid out, with good abstractions and loose coupling. The documentation is helpful even by commercial product standards. If you can afford the time investment, Tapestry is a worthwhile choice. It clearly supports building Model 2 applications, although in Tapestry they may be closer to the original Model-View-Controller paradigm. One of the most compelling reasons to use Tapestry is the reduction of the amount of code required to create applications. Because Tapestry performs so much work for you within the framework, it frees you from writing that code yourself. Once you overcome the learning curve for the API, you'll find Tapestry a productive framework.

6.7 *Summary*

In this chapter, we built our schedule application using Tapestry. Tapestry is a well-designed, mature framework that allows you to develop sophisticated applications that are built like traditional desktop applications but that run as web applications. Each artifact consists of a specification, a user interface template, and a backing class. Some of the common user interface controls (like HTML tables) rely on table and column models to supply data. Other user interface elements can generally be implemented with a built-in helper class. However, you must still understand how to supply the data to the helper class. The documentation and samples provided by Tapestry are excellent, on par or better than most commercial products. The documentation includes both JavaDoc reference help and specific help for the Tapestry components, including all their attributes.

In the next chapter, we look at another Model 2 web framework, WebWork.

WebWork

7

This chapter covers

- The architecture and design of WebWork
- Building applications using WebWork
- Evaluating WebWork

199

WebWork is an open-source web development framework for building Model 2 applications. Philosophically, it is closer to Struts than Tapestry. It works within the existing web APIs in Java rather than attempting to replace them completely. WebWork contains several concepts and constructs that are unique and that set it apart from other frameworks, such as the Pull Hierarchical Model-View-Controller design and the value stack, which supplies values to their custom JSP tags. As with the other framework chapters, we begin with a history and background of the framework. We then explore some key concepts and constructs that are vital when you're working with the framework. Of course, the centerpiece of the chapter is the schedule application, written in WebWork. As always, the principles of Model 2 development provide the guidelines for the samples and dictate a firm separation of concerns.

7.1 Overview

WebWork is produced by the Open Symphony project (www.opensymphony.com). This project includes many embedded projects; WebWork is just one of them. The framework is currently at version 1.3, and you can download it from the Open Symphony web site. It is based on best practices and design patterns that have long-standing records of accomplishment—patterns such as Model-View-Controller, the Java 2 Enterprise Edition (J2EE) Front Controller, and others. It is also based on a strong motivation to keep things as simple as possible while maintaining flexibility (which the creators acknowledge is a difficult balancing act).

WebWork implements what its documentation calls "Pull Hierarchical Model-View-Controller," or "Pull HMVC." This is the creators' own take on the Model 2 design. The "pull" part of this definition indicates that the view component is responsible for *pulling* the model information from the controller on demand. This is different from the traditional Model 2, where the view accesses information that has been placed within the model and passed to it from the controller. In this case, the view understands what information it wants and accesses it without necessarily having to wait for a controller to make it available. This architecture requires the presence of a repository of data available to all views, which access it on a just-in-time (JIT) basis.

The "hierarchical" part of the description describes the repository of view data. In the case of WebWork, the "value stack" is used to provide information to the view. (We describe this construct in section 7.2.4.) The rest of the architecture is Model-View-Controller. That means that WebWork enforces the normal semantics of Model 2, but with a different twist on how that model information is made available. WebWork is not the only project to use this approach. Turbine's documentation and white papers, discussed in chapter 1, also refer to this "pull" paradigm of Model 2.

WebWork takes advantage of the web APIs in Java rather than hiding them. However, it doesn't rely on them as much as unadorned Model 2 or Struts. Like Struts, WebWork includes a central controller, based on the J2EE Front Controller design pattern, which creates `Action` objects (thus using the Command design pattern described in chapter 4). However, the return and packaging of model information is different in WebWork.

7.1.1 *The architecture*

The architecture of WebWork follows the common architecture of most Model 2 web application frameworks. Figure 7.1 shows the overall architecture and flow.

You can configure WebWork through configuration files. When WebWork starts, the `ServletDispatcher` is invoked. This is the main controller for WebWork, similar to other Model 2 frameworks. The `ServletDispatcher` reads several configuration files (covered in section 7.1.2) and uses that information to create an `Action` object to handle the request. The action in turn creates model beans, which access data, mutate it, and otherwise perform the real work of the application. WebWork does not require the use of model beans. Properties can appear

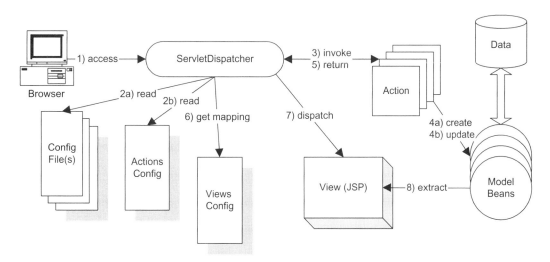

Figure 7.1   The WebWork architecture has much in common with unadorned Model 2 and Struts, with changes in information flow from the model objects.

directly in the `Action` class but shouldn't for most Model 2 applications because such an arrangement violates the separation of responsibilities.

The action returns a response code, used by the `ServletDispatcher` to look up the appropriate view. The `ServletDispatcher` dispatches control to the view component, which can be any view framework (for example, JSP or Velocity), or it can be an action chain, which will execute another action. The view extracts information needed from the value stack. The framework maintains this construct by caching information from both actions and model beans for use by the view. The value stack is discussed in section 7.2.4.

On the surface, WebWork looks just like the architectural diagram for Struts. However, the details of information flow are different. WebWork makes accessing information kept in actions and model objects easier by handling much of the information transport for you. WebWork includes numerous custom JSP tags that are savvy about the information flow within the framework.

Validation is also handled differently in WebWork. It allows you to create metadata classes around standard HTML controls to handle formatting, validation, and other facilities. In this regard, the HTML elements become much more like desktop user interface (UI) widgets.

7.1.2 The configuration

Configurability is one of the hallmarks of WebWork. The framework includes a default properties file and allows you to override these settings in additional application-specific properties files. WebWork uses the properties files shown in table 7.1 to configure the application.

Table 7.1   WebWork properties files

Properties File	Purpose
webwork	This is the primary configuration file for the framework. It includes package names, UI settings, and entries that point to the other configuration files.
default	This is the default properties file for WebWork. The framework reads all these values, then selectively overrides them from the webwork properties file.
views	This file contains all mappings for visible resources in the application. It includes mappings for actions and UI elements. The actions return values that reside in this file to point to a destination resource.

continued on next page

Table 7.1   WebWork properties files *(continued)*

Properties File	Purpose
log4j	This file is used to set up logging for WebWork. WebWork uses the Commons logging framework, whose default logging implementation is log4j. This properties file is a standard log4j file (see chapter 16 for more information on log4j).
Action-specific	Internationalization is handled through properties files mapped to actions. Each action can have a properties file that defines the visual elements exposed to that action's view.

Each of these properties files is loaded from the classpath. You can place them anywhere on the classpath (including the classes directory under WEB-INF in the web application). One of the properties in both the default and webwork properties files is `webwork.configuration.properties`, which points to all the other properties files. If you want to store most of the properties files in another location, you can point to that location from this property in the main configuration file. The framework looks for and tries to load both the default and webwork files upon startup. All the other files can load based on property settings in one of the two main files. Developers sometimes like to keep all configuration files together and away from the output classpath, so WebWork facilitates that design via its property-loading mechanism.

Some of these files may also be XML files. In particular, WebWork includes a document type definition (DTD) to use with an XML document for view mappings. If you prefer to keep view information in XML, WebWork can support that. The `webwork.configuration.xml` property in the webwork properties file allows you to specify an XML view file instead of the standard properties file.

To make it easier for you to set up the directory and configuration file structure WebWork expects, the framework install includes a "skeleton" project named skeleton-project.zip that resides in the /etc directory. This zip file includes a reasonable directory structure, libraries, an Ant build file, templates, and configuration files. This is an excellent starting point for building a WebWork project rather than setting it up on your own.

7.2 *Key concepts*

Like all nontrivial frameworks, WebWork contains some key concepts that you must understand before you can leverage the framework to its best potential. WebWork includes `Action` classes, which are an implementation of the Command design pattern; the `ServletDispatcher`, which is modeled after the Front

Controller design pattern (discussed in chapter 4); and an innovative data structure called the value stack, which makes it easy to pass information from the controller to the view.

7.2.1 *Actions*

Like most frameworks that use the Command design pattern to create a central controller servlet, WebWork includes a base class for all actions. This class, named `ActionSupport`, is a convenience class that implements the `ActionInterface`. It provides access to result view mapping, error handling, and internationalization. The Action interface includes some handy mappings (implemented as constants) to standard views that frequently reside in the view configuration document (for example, the `SUCCESS` constant).

In WebWork, the developer creates action subclasses that handle the individual page code for the application. The actions reside in a package or packages specified in the webwork.properties file and map to a particular extension (the default is .action). The names of the actions themselves appear in the views.properties file, which maps the action back to the action package. To invoke an action, the user types a URL that includes the web application name, followed by the mapping name of your action with the .action suffix. The suffix matches a URL pattern in the web.xml file, pointing it to the WebWork dispatch servlet. Once that servlet has the action, it follows the normal framework flow of events shown in figure 7.1. This structure is similar to Struts, particularly the way the controller servlet acts, but with additional configuration files.

One key difference from other frameworks lies in the fact that WebWork actions are not coupled to the servlet API. Actions are essentially just JavaBeans, with no intrinsic knowledge of constructs like `HttpServletRequest`. The actions can be made aware of these objects via interfaces, but the action itself knows nothing about what context it is running within. This makes WebWork actions more loosely coupled than Struts actions. In fact, WebWork documentation warns you when you try to use the interfaces to couple your application to the web API. While it is unlikely you would write a WebWork application that isn't a web application, a more loosely coupled application has greater flexibility.

7.2.2 *Key interfaces*

WebWork attaches behavior to actions and other classes via the use of interfaces. For example, if you need one of your actions to interact with `HttpServletRequest`, your action must implement the `ServletRequestAware` interface. This interface includes only a single method (`setServletRequest()`), which is called by the framework on any action that implements the interface. Your action can include a private `request` member variable that is set through this method. In WebWork 1.3, this interface has been replaced with a call to the static method `ServletAction-Context.getRequest()`.

An interesting variant on this theme is the `SessionAware` interface. It provides access to this user's session. Like `ServletRequestAware`, it includes a single set method (`setSession()`). However, the type passed as the user's session is a `java.util.Map`, not `HttpSession`. WebWork maintains the session information for you, keeping it in a `Map` instead of `HttpSession`. This means that you can support session tracking without being tied to the servlet API. In WebWork 1.3, this interface has been replaced with a call to the static method `ActionContext.getContext()`.

Most of the behavior that isn't intrinsic to the framework is attached to individual classes using interfaces. The interfaces are very cohesive, generally offering a single method. This provides an elegant means of enabling behavior without overburdening the framework with unneeded functionality.

7.2.3 *The value stack*

One of the built-in facilities of the framework is the *value stack*. This is a utility class that supports the access of information from the view. Semantically, it is a stack of values, implicitly placed there by actions in the course of execution. The WebWork expression language (covered next) uses the value stack heavily.

Regardless of the implementation, the value stack makes writing view elements (i.e., JSP) much easier than other frameworks do. For example, consider the use of localized properties for holding the label text for the fields on a page. As the page is loaded, the framework calls the `getText()` method on your action, passing the key, which looks up the message body from the `ResourceBundle`. It then places that value on the value stack. For example, to populate the label for a textfield (one of WebWork's UI components) with the value from the properties file, you can use the value stack method `text`:

```
<ww:textfield label="text('input.duration')"
              name="'duration'"
              value='<webwork:property value="duration"/>' />
```

As a developer, you can use the value stack as a JIT repository of data, provided by either your actions or by the framework itself. This primary underlying class supports the "pull" and "hierarchical" parts of "Pull HMVC." Generally, it is invisible, providing information through its methods just as it is needed.

The *stack* in value stack has meaning. It is implemented as a stack, with elements needed for a particular page or component pushed on the stack and then popped off when they are no longer needed. For example, consider the common case of iterating over a list of values in a JSP. In WebWork, the `iterator` tag places the value at the top of the value stack, and the `property` tag pops the value off the stack. Behind the scenes, the `property` tag looks up the `value` attribute passed to it (which defaults to .) using the stack, then pushes it back:

```
<webwork:iterator value="columns">
    <th><webwork:property/></th>
</webwork:iterator>
```

The `property` tag inside the iterator doesn't need any additional information about the property to access it. When you use the `property` tag with no attributes, it automatically pops the topmost value off the stack. In this case, the iterator pushes the current value of the `columns` collection (either a `List`, `Array`, or `Map`) on the stack, and the `property` tag pops the topmost value on the stack. Of course, the `property` tag also supports attributes for qualifying the property name, but they aren't needed in this case.

The value stack is an innovative structure, and it is used heavily and naturally throughout WebWork. As a stack, it can readily supply JIT values on the top of the stack, ready to be popped off. The developer also has more direct access to the value stack if needed, testing for the presence of values and explicitly manipulating it via push and pop methods.

7.2.4 *Expression language*

WebWork's expression language is designed to enhance the syntax of JSP to make it more programmable. It interacts with the value stack, possessing the ability to traverse the stack and flatten out objects to retrieve the desired data. It makes JSPs more readable by compressing the sometimes-verbose JSP syntax into terser, more expressive constructs. For example, it allows developers to use simpler notation when accessing a property from a JavaBean:

```
<webwork:property value="guessBean/numGuesses"/>
```

In this example, the `getGuessBean()` method of the underlying action is called, followed by a call to the `getNumGuesses()` method on the bean. The corresponding JSP syntax for this code would be

```
<jsp:getProperty name="guessBean" property="numGuesses" />
```

The expression language also has special support for standard collections in the web API. Consider this example:

```
<webwork:property value="@timer/total"/>
```

The @ symbol indicates that this object resides in page, request, or session scope. The expression language will find the most tightly scoped instance of this object, retrieve it from the scope, and call the getTotal() method on it.

The expression language may be used within any property of a WebWork custom taglib except the id property. The interaction of the expression language and the value stack create JSP pages that have much less "plumbing" code in them because the framework handles so much of it.

7.2.5 *BeanInfo classes*

WebWork borrows a convention from the JavaBeans API to add support for formatting and validation. The Action classes in WebWork are the primary active element. Each Action class can have a BeanInfo class associated with it to handle meta-property information (i.e., property information about properties). BeanInfo classes are part of the JavaBeans specification to supply meta-component information to development environments. For example, if you create a UI widget for a Swing application, you must provide support for a development environment to set and get properties. For complex properties, you can create property editors to assist the user in correctly setting the values of the properties. These editors aren't included in the code for the widget itself because they have no purpose at runtime—they are design-time-only artifacts. The JavaBeans API uses the convention for a BeanInfo class to supply property editors and other design time metadata for the component. If you create Widget.class, you can create WidgetBeanInfo.class and the development environment will automatically use the metadata class.

WebWork uses this mechanism to handle type conversions and validations for public properties of actions. The public properties (accessor and mutator pairs) for actions are made available via the value stack to the expression language elements on JSP pages. To handle validations, you can create BeanInfo classes for your actions and register editor classes for the properties. WebWork will automatically apply the editors for your fields to the input elements on the page. An example of this appears in the input elements of the schedule application in section 7.3.3.

7.2.6 *Templates*

WebWork by default is designed to create HTML-based web applications. However, the UI element rendering is governed by a set of templates. The skeleton project contains JSP pages to handle the output for Cascading Style Sheets, "normal" HTML, and Extensible Hypertext Markup Language (XHTML). These templates are used when WebWork renders the controls for display. Configuration parameters allow you to specify a different format via a set of templates. For example, you could create a set of templates for XML generation, place them in your web project, and tell WebWork to use them instead. None of the code in the application would need to change, but the output would become XML instead of HTML. The templates used by the framework are themselves WebWork pages and make heavy use of the expression language to determine property settings and internationalization options.

7.3 Scheduling in WebWork

At this point, let's build the two-page schedule application in WebWork. The boundary and entity classes are exactly the same as in the other framework chapters, preserving our goal of keeping the framework separate from the model aspect of the application. The WebWork schedule application represents a Model 2 application, built using the WebWork framework. It utilizes some of the unique features of WebWork, such as the `Action` classes and the value stack. This sample appears in the source code archive as art_sched_webwork.

7.3.1 The configuration

The first step in a WebWork application is setting up the configuration documents. For this application, we're using the default properties document and a custom webwork.properties file to override a few elements. Listing 7.1 shows the webwork.properties file, which resides in the classes directory under WEB-INF.

Listing 7.1   The webwork.properties file for the schedule application

```
# WebWork configuration
# See webwork/default.properties for full list of properties that
# can be configured here
webwork.action.packages=com.nealford.art.schedwebwork.action

# override default log4j config
# you can use .properties or .xml
# if you want to use default set property to null by an empty =
webwork.log4j.configfile=log4j.properties
```

The only two settings in the webwork.properties configuration file are the package where the actions reside and the location of the log4J configuration file.

   The next configuration document is for the views. This document contains all the mappings for user-reachable resources in the application. It defines both the action names and the result destinations for actions. This document is similar to the action mapping section in the Struts configuration file. Listing 7.2 contains the view.properties configuration document.

Listing 7.2   The view.properties for the schedule application

```
viewschedule.action=ViewSchedule
viewschedule.success=ViewSchedule.jsp

scheduleentry.action=AddScheduleEntry
scheduleentry.input=AddScheduleEntry.jsp
scheduleentry.success=viewschedule.action
scheduleentry.error=AddScheduleEntry.jsp

addscheduleitem.action=AddScheduleItem
addscheduleitem.success=AddScheduleEntry.jsp
```

The `action` suffixes indicate action objects that WebWork will create. The `input`, `success`, and `error` suffixes represent views to which the actions will dispatch. The entries in the view.properties file become the resources within the web application to which the actions can forward. The `ViewSchedule` action in the next section illustrates this.

The other configuration document in the schedule application is the log4j configuration, which contains nothing specific to WebWork, so we have omitted it.

7.3.2   *The View page*

The first page in the application is the View page, which shows all the current schedule entries. It appears in figure 7.2.

The action

The first part of the page is the `Action` class, called by the `ServletDispatcher`. Listing 7.3 shows the `ViewSchedule Action` class.

Listing 7.3   The ViewSchedule Action class defines properties and methods for the first page of the application.

```
package com.nealford.art.schedwebwork.action;

import java.io.IOException;
import java.util.Arrays;
import java.util.List;
import java.util.Map;
import javax.servlet.ServletContext;
import com.nealford.art.schedwebwork.boundary.ScheduleDb;
import org.apache.log4j.FileAppender;
```

```
import org.apache.log4j.Logger;
import org.apache.log4j.SimpleLayout;
import webwork.action.ActionContext;        Extends
import webwork.action.ActionSupport;        ActionSupport

public class ViewSchedule extends ActionSupport {  ❶
    private static final Logger logger = Logger.getLogger(  ❷  Contains
            ViewSchedule.class);                                private
    private String driverClass;                                members and
    private String dbUrl;                                       logging
    private String user;                                        definitions
    private String password;
    private ScheduleDb scheduleDb;
    private List scheduleItems;
    private String[] columns;
    private Map eventTypes;

    static {
        try {
            logger.addAppender(new FileAppender(new SimpleLayout(),
                    "c:/temp/sched-webwork.log"));
        } catch (IOException ex) {
            logger.error("Can't create log file");
        }
    }
    private void getDatabaseConfigurationParameters() {  ❸  Loads
        ServletContext sc = ActionContext.getContext().       database
                            getServletContext();              configuration
        driverClass = sc.getInitParameter("driverClass");     from
        dbUrl = sc.getInitParameter("dbUrl");                 ServletContext
```

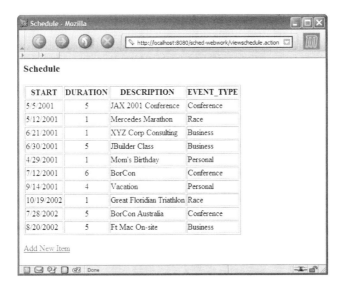

Figure 7.2
The WebWork View page shows all the schedule items, with a link for adding more.

```
        user = sc.getInitParameter("user");
        password = sc.getInitParameter("password");
    }

    protected String doExecute() throws java.lang.Exception {        ❹
        getDatabaseConfigurationParameters();
        scheduleDb = new ScheduleDb(driverClass, dbUrl, user,
                        password);                    Executes the action
        scheduleDb.populate();
        scheduleItems = scheduleDb.getList();
        columns = scheduleDb.getColumns();
        eventTypes = scheduleDb.getEventTypes();
        return SUCCESS;
    }
                                          Returns a list of ScheduleItems
    public List getScheduleItems() {    ❺ from boundary
        return scheduleItems;
    }
                                        Returns a list of columns
    public List getColumns() {    ❻ from boundary
        String[] uiColumns = new String[columns.length - 1];
        System.arraycopy(columns, 1, uiColumns, 0,
                        columns.length - 1);
        return Arrays.asList(uiColumns);
    }
}
```

❶ This class extends `ActionSupport`. It does not explicitly need access to any of the servlet API objects (such as request), so it does not implement any of the `Aware` interfaces (such as `RequestAware` or `SessionAware`). It does need access to the serv-let context object (to retrieve database parameters), but this access is provided by the `ActionContext` object.

❷ The top of the class defines private member variables and sets up log4j logging.

❸ The `getDatabaseConfigurationParameters()` method is a helper method that retrieves the database information from the web.xml file.

❹ The `doExecute()` method is the active method of this class. `ActionSupport` defines this method so that the developer can override it to perform work. This method is similar to an action method in other frameworks. It builds the boundary object, populates this action's list of schedule items, and populates both the `columns` and `eventTypes` member variables. All three of these class members (`scheduleItems`, `columns`, and `eventTypes`) are published with public accessors from this class. `scheduleItems` is the list of `ScheduleItem` entities that represent the records from the database. The `columns` array is a list of the display columns, also derived from the boundary class. The `eventTypes` map is the lookup relationship between the two tables that make up the data for this application. All three of these variables play a part in the display. The return from doExecute() is the predefined SUCCESS value defined in ActionSupport (via the Action interface). When this action returns, the ServletDispatcher looks up the value for the SUCCESS view for this action. It makes the properties of this action object available on the value stack and forwards control to that page.

❺ The getScheduleItems() accessor method returns the populated list of schedule items (courtesy of the doExecute() method) to the view.

❻ The getColumns() method returns only the displayable columns from the complete column list supplied by the boundary class.

The view

The view portion of this page makes heavy use of WebWork custom tags, the value stack, and the WebWork expression language. It appears in listing 7.4.

Listing 7.4   The view for the schedule page uses a few of the WebWork custom tags.

```
<%@ taglib uri="webwork" prefix="webwork" %>        ❶ Contains the
                                                        WebWork taglib
<html>
<head>
<title>
    <webwork:text name="'view.title'"/>            ❷ Loads text values
</title>                                               from a resource file
</head>
<body>
<h3><webwork:text name="'view.title'"/></h3>
<table border="1" >
    <tr>
        <webwork:iterator value="columns">         ❸ Outputs
            <th><webwork:property/></th>               column
        </webwork:iterator>                            headers
    </tr>

    <webwork:iterator value="scheduleItems" >
    <tr>
        <td><webwork:property value="start"/></td>
        <td align="center"><webwork:property value="duration"/></td>
        <td><webwork:property value="text"/></td>
        <td><webwork:property value="eventType"/></td>
    </tr>
    </webwork:iterator>                         Outputs table contents ❹
</table>
<p><a href="<webwork:url value="'addscheduleitem.action'"/>">
        <webwork:text name="'view.addlink'"/></a></p>
</body>
</html>
```

❶ The taglib definition at the top points to the WebWork tag library, which is the only taglib used on this page.

❷ The first tag used is the `text` tag. The `name` property makes use of a special syntax from the expression language. The single quotes around the name of the field indicate that the value should come from a properties file that defines the labels for the page. The single quotes keep the value from being evaluated by the expression language. Otherwise, it would try to use the attribute value as the property name to look up against the value stack. This is used both for separation of text values from code and for internationalization.

❸ This section of code uses the WebWork `iterator` tag. The value of `columns` automatically calls the `getColumns()` method from the action that submitted this page, accessed via the value stack. The `iterator` tag pushes the values from the columns list onto the stack and then pops it off in the `close` tag as the iteration progresses. The embedded WebWork `property` tag (with no attributes) peeks at the top value of the stack and outputs it to the page.

❹ This section is the iterator that outputs the item objects. Another feature of the expression language and value stack is the way embedded properties work. The references within the `iterator` tag are relative to the item iterated over. As the `iterator` tag works, it pulls the schedule item references from the list and uses reflection to call the accessor method using the name specified by the `property` tag. The values from the properties within the `iterator` tag are assumed to be accessors from the object pulled from the collection iterated over. The result of this combination maps the property value `start` to `scheduleItem.getStart()` on the object currently on the stack, placed there by the `iterator` tag, and so on for other properties of objects in the iterated `List`. (It takes much longer to explain it than to use it!) Once you get used to it, this approach is an intuitive way to look at the ways properties are accessed within the iterator over a collection. Of course, if one of the properties does not match an accessor on the iterator object, the `Action` class is consulted to find a matching accessor.

You should now start to see the symbiotic relationship between the value stack, the expression language, and the custom WebWork tags. The combination of all three creates a simple yet powerful display language for JSP. The underlying idea behind this facility is to simplify the job of the UI designer. Ideally, he or she shouldn't need to know anything about scoping, object references, or anything else. As long as the UI designer understands a few rules about how to access data, he or she can write pages quickly without being bogged down in programming details.

It is worth noting that WebWork provides a custom table component so that you don't have to create one by hand with iterators. Like Tapestry's table component,

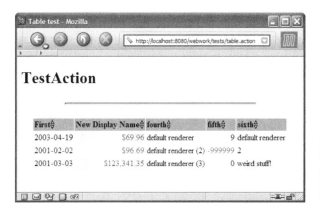

Figure 7.3
WebWork's custom table component features several advanced features. Notice that the column headers have a sort icon next to the column label.

it encapsulates several advanced features, such as sortable column heads. This custom table component is shown in figure 7.3.

7.3.3 The Add page

The Add page of the schedule application allows the user to add new schedule items. It appears in figure 7.4.

The Add page consists of three classes: a base class to handle common elements (`AddScheduleBase`), the initial add class (`AddScheduleItem`), and the save entry (`AddScheduleEntry`) class. A single UI page exists for adding records, which is shared by both the `AddScheduleItem` and `AddScheduleEntry` actions.

The AddScheduleBase class

Both the initial Add page and the Save page must have fields available to populate the UI part of the form. Rather than duplicate the same fields in two classes, we consolidated the common elements into a single base class. This class is shown in listing 7.5.

Figure 7.4
The Add page allows the user to add new schedule items.

```java
package com.nealford.art.schedwebwork.action;

import java.util.ArrayList;
import java.util.Iterator;
import java.util.List;
import java.util.Map;
import javax.servlet.ServletContext;
import com.nealford.art.schedwebwork.boundary.ScheduleDb;
import com.nealford.art.schedwebwork.entity.ScheduleItem;
import webwork.action.ActionContext;
import webwork.action.ActionSupport;

public class AddScheduleBase extends ActionSupport {
    private List events;
    protected ScheduleItem scheduleItem;
    private ScheduleDb scheduleDb;
    private String driverClass;
    private String dbUrl;
    private String user;
    private String password;

    public AddScheduleBase() {
        buildEventList();
        scheduleItem = new ScheduleItem();
    }

    public List getEvents() {
        return events;
    }

    private void buildEventList() {
        events = new ArrayList(5);
        scheduleDb = getScheduleBoundary();
        Map m = scheduleDb.getEventTypes();
        Iterator it = m.entrySet().iterator();
        while (it.hasNext()) {
            Map.Entry entry = (Map.Entry) it.next();
            EventType et = new EventType();
            et.setKey(((Integer) entry.getKey()).intValue());
            et.setEvent((String) entry.getValue());
            events.add(et);
        }
    }

    public class EventType {
        private int key;
        private String event;

        public int getKey() {
            return key;
        }
```

```
        public void setKey(int key) {
            this.key = key;
        }

        public String getEvent() {
            return event;
        }

        public void setEvent(String event) {
            this.event = event;
        }
    }
```

The `AddScheduleBase` class extends `ActionSupport`, so it is an `Action` class. The fields of the class represent database configuration information, a list of events, and an embedded entity object. Most of the details of this class involve establishing a boundary object to populate and add the entity and accessor/mutator pairs for the properties of the page. All these methods have been omitted because of space. The key methods of this class relate to the list of events.

A recurring theme in all the scheduling examples for each framework concerns how a particular framework handles the rather ugly HTML `<select>` tag, with its embedded options. Each framework has its own solution to this problem. WebWork's solution is its `select` custom tag. This tag expects a list of items that resolve to objects with a property for the key and the value. To that end, the `AddScheduleBase` class builds an embedded `EventType` class that consists solely of the key-value pairs necessary for the `select` tag to work correctly. The `build-EventList()` method gets the map of key-value pairs from the boundary object and builds the structure expected by the `select` tag, placing it in the events field of the class. The `getEvents()` method returns this list of objects.

The AddScheduleItem class

The `AddScheduleItem` class (listing 7.6) is the `Action` class first accessed when a user adds a new item. It subclasses `AddScheduleBase`.

Listing 7.6   The AddScheduleItem class is the first Add page.

```
package com.nealford.art.schedwebwork.action;

import java.io.IOException;
import org.apache.log4j.FileAppender;
import org.apache.log4j.Logger;
import org.apache.log4j.SimpleLayout;

public class AddScheduleItem extends AddScheduleBase {
```

```
    private static final Logger logger = Logger.getLogger(
            AddScheduleItem.class);

    static {
        try {
            logger.addAppender(new FileAppender(new SimpleLayout(),
                    "c:/temp/sched-webwork.log"));
        } catch (IOException ex) {
            logger.error("Can't create log file");
        }
    }

    protected String doExecute() throws java.lang.Exception {
        return SUCCESS;
    }
}
}
```

Almost all the functionality provided by the class comes from the parent class. In fact, more code is devoted to setting up logging than actual execution. Ostensibly, all this class does is immediately return the SUCCESS flag. However, it also includes the event list structure and the empty schedule item object created by its parent class.

The AddSchedule view

The view portion for adding a new schedule item appears in listing 7.7.

Listing 7.7 The View page allows the user to add new schedule items.

```
<%@ taglib uri="webwork" prefix="ww" %>
<html>
<head>
<title>
<ww:text name="'view.title'"/>
</title>
</head>
<body>
<h3>
<ww:text name="'view.title'"/>
</h3>
<form action="scheduleentry.action" method="post">
<table border="0" width="30%" align="left">
    <tr><td>
    <ww:textfield label="text('input.duration')"
                name="'duration'"
                value='<webwork:property value="duration"/>' />
    </td></tr>
    <tr><td>
    <ww:select label="text('input.eventType')"
```

```
                name="'eventType'"
                list="events"      ❶ Boundary-supplied events
                listKey="'key'"
                listValue="'event'"/>
    </td></tr>
    <tr><td>
    <ww:textfield label="text('input.start')"
                name="'start'"
                value='<webwork:property value="start"/>' />
    </td></tr>
    <tr><td>
    <ww:textfield label="text('input.text')"
                name="'text'"
                value='<webwork:property value="text"/>' />
    </td></tr>
    <tr><td align="right">
    <input type="submit" name="Submit"
                value="<ww:text name="'input.submit'"/>">
    </td></tr>
    </table>
    </form>

    </body>
    </html>
```

❶ The only dynamic values on this page are the ones placed in the HTML `<select>`. The `<select>` tag retrieves the value of events by calling `AddSchedule-Item.getEvents()`, as specified by the attribute `list`. You may notice that the `getEvents()` method is absent in `AddScheduleItem`: it is inherited from the super class `AddScheduleBase`.

The `AddScheduleEntry` JSP page makes heavy use of the WebWork custom taglibs. An interesting feature of this page is the absence of HTML text elements to identify the input fields. WebWork's `textfield` component handles that with a property value. The `name` attribute of the `textfield` becomes the label associated with the HTML input. Note that the name actually comes from the properties file that defines the values of all the text elements. The text values properties file for this page (AddScheduleItem.properties) is shown in listing 7.8.

Listing 7.8   The AddScheduleEntry.properties resource file

```
view.title=Add Schedule Item

input.start=Start
input.duration=Duration
input.eventType=Event Type
input.text=Description
```

```
input.submit=Save

error.schedule.duration=Invalid duration
error.schedule.text=Event must have description
```

The other interesting characteristic of the WebWork custom tags on the View-ScheduleEntry page is the select tag. This tag uses several attributes, which are listed with their meanings in table 7.2.

Table 7.2   Attributes of the select tag

Attribute	Value	Use
label	text('input.eventType')	The label for the field on the HTML page
name	'eventType'	The action field the value of the control will map to upon submission of the form
list	events	The list of objects that implement the name-value pair mapping
listKey	'key'	The key field of the class that implements the name-value pair mapping
listValue	'event'	The value field of the class that implements the name-value pair mapping

The AddScheduleEntry JSP page highlights the powerful triad of WebWork's value stack, custom taglibs, and expression language. The combination of these features is greater than the sum of their parts. The resulting View page is very clean and features only view elements, but it doesn't give up any flexibility.

Saving the record

The last action in the application saves the changes to the database. The AddScheduleEntry action appears in listing 7.9.

Listing 7.9   The AddScheduleEntry action saves the changes to the boundary.

```
package com.nealford.art.schedwebwork.action;

import java.io.IOException;
import java.util.Map;
import com.nealford.art.schedwebwork.boundary.ScheduleDb;
import org.apache.log4j.FileAppender;
import org.apache.log4j.Logger;
import org.apache.log4j.SimpleLayout;

public class AddScheduleEntry extends AddScheduleBase {
```

```
private static final Logger logger = Logger.getLogger(
        AddScheduleEntry.class);

static {
    try {
        logger.addAppender(new FileAppender(new SimpleLayout(),
                "c:/temp/sched-webwork.log"));
    } catch (IOException ex) {
        logger.error("Can't create log file");
    }
}

protected String doExecute() throws java.lang.Exception {
    Map errors = scheduleItem.validate();
    if (!errors.isEmpty())
        return ERROR;
    ScheduleDb scheduleDb = getScheduleBoundary();
    scheduleDb.addRecord(scheduleItem);
    return SUCCESS;
}

}
```

The `AddScheduleEntry` Action class inherits most of its capabilities from `AddSched-uleBase`. In the `doExecute()` method, it validates the `scheduleItem` and returns the `ERROR` flag upon failure. If the validations pass, the record is added to the boundary and the `SUCCESS` flag returns the user to the initial application page.

The validations performed here are perfunctory. The real validations take place in the individual field editors, which are covered in the next section.

7.3.4 *Validations*

The last topic we'll cover for the schedule application is validations. As before, the entity object contains validation code to prevent illegal values for either `duration` or `text`. You may have noticed that the View page contains no code whatsoever to handle validations. Section 7.2.5 alluded to the mechanism used by WebWork to handle validations and other field-level criteria. WebWork uses `BeanInfo` classes to attach additional behavior to the `Action` classes. The JavaBean specification allows you to register editor classes to handle validation, formatting, and any other trans-formation you want to perform on the input.

Editors

Two types of validations are needed for this application. Both of these validations ultimately map back to the entity, which is the keeper of all business rules (like val-idations). To that end, we've upgraded the entity class to include static methods that validate each field in turn. The previous validation method is still present (although we've rewritten it to take advantage of the new individual validation methods). The new methods in the ScheduleItem class are shown in listing 7.10.

Listing 7.10 The ScheduleItem class has undergone an upgrade to create more cohesive validation methods.

```java
public static String validateDuration(String duration) {
    int d = -1;
    String result = null;
    try {
        d = Integer.parseInt(duration);
    } catch (NumberFormatException x) {
        result = "Invalid number format: " + x;
    }
    if (d < MIN_DURATION || d > MAX_DURATION)
        result = ERR_DURATION;
    return result;
}

public static String validateText(String text) {
    return (text == null || text.length() < 1) ?
            ERR_TEXT :
            null;
}

public Map validate() {
    Map validationMessages = new HashMap();
    String err = validateDuration(String.valueOf(duration));
    if (err != null)
        validationMessages.put("Duration", err);
    err = validateText(text);
    if (err != null)
        validationMessages.put("Text", err);
    return validationMessages;
}
```

Now that we have cohesive validation methods, it is trivial to write custom editors that take advantage of these rules. Listing 7.11 contains the editor for duration.

Listing 7.11 The DurationEditor handles validating a duration value against the ScheduleItem's validation method.

```java
package com.nealford.art.schedwebwork.util;

import com.nealford.art.schedwebwork.entity.ScheduleItem;
import webwork.action.ValidationEditorSupport;

public class DurationEditor extends ValidationEditorSupport {
```

```
    public void setAsText(String txt) {
        String error = ScheduleItem.validateDuration(txt);
        if (error != null)
            throw new IllegalArgumentException(error);
        setValue(txt);
    }
}
```

The `DurationEditor` class extends `ValidationEditorSupport`, which is a WebWork framework class. The lone method that must be implemented is `setAsText()`. This method can either set the value of the field or throw an `IllegalArgumentException`. The WebWork framework catches the exception and associates the error string from the exception with the field. Figure 7.5 shows a validation failure for both `duration` and `text`.

No additional code was added to the View page. The framework automatically added the validation exception text to the field. The class to handle `text` validation is virtually the same, so we don't show it here.

The last step in validation is the association with the property editors with the `Action` classes. This is done through a `BeanInfo` class. The `BeanInfo` class for `AddScheduleEntry` (named, not surprisingly, `AddScheduleEntryBeanInfo`) appears in listing 7.12.

> **Listing 7.12 The AddScheduleEntryBeanInfo class registers the custom property editors to the appropriate Action class.**

```
package com.nealford.art.schedwebwork.action;

import java.beans.BeanInfo;
import java.beans.Introspector;
import java.beans.PropertyDescriptor;
import java.beans.SimpleBeanInfo;
import java.io.IOException;
import java.util.ArrayList;
import java.util.List;
import org.apache.log4j.FileAppender;
import org.apache.log4j.Logger;
import org.apache.log4j.SimpleLayout;

public class AddScheduleEntryBeanInfo extends SimpleBeanInfo {
    private static final Logger logger = Logger.getLogger(
            AddScheduleEntryBeanInfo.class);

    static {
        try {
            logger.addAppender(new FileAppender(new SimpleLayout(),
```

```
                              "c:/temp/sched-webwork.log"));
        } catch (IOException ex) {
            logger.error("Can't create log file");
        }
    }

    public PropertyDescriptor[] getPropertyDescriptors() {
        try {
            List list = new ArrayList();
            PropertyDescriptor descriptor;

            descriptor = new PropertyDescriptor("duration",
                    AddScheduleEntry.class);
            descriptor.setPropertyEditorClass(com.nealford.art.
                    schedwebwork.util.DurationEditor.class);
            list.add(descriptor);

            descriptor = new PropertyDescriptor("text",
                    AddScheduleEntry.class);
            descriptor.setPropertyEditorClass(com.nealford.art.
                    schedwebwork.util.TextEditor.class);
            list.add(descriptor);

            return (PropertyDescriptor[]) list.toArray(new
                    PropertyDescriptor[list.size()]);

        } catch (Exception x) {
            logger.error("AddScheduleEntryBeanInfo", x);
            return super.getPropertyDescriptors();
        }
    }
}
```

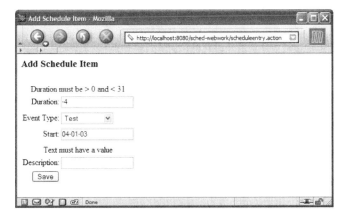

Figure 7.5
WebWork automatically associates the error text with the field whose validation failed.

Notice that the `AddScheduleEntryBeanInfo` class does not import or use any class from the WebWork framework. Everything here is either standard Java or part of the logging package. This is a standard `BeanInfo` class, just like the one you would register for a UI widget. The lone method creates an array of `PropertyDescriptors`. A property descriptor registers a property editor to the property of a particular class. In this method, we are registering the `DurationEditor` and `TextEditor` for the `AddScheduleEntry` class.

Generic validations

The validation code in the previous section reveals one of the architecture and design pitfalls faced by developers. By creating specific editors for the Duration and text fields of the `ScheduleItem` class, we can carefully tie the business logic validation to the UI. However, this becomes cumbersome if we have hundreds of fields that must be validated. If we follow this paradigm, we will have hundreds of almost identical validation editors.

Three approaches help solve this problem. First, you could create several generic editors that handle the lion's share of validations. For example, if your application needs to validate non-negative numbers in many locations, a `NonNegativeNumber` editor can easily handle the task. The second approach creates property editors that can use reflection to determine the type of the entity they are validating and call the validations automatically for the fields. Standard interfaces for entities are used to force common semantics across all entities so that they are all validated in the same way. Smart property editors can take advantage of this characteristic. The third approach uses the Decorator design pattern to decorate the entities with property editors that handle the validations.

These approaches are not mutually exclusive. It is quite common to create generic validation editors to handle common situations. Interfaces are useful when you have objects that share common semantics (usually enforced by interfaces). Decorator is useful when you have a disparate set of objects that share common validation needs.

7.4 *Evaluating WebWork*

When deciding whether to use a framework, you should consider the documentation (including the samples) and the "feel" of the framework. In WebWork, the documentation and samples go hand in hand. In fact, the best documentation for the custom tags is included in the samples.

The WebWork documentation is sufficient. (It is posted on the OpenSymphony web site and is included with the download.) The creators have even gone so far as to customize the doclet used by JavaDoc to make the API JavaDoc look more like the OpenSymphony web site. However, it is a minor change and it doesn't impede the readability. The biggest problem with the documentation is the absence of comments on many methods. The classes themselves have reasonable, if terse, comments; but many of the methods have only the standard generated JavaDoc information and nothing else. While this didn't cause me any headaches, it is a glaring deficiency in such a well-designed framework.

WebWork lacks Tapestry's excellent documentation for the custom tags. In fact, the best documentation for the custom tags was in the sample applications. This characteristic seems to be common with custom tags. The JavaDoc comments don't serve custom tags very well. JSTL suffers from this same syndrome— the samples are more useful than the documentation. The WebWork documentation for the custom tags is no worse than any other framework's documentation for the same kind of tags. However, all frameworks pale in comparison to Tapestry in this area.

I was looking for and never found a comprehensive list of the interactions between the value stack, expression language, and custom tags. The material is present; it is just scattered around a bit. It would be nice if it were summarized somewhere. As the application in this chapter shows, it is vitally important to understand the interaction between these constructs. Most of what I found concerning the interactions between these three constructs came from the tutorials and samples, not the JavaDocs.

The samples are good in WebWork. They suffer a bit from poor organization. The web application resources are in one directory and the source code is in another branch entirely. Once you figure out where everything lives, the samples help considerably.

One thing you should note: the samples are themselves WebWork pages, so they should be run through the servlet engine. Even though you can open the static HTML pages, some of the pages are dynamic. If you are looking at an example of a custom tag and it seems as if most of the tag code is missing, you are probably not running it properly.

The sample's index page categorizes the samples well. It starts with simple capabilities samples (such as how to use the taglibs) and moves to more complex, complete applications. The last samples illustrate how to incorporate UI frameworks like Velocity into WebWork.

WebWork meets its stated goals. It makes web development easier without compromising good design and reliance on design patterns. I particularly like the combination of the value stack, expression language, and custom taglibs. Once I understood how they worked, it made writing pages simple. In fact, in one case I actually wrote some code, ran it, saw that it worked, and then had to figure out why! Some of the interactions between these three elements happen so seamlessly that they seem instinctive.

7.5 Summary

This chapter covered OpenSymphony's WebWork, a "Pull Hierarchical MVC" framework for building web applications. We discussed the value stack, the expression language, and the custom properties. The interaction of these three elements is the primary distinguishing characteristic of this framework.

We built our schedule application in WebWork and explained the many configuration options, including the variety of configuration files. Then, we built the artifacts necessary to create the two pages of the schedule application. Each page in a WebWork application requires an `Action` class and a UI page. The UI page sets this framework apart from others because of the powerful behind-the-scenes behavior of the three key elements mentioned earlier.

We showed you how WebWork uses property editors and Java's `BeanInfo` mechanism to provide a way to create custom property editors for fields. We used the editors to validate the user input on the form. Finally, we discussed the documentation, samples, and the "feel" of WebWork. It is a powerful framework that does not sacrifice good design or architecture.

In the next chapter, we look at a commercial web framework, InternetBeans Express.

InternetBeans Express

8

This chapter covers

- The design and architecture of InternetBeans Express
- Building applications with InternetBeans Express
- Evaluating the framework

Most of the frameworks and tools covered in this book are open source. The Java world contains a wealth of open-source code, some of it with state-of-the-art quality. However, my emphasis on open source should not suggest that commercial frameworks don't exist. Many large organizations have undertaken huge framework initiatives. This chapter focuses on a framework supplied with a best-selling commercial integrated development environment (IDE), Borland's JBuilder. It includes a Rapid Application Development (RAD) framework called Internet-Beans Express for building web applications that leverage component-based development. It builds on the already strong components that already exist in JBuilder for building client/server applications.

This framework presents a departure in another manner as well. Most of the frameworks we've covered have been architecture and process intensive. Most of the open-source frameworks concern themselves with designing and building applications that leverage design patterns and other industry best practices. Clearly, I prefer this kind of thought and practice in designing applications. However, none of these frameworks addresses RAD development. RAD has fallen out of favor over the last few years because it doesn't necessarily address best practices and other design criteria. However, using these tools you can create applications significantly faster than without them.

The purpose of this chapter is twofold. The first is to show a RAD web development framework so that you can compare it to the others shown in the book. The other goal is to find a partial way to reconcile the worlds of RAD development with the ideas prevalent in this book. As in the other framework chapters, we'll be building the schedule application, this time with InternetBeans Express.

8.1 Overview

InternetBeans Express is a feature of the Enterprise version of JBuilder, the version that includes web development. It consists of a series of components that integrate with servlets and a custom taglib for use in JSP. These components are primarily concerned with the presentation tier of a web application. JBuilder contains other components for handling database connectivity. InternetBeans Express components use static template HTML documents and inserts dynamic content from a live data model. It is designed to make it quick and easy to generate database-aware servlets and JSPs.

The components fall roughly into three categories:

- InternetBeans, components that deal directly with the dynamic generation of HTML pages and the handling of HTTP.

- The JSP custom tag library, which uses the InternetBeans components internally. This includes JSP tag handlers that provide event-handling semantics to a web application.

- Data model support through JBuilder's DataExpress components.

The InternetBeans Express components appear in the development environment of JBuilder alongside the other components used to create desktop applications. InternetBeans Express has its own palette in the designer, as shown in figure 8.1. See section 8.3.1 for a complete discussion of these components.

Building an application with InternetBeans Express is extremely fast in the best tradition of RAD development tools. The general steps are as follows:

1. Create a new project.

2. Create a new web application.

3. Create the data model for the application (using DataExpress components).

4. Create the user interface template as an HTML document.

5. Create a servlet to act as a controller.

6. Use the designer to drop InternetBeans Express components on the servlet.

7. Use the property inspector to set the property value of the components.

8. Write any event handlers needed.

9. Add a single line of boilerplate code to the servlet's `doGet()` and `doPost()` methods.

The details of many of these steps are covered later. Before developing an application, you need to understand the architecture and some key concepts about these components.

Figure 8.1   The InternetBeans Express components appear alongside the other components in JBuilder's design view.

8.2 *The architecture*

The architecture of the InternetBeans Express components relies on other components that exist in the JBuilder development environment, primarily the DataExpress components. The DataExpress components have existed and evolved since the first version of JBuilder. They represent a solid, well-architected wrapper around Java Database Connectivity (JDBC). Most of the behavior in DataExpress started as support for building client/server applications. As the focus in Java has moved more to the server side, the DataExpress components have migrated as well.

8.2.1 *DataExpress*

To use the DataExpress components, you must understand the relationship between these controls and standard JDBC and the support classes JBuilder provides to handle containership and instancing. The DataExpress components provide a component-based alternative to writing JDBC code by hand. JBuilder also contains support classes, such as `DataModules`, to make it easy to use DataExpress in both desktop and web applications.

DataExpress and JDBC

DataExpress is a moniker for the components in JBuilder that encapsulate standard JDBC classes. Figure 8.2 shows the relationship between the DataExpress components and JDBC classes.

The DataExpress Database component contains both the `DriverManager` and `Connection` classes. It holds a persistent connection to the database tied to a

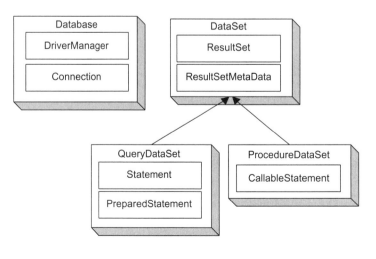

**Figure 8.2
The DataExpress components encapsulate the JDBC classes.**

particular user's login. DataSet is an abstract class that encapsulates both Result-Set and ResultSetMetaData. This class also includes numerous DataExpress-specific classes that manipulate data from a database server. The concrete subclasses of DataSet are QueryDataSet, which encapsulates both Statement and Prepared-Statement, and ProcedureDataSet, which encapsulates CallableStatement.

When using the DataExpress components, you never have to write any SQL or other low-level JDBC code. The components generate all the code for you. Designers exist within JBuilder that help you build SQL statements for queries and set properties for the DataSets and the individual columns returned from the DataSets. DataExpress also defines a series of events for these controls, allowing the developer to attach code to events within the lifecycle of the component.

DataModules

A DataModule is a class created by JBuilder for managing DataExpress components. The original purpose for DataModules was to allow multiple user interface frames in a desktop application to share the same database connection. A Data-Module is a class that acts as a factory for either creating instances of itself or returning a shared instance of itself. Thus, a DataModule is a factory implemented as a singleton object. DataModules also automatically generate accessor methods for any DataExpress component added to it. Listing 8.1 shows a DataModule with a single database component on it.

Listing 8.1 A simple DataModule with a single database component on it

```
package com.nealford.art.ixbeans.servlet.db;

import com.borland.dx.dataset.DataModule;
import com.borland.dx.sql.dataset.ConnectionDescriptor;
import com.borland.dx.sql.dataset.Database;

public class DataModuleSched implements DataModule {
    static private DataModuleSched myDM;
    private Database dtbsSchedule = new Database();

    public DataModuleSched() {
        try {
            jbInit();
        } catch (Exception e) {
            e.printStackTrace();
        }
    }

    private void jbInit() throws Exception {
        dtbsSchedule.setConnection(new ConnectionDescriptor(
                "jdbc:mysql://localhost/schedule", "root",
```

```
                    "marathon", false, "com.mysql.jdbc.Driver"));
    }

    public static DataModuleSched getDataModule() {
        if (myDM == null) {
            myDM = new DataModuleSched();
        }
        return myDM;
    }

    public com.borland.dx.sql.dataset.Database getDtbsSchedule() {
        return dtbsSchedule;
    }
}
```

Typical for a singleton object, the class includes a static reference to itself named myDM. However, this class has a public constructor instead of the more typical private one. A DataModule is not a true singleton because situations may arise when a new instance is required. Thus, the DataModule supports both kinds of instantiation. The jbInit() method is common in any class whose component properties are set through the JBuilder designer. With this method, JBuilder writes all the code generated by the design tools. Finally, the database component automatically generates an accessor method when the component is dropped on the Data-Module in the designer.

DataModules can contain any component, though the designer creates accessors only for DataExpress components. Because they are normal classes, you can have as many as you like in your application. For large applications, it is typical to have a main DataModule that contains the database component and many other DataModules that contain DataSet components. However, in small applications you may place the database and DataSet components on the same DataModule. JBuilder has special designers that make it easy to generate a database component and several DataSets that use it.

Other classes use the DataModule to connect to the database. Typically, a class that contains user interface elements (either a client/server desktop or Internet-Beans Express class) connects to the DataModule by creating a reference to it. The data-aware components then use their DataSet property to connect to one of the controls on the DataModule. This process is shown in figure 8.3.

The user interface element class contains a reference (either shared or unique) to the DataModule, and the data-aware controls point to a DataSet on the DataModule.

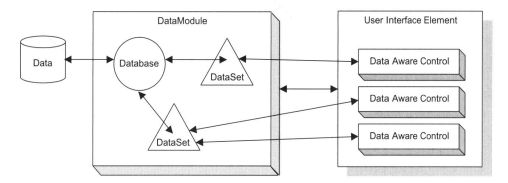

Figure 8.3   DataModule contains DataExpress components, which are set as property values for the data-aware controls in the user interface class.

Disconnected updates

One of the features of DataExpress is the concept of *cached data.* When a `DataSet` is connected to a database, it does not keep a database cursor open for the table. It instead caches a set of the rows locally, either in memory or on disk. The local cache contains three sections: metadata, data, and deltas. The *metadata* keeps column information locally. The *data* is the snapshot of the data in the underlying table. The *deltas* are changes that have been made to the local data but have not been resolved to the database yet. Changes made to the local cached data (kept in the deltas) are not updated in the database until the `saveChanges()` method on the `DataSet` is called.

It is important to realize that a call to the `post()` method of the `DataSet` posts the changes only to the local cache. To make the changes permanent, you must call `saveChanges()`. This architecture is in place to make client/server applications more flexible and to allow for disconnected data applications. This has little impact on web applications because typically you post and save changes at the same point in time.

8.2.2 *InternetBeans Express*

The InternetBeans Express controls are data-aware controls that are declared in a servlet and that replace HTML template elements when the servlet renders the page. The component that controls the rendering process and binds the various data-aware controls together is the `PageProducer`. The relationship among the various controls is shown in figure 8.4.

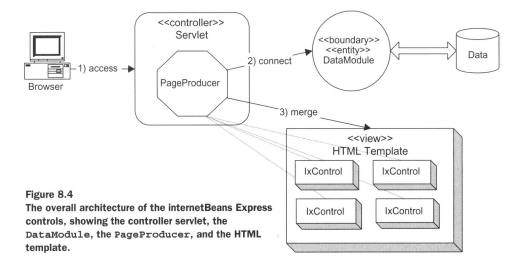

Figure 8.4
The overall architecture of the internetBeans Express controls, showing the controller servlet, the `DataModule`**, the** `PageProducer`**, and the HTML template.**

The controller servlet contains the `PageProducer` component as well as the declarations and property settings for the Internet Express Controls (known generically as "ixControls"). When the user connects to the web application, the controller servlet creates a reference to the `DataModule`, which in this case acts as both a boundary and entity class. It encapsulates both the database connectivity and the data from the table into a single component. The `PageProducer` then merges the contents of the ixControls with their corresponding controls on the HTML template to produce output.

8.3 InternetBeans Express components

The InternetBeans Express components consist of the `PageProducer` and all the user interface controls. The `PageProducer` acts as the driving force in the application, controlling rendering and dispatching. The user interface controls connect to the `PageProducer` for event notification and coordination.

8.3.1 ixPageProducer

The `PageProducer` is the key component in InternetBeans Express. This component acts as the glue between the DataExpress components and the other InternetBeans Express components. Only this component is both data and servlet aware. It is typically instantiated as a member of a servlet along with the other ixControls. The other controls have a `PageProducer` property that associates them with a particular producer. The `PageProducer` has three distinct roles in an InternetBeans Express application: rendering pages, handling request parameters, and handling events.

Rendering pages

The `PageProducer` handles the merging of the other ixControls with the static HTML template used for the user interface. The HTML elements are placeholders for the dynamically generated, data-aware ixControls. This is similar to the way that Tapestry handles user interface elements and templates. The relationship between the `PageProducer` and the controls it renders is established at design time. Each ixControl has a `PageProducer` property that points to its rendering control.

To invoke the rendering, the servlet's `doGet()` method should call the `PageProducer`'s `servletGet()` method. Typically, the only line of code in the `doGet()` method of a servlet acting as the controller for an InternetBeans Express application is

```
ixPageProducer.servletGet(this, request, response);
```

The parameters to this method are the servlet itself and the normal request/ response pair passed to the `doGet()` method.

Handling request parameters

To handle the parameters passed to the servlet from a form post, the `doPost()` method of the servlet calls the `servletPost()` method of the `PageProducer`:

```
ixPageProducer.servletPost(this, request, response);
```

This call to `servletPost()` automatically applies the request parameters to the matching controls governed by the `PageProducer`. Generally, this method call is followed by whatever action you want to take after the posting operation. If you're updating the current page, a call to the `doGet()` method of the servlet will update the fields by chaining to the `PageProducer`'s `servletGet()` method. Alternatively, you can redirect to another page in the application.

A great deal of behavior is encapsulated within the call to `servletPost()`. If the controls attached to the `PageProducer` are data aware, their values are automatically updated by the values passed as form parameters. Creating an application that shows values from a database query on a page, allowing the user to change the values, and updating the database is largely taken care of by the framework. To complete the update, you need only call the `post()` and `saveChanges()` methods on the `DataSet` bound to the controls.

Handling submit events

The last action of the `servletPost()` method is to determine if there is a request parameter matching an ixSubmitButton associated with the `PageProducer`. If so, the `PageProducer` calls the `submitPerformed()` method of the button. This mechanism allows the post of the servlet to act as an event in a desktop application. Each Submit button may have an associated event handler. The parameter passed to the event handler (of type `SubmitEvent`) gives the developer access to session-specific data.

The `PageProducer` handles a session-specific `DataModule` (and the associated `DataSets`) for the user. To access this user's instance of the `DataModule`, you use the `SubmitEvent`'s methods. For example, to get access to a user-specific `DataModule` instance, you can use the following code in the `submitPerformed()` event handler:

```
DataModuleSched dm = (DataModuleSched)
        ixPageProducer.getSessionDataModule(e.getSession());
```

The framework automatically handles generating a new instance of the `DataModule` per user, in effect giving each user a connection to the database. For scalability purposes, it is possible to override this behavior. However, it is in tune with this framework's attempt to make web development mimic desktop application development.

8.3.2 ixComponents

The other ixComponents all function in the same manner. They all encapsulate (and replace) their corresponding HTML controls on the user interface template when rendered by the `PageProducer`. Table 8.1 contains a listing of the components and their purpose.

Table 8.1   The ixComponents

Component	Description
ixControl	A generic control that can take on the characteristics of any HTML control when rendered. This component may be used in a JSP without a `PageProducer`.
ixTable	Generates an HTML table from a `DataSet` or table model.
ixImage	Represents an image used for display or as a link.
ixLink	Represents a link. If URL Rewriting is necessary, this component handles it by calling `response.encodeURL()`.
ixSpan	Replaces read-only content on the HTML template page.
ixCheckBox	Represents a check box.

continued on next page

Table 8.1   The ixComponents *(continued)*

Component	Description
ixComboBox	Represents a combo box.
ixHidden	Represents a hidden HTML input field.
ixImageButton	Represents an image that submits the form when clicked.
ixListBox	Represents a list box.
ixPassword	Represents a password field.
ixPushButton	Represents a client-side button (that executes JavaScript).
ixRadioButton	Represents a radio button.
ixSubmitButton	Represents a form submit button. If the button that matches this component is the button that submits the form, the `submitPerformed()` method of the servlet will fire.
ixTextArea	Represents a text area.
ixTextField	Represents an input field.

Virtually all of these controls are data aware, meaning that they have properties that point them to a `DataSet` and a column. When the contents of the control change, the underlying value in the row of the `DataSet` changes as well. However, the changes are not made permanently to the cached `DataSet` until the row pointer is changed (in other words, the `DataSet` moves to another row) or the `post()` method of the `DataSet` is called. The changes are not permanent in the database until the `saveChanges()` method on the `DataSet` is called.

8.4 *Scheduling with InternetBeans*

This section features the ubiquitous schedule application, written using Internet-Beans Express. The major change in this version of the application is the RAD nature of the framework. This will not be a Model 2 application—this framework is not designed to work in that context. However, a reasonable separation of concerns is still possible without doing battle with the framework. For the most part, we're going to let the RAD nature of the framework dictate the architecture of the application and retrofit it to improve the structure.

Unlike all the previous versions, this schedule application does not use the boundary and entity classes created for the generic Model 2 application. Instead, it uses a DataExpress `DataModule` to handle both boundary and entity responsibilities. None of the infrastructure (except the database itself) from the previous version is used in this one. Yet developing this application from scratch takes much less time than developing in one of the other frameworks using the existing infrastructure. Welcome to the world of RAD!

8.4.1 Data connectivity

The first piece of the application is the data connectivity. Let's create a Data-Module with a database and two QueryDataSet components (for event and event_type) on it. The first part of the DataModule is used for the basic connectivity and the first page of the application. The latter part of the DataModule is needed for validation and user input, so it will appear later. Listing 8.2 shows the first part of the DataModuleSchedule.

Listing 8.2   The first portion of the Schedule DataModule

```
package com.nealford.art.ixbeans.servlet.db;

import java.util.ArrayList;
import java.util.ResourceBundle;
import com.borland.dx.dataset.CalcFieldsListener;
import com.borland.dx.dataset.Column;
import com.borland.dx.dataset.ColumnChangeAdapter;
import com.borland.dx.dataset.DataModule;
import com.borland.dx.dataset.DataRow;
import com.borland.dx.dataset.DataSet;
import com.borland.dx.dataset.DataSetException;
import com.borland.dx.dataset.Locate;
import com.borland.dx.dataset.ReadRow;
import com.borland.dx.dataset.Variant;
import com.borland.dx.sql.dataset.ConnectionDescriptor;
import com.borland.dx.sql.dataset.Database;
import com.borland.dx.sql.dataset.Load;
import com.borland.dx.sql.dataset.QueryDataSet;
import com.borland.dx.sql.dataset.QueryDescriptor;
import com.borland.jb.util.TriStateProperty;
import com.nealford.art.ixbeans.servlet.entity.ScheduleItemBizRules;

public class DataModuleSchedule implements DataModule {        ❶  The class that
    ResourceBundle sqlRes = ResourceBundle.getBundle(              implements
            "com.nealford.art.ixbeans.servlet.db.SqlRes");        DataModule
    static private DataModuleSchedule myDM;
    private Database dbSchedule = new Database();
    private QueryDataSet qryEvents = new QueryDataSet();
    private QueryDataSet qryEventType = new QueryDataSet();
    private Column column2 = new Column();
    private Column column3 = new Column();
    private Column column4 = new Column();
    private java.util.List errorList;
    private Column column5 = new Column();
```

```
public DataModuleSchedule() {        ❷ | Public constructor
    try {                                  that calls jbInit()
        jbInit();
        errorList = new ArrayList(2);
    } catch (Exception e) {
        e.printStackTrace();
    }
}                                          jbInit() method,
                                           including all designer-
private void jbInit() throws Exception {  ❸ | generated code
    column5.setColumnName("description");
    column5.setDataType(com.borland.dx.dataset.Variant.STRING);
    column5.setPrecision(50);
    column5.setEditable(true);
    column5.setTableName("event");
    column5.setServerColumnName("description");
    column5.setSqlType(12);
    column5.addColumnChangeListener(new  ColumnChangeAdapter() {
        public void validate(DataSet dataSet, Column column,
                Variant value) throws Exception,
                DataSetException {
            column5_validate(dataSet, column, value);
        }
    });
    column4.setColumnName("duration");
    column4.setDataType(com.borland.dx.dataset.Variant.INT);
    column4.setRequired(true);
    column4.setTableName("event");
    column4.setServerColumnName("duration");
    column4.setSqlType(4);
    column4.addColumnChangeListener(new ColumnChangeAdapter() {
        public void validate(DataSet dataSet, Column column,
                              Variant value) throws Exception,
                DataSetException {
            column4_validate(dataSet, column, value);
        }
    });
    column3.setColumnName("event_type");
    column3.setDataType(com.borland.dx.dataset.Variant.INT);
    column3.setTableName("event");
    column3.setVisible(TriStateProperty.FALSE);
    column3.setServerColumnName("event_type");
    column3.setSqlType(4);
    column2.setCalcType(com.borland.dx.dataset.CalcType.CALC);
    column2.setCaption("Event Type");
    column2.setColumnName("Event Type");
    column2.setDataType(com.borland.dx.dataset.Variant.STRING);
    column2.setPreferredOrdinal(2);
    column2.setServerColumnName("NewColumn1");
    column2.setSqlType(0);
    qryEventType.setQuery(new QueryDescriptor(dbSchedule,
```

```
                        sqlRes.getString("event_types"), null, true,
                    Load.ALL));
        qryEvents.setQuery(new QueryDescriptor(dbSchedule,
                "select * from event", null, true, Load.ALL));
        qryEvents.addCalcFieldsListener(new CalcFieldsListener() {
            public void calcFields(ReadRow changedRow,
                    DataRow calcRow, boolean isPosted) {
                qryEvents_calcFields(changedRow, calcRow, isPosted);
            }
        });
        dbSchedule.setConnection(new ConnectionDescriptor(
                "jdbc:mysql://localhost/schedule", "root",
                "marathon", false, "com.mysql.jdbc.Driver"));
        qryEvents.setColumns(new Column[] {column2, column4,
                            column5, column3});
    }
    public static DataModuleSchedule getDataModule() {
        if (myDM == null) {
            myDM = new DataModuleSchedule();
        }
        return myDM;
    }
    public Database getDbSchedule() {
        return dbSchedule;
    }

    public QueryDataSet getQryEvents() {
        return qryEvents;
    }

    public QueryDataSet getQryEventType() {
        return qryEventType;
    }

    void qryEvents_calcFields(ReadRow changedRow, DataRow calcRow,
                            boolean isPosted) {
        if (!qryEventType.isOpen())
            qryEventType.open();
        if (!qryEvents.isOpen())
            qryEvents.open();
        DataRow locateRow = new DataRow(qryEventType,
                                        "event_type_key");
        locateRow.setInt("event_type_key",
                    changedRow.getInt("event_type"));
        qryEventType.locate(locateRow, Locate.FIRST);
        calcRow.setString("event type",
                    qryEventType.getString("event_text"));
    }
```

4 Static factory method for shared instancing

5 Accessor for Database component

6 Calculated field definition

❶ This class implements the `DataModule` interface, which is all that is required for the designer to implement its special behaviors (such as the automatic generation of accessor methods).

❷ The constructor is public (whereas a "true" singleton class would have a private constructor) to give the users of the class a choice as to how it is instantiated. The constructor primarily calls the `jbInit()` method.

❸ The `jbInit()` method contains all the code generated by the design tool. All property settings created through the object inspector in the designer generate code in this method.

❹ This method is the static factory method for returning the shared, singleton instance of the `DataModule`.

❺ JBuilder generates accessor methods automatically whenever a DataExpress component is dropped on a `DataModule`. These three methods represent generated accessors for the three corresponding controls. The designer is not intelligent enough to remove the accessors if you remove one of the components—you must delete the accessor by hand.

❻ The only code not generated by the designer is the definition of the calculated field. The information from the database resides in two tables, but we need the foreign key lookup to be transparent for the data-aware controls. To achieve that goal, we created a calculated column. `DataSets` contain a collection of `Column` objects, and the developer can create new calculated columns that behave exactly like the intrinsic columns. In the `qryEvents_calcFields()` method, we first make sure both `DataSets` are open. Then, we create a scoped `DataRow`. A scoped `DataRow` is an empty row of data that takes on the metadata structure of a table. To create a scoped `DataRow` that contains a single column from the referenced `DataSet`, we call the constructor that expects the `DataSet` and the column that we want in our scoped `DataRow`. If we needed all the rows to be present, we would use a different constructor. Once we have the scoped `DataRow`, we can fill in the value of the field for which we are looking. The `locate()` method will move the record pointer to the first row whose column matches the value in `locateRow`. We set the value of the calculated column to the matching column value in the lookup `DataSet`. The data-aware controls can now use this column.

One of the options you have available when creating a `DataModule` is to isolate the SQL statements in a list resource bundle. This arrangement makes it easier to find and change them in the future. We selected this option, and JBuilder automatically created the `SqlRes` class in the same package as the `DataModule`. This class appears in listing 8.3.

Listing 8.3   The SqlRes class

```
package com.nealford.art.ixbeans.servlet.db;

public class SqlRes extends java.util.ListResourceBundle {
    private static final Object[][] contents = new String[][]{
            { "event", "select * from event" },
            { "event_types", "select * from event_types" }};
    public Object[][] getContents() {
        return contents;
    }
}
```

JBuilder automatically maintains this file for the application and places references to it in the appropriate locations in the `DataModule`.

8.4.2 *The View page*

The View page for the InternetBeans Express schedule application consists of two parts: the servlet with the ixComponents and the HTML template. It is shown in figure 8.5.

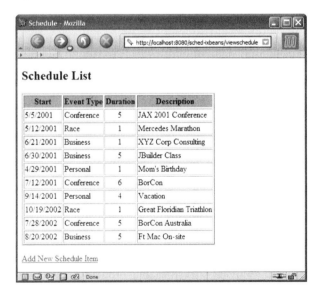

Figure 8.5
The InternetBeans Express schedule application's View page is the combination of DataExpress, InternetBeans Express components, and an HTML template.

The View servlet

The ViewSchedule servlet appears in listing 8.4.

Listing 8.4   The ViewSchedule servlet

```
package com.nealford.art.ixbeans.servlet.ui;

import java.io.IOException;
import javax.servlet.ServletException;
import javax.servlet.http.HttpServlet;
import javax.servlet.http.HttpServletRequest;
import javax.servlet.http.HttpServletResponse;
import com.borland.internetbeans.IxLink;
import com.borland.internetbeans.IxPageProducer;
import com.borland.internetbeans.IxTable;
import com.nealford.art.ixbeans.servlet.db.DataModuleSchedule;

public class ViewSchedule extends HttpServlet {                    ❶
    IxPageProducer ixPageProducer1 = new IxPageProducer();
    IxTable ixTable1 = new IxTable();                         ViewSchedule, a
    DataModuleSchedule dataModuleSchedule;                    standard servlet
    IxLink ixLink1 = new IxLink();
                                                              Standard doGet()
    public void doGet(HttpServletRequest request,      ❷    method
                      HttpServletResponse response) throws
            ServletException, IOException {
        ixPageProducer1.servletGet(this, request, response);
    }
                                                              Standard doPost()
    public void doPost(HttpServletRequest request,     ❸    method
                       HttpServletResponse response) throws
            ServletException, IOException {
        DataModuleSchedule dm =
                (DataModuleSchedule) ixPageProducer1.
                getSessionDataModule(request.getSession());
        dm.getQryEvents().refresh();
        ixPageProducer1.servletGet(this, request, response);
    }

    public ViewSchedule() {
        try {
            jbInit();
        } catch (Exception e) {
            e.printStackTrace();
        }
    }
                                                              Designer-generated
    private void jbInit() throws Exception {           ❹    jbInit() method
        dataModuleSchedule = com.nealford.art.ixbeans.servlet.db.
                             DataModuleSchedule.getDataModule();
        ixTable1.setDataSet(dataModuleSchedule.getQryEvents());
        ixTable1.setRowCount(20);
```

```
            ixPageProducer1.setDataModule(dataModuleSchedule);
            ixLink1.setPageProducer(ixPageProducer1);
            ixTable1.setPageProducer(ixPageProducer1);
            ixPageProducer1.setHtmlFile("root/sched-template.html");
            ixPageProducer1.setRootPath(".");
            ixTable1.setElementId("scheduletable");
            ixLink1.setElementId("addlink");
            ixLink1.setLink("/sched-ixbeans/addscheduleentry");
    }
}
```

❶ This servlet extends `HttpServlet` and includes several ixComponents.

❷ The `doGet()` method is characteristic for InternetBeans Express applications—it calls the `servletGet()` method on the `PageProducer`.

❸ The `doPost()` method first retrieves the session-specific `DataModule` and refreshes the data. This code handles the case when this page is posted from another servlet (for example, the successful result of the Add servlet). The last thing the `doPost()` method does is call `servletGet()`, causing the control to be rendered.

❹ The remainder of this class consists of the designer-generated `jbInit()` method. Notice the relationship between the `PageProducer`, `DataModule`, and ixComponents. The `PageProducer` points to the `DataModule` (to handle the session-specific instancing), and the ixComponents point to the `PageProducer`.

The View template

The template for this page (listing 8.5) is also simple. The HTML controls act as placeholders for the ixComponents.

Listing 8.5   The HTML template (sched-template.html) for the View page

```html
<html>
<head>
<title>
Schedule
</title>
</head>
<body>
<p><h2>Schedule List</h2></p>
<table id="scheduletable" border="2">

    <tr bgcolor="yellow">
        <th>Start</th>
        <th>Event Type</th>
        <th>Duration</th>
        <th>Description</th>
    </tr>
```

```
<tr>
  <td>01-01-2003</td>
  <td>Conference</td>
  <td align="center">3</td>
  <td>Template Text</td>
</tr>
</table>

<p>
<span id="addlink">Add New Schedule Item</span>
</body>
</html>
```

The sched-template HTML page includes dummy data to serve as placeholders for the dynamic controls. This makes it easier to design; the dynamic controls pay no attention to the contents but only to the relative location of the static controls on the page. However, the controls do respect meta-information embedded in the tags. The third column of the table includes an `align` attribute, and the resulting dynamic table respects that attribute. The servlet (in this case, `ViewSchedule`) uses the `id` attribute to match dynamic controls to their static counterparts, using the `setElementId()` method of each dynamic control.

8.4.3 *The Add page*

The Add page uses the same `DataModule` as the View page. The two unique items for this page are the Add servlet and the HTML template.

The Add servlet

The Add servlet has two modes of operation. When the `doGet()` method is called, it must display the controls, using the `PageProducer` to render the dynamic controls. The Add page appears in figure 8.6.

Figure 8.6
The Add page allows the user to add new items.

The first portion of the servlet handles the initial display. Listing 8.6 contains this code.

Listing 8.6   The first portion of the Add servlet

```
package com.nealford.art.ixbeans.servlet.ui;

import java.io.IOException;
import java.io.PrintWriter;
import java.util.ArrayList;
import java.util.Iterator;
import java.util.List;

import javax.servlet.RequestDispatcher;
import javax.servlet.ServletException;
import javax.servlet.http.HttpServlet;
import javax.servlet.http.HttpServletRequest;
import javax.servlet.http.HttpServletResponse;

import com.borland.dx.dataset.DataRow;
import com.borland.dx.dataset.Locate;
import com.borland.dx.sql.dataset.QueryDataSet;
import com.borland.internetbeans.IxComboBox;
import com.borland.internetbeans.IxPageProducer;
import com.borland.internetbeans.IxPushButton;
import com.borland.internetbeans.IxSubmitButton;
import com.borland.internetbeans.IxTextField;
import com.borland.internetbeans.SubmitEvent;
import com.nealford.art.ixbeans.servlet.db.DataModuleSchedule;

public class AddScheduleEntry extends HttpServlet {
    private IxPageProducer ixPageProducer1 = new IxPageProducer();
    private IxSubmitButton ixSubmitButton1 = new IxSubmitButton();
    private IxTextField ixtxtDuration = new IxTextField();
    private IxTextField ixtxtStart = new IxTextField();
    private IxTextField ixtxtText = new IxTextField();
    private IxComboBox ixcbEventType = new IxComboBox();
    private DataModuleSchedule dataModuleSchedule;
    private QueryDataSet referenceForInsert;
    private IxPushButton ixPushButton1 = new IxPushButton();

    public AddScheduleEntry() {
        try {
            jbInit();
        } catch (Exception e) {
            e.printStackTrace();
        }
    }

    private void jbInit() throws Exception {
        dataModuleSchedule = com.nealford.art.ixbeans.servlet.db.
                    DataModuleSchedule.getDataModule();
        ixcbEventType.setColumnName("Event Type");
```

```
        ixcbEventType.setDataSet(dataModuleSchedule.getQryEvents());
        ixcbEventType.setControlName("eventTypeKey");
        ixtxtStart.setColumnName("start");
        ixtxtStart.setDataSet(dataModuleSchedule.getQryEvents());
        ixtxtStart.setControlName("start");
        ixtxtText.setColumnName("description");
        ixtxtText.setDataSet(dataModuleSchedule.getQryEvents());
        ixtxtText.setControlName("text");
        ixSubmitButton1.setControlName("submit");
        ixSubmitButton1.setElementId("submit");
        ixSubmitButton1.addSubmitListener(new com.borland.
                internetbeans.SubmitListener() {
            public void submitPerformed(SubmitEvent e) {
                ixSubmitButton1_submitPerformed(e);
            }
        });
        ixtxtDuration.setColumnName("duration");
        ixtxtDuration.setDataSet(dataModuleSchedule.getQryEvents());
        ixPushButton1.setPageProducer(ixPageProducer1);
        ixSubmitButton1.setPageProducer(ixPageProducer1);
        ixcbEventType.setPageProducer(ixPageProducer1);
        ixtxtText.setPageProducer(ixPageProducer1);
        ixtxtStart.setPageProducer(ixPageProducer1);
        ixtxtDuration.setControlName("duration");
        ixtxtDuration.setPageProducer(ixPageProducer1);
        ixPageProducer1.setHtmlFile(
                "/root/AddScheduleEntry.html");
        ixPageProducer1.setRootPath(".");
        ixPageProducer1.setDataModule(dataModuleSchedule);
}
public void doGet(HttpServletRequest request,
                  HttpServletResponse response) throws
        ServletException, IOException {
    ixcbEventType.setOptions(getEventTypeList(request));
    ixPageProducer1.servletGet(this, request, response);
}

private List getEventTypeList(HttpServletRequest request) {
    DataModuleSchedule dm = (DataModuleSchedule)
            ixPageProducer1.getSessionDataModule(
            request.getSession());
    dm.getQryEventType().open();
    dm.getQryEventType().first();
    List items = new ArrayList(10);
    while (dm.getQryEventType().inBounds()) {
        items.add(dm.getQryEventType().getString("event_text"));
        dm.getQryEventType().next();
    }
    return items;
}
```

➊ Populates the combobox

➋ Builds a list of events mapped to event types

❶ Before the requisite call to `servletGet()` to render the controls, the values for the combo box must be populated. The IxComboBox control has a `setOptions()` method, which accepts either a `List` or an `Array` of items to appear in the pull-down list.

❷ To generate the list required by the IxComboBox, the `getEventTypeList()` method iterates through the `DataSet` associated with the event_type table. First, it opens the `DataSet`, moves the row pointer to the first row, and loops over the `DataSet` while there are more records remaining. The `inBounds()` method of the `DataSet` returns true until the row pointer is beyond the last record.

Notice in figure 8.6 that the fields are already populated with values. When the user selects this page, the bound controls show the record where the `DataSet` is currently pointing. The bound controls go so far as to generate the `selected` attribute on the HTML select control generated from the IxComboBox control. This is the effect of data-aware controls.

The Add template

The Add template consists of simple HTML placeholders for the dynamic controls. It appears in listing 8.7.

Listing 8.7 The Add page's HTML template

```
<html>
<head>
<title>
Add Schedule Entry
</title>
</head>
<body>
<h3>
Add New Schedule Entry
</h3>
<hr>
<form method="post">
<table border="0" width="30%" align="left">
    <tr><th align="right">Duration</th>
        <td align="left">
        <input id="duration" name="duration" size="16" value="12">
        </td>
    </tr>
    <tr><th align="right">Event Type</th>
        <td align="left">
        <input id="eventType" name="eventTypeKey" />
        </td>
    </tr>
    <tr><th align="right">Start</th>
```

❶ Event type appears here as an input field

```
            <td align="left">
            <input id="start" name="start" size="16" value="01-01-03"/>
            </td>
        </tr>
        <tr><th align="right">Text</th>
            <td align="left">
            <input id="text" name="text" size="16" value="Description"/>
            </td>
        </tr>

        <tr>
            <td align="right">
                <input id="submit" type="submit" value="Save Changes" >
            </td>
        </tr>
    </table>
    </form>
    </body>
    </html >
```

❶ The eventType field is not even a `select` component. The type of the component in the HTML template is not important. The `id` attribute is the property binding the dynamic control to the HTML element. It is the only attribute required of the template fields for the dynamic rendering to occur.

8.4.4 *Validations*

Validations in InternetBeans Express cover three areas. First, the events tied to the columns in the `DataModule` fire as the record is inserted. Second, the appropriate validation code is executed, preferably on the entity classes. Third, the errors must be displayed to the user.

The validation for the columns happens in the `DataModule` as the attempt is made to insert the record. The remainder of the `DataModule` (including the validation methods) is shown in listing 8.8.

Listing 8.8   The DataModule contains the code for validating the inserted data.

```
    public java.util.List getErrorList() {
        return errorList;
    }

    void column4_validate(DataSet dataSet, Column column,
                          Variant value)
            throws Exception, DataSetException {
        ScheduleItemBizRules bizRule = ScheduleItemBizRules.getInstance();
        String error = bizRule.validateDuration(value.getAsInt());
        if (error != null)
```

```
                errorList.add(error);
        }

    void column5_validate(DataSet dataSet, Column column,
                          Variant value)
            throws Exception, DataSetException {
        ScheduleItemBizRules bizRule = ScheduleItemBizRules.getInstance();
        String error = bizRule.validateText(value.getString());
        if (error != null)
            errorList.add(error);
    }
  }
```

The `DataSet` in `DataExpress` defines column objects, based on the metadata for the query. The columns have properties (such as the data type and display name) as well as events. The events are automatically fired at the appropriate time in the lifecycle of the `DataSet`. One of the events for each column is the `validate()` event. This event handler is fired any time the user attempts to update the column. In a client/server application, this takes place as the user types a new value and moves away from the field. However, a web application cannot be as event driven as a desktop application. Therefore, for web applications the column validations occur as the information is moved from the data-aware control into the inserted row in the `DataSet`. For our schedule application, two columns must be validated: the duration and text columns. The event handlers `column4_validate()` and `column5_validate()` handle these validations. If an error occurs, it updates a `List` kept by the `DataModule` indicating the error. This too is contrary to how these event handlers work in a client/server application, where exceptions are thrown from the events to instruct the `DataSet` not to post the records.

The natural location to place the validation rules are in these event handlers. However, that arrangement violates all the best practices that have driven the development of the applications in this book so far. Placing these validations in the boundary class means that they are hopelessly scattered throughout the application, losing the good separation of responsibilities. The `DataModule` already handles all the data for the entities. What is needed is a way to decouple the business rules activities away from the `DataModule`'s event handlers.

The solution to this problem lies in a business rules class. This class acts as an adjunct to the `DataModule` and supplies behaviors for the entities in the application. It contains the business rules methods that pertain to the data values kept in the `DataModule` and `DataSets`. Listing 8.9 shows the business rules class for this application.

Listing 8.9   The business rules for our entities reside in a class separate from the DataModule.

```
package com.nealford.art.ixbeans.servlet.entity;

public class ScheduleItemBizRules {
    private static ScheduleItemBizRules internalInstance;
    private static final int MIN_DURATION = 0;
    private static final int MAX_DURATION = 31;
    private static final String ERR_DURATION = "Duration must be " +
            "between " + MIN_DURATION + " and " + MAX_DURATION;
    private static final String ERR_TEXT = "Text must have a value";

    private ScheduleItemBizRules() {
    }

    public static ScheduleItemBizRules getInstance() {
        if (internalInstance == null)
            internalInstance = new ScheduleItemBizRules();
        return internalInstance;
    }

    public String validateDuration(int duration) {
        String result = null;
        if (duration < MIN_DURATION || duration > MAX_DURATION)
            result = ERR_DURATION;
        return result;
    }

    public String validateText(String text) {
        String result = null;
        if (text == null || text.length() == 0)
            result = ERR_TEXT;
        return result;
    }
}
```

This class is a singleton with two methods, one for each validation rule. The criteria for the validation (the minimum and maximum durations) appear in this class as constants along with the error strings. When the `DataModule`'s `validate()` methods validate the data fields, it creates an instance of this class and calls these methods. While not the ideal separation of concerns, this is the most expedient way to take advantage of the framework without hopelessly compromising the overall architecture of the application.

InternetBeans Express attempts to create an event-driven paradigm for web applications, mimicking desktop applications. However, it doesn't go as far as Tapestry, which replaces the entire web API with its own. InternetBeans Express allows the developer to tie event-handling code to a Submit button on a form. The last job of `servletPost()` is to check whether the button that submitted the form has an associated event handler. If so, it dispatches to that event handler. The servlet's `doPost()` method is still called first (after all, this is a servlet responding to an HTML POST). Therefore, you must understand the interaction between `doPost()` and the event handler.

The remainder of the `AddScheduleEntry` servlet relates to validating and adding a new record. It appears in listing 8.10.

Listing 8.10   The remainder of the AddScheduleEntry servlet

```
public void doPost(HttpServletRequest request,
                   HttpServletResponse response) throws
        ServletException, IOException {
    DataModuleSchedule dm = (DataModuleSchedule)
            ixPageProducer1.getSessionDataModule(
            request.getSession());
    List errorList = (List) request.getAttribute("errorList");
    if (errorList != null)
        outputErrors(request, response, errorList);
    else {
        dm.getQryEvents().insertRow(false);
        ixPageProducer1.servletPost(this, request, response);
    }
}

private void outputErrors(HttpServletRequest request,
                          HttpServletResponse response,
                          List errorList) throws
        IOException {
    PrintWriter out = response.getWriter();
    Iterator err = errorList.iterator();
    out.println("<font color='red'>");
    while (err.hasNext())
        out.println(err.next() + "<br>");
    out.println("</font>");
    errorList.clear();
    ixPageProducer1.servletGet(this, request, response);
}

void ixSubmitButton1_submitPerformed(SubmitEvent e) {
    DataModuleSchedule dm = (DataModuleSchedule)
            ixPageProducer1.getSessionDataModule(
            e.getSession());
    lookupEventKeyAndUpdateRowValue(e, dm);
    RequestDispatcher rd = null;
    List errors = dm.getErrorList();
    if (errors.size() > 0) {
        forwardToErrorView(e, rd, errors);
        return;
```

❶ Routes to a page depending on successful validation

❷ Outputs the errors to the servlet

❸ Handles errors for the form's Submit button

```
        }
        saveChangesToDatabase(dm);
        dm.getErrorList().clear();
        rd = e.getRequest().getRequestDispatcher(
                "/viewschedule");
        try {
            rd.forward(e.getRequest(), e.getResponse());
        } catch (ServletException ex) {
            ex.printStackTrace();
        } catch (IOException ex) {
            ex.printStackTrace();
        }
    }

    private void saveChangesToDatabase(DataModuleSchedule dm) {
        dm.getQryEvents().post();
        dm.getQryEvents().saveChanges();
    }

    private void lookupEventKeyAndUpdateRowValue(SubmitEvent e,
                            DataModuleSchedule dm) {
        DataRow lookupRow = new DataRow(dm.getQryEventType(),
                                "event_text");
        DataRow resultRow = new DataRow(dm.getQryEventType());
        lookupRow.setString("event_text",
                        e.getRequest().
                        getParameter("eventTypeKey"));
        if (dm.getQryEventType().lookup(lookupRow, resultRow,
                                Locate.FIRST))
            dm.getQryEvents().setInt("event_type",
                    resultRow.getInt("event_type_key"));
    }

    private void forwardToErrorView(SubmitEvent e,
                                RequestDispatcher rd,
                                List errors) {
        e.getRequest().setAttribute("errorList", errors);
        rd = e.getRequest().getRequestDispatcher(
                "/addscheduleentry");
        try {
            rd.forward(e.getRequest(), e.getResponse());
        } catch (ServletException sx) {
            e.getSession().getServletContext().log(
                "Forward error from submit", sx);
        } catch (IOException ix) {
            e.getSession().getServletContext().log(
                "Forward error from submit", ix);
        }
    }
}
```

Updates the database

④

Handles updating data

⑤

⑥ **Reposts back to same page with errors added**

❶ When a user is entering a new schedule item, the post method must determine whether an error has already been generated. When the new record is validated and fails, it returns to the same page so that the user can correct the errors. When the user clicks the Submit button again, the servlet must decide if this is a re-post from an error listing or a new post request. The doPost() method of this servlet handles this contingency by looking at the contents of the list of errors. If there are no errors, the method assumes that this is a first-time post and that it should try to add a new record. It does so by inserting a new row into the database and calling servletPost(), which activates the event handler.

❷ This method iterates over the errors collection and prints each error to output stream.

❸ The ixSubmitButton1_submitPerformed() method does the work of trying to insert a new record. It gets the key value for the selected eventType using the lookupEventKeyandUpdateRowValue() method (which appears at #5). It then gets the list of errors from the DataModule. Notice that we didn't have to call any methods to generate this list. It is automatically generated when the servletPost() method binds the request parameters back to the data-aware controls.

❹ If the error list is empty, we call the saveChangesToDatabase() method, which performs the post() and saveChanges() methods on the DataSet. The last order of business is to redirect to the View page.

❺ This method performs a lookup to get the key for the selected eventType using a scoped DataRow.

❻ If errors are discovered, the servlet redirects back to itself, performing a postback and using the error list as a request attribute. The doPost() method checks to see whether the errorList attribute is present. If it is, it calls the outputErrors() method. The result of this call is shown in figure 8.7.

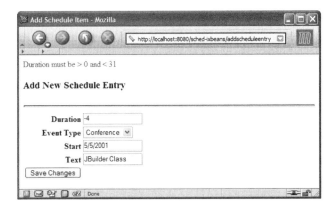

Figure 8.7
If validation errors occur, the servlet posts back to itself and displays the errors at the top of the page.

The error list appears at the top of the page. This is one of the disadvantages of using a servlet-only framework. To generate the error list, we hijacked the normal response stream, placing our elements at the top. Although this approach works, it doesn't provide many options for placement. An improved version of this is possible if we use JSP and custom tags to handle the error processing.

This completes the servlet-based InternetBeans Express schedule application. This application generated a lot of source code but, ironically, you had to type much less code for this application than for the other versions of the schedule application. The RAD framework generated most of the code, either automatically or through properties and events.

8.5 JSP custom tags

The schedule application in this chapter was created solely with the servlet-based controls in InternetBeans Express. InternetBeans Express also contains a collection of custom JSP tags. They are similar in intent to the SQL tags in the JSP Standard Tag Library (JSTL), but they predate the JSTL tags. To provide a flavor of these tags, we'll show the initial schedule page, written as a JSP and using the InternetBeans Express taglib. The output of this page (see figure 8.8) resembles that of most of the schedule View pages.

The source for this page (the only artifact in the application) appears in listing 8.11.

Figure 8.8
We used the JSP custom tags from InternetBeans Express to generate the View page of the schedule application.

Listing 8.11 The JSP page that generated the InternetBeans Express taglib Schedule page

```
<%@ page import="com.borland.internetbeans.*,
        com.borland.dx.dataset.*,
        com.borland.dx.sql.dataset.*" %>
<%@ taglib uri="/internetbeans.tld" prefix="ix" %>

<ix:database id="scheduleDb" driver="com.mysql.jdbc.Driver"
    url="jdbc:mysql://localhost/schedule" username="root"
    password="marathon">

<ix:query id="qryEvent"
    statement="select e.duration as 'Duration', et.event_text as
    'Event Type', e.start as 'Start', e.description as 'Description'
    from event e,  event_types et where e.event_type =
    et.event_type_key" >
<html>
<head>
<title>
Schedule Items
</title>
</head>
<body>

<p><h2>Schedule List</h2></p>
<ix:table dataSet="qryEvent">
<table border="1">

    <tr bgcolor="yellow">
        <th>Duration</th>
        <th>Event Type</th>
        <th>Start</th>
        <th>Description</th>
    </tr>
    <tr>
    <td>5</TD>
    <td>Conference</td>
    <td>01-01-01</td>
    <td>Description</td>
  </tr>
</table>
</ix:table>
<p>

<a href="scheduleentry">Add New Schedule Item</a>
</ix:query>
</ix:database>

</body>
</html>
```

The custom tags instantiate ixComponents underneath. So, the `ixTable` custom tag is using the same `ixTable` component used in the servlet-based version of this application. The tags used on this page are the `ixDatabase`, `ixQuery`, and `ixTable` components. The containership of the tags is important. The query uses the database that the tag is nested within. Similarly, the `ixTable` component only has access to the query that it is nested within.

We provided this example to show that InternetBeans Express does have a JSP collection of tags. However, this application violates many of the rules of separation touted in the other chapters of this book. This approach might suffice for a quick-and-dirty application, but it is not suitable for serious development. The same applies to the similar JSTL tags mentioned in chapter 3.

8.6 *Evaluating InternetBeans Express*

This evaluation of InternetBeans Express is a little different from the other evaluations. I conceded at the beginning of this chapter that this framework does not embody the criteria used to judge many of the frameworks in this book. However, given that limitation, I will discuss the documentation, samples, and the use of InternetBeans Express.

8.6.1 *Documentation and samples*

The documentation is of special interest because InternetBeans Express is generally considered the Achilles heel of open-source frameworks. A commercial product's offering should surpass the open-source efforts. The documentation of InternetBeans Express is a part of the overall documentation of JBuilder. It is a subset of the "Building Web Applications" help book included with the JBuilder help system. The documentation is good, with a polished look and feel that matches the rest of the JBuilder documentation. The coverage is well done but brief. However, this isn't a large framework, so a lot of verbiage isn't necessary.

The documentation consists of a narrative introduction to the topic, with links to the sample application and links to the appropriate JavaDoc documentation. It is informative and well done. It doesn't feature any of the "TO BE DONE" entries that you sometimes see in open-source documentation. The JavaDoc is very comprehensive and complete. Even though it is good, I don't think it is significantly better than the documentation for some open-source frameworks (Velocity is the gold standard in that respect).

A single sample application is available for the servlet InternetBeans Express controls and another for the InternetBeans Express JSP taglibs. The examples are sufficient to lead to a good understanding of the framework but could have been better. They were single-page applications with postbacks, so some of the coupling issues we dealt with in the schedule application didn't come up. Both of these frameworks are fairly simple, and the sample application is sufficient to illustrate the main points.

8.6.2 *Using InternetBeans Express*

The $64,000 question is: Does the speed of development using the RAD framework overcome the compromises imposed by it? This problem is common in the RAD world and one of the reasons that it has fallen somewhat out of favor. There is no question about the productivity of using a RAD framework: building an application is much faster than with other frameworks. That makes it eminently suitable for quick-and-dirty applications that don't need the industrial strength underpinnings of Model 2 and other best practices.

The problem with this mindset is that applications never exist in a vacuum. If they are useful, they tend to outlive their supposed lifetime. The developers who wrote COBOL code in the 1960s never imagined that their code would still be running in 2000. Applications tend to grow over their lifetimes. Even if it is designed to be quick and dirty at the outset, it is hard to predict how it might evolve. This is exactly the trouble faced by RAD today. Many developers have been burnt by using frameworks that started to collapse as the application outgrew the framework.

This is particularly true with web applications. At least with client/server applications, you could reasonably predict the number of users it needed to support. With web applications, the number of users can multiply overnight. Using a framework because it is quick becomes the death toll for the application if it lacks reasonable design.

Given this dire warning, if you still decide to use a framework like this one, you have ways to mitigate the risk. All RAD frameworks lay out a path of least resistance for development. This is the path the designers thought would yield the best results in the shortest amount of time. The problem arises when you try to get *underneath* the framework. For example, you could design a completely Model 2 application using InternetBeans Express. However, you will spend a great deal of time trying to get the framework to do things it wasn't meant to do. In such a case, you have stepped off the path of least resistance.

The trick is to find a way to stay on the path without hopelessly compromising your design. In this chapter, we used business rules classes. While not as pure a design as Model 2, this approach still achieved some of the goals of Model 2 (separation of business rules from the main line of development) without stepping off the path. To use a framework like this one successfully, you must find an effective way to work *within* the framework rather than fight it.

We've used InternetBeans Express as an example of RAD-based application frameworks. It is certainly not the only one available. We also don't want to leave you with the impression that it is the only game in town if you use JBuilder. The latest versions of JBuilder include JSTL and Struts libraries and designers. Borland is leveraging open-source frameworks like the rest of the world.

8.7 *Summary*

This chapter covered the InternetBeans Express framework that is included with Borland's JBuilder. To understand the framework, you must understand other parts of JBuilder's component hierarchy. The DataExpress components in JBuilder encapsulate the lower-level JDBC classes to make data access easier. InternetBeans Express attempts the same with the web API, creating a component layer over the lower-level classes and interfaces.

The InternetBeans Express schedule application demonstrated how to build HTML templates for user interfaces, how to handle display and update of data, and how validations are performed. It utilized the event-handler infrastructure, dealing with both strengths and weaknesses in its implementation. In particular, the servlet-only framework presents limited options for outputting errors and other non-ixControl-based output.

InternetBeans Express also includes a set of custom JSP tags, which we used to build only the first page of the schedule application. These tags are similar in intent to the SQL tags that are part of JSTL, which don't easily support building Model 2 applications.

InternetBeans Express features good documentation and reasonable but small sample applications. It is a good framework for small applications or where a clean Model 2 architecture isn't needed. It is extremely productive, reflecting the RAD philosophy that underlies its design.

In the next chapter, we cover the template language Velocity and how it contributes to Model 2 applications.

Velocity

This chapter covers

- The design of Velocity
- Building web applications with Velocity
- Evaluating Velocity

The frameworks we've covered in this book so far have been multifaceted. In other words, they have included several areas of web development: connection pooling, resource management, page generation, and so forth. Different frameworks varying degrees of comprehension. The next framework we'll cover is more cohesive and includes only a single area of web development. Technically, it might not be considered an entire framework. However, it justifies treatment here because it elegantly solves a common problem in web development and is very popular. In fact, its popularity verges on cult status in some circles of Java web development. It is also orthogonal to the other frameworks we've discussed, meaning that it can be used in conjunction with, not as a replacement for, most of the other frameworks.

Velocity is a replacement for JSP and other view technologies. Most of the frameworks can use Velocity as a plug-in replacement instead of whatever technology they are using to generate user interfaces. Some frameworks strongly favor Velocity over the alternatives, such as JSP. For example, the Turbine framework developers prefer Velocity over JSP.

Velocity is a template language designed to replace JSP, PHP Hypertext Preprocessor (PHP), and other presentation techniques. It is designed to work hand in hand with servlet-based web development (although it may work in other environments as well). If you are using open-source web development tools and frameworks, you should at least be familiar with Velocity.

This chapter discusses the Velocity architecture, some key concepts (such as how to set it up and some of the language elements), and building applications. As in the other framework chapters, we build the Velocity version of the schedule application. It uses the generic Model 2 application as the base, replacing the presentation layer with Velocity.

9.1 *Overview*

Velocity is a Java-based template engine. It is useful as a stand-alone utility for generating any text-based information, such as source code, HTML, XML, SQL, and reports. It also includes facilities for incorporating itself into Java web applications via a servlet. It is an open-source project, hosted on the Jakarta site at Apache. You can download it at http://jakarta.apache.org/velocity. The first (beta) release was on March 26, 2001, and the current version as of this writing is 1.3.1, released on March 31, 2003.

Velocity provides an implementation for something that is elusive in the development world: a simple, powerful scripting language that handles presentation chores in a web application. It is easier and friendlier than either JSP or JSTL but provides a superset of the capabilities of those techniques. It has found that sweet spot of unobtrusive usefulness without compromising the performance or design of the web application, which is no small feat.

Velocity allows web user interface designers to embed simple Velocity scripting elements in web pages. It is not like JavaScript, which is interpreted by the browser. Instead, all processing takes place as the page is rendered so that the end result is a simple HTML page. It helps enforce Model 2 architecture, allowing straightforward user interface scripting. It does not violate the separation of concerns important to good design. Velocity does not encourage placing business logic or other model code within the page because the scripting language is not well suited to writing that type of code. Rather, it helps make the job of the user interface designer easier by providing a simple scripting language for automating presentation.

9.2 *The architecture*

Velocity works either as a stand-alone template engine or through a servlet. When using it as a servlet, the developer extends the `VelocityServlet` included with the framework. This servlet becomes the controller for a page. Generally, each page has its own controller servlet. The developer adds code to the context object (which the template language uses to store name-value pairs) and merges the template and the context object to produce output. The template is an HTML document that includes Velocity template language constructs. The process of building a web application using Velocity is shown in figure 9.1.

The general steps to using Velocity are:

1 Initialize Velocity. The `VelocityServlet` handles this for you for web applications. Initialization parameters are specified in a properties file.

2 Create a `Context` object. This is passed as one of the parameters for the method you override in the servlet.

3 Add data objects as name-value pairs to the `Context`.

4 Choose a template.

5 Merge the template and the `Context` to produce output.

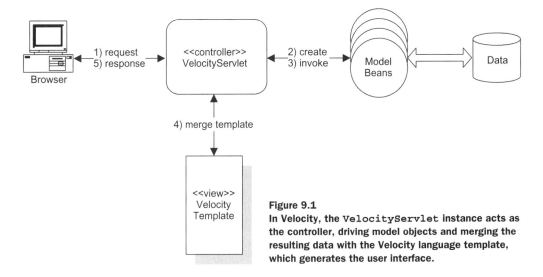

Figure 9.1

In Velocity, the `VelocityServlet` instance acts as the controller, driving model objects and merging the resulting data with the Velocity language template, which generates the user interface.

When extending `VelocityServlet`, you must override a single method, `handleRequest()`, which returns a template. This method takes as parameters the `HttpServletRequest`, `HttpServletResponse`, and a `Context` object.

If you do not want to extend the Velocity servlet, you can create and initialize the Velocity engine yourself. You should do this if you are using Velocity outside the web API or if you are implementing another framework that takes the place of servlets. For example, you could initialize the Velocity engine within an action in Struts, bypassing the JSP presentation layer. To create the Velocity engine yourself, the steps are the same as the ones we listed previously. Listing 9.1 shows the general template used to bootstrap Velocity.

Listing 9.1 Instantiating the Velocity engine

```
import java.io.StringWriter;
import org.apache.velocity.Template;
import org.apache.velocity.VelocityContext;
import org.apache.velocity.app.Velocity;
import org.apache.velocity.exception.MethodInvocationException;
import org.apache.velocity.exception.ParseErrorException;
import org.apache.velocity.exception.ResourceNotFoundException;

public class Test {
    public doIt() {
        Velocity.init();          ← Initializes the Velocity engine

        VelocityContext context = new VelocityContext();    ← Creates the Velocity context
```

```
        context.put("name", new String("Velocity"));    ◁──┐ Inserts a string
                                                            │ into the context
        Template template = null;

        try {
            template = Velocity.getTemplate("mytemplate.vm");   ◁──┐
        } catch (ResourceNotFoundException rnfe) {               Gets the
            // couldn't find the template                        template
        } catch (ParseErrorException pee) {
            // syntax error : problem parsing the template
        } catch (MethodInvocationException mie) {
            // something invoked in the template
            // threw an exception
        } catch (Exception e) {
        }                                          │ Creates the
        StringWriter sw = new StringWriter();   ◁──┘ output buffer

        template.merge(context, sw);   ◁──┐ Merges the template
    }                                     │ with the context
}
```

9.3 Key concepts

As with any framework, Velocity contains some concepts that are critical to successfully using it. To start using Velocity, you must first configure it by installing library JAR files and configuration documents. You should become familiar with the Velocity language as well as the Context object, which allows you to pass information to the page.

9.3.1 Setting up Velocity

The Velocity distribution contains quite a few directories when unzipped, but the only two items you must have are the two JAR files: velocity-1.3.1.jar and velocity-dep-1.3.1.jar. The first JAR file contains the Velocity classes, and the other file contains all the classes Velocity depends on. When used in a web application, the two JAR files should end up in the web application's WEB-INF/lib directory.

Configuration

A properties file is used to configure Velocity. In a web application, it may appear as an initialization parameter for the servlet that extends VelocityServlet:

```
<servlet>
  <servlet-name>SaveEntry</servlet-name>
  <servlet-class>
      com.nealford.art.schedvelocity.controller.SaveEntry
```

```
    </servlet-class>
    <init-param>
      <param-name>properties</param-name>
      <param-value>/velocity.properties</param-value>
    </init-param>
  </servlet>
```

Resource loading

The properties file contains entries for resource loading and logging. You have four ways to load resources (which encompasses both templates and other resources loaded via Velocity's `#include()` directive). Table 9.1 summarizes the resource-loading options.

Table 9.1   Velocity's resource loading options

Loader	Description
FileResourceLoader	This loader is the default. It loads files directly from the file system. The loader is inflexible when used with servlets because the template location must be relative to the servlet engine. The servlet engine has the option not to expand the WAR file housing the application, which causes this loader to fail.
JarResourceLoader	This loader gets resources from specific JAR files. It is similar in use to the `FileResourceLoader`.
ClasspathResourceLoader	This loader gets its resources from the class loader used by the application. It loads template JAR files from the classpath. It is the most convenient option for web applications because the templates can reside in a JAR file in the WEB-INF/lib directory or in any other directory under WEB-INF. Notice that it is not a good idea to put template files outside the WEB-INF directory because the WEB-INF directory ensures that the templates will not be reachable from the client browser.
DataSourceResourceLoader	This loader loads resources from a `DataSource`. To use this loader, you must configure Velocity to include the J2EE JAR files.

It is possible to use a combination of different resource loaders in an application. For web applications, the easiest resource loader is the `ClasspathResourceLoader`. The templates and other resources are placed in a JAR file and deployed to the WEB-INF/lib directory.

Instancing options

Velocity gives the developer options for how the Velocity engine itself is instanced in the application. The typical approach is to treat the Velocity engine as a singleton object. In this model, a single instance of the engine handles all requests for the application. Prior to version 1.2, this was the only model available. However, developers now have the choice of creating multiple instances of the engine. This approach is useful when you need to support multiple configurations (different resource loaders, log files, etc.). This is also useful in a clustered environment in which you must provide load balancing for the engine.

To create a new instance rather than rely on the singleton model, you need only fire the constructor on the VelocityEngine class, a sample of which appears in listing 9.2.

Listing 9.2   The VelocityEngine separate instancing

```
import org.apache.velocity.Template;
import org.apache.velocity.app.VelocityEngine;

public class Test {
    public doIt() {
        //-- create a new instance of the engine
        VelocityEngine ve = new VelocityEngine();

        //--  configure the engine.  In this case, we are using
        //--  ourselves as a logger (see logging examples..)
        ve.setProperty(VelocityEngine.RUNTIME_LOG_LOGSYSTEM, this);

        //--  initialize the engine
        ve.init();

        Template t = ve.getTemplate("foo.vm");
    }
}
```

When you use the VelocityServlet, always select the singleton model. If you don't want to use this model, you must not use the VelocityServlet and should instead create the engine yourself.

Because Velocity acts as a singleton, make sure that the Velocity JAR files are deployed separately with each web application that uses Velocity. For example, if you place the Velocity JAR files in the servlet engine's classpath (rather than in the WEB-INF/lib directory of your web applications), the singleton instance will execute across web applications. While it will still function, it will not allow you to have separate configurations for different web applications and will limit your options for template and resource locations.

9.3.2 *The Velocity Template Language*

The Velocity Template Language (VTL) is a scripting language meant to be simple enough for nonprogrammers (i.e., web designers) to learn quickly. It consists of references, directives, and statements. This section discusses only a few of these constructs. Velocity comes with an excellent user's guide that acts as a language reference.

References

Three types of references exist in VTL: variables, properties, and methods. Everything coming from a reference is treated as a String. Variables in VTL are preceded with $. Here are some examples of VTL variables:

```
$foo
$hyphen-var
$under_score
```

The second type of reference is a property. Properties use the familiar dot notation used by Java with the $ character indicating a VTL variable name. Examples of property references are

```
$scheduleItem.Start
$customer.Balance
```

A property notation may have two meanings. It could represent a Hashtable name-value pair. For example, the notation would be the same as the Java code if `customer` was a Hashtable and `Balance` was the key:

```
customer.get("Balance");
```

It may also refer to the accessor method for the `customer` object. For example, the previous example could also evaluate to

```
customer.getBalance();
```

This is an example of a method reference. Other methods (not just accessors) are called in the same way.

Directives

Directives are the basic programming constructs in VTL. VTL contains a variety of directives to handle looping, conditional statements, setting of variables, and other tasks. Directives are distinguished by the # prefix. To use the #set directive, you write

```
#set ($ravenSpeak = "nevermore")
#set ($raven.Quote = $ravenSpeak)
```

The first statement sets the value `nevermore` to the VTL variable `ravenSpeak`. The second calls the `setQuote()` method on the `raven` object to the string `nevermore`.

Directives also encompass conditional statements and looping. Here is an example of an `if` construct:

```
#if ( $foo < 10 )
    <strong>Go North</strong>
#elseif( $foo == 10 )
    <strong>Go East</strong>
#elseif( $bar == 6 )
    <strong>Go South</strong>
#else
    <strong>Go West</strong>
#end
```

Examples of the `foreach` directive appear in section 9.4.1.

Statements

A *statement* is a combination of a directive and variable references, similar to a statement in Java. VTL also contains a number of other constructs and rules for handling string literals, math operations, and so forth.

9.3.3 Context

The last of the key concepts in Velocity is the `Context` object. `Context` is defined as an interface that mimics the behavior (but not the implementation) of a `Map`. The primary use of the `Context` interface in Velocity is through the `VelocityContext` instance of the interface. It is used to pass information from the Java layer into VTL, where references can access the contents of the `Context`.

It is used just like a `Map` in Java. The primary methods are `put()` and `get()`, both of which act like their `Map` counterparts. The same restrictions exist for the `Context`: every value must derive from `Object`, you cannot use primitives (you must wrap them in type wrappers), and you cannot use null as a value.

The `Context` has special support for the `foreach` directive. This directive supports several collection types when pulled from the `Context`. These are summarized in table 9.2.

9.4 Scheduling with Velocity

Now that we've covered the basic characteristics of Velocity, it is time to put it to work. As the starting point of the Velocity schedule application, we're using the generic Model 2 application from chapter 4 (section 4.1.1). The boundary and

Table 9.2 `foreach` **collection types**

Collection	Description
Object[]	No special treatment required. VTL iterates over the array from first to last.
java.util.Collection	Velocity creates an `iterator()` over the collection. If you have implemented your own collection, you must ensure that your `iterator()` method returns a proper iterator.
java.util.Map	Velocity uses the `values()` method of the interface to get a `Collection` reference. It then uses this reference to get an iterator over the values.
java.util.Iterator	You can pass a "raw" iterator into the `foreach` directive. However, if you try to use it from the `Context` for more than one `foreach`, it will fail because iterators have no semantics for "rewinding" themselves.
java.util.Enumeration	Same as above. You can place it in the `Context`, but you must avoid using it in more than one `foreach` loop because the Enumeration cannot rewind itself.

entity classes are exactly the same. The differences in this application are the new controller servlets (utilizing Velocity) and the Velocity user interface. The Velocity schedule application appears in the source code archive as art_sched_velocity.

The first step in using Velocity is the configuration of the engine. We discussed the configuration issues in section 9.3.1, and there is no special setup needed beyond what we described in that section.

**Figure 9.2
The schedule application
written in Velocity looks like
the other versions.**

9.4.1 The View page

The first page of the schedule application displays the list of schedule items (see figure 9.2).

This page consists of two elements: the VelocityServlet and the template.

The Velocity servlet

The first item of interest is the Velocity servlet, which appears in listing 9.3.

Listing 9.3 The ViewSchedule servlet extends the VelocityServlet.

```
package com.nealford.art.schedvelocity.controller;

import java.io.IOException;
import javax.servlet.ServletException;
import javax.servlet.http.HttpServletRequest;
import javax.servlet.http.HttpServletResponse;
import javax.servlet.http.HttpSession;
import com.nealford.art.schedvelocity.boundary.ScheduleDb;
import org.apache.velocity.Template;
import org.apache.velocity.context.Context;
import org.apache.velocity.exception.ParseErrorException;
import org.apache.velocity.exception.ResourceNotFoundException;
import org.apache.velocity.servlet.VelocityServlet;       Acts as the primary
                                                          servlet method
public class ViewSchedule extends VelocityServlet {
    private final String BOUNDARY_SESSION_KEY = "scheduleDb";

    public Template handleRequest(HttpServletRequest request,      ❶
                                  HttpServletResponse response,
                                  Context context) throws
            ServletException, IOException {

        ScheduleDb scheduleDb = getOrCreateBoundary(request);
        String[] displayColumns = buildDisplayColumns(scheduleDb);
        populateContext(context, scheduleDb, displayColumns);
        Template template = null;
        try {
            template = getTemplate("ViewSchedule.vm");       ❷ Retrieves the
        } catch (ParseErrorException pex) {                      Velocity page
            log("ViewSchedule: ", pex);                          for return
        } catch (ResourceNotFoundException rnfx) {
            log("ViewSchedule: ", rnfx);
        } catch (Exception x) {
            log("ViewSchedule: ", x);
        }
        return template;                                    Populates the
    }                                                       items to be passed
                                                       ❸   to the view
    private void populateContext(Context context,
                                 ScheduleDb scheduleDb,
```

```
                                String[] displayColumns) {
      context.put("columnHeaders", displayColumns);
      context.put("scheduleList", scheduleDb.getList());
  }

  private ScheduleDb getOrCreateBoundary(HttpServletRequest
          request) {
      HttpSession session = request.getSession(true);
      ScheduleDb scheduleDb = (ScheduleDb) session.getAttribute(
              BOUNDARY_SESSION_KEY);
      if (scheduleDb == null) {
          scheduleDb = new ScheduleDb();
          session.setAttribute(BOUNDARY_SESSION_KEY, scheduleDb);
      }

      try {
          scheduleDb.populate();
      } catch (Exception x) {
          log("Error: ScheduleBean.populate()", x);
      }
      return scheduleDb;
  }

  private String[] buildDisplayColumns(ScheduleDb scheduleBean) {
      int numOfDisplayColumns = scheduleBean.
              getDisplayColumnHeaders().length -1;
      String[] displayColumns = new String[numOfDisplayColumns];
      System.arraycopy(scheduleBean.getDisplayColumnHeaders(),
                  1, displayColumns, 0, numOfDisplayColumns);
      return displayColumns;
  }
}
```

Gets (or creates) a populated boundary object ❹

Builds a list of column heads from boundary ❺

❶ The required method when extending `VelocityServlet` is `handleRequest()`, which is the first method of this servlet. It is the responsibility of this method to perform the work of the page, build the `Context` object, and retrieve the template.

❷ The `getTemplate()` method retrieves the named template from the JAR file. The last order of business is to return the template.

❸ The first method called in `handleRequest()` is the `getOrCreateBoundary()` method, which either creates a new instance of the boundary class or retrieves it from the session.

❹ This method is the first Velocity-specific method call. The `populateContext()` method takes the two objects that contribute to the display and places them in the `Context` object. This context is passed as a parameter of `handleRequest()`, so we don't have to create it. The two passed objects are the list of column headers and the list of schedule item records.

❺ This method builds a list of display columns. This method takes the "raw" list of all columns from the boundary class and creates an array of just the columns that are displayed.

After the Context has been populated with the data coming from the model, the handleRequest() method returns the template. The VelocityServlet.service() method merges the Context with the template.

The template

The template for the View page appears in listing 9.4.

Listing 9.4   The ViewSchedule template contains a mixture of HTML and VTL.

```
<html>
<head>
<title>
Schedule Items
</title>
</head >
<body >
<p><h2>Schedule List</h2></p>
<table border="2">
    <tr bgcolor="yellow">
        #foreach ($columnHead in $columnHeaders)    ❶ Generates column headers
            <th>$columnHead</th>
        #end
    </tr>
    <tr>
    #foreach ($scheduleItem in $scheduleList)
    <tr>
        <td>$scheduleItem.Start</td>
        <td align="center">$scheduleItem.Duration</td>    ❷ Generates table data
        <td>$scheduleItem.Text</td>
        <td>$scheduleItem.EventType</td>
    </tr>
    #end
</table>
<p>
<a href="scheduleentry">Add New Schedule Item</a>
</body>
</html>
```

❶ The foreach directive iterates over the array of column headers placed in the Context object from the view servlet. It allows you to reference the collection element by the variable named in the foreach directive within the body of the directive.

❷ The second use of foreach is the body of the table. In this case, we pull the list of schedule items from the List placed in the Context. For each of the elements, we use the property notation to invoke the accessor methods for each of the properties.

As you can see, the use of the foreach construct in Velocity is like the foreach construct in JTSL. However, the syntax in Velocity is cleaner because Velocity doesn't have to produce proper HTML. The template generates the eventual HTML page after interpreting the VTL and merging the results.

9.4.2 *The Add page*

The Add page is also similar to previous versions of the schedule application. It appears in figure 9.3.

As does the View page, this page consists of a servlet and a template document. However, two separate pages—one for data entry, the other for validation and saving—handle this page's functionality. Both pages have in common the need to access the boundary class. Rather than create the same code in two different servlets, we created a base class. The ScheduleSaveBase class appears in listing 9.5.

Listing 9.5   The ScheduleSaveBase servlet

```
package com.nealford.art.schedvelocity.util;

import javax.servlet.http.HttpSession;
import com.nealford.art.schedvelocity.boundary.ScheduleDb;
import org.apache.velocity.servlet.VelocityServlet;

public abstract class ScheduleSaveBase extends VelocityServlet {
    protected final String BOUNDARY_SESSION_KEY = "scheduleDb";

    protected ScheduleDb getBoundary(HttpSession session) {
        if (session == null)
            return null;
        return (ScheduleDb) session.getAttribute(
                BOUNDARY_SESSION_KEY);
    }
}
```

This is a simple class that extends VelocityServlet and has a single protected getBoundary() method that returns the boundary class from the session.

Now that we have the base class, the next page is the one that generates the input page. It appears in listing 9.6.

Figure 9.3
The Add page allows the users to add new items.

Listing 9.6   The ScheduleEntry servlet

```
package com.nealford.art.schedvelocity.controller;

import java.io.IOException;
import javax.servlet.ServletException;
import javax.servlet.http.HttpServletRequest;
import javax.servlet.http.HttpServletResponse;
import com.nealford.art.schedvelocity.boundary.ScheduleDb;
import com.nealford.art.schedvelocity.entity.ScheduleItem;
import com.nealford.art.schedvelocity.util.ScheduleSaveBase;
import org.apache.velocity.Template;
import org.apache.velocity.context.Context;
import org.apache.velocity.exception.ParseErrorException;
import org.apache.velocity.exception.ResourceNotFoundException;

public class ScheduleEntry extends ScheduleSaveBase {

    public Template handleRequest(HttpServletRequest request,
                                  HttpServletResponse response,
                                  Context context) throws
            ServletException, IOException {
        ScheduleDb scheduleDb =
                getBoundary(request.getSession(false));
        context.put("eventTypes", scheduleDb.getEventTypes());
        context.put("scheduleItem", new ScheduleItem());
        Template template = null;
        try {
            template = getTemplate("ScheduleEntryView.vm");
        } catch (ParseErrorException pex) {
            log("ScheduleEntryView: ", pex);
        } catch (ResourceNotFoundException rnfx) {
            log("ScheduleEntryView: ", rnfx);
        } catch (Exception x) {
            log("ScheduleEntryView: ", x);
```

```
        }
        return template;
    }
}
```

This Velocity servlet implementation gets the schedule boundary class from the session and adds two items to the Context: the map of event types and a new instance of a ScheduleItem object. It then merges with the Velocity page to show the input.

Listing 9.7 contains the template for adding new records.

```
<html>
<head>
<title>
Add Schedule Item
</title>
</head>
<body>
<h3>
Add New Schedule Entry
</h3>
#if ($errors)
    <hr>
    <b><u>Validation Errors</u></b><br>
    <font color="red">
    #foreach ($error in $errors)
        $error <br>
    #end
    </font>
    <hr>
#end
<form action="saveentry" method="post">
<table border="0" width="30%" align="left">
    <tr>
        <th align="right">Duration</th>
        <td align="left">
        <input name="duration" size="16"
                value="$scheduleItem.Duration">
        </td>
    </tr>
    <tr>
        <th align="right">Event Type</th>
        <td align="left">
        <select name="eventTypeKey"
                value="$scheduleItem.EventTypeKey" >
```

```
            #foreach ($key in $eventTypes.keySet())
                #set ($eventType = $eventTypes.get($key))
                <option value="$key"
                #if ($key == $scheduleItem.EventTypeKey)
                    "selected"
                #end
                >$eventType</option>
            #end
        </select>
        </td>
    </tr>
    <tr>
        <th align="right">Start</th>
        <td align="left">
        <input name="start" size="16" value="$scheduleItem.Start"/>
        </td>
    </tr>
    <tr>
        <th align="right">Description</th>
        <td align="left">
        <input name="text" size="16" value="$scheduleItem.Text"/>
        </td>
    </tr>
    <tr>
        <td align="right">
        <input type="submit" name="Submit" value="Submit">
        </td>
        <td align="right">
        <input type="reset" value="Reset">
        </td>
    </tr>
</table>
</form>

</body>
</html>
```

Most of this page is straightforward HTML mixed with VTL. The new `Schedule Item` object sent to this page (with no values for the fields) shows up as empty fields, ready for input. This is necessary, not for this page but the next, when validations must refill the values as it generates the page again.

Unlike some of the other frameworks we've examined, Velocity has no substitute for the standard HTML `<select>` tag. You must still generate the list of items by hand. However, compare this to the code from chapter 4, listing 4.11 (duplicated here), which uses standard HTML and JSP to generate this same list:

```
      <select name="eventTypeKey">
  <%
          int currentValue = scheduleItem.getEventTypeKey();
          Map eventMap = scheduleBean.getEventTypes();
          Set keySet = eventMap.keySet();
          Iterator eti = keySet.iterator();
          while (eti.hasNext()) {
              int key = ((Integer) eti.next()).intValue();
  %>
              <option value='<%= key %>'<%= (currentValue == key ?
                  "selected" : "") + ">" +
                  eventMap.get(new Integer(key)) %>
  <%
          }
  %>
      </select>
```

In JSP, it takes 17 lines of mixed Java and HTML to generate the select. In Velocity, it takes 11 lines of code with mixed HTML and VTL, which is easier to read because you don't have to worry as much about delimiters.

One possible pitfall lies in Velocity's handling of special characters, such as double quotes. If one of the strings merged by the template engine includes double quotes, the result does not render correctly. For example, if the schedule-Item.getText() method returns the string "Hello, \"World", Velocity produces the following HTML output:

```
<input name="text" size="16" value="Hello, "World/>
```

The output on the page does not show "World," only "Hello," because the second double quote isn't escaped in HTML—it appears as a double quote. To handle this correctly, Velocity should encode the embedded double quote as ".

If the possibility exists that your users might include problem characters (i.e., characters not permitted in HTML, such as double quotes, ampersands, and brackets), you must code defensively to prevent improper output. You could use the Decorator design pattern to add functionality to Velocity's Context object to automatically encode special HTML characters.

9.4.3 *Validations*

The foreach at the top of the page in listing 9.7 prints out a list of errors if they are present. Figure 9.4 illustrates this behavior.

Notice that the if directive will accept a null value as false and non-null as true. This is contrary to the Java language, but a convenience in a scripting language. The error list is generated by the SaveEntry servlet, which is shown in listing 9.8.

Figure 9.4
Validation errors appear at the top of the page, indicating that the record did not post and that the user should correct the errors.

Listing 9.8 The SaveEntry servlet

```
package com.nealford.art.schedvelocity.controller;
import java.io.IOException;
import java.util.List;
import javax.servlet.RequestDispatcher;
import javax.servlet.ServletException;
import javax.servlet.http.HttpServletRequest;
import javax.servlet.http.HttpServletResponse;
import com.nealford.art.schedvelocity.boundary.ScheduleDb;
import com.nealford.art.schedvelocity.entity.ScheduleItem;
import com.nealford.art.schedvelocity.util.ScheduleAddException;
import com.nealford.art.schedvelocity.util.ScheduleSaveBase;
import org.apache.velocity.Template;
import org.apache.velocity.context.Context;
import org.apache.velocity.exception.ParseErrorException;
import org.apache.velocity.exception.ResourceNotFoundException;

public class SaveEntry extends ScheduleSaveBase {

    public Template handleRequest(HttpServletRequest request,
                                  HttpServletResponse response,
                                  Context context) throws
            ServletException, IOException {
        ScheduleItem newItem = populateItemFromRequest(request);
        Template template = null;
        try {
            ScheduleDb scheduleDb = getBoundary(
                    request.getSession(false));
            List validationErrors = newItem.validate();
            if (! validationErrors.isEmpty()) {
                populateContext(context, newItem, scheduleDb,
                                validationErrors);
```

❶ Dispatches based on validation errors

```
                  template = getTemplate("ScheduleEntryView.vm");
            } else {
                scheduleDb.addRecord(newItem);
                RequestDispatcher dispatcher = request.
                        getRequestDispatcher(
                        "/viewschedule");
                dispatcher.forward(request, response);
            }
        } catch (ScheduleAddException sax) {
            log("Add error", sax);
        } catch (ParseErrorException pex) {
            log("SaveEntry: ", pex);
        } catch (ResourceNotFoundException rnfx) {
            log("SaveEntry: ", rnfx);
        } catch (Exception x) {
            log("SaveEntry: ", x);
        }
        return template;
    }

    private void populateContext(Context context,
                                 ScheduleItem newItem,
                                 ScheduleDb scheduleDb,
                                 List validationErrors) {
        context.put("scheduleItem", newItem);
        context.put("errors", validationErrors);
        context.put("eventTypes", scheduleDb.getEventTypes());
    }

    private ScheduleItem populateItemFromRequest(HttpServletRequest
            request) {
        ScheduleItem newItem = new ScheduleItem();
        String duration = request.getParameter("duration");
        try {
            if (duration != null)
                newItem.setDuration(Integer.parseInt(duration));
        } catch (NumberFormatException nfx) {
            log("Conversion error:duration", nfx);
        }
        String typeKey = request.getParameter("eventTypeKey");
        try {
            if (typeKey != null)
                newItem.setEventTypeKey(Integer.parseInt(typeKey));
        } catch (NumberFormatException nfx) {
            log("Conversion error:eventTypeKey", nfx);
        }
        String start = request.getParameter("start");
        if (start != null)
            newItem.setStart(start);
        String text = request.getParameter("text");
        if (text != null)
```

**Populates the
ScheduleItem
from request
parameters**

❷

```
            newItem.setText(text);
         return newItem;
      }
   }
```

❶ This servlet extends `ScheduleSaveBase` to provide access to the boundary class. The primary method in this class is `handleRequest()`. It populates the new item from request parameters via the `populateItemFromRequest()` method and validates the new item, using the validation code in the entity class. If the validation fails, it populates the context with the invalid schedule item entity, the error list, and the list of event types (to populate the select field). It then re-merges with the user interface template. If the record validates successfully, the servlet redirects to the main view page. Notice that, in the successful case, the Velocity servlet returns null. The framework handles this, not by merging with a template, but by respecting any redirects or forwards.

❷ This method matches request parameters to the fields of the `scheduleItem` entity object, populating it with the values entered by the user.

9.5 *Evaluating Velocity*

If Velocity is considered a framework, it is a very small one. However, it is a cohesive way to handle user interface generation. As with any framework, the quality of the documentation and samples dictates how easy it is to learn. Each framework must also justify its existence either by making a hard job easier or by creating something you couldn't create without it. Velocity takes the former approach.

9.5.1 *Documentation and samples*

The documentation for Velocity sets the gold standard for any product, commercial or open source. It consists of a few "getting started" guides and similar documents. However, the meat of the documentation is the developer's and the user's guides. The developer's guide walks through setup, architecture, and issues like "To Singleton or Not to Singleton." It is well written and easy to follow.

The heart of the documentation for the Velocity Template Language is in the user's guide. It is a narrative-style reference that explains the capabilities and characteristics of the language. It is easy to follow and written at a level that makes it easy for web-savvy nonprogrammers (for example, web designers) to learn everything they need to know about Velocity.

The samples are also excellent. The user's guide has numerous embedded samples, and the framework itself includes samples for more esoteric uses of Velocity (such as generating XML using Velocity or using Velocity outside web applications).

9.5.2 *Using Velocity*

Velocity successfully straddles the line between power and ease of use. It is easy to use yet yields more benefits than JSTL or "vanilla" JSP. It doesn't try to encapsulate HTML controls into custom tags like most of the frameworks do, so it does require extra coding for complex elements like tables and selects.

Unfortunately, no good debugging support is available for Velocity except the log files maintained by Velocity itself. However, that is sufficient. Velocity never attempts to do anything complex enough for serious debugging.

Velocity can replace virtually any of the user interface elements present in the other frameworks we've covered (except perhaps Tapestry). If you use Velocity in Struts, the actions create the template engine and perform the merge instead of forwarding to a JSP. WebWork has a property setting for using Velocity as the user interface layer. This highlights one of the best things about Velocity: it is highly cohesive and doesn't have a big impact on the other parts of the architecture of the application. The primary difference (besides the use of VTL on the page) is the presence of the `Context` object. However, you must pass information from the controller to the user interface somehow, and the `Context` is as good as any other mechanism.

9.6 *Summary*

This chapter discussed Velocity, the Java-based template language for generating user interface elements. Velocity defines a simple but powerful scripting language that is executed on the server during page render, generating HTML or other markup, such as XML.

The schedule application we built in this chapter used Velocity as the user interface layer. We demonstrated several techniques, including building an HTML `<select>` control using the Velocity Template Language and iterating over collections.

Velocity is a highly cohesive tool for assisting in the user interface portion of Model 2 applications. It doesn't impose itself on the application to the exclusion of other technologies. It is a popular framework for exactly those reasons.

In the next chapter, we look at Cocoon, a publishing framework and a web application framework.

10

Cocoon

283

Cocoon is more than one type of framework. It provides some of the same facilities as the other web frameworks we've discussed, but Cocoon contains an entire additional personality: that of a *publishing* framework. Cocoon automatically transforms documents based on the request context. It presents a new kind of application service, leveraging XML technologies to create web sites with unprecedented flexibility. It also embodies another dimension of Model-View-Controller, in which the framework handles all the view generation automatically.

Cocoon is also a complicated framework. It relies on XML technologies, such as Extensible Stylesheet Transformation Language (XSLT). Because it does so much, there are myriad configuration and development issues. As such, this chapter serves only as an introduction to Cocoon in both its guises as a publishing framework and as a web application framework.

A working knowledge of XML technologies will help but shouldn't be necessary. Because of the complexity of the framework, we're going to build only a part of the schedule application with this framework.

10.1 *Overview*

Stefano Mazzocchi founded the Cocoon project in 1999 as an open-source Apache project. It started as a simple servlet for on-the-fly transformations of XML documents using Extensible Stylesheet Language (XSL) stylesheets. It was based on the memory-intensive Document Object Model (DOM) API, which loaded the entire document in memory to process it. This quickly became a limiting factor. To drive the transformations, the XSL stylesheet was either referenced or embedded inside the XML document. While convenient, it caused maintenance problems for dynamic web sites.

To solve these problems, Cocoon 2 included a complete rewrite of the framework, incorporating the lessons learned from Cocoon version 1. Cocoon 2 changed from DOM to the much more memory- and processing-thrifty Simple API for XML Processing (SAX) technique of parsing the XML documents. It also created the concept of a *pipeline* to determine the processing stages that a document must traverse, and included numerous performance and caching improvements. Legend has it that the time elapsed between the two releases was partially due to the principal developer deciding to go back to college to complete his degree. Only in the open-source world can this happen to a state-of-the-art piece of software!

For this chapter, we're using Cocoon version 2.0.4. You can download Cocoon at http://xml.apache.org/cocoon/. This site allows you to download either Cocoon 1 or 2, although Cocoon 1 is provided only for backward compatibility.

10.2 The architecture

Cocoon's two parts, the publishing and web application frameworks, are related at the core level but may not seem so from the surface. It turns out that the web framework is another aspect of the publishing framework. For the purposes of architecture, we'll show them as distinct elements. First, we'll discuss the architecture of the publishing framework, then of the web framework.

10.2.1 The publishing framework

A publishing framework is a tool that automates part of the generation of client-specific documents from a common base. Figure 10.1 shows this architecture.

In the diagram in figure 10.1, two separate client devices are making a request of the publishing framework, which is running as part of a web application. The browser requests the document. The publishing framework notifies the user agent of the request (which is part of the HTTP header information) and the requested resource. Once it starts to return the resource, it applies an XSLT transformation to it and generates an HTML document suitable for the browser. A wireless device (like a cell phone) makes a request for the same resource from the same publishing framework. However, because the user agent is different, a different stylesheet

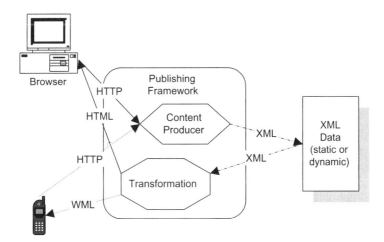

Figure 10.1
A publishing framework performs automatic transformations depending on the device making the request.

transformation is applied and the cell phone receives a Wireless Markup Language (WML) document.

The benefits of a publishing framework are twofold. First, for the developers of the content, they no longer have to worry about creating different types of content for different devices. The developers produce XML documents. Stylesheet designers create XSLT stylesheets for the various types of devices the application must support. This step is completely separate from the content-generation step. The second benefit is the flexibility of the application. When a new device appears, the content designers don't have to change anything about the application. A new stylesheet is all that is required to support the new device.

The problems with this approach are also twofold. First, the transformation process is very resource intensive on the servlet engine. Parsing text and applying transformations in XML takes a great deal of processor resources. Memory management has gotten better with Cocoon moving to SAX instead of DOM, but it is still an issue. The other problem lies with the complexity of the XSLT stylesheets. It is an entirely new language for developers to learn, and it is not very readable or friendly. Currently, few tools do anything to ease the process of creating the stylesheets. For the time being, developers must create the stylesheets by hand. Because good stylesheet developers are hard to find, the practicability of wide use of publishing frameworks is limited. However, tool support will eventually come and the process will become much easier.

Pipelines

Cocoon 2 introduced the idea of a *pipeline* to handle a request. A pipeline is a series of steps for processing a particular kind of content. Usually, a pipeline consists of several steps that specify the generation, transformation, and serialization of the SAX events that make up the generated content. This is shown in figure 10.2.

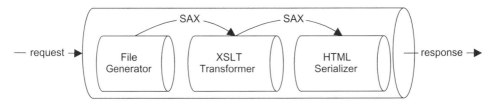

Figure 10.2   A pipeline is a series of steps that contribute to the transformation of one type of content to another.

As the request is processed, it moves from stage to stage in the pipeline. Each stage is responsible for a part of the generation or transformation of the content. Cocoon allows you to customize the steps a particular type of content incurs. Between each stage of the pipeline, SAX events are fired so that you can further customize the processing of the content. In figure 10.2, a file is generated, passed to an XSLT transformation, and then passed to an HTML serializer to produce the output file. The result is the automated transformation of an XML document into an HTML document.

A pipeline may consist of four types of steps (generator, transformer, aggregator, and serializer), which always occur in the same order. You can, however, apply multiple processing steps of the same type at each stage. This is shown in figure 10.3.

The types of processing to which content is subjected is defined in a *sitemap*. It is the major configuration document for the publishing framework. The format of this document is covered in section 10.3.2.

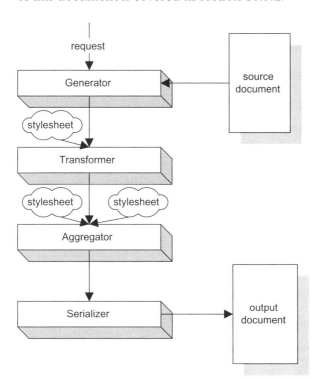

Figure 10.3
A document goes through up to four steps (with as many iterations as possible through each step) during the transformation.

10.2.2 *The web framework*

As a web framework, Cocoon is also a publishing framework. You could configure Cocoon on a case-by-case basis to apply custom stylesheets to your content to produce HTML documents. If this were the extent of the web framework, you would spend most of your time getting the plumbing correct. In addition, you would have to write all the stylesheets yourself. Wouldn't it be better to create a set of stylesheets that always apply to web-development content? That is what the designers of Cocoon have done. You can create Model 2 web applications using built-in classes and stylesheets, relying on the existing transformers for most work, and then customize them for special circumstances. The web framework aspect of Cocoon is shown in figure 10.4.

For a Cocoon web application, the user makes a request to the Cocoon servlet. The servlet determines that it is a request for web-application content via the sitemap and instantiates a matching action. In this case, the sitemap serves the same purpose as the Struts configuration document. The action references model beans, both boundary and entity, and performs work. The resulting information is packaged into a standard web collection (request, session, or application) and

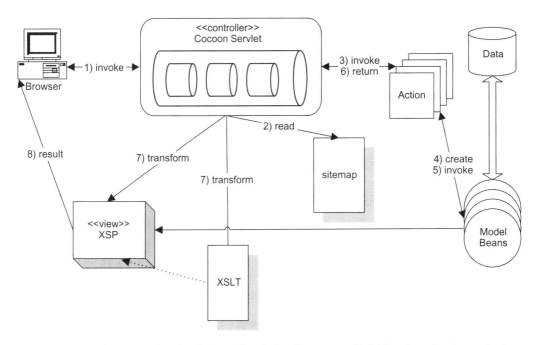

Figure 10.4   The Cocoon servlet already knows how to handle common Model 2 web-application content.

passed back to the Cocoon servlet. It then selects the appropriate user interface file and transformation from the sitemap and forwards the request to it. The transformation is applied, and the response is sent back to the user.

Cocoon has created the concept of Extensible Server Pages (XSP). These pages are similar to JSPs but use a stricter XML syntax and some different constructs on the page themselves. The differences are covered in section 10.3.3.

10.3 Key concepts

To understand the web framework aspect of Cocoon, you must understand some of the publishing framework as well. In this section, we discuss some key concepts of the publishing framework, move to configuration and the sitemap, and then examine web actions and XSP.

10.3.1 The publishing framework

XML is a data-centric document format, whereas HTML is view-centric. The problem with the data in HTML documents is that it has no intrinsic meaning beyond the presentation tags. For example, if you search the World Wide Web for information on "cardinals," you will find documents on birds, baseball, and churches. The search engines cannot determine what kind of "cardinal" you are searching for because the documents returned contain only presentation markup. XML solves this problem by creating tags that have inherent meaning.

Eventually, XML needs to be displayed or transformed into another document format, which is the purpose of XSL and XSLT. XSL defines a syntax for transforming XML documents into other formats, such as other XML or HTML documents. This transformation is the core of how a publishing framework functions.

Transformations

To understand the publishing framework aspect of Cocoon, you must understand how XSLT transformations work. XSL is an open standard for applying transformations to XML documents to change them into another document type. It is used for XML to XML, XML to HTML, XML to WML, and XML to binary format (like PDF) transformations. XSL can take any XML document and transform it into another document with the same information (or a subset of it).

Consider the XML document in listing 10.1. It contains a short list of planetary information. (I'll bet you didn't already know that most of the moons of Uranus were named after Shakespearean characters!)

Listing 10.1 An XML document containing planetary information

```
<Planets>
<Planet Rings="no">
    <Name>Venus</Name>
    <Diameter Units="km">12104</Diameter>
    <Mean-Orbital-Velocity Units="km/sec">
        35.03
    </Mean-Orbital-Velocity>
    <Rotation-Period Units="Earth days">
        -243
    </Rotation-Period>
    <Gravity>0.9</Gravity>
    <Escape-Velocity Units="km/sec">
        10.36
    </Escape-Velocity>
</Planet>

<Planet Rings="no">
    <Name>Earth</Name>
    <Diameter Units="km">12756</Diameter>
    <Mean-Orbital-Velocity Units="km/sec">
        29.79
    </Mean-Orbital-Velocity>
    <Rotation-Period Units="Earth days">
        1
    </Rotation-Period>
    <Gravity>1.0</Gravity>
    <Escape-Velocity Units="km/sec">
        11.18
    </Escape-Velocity>
    <Moon><Name>Moon</Name></Moon>
</Planet>

<Planet Rings="yes">
    <Name>Uranus</Name>
    <Diameter Units="km">51118</Diameter>
    <Mean-Orbital-Velocity Units="km/sec">
        6.81
    </Mean-Orbital-Velocity>
    <Rotation-Period Units="Earth days">
        -0.72
    </Rotation-Period>
    <Gravity>0.89</Gravity>
    <Escape-Velocity Units="km/sec">
        21.29
    </Escape-Velocity>
    <Moon><Name>Cordelia</Name></Moon>
    <Moon><Name>Ophelia</Name></Moon>
    <Moon><Name>Bianca</Name></Moon>
    <Moon><Name>Cressida</Name></Moon>
    <Moon><Name>Desdemona</Name></Moon>
```

```
<Moon><Name>Juliet</Name></Moon>
<Moon><Name>Portia</Name></Moon>
<Moon><Name>Rosalind</Name></Moon>
<Moon><Name>Belinda</Name></Moon>
<Moon><Name>Puck</Name></Moon>
<Moon><Name>Miranda</Name></Moon>
<Moon><Name>Ariel</Name></Moon>
<Moon><Name>Umbriel</Name></Moon>
<Moon><Name>Titania</Name></Moon>
<Moon><Name>Oberon</Name></Moon>
<Moon><Name>Caliban</Name></Moon>
<Moon><Name>Sycorax</Name></Moon>
<Moon><Name>Prospero</Name></Moon>
<Moon><Name>Setebos</Name></Moon>
<Moon><Name>Stephano</Name></Moon>
<Moon><Name>1986 U 10</Name></Moon>

</Planet>
</Planets>
```

To transform this document into an HTML document containing a list of planets, you apply the stylesheet in listing 10.2.

Listing 10.2 A stylesheet that transforms the planets document into an HTML document

```
<?xml version="1.0"?>
<xsl:stylesheet version="1.0"
  xmlns:xsl="http://www.w3.org/1999/XSL/Transform">

  <xsl:template match="Planets">        ❶ Rule that
    <html>                                 encompasses the
      <body>                               whole document
        <xsl:apply-templates/>
      </body>
    </html>
  </xsl:template>

  <xsl:template match="Planet">                              ❷ Rule for
    <P>                                                        processing
      <ul>                                                     Planet
      Name is: <b><xsl:value-of select="Name"/></b><br/>
      Diameter is: <i><xsl:value-of select="Diameter"/></i>
      <xsl:apply-templates select="Moon"/>
      </ul>
    </P>
  </xsl:template>

  <xsl:template match="Moon">        ❸ Rule for
    <li><xsl:apply-templates/></li>    Moon
  </xsl:template>
```

```
<xsl:template match="Name">
  <b>
    <xsl:apply-templates/>
  </b>
</xsl:template>
</xsl:stylesheet>
```

❹ **Rule for any Name**

❶ This first rule creates the HTML header and body elements, and then applies the remaining templates. The resulting HTML document must start with the <html> tag and end with the corresponding </html> tag.

❷ The rule for Planet selects the name and diameter, then applies the transformations for Moon inside a list.

❸ The rule for the Moon element places the moon names within a list.

❹ The rule for Name applies the bold font to all names, whether for planets or moons.

The result of this transformation is shown figure 10.5.

Taking the same root document, let's apply the transformation that appears in listing 10.3, which generates a comparison table.

Listing 10.3 This stylesheet generates an HTML table

```
<?xml version="1.0"?>
<xsl:stylesheet version="1.0"
   xmlns:xsl="http://www.w3.org/1999/XSL/Transform">

  <xsl:template match="/">
    <html>
      <head>
        <title>
            Planetary Diameter and Escape Velocity
        </title>
      </head>
      <body>
        <xsl:apply-templates select="Planets"/>
      </body>
    </html>
  </xsl:template>

  <xsl:template match="Planets">
    <h1>Diameter vs. Escape Velocity</h1>
    <table border="1" >
      <th>Planet</th>
      <th>Diameter</th>
      <th>Escape Velocity</th>
        <xsl:apply-templates select="Planet"/>
```

```
      </table>
    </xsl:template>

    <xsl:template match="Planet">
      <tr>
        <td><xsl:value-of select="Name"/></td>
        <td align="right">
            <xsl:value-of select="Diameter"/>
        </td>
        <td align="right">
            <xsl:value-of select="Escape-Velocity"/>
        </td>
      </tr>
    </xsl:template>

</xsl:stylesheet>
```

The transformation in listing 10.3 defines a table, with elements from the base XML document selected to fill the table cells. The result of this transformation appears in figure 10.6.

This is a simple example, and it utilizes only a small portion of the capabilities (and complexity) of XSLT. However, it demonstrates the underlying concept for a publishing framework. The same core data documents can drive a variety of completely different user interfaces. In these examples, we were generating only HTML. You can easily generate other document formats, even binary ones.

This is a new spin on the Model-View-Controller design pattern. Now the model becomes the XML document (whether static or dynamic), the controller is

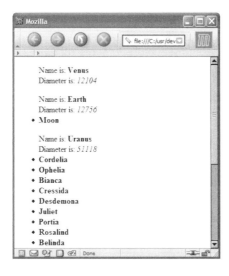

Figure 10.5
The XSLT transformation of the Planets XML document yields a very different HTML document.

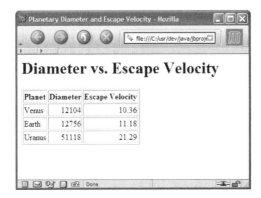

Figure 10.6
If we use the same source document, vastly
different results are possible by applying
different stylesheets.

the publishing framework, and the view is automatically generated based on just-in-time information about the client making the request. Many developers believe this concept will eventually replace much of the content generation as we know it now.

Pipeline

The pipeline model adopts an assembly-line approach to generating content. The pipeline in Cocoon always begins with a generator, continues with one or more transformers, and ends with a serializer. This is similar to the servlet-chaining concept for a web application, in which each servlet contributes one service to the overall request.

Generator

A *generator* is always the starting point for a pipeline. It is responsible for delivering the document and SAX events along the subsequent stages of the pipeline. The simplest example of a generator is the FileGenerator, which loads an XML document from a file system, parses it, and sends the SAX parsing events down the pipeline. Generators do not have to be file based. They can be network streams, sockets, or any other source that can generate SAX events (even if they don't originate from an XML document).

Transformer

A *transformer* is the Cocoon equivalent to an XSL transformation. It accepts an XML document (or a stream of SAX events) and generates another XML document (or SAX events). The simplest transformer is based on the XSLT engine Xalan, which is maintained by the Apache site. The XalanTransformer applies XSL to the SAX events it receives.

Serializer

A *serializer* is responsible for generating output from a stream of SAX events. Cocoon includes serializers for generating HTML, XML, PDF, Virtual Reality Modeling Language (VRML), and Wireless Application Protocol (WAP). It also includes the API that allows you to create your own. The simplest of the serializers is the `XMLSerializer`. It receives SAX events and returns an XML document that is indented and formatted so that it is human readable.

10.3.2 The sitemap

One of the main changes from Cocoon 1 to Cocoon 2 was the advent of the *sitemap*. This document defines all the pipelines, generators, and other configuration information for a Cocoon application. It also maps URIs to resources. A complete sitemap for even a trivial application is too long to show here; for example, the sitemap accompanying Cocoon that defines its samples is 1482 lines long! It contains a fair number of comments, but there is still more content than comments. Even a simple sitemap can easily stretch to hundreds of lines. Fortunately, Cocoon documents the contents of the sitemap well. You'll learn about the pertinent parts of the sitemap for the schedule application in section 10.4.1.

The sitemap consists of two parts—components and pipelines—and pipelines are made up of components. The first part of the sitemap contains the component definitions, broken down into component types. The following sections highlight some important portions of the sitemap but are not an exhaustive treatment. The sitemap included with the samples is well documented.

Generator configuration

Generators are components; thus, they are defined within the sitemap. All pipelines consist of at least two components:

- A generator, which produces the content
- A serializer, which is responsible for persisting the document and delivering it to the requesting client

Within a sitemap, each generator must have a unique name, and one generator is declared as the default, which acts if no specific generator is associated with a pipeline. A small portion of the components section in a sitemap appears in listing 10.4.

Listing 10.4 The components section of the sitemap defines components that are used in pipelines.

```
<map:generators default="file">
  <map:generator label="content,data"
                 logger="sitemap.generator.file"
                 name="file"
                 pool-grow="4"                    Contains an
                 pool-max="32"                     optional attribute
                 pool-min="8"
       src="org.apache.cocoon.generation.FileGenerator"/>

  <map:generator label="content,data"             ❶
                 logger="sitemap.generator.serverpages"  ❷  Configures
                 name="serverpages"                           logging
                 pool-grow="2"  ❸  Configures pool
                 pool-max="32"      resources        Defines the
                 pool-min="4"                         generator class
       src="org.apache.cocoon.generation.ServerPagesGenerator"/>  ❹
```

❶ The `label` attribute is optional (it relates to one of the later categories in the sitemap).

❷ The `logger` attribute allows you to specify a different logging mechanism for each component. If the component doesn't specify a logger, it uses the default for the application.

❸ The `pool` attributes are used by the component manager part of the framework to specify resource allocation.

❹ The `src` attribute is poorly named—it is not the source code but rather the fully qualified class name of the generator class.

Transformers

Transformers also appear in the component section. They sit in the pipeline between the generator and the serializer, and each pipeline can have as many transformers as needed. Some of the transformers have custom configuration information associated with them as child attributes. These custom components are declared in another file, Cocoon.xconf, which is the configuration file format for the Avalon meta-framework on which Cocoon is based. This file defines the components and specifies additional information (like configuration parameters) for them. Listing 10.5 shows a couple of transformer declarations in the sitemap file.

Listing 10.5 Transformers consume SAX events and emit SAX events.

```
<map:transformers default="xslt">
  <map:transformer logger="sitemap.transformer.xslt"
                   name="xslt"
                   pool-grow="2"
                   pool-max="32"
                   pool-min="8"
         src="org.apache.cocoon.transformation.TraxTransformer">
    <use-request-parameters>false</use-request-parameters>
    <use-browser-capabilities-db>
        false
    </use-browser-capabilities-db>
    <use-deli>false</use-deli>
  </map:transformer>

  <map:transformer logger="sitemap.transformer.log"
                   name="log"
                   pool-grow="2"
                   pool-max="16"
                   pool-min="2"
         src="org.apache.cocoon.transformation.LogTransformer"/>
```

Actions

Actions are executed during pipeline setup. Their purpose is to execute code necessary for the pipeline to execute. For example, the action might pull information from a database to populate the document consumed by the generator. Their execution may succeed or fail. If the action fails, the pipeline segment defined inside the action will not execute.

Actions are the prime execution context in Cocoon. They are used in web-application development, much like the actions in Struts. Defining a pipeline with embedded actions provides most of the programmability for the way the pipeline execution proceeds. A couple of example action declarations are shown in listing 10.6.

Listing 10.6 Actions are the execution context of a Cocoon pipeline.

```
<map:action name="sunRise-login"
    src="org.apache.cocoon.sunshine.sunrise.acting.LoginAction"/>
<map:action name="sunRise-logout"
    src="org.apache.cocoon.sunshine.sunrise.acting.LogoutAction"/>
```

Pipelines

The second part of the sitemap consists of the pipeline definitions. Pipelines specify how the processing of content is done. In most cases, pipelines consist of a generator, zero or more transformers, and a serializer. The invocation of a pipeline depends on a URI mapping either of a single document or by extension or wildcard, if you want a particular pipeline to apply to a variety of content. Examples of several pipeline definitions appear in listing 10.7.

Listing 10.7 Pipelines define content processing.

```
<map:match pattern="sample-*">       ❶ Pipeline URI       Pipeline
    <map:generate src="docs/samples/sample-{1}.xml"/>  ❷  generator
    <map:transform src="stylesheets/simple-samples2html.xsl"/>  ❸
    <map:serialize/>    ❹ Default serializer       Pipeline
</map:match>                                         transformer


<map:match pattern="news/slashdot.xml">
    <map:generate src="http://slashdot.org/slashdot.xml"/>
    <map:transform src="stylesheets/news/slashdot.xsl"/>
    <map:serialize/>
</map:match>
```

❶ This pipeline matches the URI "sample-*"—meaning any URI that starts with "sample-" followed by anything matches this pipeline.

❷ The generator is a document located at docs/samples/sample-{1}.xml. The {1} token matches the part of the URI handled by the asterisk. For example, if the user requested the URI http://localhost:8080/cocoon/sample-foo, the pipeline generator would use the document docs/samples/sample-foo.xml as the source for the pipeline.

❸ The transformation is the standard transformation for sample documents to HTML.

❹ The serializer is the default serializer (which generates the output of the transformation directly).

The second pipeline example utilizes a feature of the SlashDot web site, which returns the current front page news as an XML document. Cocoon uses a stylesheet defined in its examples to perform a transformation on the content to produce the page shown in figure 10.7.

Figure 10.7
The Cocoon pipeline defines the Slashdot news site as an XML generator and applies a stylesheet to create an alternate view of the new.

Editing the sitemap

The Cocoon sitemap is a large, complex XML document. Editing XML by hand is error prone and not anyone's idea of fun. It is particularly cumbersome for a configuration document like this one because you can't tell whether the document is broken until you deploy and run the application, which is time consuming.

To solve this problem, an open-source XML editor named Pollo, which resides at SourceForge, "understands" the sitemap format of Cocoon. (Pollo is available for download at http://sourceforge.net/projects/pollo/.) It is a desktop application, written in Java and Swing, which allows drag-and-drop editing of XML documents. It was written especially for Cocoon and has special support for it. Figure 10.8 shows the Cocoon sitemap in Pollo.

10.3.3 *The web framework*

The web framework in Cocoon is one aspect of the publishing framework. It encompasses two areas suited for web development. The first, actions, applies to any pipeline. The second, XSP, is aimed at web development.

Actions

Cocoon uses the concept of an action as an execution context, which is similar to Struts' actions. A pipeline invokes an action to perform some processing before the rest of the pipeline takes over. Actions are used as the active elements for pipelines in the publishing framework. They are used in the web

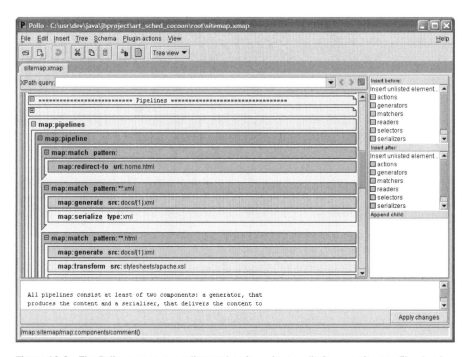

Figure 10.8   The Pollo open-source editor makes it easier to edit Cocoon sitemap files (and other XML documents as well).

framework side of Cocoon as controller proxies to perform work before forwarding to a view component.

Actions are executed during pipeline setup. Therefore, the action itself has no effect on the pipeline once the processing has started. The action is used to set up conditions suitable for the pipeline to work, passing dynamic content over to the generator to process.

Actions are based on the Cocoon `Action` interface, which defines a single `act()` method. Cocoon also includes an `AbstractAction` class, which implements the interface and extends the `AbstractLoggable` class. This class provides access to the logger defined for this component via the `getLogger()` method.

Actions return a `java.util.Map` object. The contents of this map are used in the pipeline as replaceable variables (like the ones shown in the pipeline example in listing 10.7). Any name-value pairs returned by the action become parameters. If a particular action does not need to supply any values, it should return an empty Hashmap (the `AbstractAction` has a constant defined for this purpose). If the action needs to indicate failure, it should return null.

XSP

XSP is a Cocoon technology built on the ideas behind JSP. XSP is similar to JSP with two exceptions. First, the pages are all XML pages, not necessarily HTML. Therefore, they can undergo the same kind of transformations as XML documents in the Cocoon publishing framework. Second, XSP pages are not tied to Java as the underlying language. An implementation exists in Cocoon for a JavaScript version of XSP. Listing 10.8 shows an example of a simple XSP page.

Listing 10.8 XSP pages resemble JSP pages.

```
<xsp:page language="java">

  <page>
  <log:logger filename="xsp-sample.log" name="xsp-sample"/>
  <log:debug>Processing the beginning of the page</log:debug>

  <title>A Simple XSP Page</title>

  <content>
  <para>Hi there! I'm a simple dynamic page generated by XSP
  (eXtensible Server Pages).</para>

  <para>I was requested as the URI:
        <b><xsp-request:get-uri as="xml"/></b></para>

  <para>The following list was dynamically generated:</para>

  <ul>
    <xsp:logic>
      <![CDATA[
      for (int i=0; i<3; i++) {]]><![CDATA[
      ]]>
        <li>
          Item <xsp:expr>i</xsp:expr>
        </li>
      <![CDATA[
      } ]]><![CDATA[
      ]]>
    </xsp:logic>
  </ul>

  <xsp:element>
    <xsp:param name="name">
      <xsp:expr>"P".toLowerCase()</xsp:expr>
    </xsp:param>
    <xsp:attribute name="align">left</xsp:attribute>
    <i>
      This paragraph was dynamically generated by logic
      embedded in the page
    </i>
  </xsp:element>
```

```
    <para>
      Request parameter "name" as XML:
      <xsp-request:get-parameter as="xml"
            default="Not provided" name="name"/>
    </para>

    <para>
      Request parameter "name" as String:
      <xsp-request:get-parameter
            default="Not provided" name="name"/>
    </para>

  </page>
</xsp:page>
```

While XSP is similar to a JSP, there are notable differences. First, notice that the `<para>` tags used to delimit the paragraphs and other elements are not HTML; they are instead defined as XSP. Second, embedded code in XSP appears in a `<logic>` tag. An unfortunate side effect of XSP pages adhering strictly to the XML standards is that the normal operators in Java for "less than" and "greater than" are illegal within tags. To use them (as in a `for` loop), you must either escape them within a CDATA block or use the XML-friendly equivalent (for <, use <).

XSP pages have a transformer predefined by Cocoon. To create a web application in Cocoon, the developer defines a pipeline that includes one or more actions that place items in a standard web collection. Then, the pipeline forwards to an XSP document, which is picked up by the XSPGenerator and passed to the XSP-to-HTML transformer, which generates the output for the user. This sequence occurs in the schedule application in the next section.

10.4   Scheduling in Cocoon

The schedule application in Cocoon takes advantage of the web application framework. However, as you have seen, you can't use that framework without also using the publishing framework. For this example, we're using pipelines, actions, and XSP pages. Unlike the other versions of scheduling, we're implementing only the first (View) page of the application because of space considerations. This project consists of sitemap definitions, the action class, and the XSP. The running Cocoon schedule application appears in figure 10.9.

Figure 10.9
The Cocoon schedule application uses custom actions and an XSP for generating the user interface.

10.4.1 *The sitemap*

The first step in a Cocoon project is the creation of the sitemap. More accurately, the first step is the modification of an existing sitemap. (Complex XML documents like this are never created from scratch; they are always "borrowed" and modified.) For this application, we register an action component and define the pipeline for the application. These declarations appear in separate sections of the sitemap, but we've compressed them here to fit into a single listing. The sitemap elements required for this application are shown in listing 10.9.

Listing 10.9 The sitemap for the schedule application

```
<map:actions>
    <map:action name="view-schedule"          ❶ Action definition
      src="com.nealford.art.schedcocoon.action.ViewSchedule" />
</map:actions>

<!-- sections of sitemap omitted -->                    Pipeline pattern
                                                         definitions          Default
<map:pipeline>                                      ❷                          pattern
    <map:match pattern="">                               ❸
        <map:redirect-to uri="home.html" />
    </map:match>
                                                         viewschedule
    <map:match pattern="viewschedule">              ❹   pattern
        <map:act type="view-schedule">
            <map:generate type="serverpages"
                        src="viewschedule.xsp" />
```

```
            </map:act>
            <map:serialize/>
        </map:match>                    |  Error
                                        |  mapping
        <map:handle-errors>      ❺      |
            <map:transform src="stylesheets/system/error2html.xsl"/>
            <map:serialize status-code="500" />
        </map:handle-errors>
    </map:pipeline>
```

❶ The action definition registers the action from section 10.4.3 as a component.

❷ The pipeline creates three patterns to match.

❸ The first pattern is a stopgap for any unrecognized content to map to a Home page.

❹ The second pattern is the important one for this application. Any URI that maps to viewschedule will go through this pipeline. It creates an instance of the custom action. If the action succeeds, it uses the XSP generator to point to the XSP for this page.

❺ The last mapping handles error conditions, taking the default XML error message from Cocoon and generating an HTML document. It is a good idea to include this mapping in every project because it makes the error messages while debugging much more readable.

10.4.2 *The action*

The action is similar in intent to an action in Struts or any other web framework that uses the Command design pattern. The ViewSchedule action appears in listing 10.10.

Listing 10.10 The ViewSchedule action builds the dynamic content needed for the view XSP

```
package com.nealford.art.schedcocoon.action;

import java.util.HashMap;
import java.util.Map;
import com.nealford.art.schedcocoon.boundary.ScheduleDb;
import org.apache.avalon.framework.parameters.Parameters;
import org.apache.cocoon.acting.AbstractAction;
import org.apache.cocoon.environment.ObjectModelHelper;
import org.apache.cocoon.environment.Redirector;
import org.apache.cocoon.environment.Request;
import org.apache.cocoon.environment.SourceResolver;

public class ViewSchedule extends AbstractAction {
```

```
    public Map act(Redirector redirector, SourceResolver resolver,
                Map objectModel, String source, Parameters par)
          throws java.lang.Exception {
      ScheduleDb scheduleDb = new ScheduleDb();
      scheduleDb.populate();
      Request request = ObjectModelHelper.getRequest(objectModel);
      request.setAttribute("scheduleItemList",
                          scheduleDb.getList());
      request.setAttribute("columnHeaders",
                          generateDisplayColumns(scheduleDb));
      return EMPTY_MAP;
    }

    private String[] generateDisplayColumns(ScheduleDb scheduleDb) {
      int numDisplayHeaders =
              scheduleDb.getDisplayColumnHeaders().length;
      String[] displayColumns = new String[numDisplayHeaders - 1];
      System.arraycopy(scheduleDb.getDisplayColumnHeaders(), 1,
                      displayColumns, 0, numDisplayHeaders - 1);
      return displayColumns;
    }
}
```

The `ViewSchedule` class extends the Cocoon `AbstractAction` class and overrides the lone abstract method, `act()`. This method builds a new boundary object and populates it. To pass information to the XSP, the action must have access to one of the standard collections. The `ObjectModelHelper` class is a Cocoon class that returns an instance of the Cocoon request object. This is not an `HttpServletRequest` object but rather one defined by Cocoon, though it does have the same collection semantics.

Once we have the request, we can add the two pieces of information to it (namely, the list of items and the column headers to display) and return. This action does not need to supply any parameter values to the pipeline, so we return an empty map, using the predefined protected field from the parent class.

10.4.3 *The view*

The View page of the schedule application is an XSP page. It appears in listing 10.11.

Listing 10.11 The view portion of the application is an XSP page.

```
<xsp:page
    xmlns:xsp="http://apache.org/xsp"
    xmlns:xsp-request="http://apache.org/xsp/request/2.0">
  <xsp:structure>
```

```
    <xsp:include>java.util.Iterator</xsp:include>
    <xsp:include>

  com.nealford.art.schedcocoon.entity.ScheduleItem
    </xsp:include>
  </xsp:structure>
<page>
<html>
<head>
<title>
Schedule Items
</title>
</head>
<body>

<p><h2>Schedule List</h2></p>
<table border="2">

    <tr bgcolor="yellow">
        <xsp:logic>{
            String[] headers = (String [])
            <xsp-request:get-attribute name="columnHeaders"/>;
            for (int i = 0; i &lt; headers.length; i++) {
                <th><xsp:expr>headers[i]</xsp:expr></th>
            }
        }</xsp:logic>
    </tr>
    <xsp:logic>{
        List itemList = (List)
            <xsp-request:get-attribute name="scheduleItemList"/>;
        Iterator it = itemList.iterator();
        while (it.hasNext()) {
            ScheduleItem item = (ScheduleItem) it.next();
            <tr>
                <td><xsp:expr>item.getStart()</xsp:expr></td>
                <td><xsp:expr>item.getDuration()</xsp:expr></td>
                <td><xsp:expr>item.getText()</xsp:expr></td>
                <td><xsp:expr>item.getEventType()</xsp:expr></td>
            </tr>
        }
    }</xsp:logic>
</table>
<p/>

<a href="scheduleentry">Add New Schedule Item</a>

</body>
</html>
</page>
</xsp:page>
```

1 XSP import

2 Iteration with the logic tag

❶ XSP has tags that are defined to perform imports (which XSP calls *includes*) within a `<structure>` tag.

❷ The dynamic parts of this page resemble the same parts from a JSP. We chose in this example to escape the < sign within the `for` loop for the column headers to avoid the equally ugly CDATA section. One benefit of the nature of XML and the `<logic>` tag is that you can freely mix presentation and markup within the `<logic>` tag. This makes the blocks less scattered than in JSP.

While not the complete schedule application, this example should give you a feel for what web development looks like in Cocoon. Once you understand how to set up pipelines and the interaction of the publishing framework with the web framework, the web coding is straightforward.

10.5 *Evaluating Cocoon*

Cocoon is the most complex framework in this book. Of course, it is more than just a web-application framework, which is almost an afterthought. However, the criteria used to evaluate Cocoon are the same as those for the other frameworks. Let's look at the documentation and samples, the source code, and how to debug Cocoon applications.

10.5.1 *Documentation and samples*

The documentation for Cocoon is rather scattered. It isn't well organized at all (ironic for a publishing framework). I frequently had the experience of knowing that I had seen a topic but not being able to remember where it was or how I got to it. The documentation is separated into categories, but some of them are incomplete. The phrase "Here will soon appear an overview of ..." turns up in numerous places.

The documentation proceeds in a narrative fashion that is useful as a tutorial but frustrating as reference material. I could not find a comprehensive index for all the topics. The table of contents page includes numerous side-panel topics. The side-panel topics include hyperlinks to other topics, which also have side-panel topics, which have hyperlinks to other topics, and so on. The best documentation for the sitemap is in the sample sitemap file itself as comments. This file features a good overview of each section and embedded comments when something out of the ordinary pops up.

The samples are good but not voluminous enough for my taste. I like numerous samples, which is particularly important for a complex framework like

Cocoon. One of the problems with the samples is the way they are packaged. All the samples reside in a single web application (which also contains all the documentation). Configuring Cocoon is no simple matter, and it makes it difficult to look at the configuration for the samples because they are all in one place. I would like to have a few simple sample applications that stand alone from the large archive.

10.5.2 *Source code*

Like any open-source project, the source code is downloadable as well. When evaluating a framework, the only time I mention the source code explicitly is when I see frightening things. In several places as I was debugging in Cocoon, I saw large areas of code commented out. Comments often appear in a release version, but not in a beta. While this isn't a crime, it is usually a sign of undisciplined developers. Every project of this size uses version control, so it is never necessary to leave commented code lying around. If you need to get back to it, get it out of version control.

In a specific example, the following comment appears in the sample sitemap, under the Pipelines section:

```
1) The top level elements are executed in order of appearance until
   one signals success. These top level elements are usually
   matchers. AFAIK other components are not supported for this.
```

The "AFAIK" comment frightens me a little (in case you don't know, it is an acronym for "As Far As I Know"). If the commenter of the sample sitemap file doesn't know, I'm afraid to ask who does. This is in the pipelines section, which is not a trivial section, of this critical file. I don't dispute the information—it is probably true that this is a rare or never seen situation. However, the comment is still disconcerting because it indicates that there may be other sections in the code like this.

10.5.3 *Debugging*

Debugging a Cocoon application is nice because the error messages are very informative. The errors come back as XML, and they are transformed to HTML for debugging web applications. It is certainly a good idea to include the `handle-errors` mapping in your pipeline:

```
<map:handle-errors>
    <map:transform src="stylesheets/system/error2html.xsl"/>
    <map:serialize status-code="500" />
</map:handle-errors>
```

This will ensure that all the errors appear as nicely formatted HTML instead of the raw XML error output.

10.6 *Summary*

Cocoon is a very powerful idea. It takes the concept of separation of content and presentation to a completely new level. It is also complex. In its current incarnation, it is more suited for certain web applications than others. If your web application already has the need to generate different output based on requests (in other words, it has a need for a publishing framework), Cocoon is the obvious choice. In the near future, it won't be an option any more—every web application will need to handle this kind of functionality.

The main problem that hampers Cocoon now is the complexity of the underlying open standards it is built on. XSLT is a complex transformation language, and not much expertise or enough tools exist to mitigate that. Including transformations in your content generation adds a significant layer of complexity to your web application. Of course, you don't have to do this—you can use the web framework as it is and use XSP as a substitute for JSP or some other presentation technology. But if you do that, you aren't taking advantage of the strengths of Cocoon.

In the next chapter, we turn to the evaluation of web frameworks.

Evaluating frameworks

This chapter covers
- Evaluation criteria for frameworks
- Design considerations
- What I like in frameworks

311

The previous chapters have focused on a single framework, highlighting its design and unique characteristics. That works fine for you if the framework you are considering appears in one of those chapters and I hit on all the high points that interest you. Chances are good, though, that I didn't cover exactly the features or even the frameworks that interest you, so this chapter provides some tips on evaluating frameworks on your own. These are the factors I take into account when deciding whether I want to use a new framework. I work as the Chief Technical Officer at a small consulting company. I bring this up because consultants in my position have a unique advantage over people who work for a single company. I have seen hundreds of projects over the years and contributed significantly to dozens. Just as learning new languages provides insights into your primary language, seeing numerous development efforts teaches firsthand what works and what doesn't work. Most of the opinions I have formed concerning design and architecture come from direct experience: Some designs look great at the start, and then get uglier as time progresses. In this chapter, I am sharing some of the lessons I've learned as they apply to using frameworks.

I've used all of the frameworks described in this book to one degree or another, and I've seen many more. It is my job to figure out what framework and architecture should be used for various projects my company undertakes. Thus, evaluating the quality of frameworks and other tools isn't a hobby. It is the difference between six months to a year of hassle and grief versus happiness and light.

This chapter is devoted to generating an objective and a subjective view of a web application framework. Many of these criteria work for other frameworks and tools as well, but the primary focus is on web development frameworks. At the end, I've included a section in which I tell what my favorites are and why.

11.1 Evaluation criteria

A developer comes to you and wants to start using "Bob's Framework" for developing an application. Never having seen Bob's Framework, you must evaluate it to determine whether it's a good idea to trust your application to it. To make an educated judgment, you need objective criteria you can apply to the framework to see if it is suitable for the task.

11.1.1 Suitability to the application

Unfortunately, there is no one-size-fits-all framework, especially for web application development. Different applications have different needs. Making the right decision for a distributed application is harder than for a desktop or client/server application because of the uncertain nature of scalability. The following sections highlight some decision points.

Speed of development

How long do you have to build the application? Some applications will be useless if they take a year to produce. Of course, every manager in the world will tell you that he or she wants it "yesterday" with more features than an operating system and fewer bugs than NASA software. Once you return your manager to this planet, the speed of development versus complexity is one of the primary factors. For example, you can build an application much faster using a Rapid Application Development (RAD) framework than you can using a more architecturally pure framework. However, if the application must live for a long time, you end up spending more time on patching and workarounds toward the end of the lifecycle than you saved at the beginning.

This is a sticky question and one that has haunted client/server development for years. Back in the mid-1990s, everyone built applications using RAD tools (and their corresponding frameworks), where the greatest concern was speed of development. However, as these applications' maintenance and upgrade cycle lengthened, many of them started collapsing under the weight of the framework. Even in cases where raw speed wasn't an issue (for example, compiled versus interpreted languages), the design and architecture couldn't support changes without Herculean effort. Generally, this reveals itself as super high coupling and poor separation of responsibilities. Most of you have probably worked on a project with The Guy, who knew that if you changed this part of the application, then that would affect Part A, Part D, Part E, and Part W. And, of course, it's a dependency tree, so Part A's dependencies must be managed, and Part D's, and so on. For many organizations, if a bus hits The Guy, they need to rewrite the application from the ground up.

This is the dark side of RAD development. However, that isn't to say it is always a bad thing. If you have a web application that

- Is small in scope
- Doesn't need to be scalable
- Won't have a long lifetime

then using a RAD framework is the best choice. You can write the application quickly, glossing over the design compromises that come up, and move on to other projects. If you do this, you need to get guarantees from The Boss (preferably written in stone) that those characteristics will not change. You might get an agreement stating that when they do change (and they always do), you get to rewrite the application in a more suitable framework.

Some development falls in between RAD frameworks and more methodologically pure ones. As an example, consider the "forbidden" SQL tags in JSTL. It isn't that these tags are inherently bad. They are certainly a bad idea if you are building a large application because it mixes presentation, SQL access, and business logic all on the same page. However, for a small application that meets the criteria we just listed, these tags might be the perfect tool to do the job. Few things are *always* bad. Ultimately, they are all tools. Finding the right tool for the job is better than forcing a tool to perform a task for which it is not suited.

Even if you are short on time, it pays on the back end to use good design up front. Unless the application meets all the criteria, you should do it right. Even though there is constant schedule pressure, you end up using less time for good design than you do by hurrying through a bad design. If speed of development is a critical risk factor, you might choose one of the lighter-weight frameworks (like Struts) rather than invest the time in learning one of the heavier-weight ones (like Tapestry). You will probably end up writing many of the same services by hand that Tapestry already provides, but the ramp-up time is shorter for a simpler framework.

Scalability

Scalability is a killer for web applications and techniques to mitigate. Generally, *more* scalable is better than *less*, even if that scalability comes with some added complexity. You should look at the scalability of the framework to make sure it meets your needs. Of course, the framework isn't going to publish a report showing how scalable it is, but, you can look at the architecture and glean some insight into this aspect. If you have serious scalability needs, you might consider writing a small representative proof-of-concept application and load-test it, using either one of the open-source tools (like HttpUnit, covered in chapter 14) or one of the commercial tools. Chapter 14 covers performance and profiling.

Of course, the ultimate scalability solution lies with Enterprise JavaBeans (EJBs) because the application server that hosts them provides the necessary infrastructure to support caching, pooling, and other scalability services. If you go that route, make sure that the framework fits nicely into that environment. For example, InternetBeans Express's reliance on DataExpress doesn't work as nicely as Struts for EJBs.

Lifetime and maintainability

Application lifespan and maintainability is the other side to our RAD discussion. You are free to use a more RAD-based framework if the application is going to have either a short lifetime or it isn't going to evolve much. If you expect your application to have a long life, consider using a framework in which it is easy to move to EJB because the longer the application lives, the more likely it will eventually need the scalability provided by EJB. All the frameworks that support Model 2 apply here (and that encompasses most of the frameworks in this book).

11.1.2 Documentation

We covered this topic individually for each of the frameworks in previous chapters. Particularly for open-source projects, the quality of the documentation is critical because producing it is not the most enjoyable part of building the framework. As the complexity of the framework increases, the documentation should follow suit. I firmly believe that the reason more people don't use the Turbine framework is the format of the documentation. Because open-source projects don't have marketing departments, they must rely on developers picking up their framework and understanding enough to use it. Documentation exists in two different formats for frameworks: the written documentation (including tutorials) and JavaDocs.

Developer guides

As you look at the documentation, make sure that it is complete. Several open-source documents have "TBD" (To Be Done") sections, some of which have survived several iterations of the framework. If that covers a complex part of the framework, you are on your own.

The *quality* of the documentation is more important than the *quantity*. Some frameworks have both (like Velocity), but that is rare. Well-written documentation is as hard (or harder) to come by as well-written code. One of the shortcomings of Cocoon is the confusing format of the documentation.

Another documentation pitfall is out-of-date material. Sometimes the documentation doesn't stay current with the code base. The reverse is true in Cocoon. In several sections on web development, the documentation is ahead of the release of the framework. To take advantage of some of the documented features in the significantly updated web framework, you must download and build the latest nightly releases. This is at least better than lagging documentation, but not very helpful if you are using the current release version of the framework.

Some frameworks have documentation that comes in several formats. Most of the frameworks covered in this book have both formal reference documentation and tutorials. Tutorials are best for getting the flavor of a framework because they let developers see what they want to see most: code. However, by their nature tutorials don't delve into the complexity or real feature set of the framework.

The Tapestry framework goes the extra mile as far as documenting its custom tags. The tags are complex and have two aspects: the Java code that implements the tag (which is documented with JavaDocs) and the usage documentation. The usage documentation is valuable because it shows you which properties are available for the control and some examples of use. The usage documentation is linked within the JavaDoc, so finding it is easy. Tapestry sets the gold standard for documenting custom tags.

JavaDocs

Every Java project uses JavaDocs to one degree or another. JavaDocs are the primary reference documentation for many projects. The key to a good JavaDoc is the level of detail. Most projects have adequate class-level JavaDocs. The real differentiating factor is the method-level JavaDoc. Some of the frameworks don't have anything at the method level. This is unfortunate because even the simplest method should tell something about itself. The exceptions to this rule are accessors and mutators, which are well-understood entities in the Java world and don't require documentation unless they have side effects of which the developer should be aware.

Generally, your development tool of choice will allow you to include the Java-Doc (and the source) along with the classes that make up the project. This places the JavaDoc under your fingertips, making it easier to access, particularly when you're debugging. For example, the Configure Libraries dialog box in JBuilder allows you to define the binaries, source, and documentation that should be included with a framework, as shown in figure 11.1.

11.1.3   Source code

An advantage of the open-source frameworks is the availability of the source code. For either open-source or commercial frameworks, if you have the source code you should browse through it. This doesn't mean that you should try to read all the code. Just open it up at some random locations and see what you find. It should be well organized, from both a class-hierarchy level and individual-file level. Check for consistent indentation and brace matching across files, particularly ones not written by individual developers. This consistency isn't critical to the

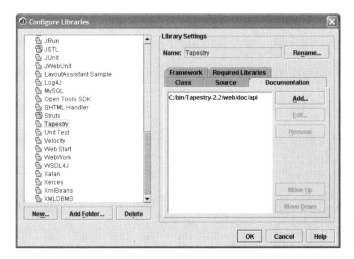

Figure 11.1
JBuilder allows you to associate the JavaDocs with the binaries.

function of the framework, but most open-source projects have coding guidelines. If some developers are not following the guidelines, in what other ways are they not cooperating with the overall vision of the project?

One red flag in source code is the presence of commented-out code. Every project the size of a framework uses version control, which allows developers to retrieve previous versions of code if needed. Especially for a release version of the software, commented-out code is bad sign because it shows a lack of organization. Again, this might not affect the functioning of the framework, but it raises questions.

11.1.4   Tool support

The question of tool support may be more of a luxury than a hard requirement. Some frameworks have tools that other developers have built to make it easier to use the framework. For example, several tools have emerged that make it easier to edit Struts configuration files. The goal of the Pollo project is to assist in creating XML files generally and Cocoon sitemaps specifically. Many of the integrated development environments (IDEs) now support specific frameworks. For example, the latest version of JBuilder supports Struts development with editors and wizards.

Even if the tool doesn't directly support it, most Java IDEs and editors feature a plug-in architecture, which enables developers to write tools that plug into the IDE. Numerous such plug-ins exists for JBuilder, JEdit, Eclipse, and a host of other development tools.

User interface designer tools are getting smarter about frameworks as well. Macromedia's Dreamweaver supported JSP custom tags in its version 4 with a plug-in from Apache's site. The newest version (Dreamweaver MX) supports custom tags natively. When you're using a framework that implements custom tags (JSTL, Struts, Tapestry), it makes a big difference if the user interface designer can use the tool to generate exactly the kind of user interface elements supported by the library.

You shouldn't base your decision on whether to use a particular framework on tool support alone. But tool support—or the lack thereof—can help you distinguish between two frameworks that have similar characteristics.

11.1.5 External criteria

External criteria are those criteria that don't necessarily reflect technical aspects of the framework. These are factors beyond the control of the authors of the framework but can still contribute to your decision.

Critical mass

For open-source projects, critical mass is important. They don't have to sell more copies to stay in business, but popularity is important. No matter how technically brilliant, would any project stay afloat if no one used it? The more popular an open-source project is, the more likely that an active community exists to answer questions and that tool support will appear. In addition, it is easier to hire developers who are already familiar with a framework. Struts has practically become a standard in Java web development, and the more success it has, the more entrenched it becomes. Most developers have at least heard of Struts, and many have experience with it.

At the same time, one of the problems with open source is companies' fears that the developers will lose interest and just stop working on it. Because of the nature of open source, you have the source code. In the worst-case scenario, the developers stop making enhancements. However, if a framework does the job that you need now and it is relatively free of bugs, this fear shouldn't stop you from using it. A mentality of upgrade-or-die exists because of commercial software. I know of many software packages that should never have been upgraded past a certain point. I believe that a piece of software, particularly if it is highly cohesive, can reach a point of equilibrium where it doesn't need enhancements anymore. This is particularly true of infrastructure software like frameworks.

The developer community

A strong developer community is also an asset for any framework. This relates to how easy it is to get answers to questions. Open-source software doesn't have tech support lines. The best way to get answers to questions are mailing lists and newsgroups. The more developers using a framework, the more likely that someone can (and will be willing) to answer your question. Some of the framework sites contain a link to point you to a gathering place for like-minded developers.

Places in use

Some framework developers have a list of success stories or sites that are using their framework. It is interesting to browse those sites to see what kinds of things they have gotten the framework to do. It can give you ideas for your own sites. Because they were written in the framework, you know that it is possible (just not how difficult). A framework with many success stories can indicate how much penetration the framework has out in the world.

11.2 Design considerations

No matter how good the documentation or how many people are using it, a poorly designed framework is still not a bargain. Just because it enjoys wide use doesn't mean it is good. It is important to know what constitutes good design and apply that knowledge to the framework to see whether the framework supports good design principles.

   Some frameworks have multiple modes of operation. For example, it is a bad idea for a large project to mix presentation logic and user interface. Yet JSTL has custom tags that allow you to place business logic and database access right on the page. While the user interface elements of JSTL are useful, it would be a mistake to use the other tags. Using a framework doesn't absolve you of policing the design and architecture of what you produce.

11.2.1 Adherence to good design principles

Practicing good design applies to both the source code of the framework and the kind of code you can produce with the framework. These are two completely different issues. The most elegantly crafted framework in the world that forces you to write poorly designed applications is a disaster for you.

   You must understand what constitutes good design. That type of information is littered throughout this book. However, I certainly don't claim to be the last word on the topic. Understanding object-oriented programming is the first step—and I mean really understanding it, beyond just the syntax for making objects work. You should know why high cohesion and low coupling are desirable, how to use interfaces to create loosely coupled systems, when inheritance is suitable, and various other things. Most developers today should be well versed in design patterns and other industry-accepted best practices.

Once you understand these issues, you should apply them to the design of your application and see whether the framework you are considering helps or hampers that goal. Some frameworks won't help or hurt your design. Some will actively interfere, and some will force you toward the right direction. However, I don't know of any that are foolproof. You must always be diligent to make sure that the architecture and design are what you want.

Setting the architecture and design early and forgetting about it is also dangerous. You must constantly police the use of the framework, particularly if you have developers who are new to it. Once a group of developers has used a framework correctly and successfully for a while, the policing becomes easier.

11.2.2 *The user interface*

Most of the frameworks covered in this book contain a user interface element. It is evaluated along with the rest of the framework. User interfaces have their own criteria for deciding suitability for a given project.

Ease of use

This section might be more appropriately titled "Not Too Hard to Use," which is more important than how *easy* it is to use. This topic and the next ("Power") go hand in hand and are sometimes at opposite poles. The user interface part of the framework should be easy to use without compromising the overall design. Most of the frameworks covered in this book feature custom tags for user interface development.

If you are working in specialized groups in which the user interface designers are not Java developers, you should evaluate how hard it will be for the designers to make use of the tags. Tool support is nice here because if the tool allows you to use the tags invisibly, the web designers don't have to know much about the internal workings. For the frameworks that use templates instead of custom tags, the job of user interface designers becomes easier because they are back doing the work of pure HTML. However, they don't get as good a sense of what the result will be because the template replacement sometimes generates a different look than what it replaces.

Power

Power is the other side of "ease of use." A set of powerful user interface components can make the job of designing the user interface more difficult. Alternatively, the components can provide the kind of powerful user interface that is virtually impossible with lesser components.

Most of the frameworks covered in this book use custom tags to perform their work, and the others use replaceable templates. Generally, the ones that use templates can't get the behavior they want through the tag API. A good example of this is Tapestry. This framework attempts to mimic the development of desktop applications. It goes to the extent of enabling you to create user interface components that resemble the corresponding Swing controls. The Tapestry controls offer a lot of power but are much more difficult to create. Tapestry is excellent for developers who have a strong background in building desktop applications and models for Swing controls. The framework hides many of the details of web development, even in the controls. Tapestry is powerful, but easy to use for only a certain type of developer.

Flexibility

Frequently, you are not required to use the user interface portion of the framework. Several of the frameworks we discussed give you the option of plugging in some other user interface element. Some of the ones that don't explicitly give you that option support alternative user interface frameworks anyway. The most likely candidate to displace the user interface part of another framework is Velocity. If the framework supports this, you have the option of using a best-of-breed approach.

One replacement element that is useful in all the custom tags–based frameworks is JSTL. The iterators and other controls in JSTL are sometimes better than the ones in other frameworks. Because they are all just custom tags, you can easily substitute one for the other. Of course, if you are using a framework that has special support for its tags (like WebWork and its value stack), you can't drop in a replacement.

11.2.3 Innovative features

Some of these frameworks have clever features that make them easier to use. One of my favorites among the frameworks presented in this book is the value stack concept in WebWork. It is a good combination of power and ease of use because it generally works just the way you would want it to. Another example of an innovative feature is the way that Tapestry wrestles control away from the servlet API and creates its own world.

These features are ultimately the distinguishing characteristics between frameworks. You can compare them head to head on such criteria as support for Model 2, whose custom tags are better. However, the unique features of the framework set one apart from another. This is where the decision gets tough—you will almost certainly like *some* of the features of *all* the frameworks. One way to help decide is to "grade" the value of a particular feature. In other words, have your developers assign a numerical value to the features they like. Whichever framework gets the best grade wins.

11.2.4 *Insularity*

Insularity is a measure of how tightly the framework holds its grip on you. Some frameworks are very insular. Once you are in the code of the framework, you can't get out. The most likely candidate in this book is Tapestry. Because it is such an elaborate framework, once you are running in the framework it doesn't seem as if you are writing a web application anymore. Many of these frameworks replace the common `HttpServletRequest` with their own `Request` object. Some of the behavior is the same, but not all of it. Most of the frameworks (including Tapestry) provide hooks to get you back to the web world. A stark contrast is a framework like Struts, which relies on the web API to perform its work.

Insularity itself is not an undesirable characteristic. How much the insularity is enforced is the issue. You may have had the experience of writing within a framework where 80 percent of what you wanted was easy, the next 10 percent was difficult but possible, and the last 10 percent could not be done within the confines of the framework. You must watch out for frameworks that don't give you any access to the world outside (or make it so difficult that you never try).

11.2.5 *"Feel"*

This last criterion is strictly subjective. No matter how objective you try to be, some frameworks will "feel" better than others will. Your experience with other frameworks, your personality, your last project, and what you had for breakfast all feed into this evaluation criterion. This probably has something to do with the nonverbal, pattern-matching part of your brain recognizing something you like. Ultimately, this is why so many frameworks are available. If everyone went by strictly objective criteria, we would probably have only one framework (and one language for that matter).

You shouldn't discount this as a measurement. If you pick a framework for all the right reasons but it "feels" wrong, you aren't going to be happy. On the other hand, don't pick a framework that has nasty characteristics just because it "feels" good. Some things that feel good aren't good for you.

11.3 What I like

As a developer, I have been living with frameworks (and building some of my own) for a while and have formed some opinions on what I like. I've tried to be objective in the chapters on frameworks, yet I tend to like some things more than others. This certainly has more to do with my personality than anything else.

Having stated my disclaimer, here are my criteria for choosing a framework. I don't mean to "disrespect" any of these frameworks. All the ones we covered in this book are excellent works of craftsmanship.

11.3.1 Transparent infrastructure

I tend to like frameworks that have a virtually transparent infrastructure. Struts falls nicely into this category. If you understand web development and design patterns, you can understand how Struts works after using it for an afternoon. This probably stems from the fact that I've used too many annoying heavyweight frameworks, mostly predating Java. Struts is a nice mixture of transparent power and ease of use. I suspect that this is one of the reasons it is so popular. Struts combined with either JSTL or Velocity is a favorite combination of mine.

Tapestry, Cocoon, and Turbine are the polar opposites of this principle. All of these frameworks are powerful but have a huge amount of code backing up that power. You must surrender yourself to the framework to use them. For building complex sites, I firmly believe that you could get it done faster, with less code, using one of these heavier frameworks. However, I can't help but think that I'll eventually find myself in a corner that I can't escape. In other words, I'll reach a point where I need to do something and the support offered by the framework becomes a prison. Of these heavier-weight frameworks, Tapestry is the best because of its attention to detail (like the documentation) and the excellent design. Tapestry is a case study in low coupling.

11.3.2 Innovative ideas

I tend to be drawn to innovative ideas, especially ones that are obvious in hindsight. The winner in this category is WebWork and the combination of the value stack and the expression language. Of the medium-weight frameworks, I'm drawn to this one more than the others. It still uses JSP for the presentation layer (opening the door to mix and match JSTL). I think Cocoon also fits into this category but has other characteristics for which I don't care.

11.3.3 *Ultra-high cohesion and low coupling*

I am very enthusiastic about high cohesion and low coupling. I have seen the benefits for these two principles too much not to admire any framework (or piece of software) that exhibits these characteristics. Velocity fits into this category. It is a single-purpose tool for creating the user interface of web applications. It plugs into a variety of different frameworks because it is so modular.

Struts also falls into this category. It does one thing and does it well: it offers plumbing for Model 2 applications. Again, I think this is one of the reasons it is so popular. The code in Tapestry also exhibits low coupling. Everything in Tapestry that the developer sees is an interface, with backing concrete classes. From a coding standpoint, I think Tapestry has done a good job of creating a flexible architecture.

11.3.4 *Evaluating frameworks as a hobby*

On a personal note, I must say that it has been fascinating delving into the details of all these frameworks. For the ones I already knew about, it is interesting to see how my perspective changed once I started digging into them, sometimes for the better and sometimes for the worse. Each one is like an admittedly geeky birthday gift, with surprises around every corner. It is fascinating to see all the ways developers have taken the core problem (creating Model 2 web applications) and spawned so much variety. While evaluating frameworks is enormously time consuming, it yields much insight into building a certain type of software.

11.4 *Summary*

This chapter details the characteristics used to evaluate frameworks. If you must evaluate one of the frameworks not covered in this book, this chapter gives you guidelines. First, you must choose the right type of framework for the job at hand. If you have a simple web application, you may be better off picking either a RAD or user interface-centric framework like JSTL with its SQL tags. Next, you must consider the documentation, including tutorials and JavaDocs. Then, read the source code of the framework to get a feel for the structure of the code and its adherence to standards. Be sure to evaluate the tool support for a given framework and determine the importance of this factor for your project.

Next, you should evaluate which design criteria and what kind of design elements appear in a framework. This includes an adherence to good design principles. Also consider the user interface portion of web frameworks, including the option of replacing this entire layer. Weigh the importance of innovative features like WebWork's value stack and expression language, and consider how the insularity of the framework affects your efforts and whether the benefits of the framework offset the restrictions. Finally, don't disregard the "feel" of the framework, which may not be objective but is still an important criterion.

I tend to like frameworks that are highly cohesive and feature low coupling. I generally don't enjoy using frameworks that are overly insular because I suspect that they will eventually keep me from implementing something that should be possible. I appreciate innovative ideas and try to leverage them whenever possible. I like modular systems that can be used as a replacement for other framework pieces, such as user interface elements.

In chapter 12, we begin looking at best practices and how to partition the concerns of your applications.

Part III

Best practices

Once you understand the architecture and have decided on a framework (or decided not to use one), you still have to solve some common problems to implement the application. A host of issues arises when you build sophisticated web applications that address caching, resource management, resource allocation, and other strategies.

Part 3 covers a collection of best practices and related materials that pertain to building web applications. These chapters differ from similar best practices books in that we rely on the knowledge you've gathered thus far in the book. The best practices we present are written with the correct architecture in mind, and not as an afterthought. Web applications are coupled to their architecture, so providing a best practice or technique without a consideration of the surrounding code is a disservice.

The chapters that follow cover topics that contributed to the idea of *Art of Java Web Development*. The goal of the book is to provide a well-rounded coverage of Java web development, leaving no stone unturned. It is time to turn over the stones of best practices.

Separating concerns

One of the modern trends in software engineering is the separation, or partitioning, of responsibilities. Modern languages such as Java support this concept via interfaces. Even languages that don't facilitate this separation still strive for this ideal. When you separate the concerns of an API, you free the writers of the API from too much specificity. The concerns of an application may include many things: caching, persistence to permanent storage, interaction with a framework, and others. By "concern," we mean anything that developers must concern themselves with when building the application. As long as you know how something is supposed to work, you shouldn't care *how* it works. The concept of encapsulation in object-oriented languages reflects this notion.

This chapter investigates many ways to separate the concerns of an application. You will notice that this further extends the ideas put forth in chapter 4's discussion of Model 2 about separating logic from the user interface. This chapter describes how to use JavaBeans correctly and shows you how to avoid potential misuses. We also discuss how to port the models in your Model 2 application to Enterprise JavaBeans (EJBs), enhancing the application's scalability. Finally, we explore separating your business rules from the user interface even if you need the immediacy of client-side validations.

12.1 Using interfaces to hide implementation

Interface-like mechanisms appeared before the concept of an interface officially appeared in languages. In C++, a pure virtual class was used for the same behavior that interfaces support now. A pure virtual class was an abstract class that contained no implementation code whatsoever. While this functioned as an interface does, it required the developer to enforce the convention that it contain only method signatures and no code. In other words, nothing prevented a developer from coming along and adding code to the class.

The advantage of using interfaces to hide implementation details lies in the potential to decouple the behavior of an API from its implementation. If you always interact with an API through an interface, you cannot know how the authors of the API actually implemented it. This frees the authors of the API to change how the internals work without breaking code written against the API (as long as they don't break the interface). Tapestry and WebWork do an excellent job of using interfaces to hide implementation details.

12.1.1 *JDBC interfaces*

Most of the APIs that extend Java's core behavior also rely on interfaces to hide implementation details. One of the most common encounters with the concept appears in the JDBC API. The `java.sql` package contains the interfaces that make up a large part of JDBC. Why didn't the developers of the Software Development Kit (SDK) write concrete classes to handle all these responsibilities? Because they couldn't (and didn't want to) distinguish all the possible types of database details required to create concrete classes.

By developing a carefully crafted API, the SDK creators allow the Java developer to write to JDBC without regard to the database running at the back end. In fact, the actual implementation of one of the classes (for example, the `Driver` class) is vastly different between Oracle and MySQL. As a developer, you don't care about the internal differences between the `Driver` class implementations because you always access it via JDBC.

Not all the classes in JDBC are interfaces or abstract classes. The key to creating a useful API lies in understanding what can be a concrete (in other words, a non-abstract) class and what can be deferred to the implementer of the API. For example, the `java.sql.Date` class is a concrete subclass of `java.util.Date`. If the JDBC developers left the entire API as a set of interfaces, it would hamper the interrelationship with the other parts of the SDK because other parts of the API depend on certain behaviors (not just method signatures) of the concrete classes. Building a well-designed API as a mix of interfaces and classes is difficult because the implications of design decisions (such as what should be an interface) have a broad impact on both usability and flexibility.

12.1.2 *Interfaces in frameworks*

Several of the frameworks featured in part 2 make excellent use of interfaces to hide implementation details. The best example of this technique is Tapestry. Everything in Tapestry is represented as an interface, creating a highly decoupled architecture.

The problem with building so many interfaces to define characteristics is the rigidity of the interface as a contract. In Java, you have no choice as to which of the methods of the interface you implement; you must implement them all. To solve this problem, both the SDK and Tapestry create abstract "helper" classes based on their interfaces. The abstract class implementing the interface handles the most common behavior and leaves the specialization to the developer. You get the best of both worlds because you still have the full decoupling power of the interface for unique situations but can rely on the abstract helpers most of the time. Swing uses the same technique for its user interface models. The `TableModel` interface is the "pure" interface, but `AbstractTableModel` implements the most common behaviors for you. Look at chapter 6 (sections 6.4.1 and 6.4.2) for examples of Tapestry's use of interfaces, both for the framework itself and for building user interface components in Tapestry.

Generally, state-of-the-art frameworks (such as the ones covered in this book) rely on interfaces a great deal. Good examples of implementation hiding using interfaces can be found in virtually every framework.

12.1.3 *Decoupled classes*

Using interfaces to decouple the implementation from the semantic definition is a useful technique when you're creating your own applications. For example, imagine that you are writing an application that must support a wide range of types of users. They all have common characteristics, and you must perform the same kinds of operations on all users. Rather than create a concrete "User" interface, you should create an interface that encapsulates all the common properties (implemented via accessor and mutator pairs) and operations on all users. Then, write the entire application in terms of the `User` interface instead of a particular instance of the interface, as illustrated in figure 12.1

In this example, the entire API (wherever possible) is written in terms of the `UserIntf` interface, not one of the concrete classes that implement the interface. This makes it easy to write new kinds of users into the application by subclassing an existing concrete class or implementing the interface directly.

This type of decoupling may be performed with abstract classes as well. However, using interfaces gives you more power because they allow you to create cross-cutting APIs. A *cross-cutting API* is a relationship that isn't limited to the single-inheritance relationship of classes, but instead may be used in a variety of scenarios, thus cutting across the inheritance hierarchy. For example, in figure 12.1 the concrete classes may implement any number of interfaces. When it is convenient, the `Military` class can appear to the rest of the API as a `UserIntf` type. In other parts of the API, the `Military` class appears as a `MediatorIntf`. The single-inheritance model in Java limits the number of ways you can create APIs with inheritance, but you can create as many relationships between classes and interfaces as you like using interfaces.

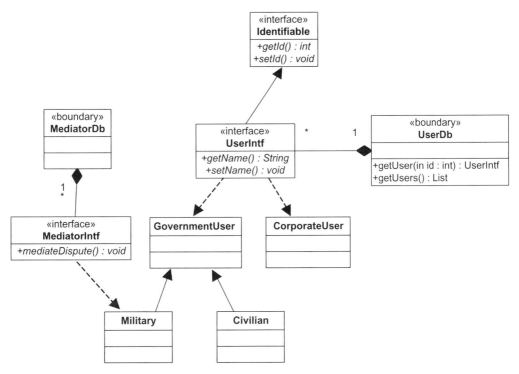

Figure 12.1 **Using interfaces to build the API decouples the supporting classes from the direct implementation of the classes.**

12.2 Using JavaBeans

The servlet and JSP specifications stipulate that the requirements for a Java class be considered a JavaBean and describe how JavaBeans behave in web applications. Every book on the basics of Java web development covers these topics. However, some topics do not appear in introductory materials that are nevertheless important to the effective construction of web applications.

The characteristics found in table 12.1 define the difference between a "regular" Java class and a JavaBean. Any class that meets these criteria is considered a JavaBean.

The requirements in table 12.1 mandate what it takes to be a JavaBean. However, the table doesn't cover some of the nuances that developers of web applications encounter. It turns out that there are some often-overlooked aspects of using JavaBeans in web applications.

Table 12.1   Criteria for JavaBeans

Requirement	Description
Parameterless constructor	The class must include a no-parameter public constructor.
Standard property management	The class must use standard accessor and mutator methods (i.e., getters and setters) to access the properties of the class.
JDK 1.1 or greater event model	The class must support the JDK 1.1 event model. (This appears primarily to prevent classes from implementing the deprecated JDK 1.02 event model.)
Persistence	The class must support persistence, the ability to save a snapshot of an object instance to external storage (memory, disk, file stream, etc.) and restore it. Except in extraordinary cases, Java handles this automatically through serialization (i.e., the bean should implement the `java.io.Serializable` interface).
Introspection	The class must support the ability for another Java class to discover at runtime the methods and types defined by the class. This behavior appears automatically in Java classes via the Reflection API. The requirement appears here to support JavaBeans written in other languages (for example, JPython).
Application builder support	The class must support standard application builder helper behaviors. For example, it must support the packaging of design-time artifacts such as editors and icons in a `BeanInfo` class to assist automated design tools (like Borland's JBuilder or Sun's NetBeans). This requirement generally has little effect on JavaBeans used in web development.

12.2.1 *Model beans*

In chapters 1 and 4, we discussed the concept and definition of the "model" class, from Model-View-Controller. In Model 2 applications, the model encapsulates all the details of the data and rules for the application. In formal terms, two types of model objects exist. The first is a value object; the second is a boundary, or aggregator. It is important to understand the formal definition and use of these terms to facilitate standardization and communication.

Value objects (entity classes)

Value objects (sometimes also called Data Transfer Objects, or DTOs) represent individual entities in the application. Frequently, a value object encapsulates the data from a single row in a table from a relational database. Up until this point, we have referred to these objects simply as value objects. However, there is a more formal definition of objects in this role from the Unified Modeling Language

(UML). UML is the standard object-oriented diagramming notation, created by the "three amigos" (Grady Booch, James Rumbaugh, and Ivar Jacobson) of Rational Software. In UML, a class diagram consists of a three-sectioned rectangle. The top of the rectangle represents the class name, the middle contains the attributes (properties), and the bottom contains the method signatures. Figure 12.2 shows a typical UML diagram of a class. The indicator before the name of the attribute or operation shows the scoping of that element. The plus sign (+) indicates public, the minus sign (–) indicates private, the number sign (#) indicates protected, and the tilde (~) indicates a package.

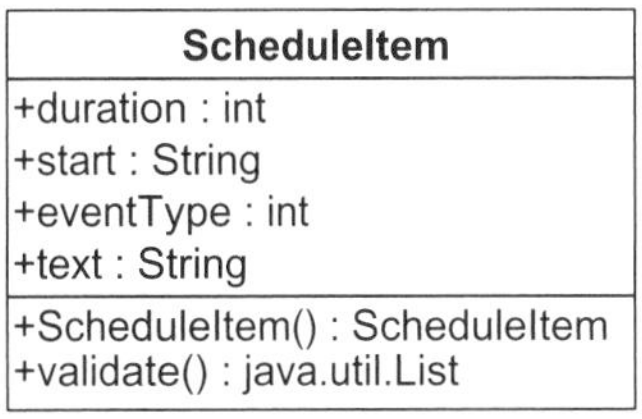

ScheduleItem
+duration : int
+start : String
+eventType : int
+text : String
+ScheduleItem() : ScheduleItem
+validate() : java.util.List

Figure 12.2   UML notation for a class shows the name at the top, the attributes (properties) in the middle, and the operations (methods) at the bottom.

Technically, a UML diagram shows all the attributes and operations of a class. However, most Java classes contain private internal member variables and public accessor and mutators. To prevent excessive clutter in the class diagrams, a common practice omits the accessors and mutators and instead shows the attributes as public. While not absolutely accurate, this strategy improves the readability of the diagram. Any special cases (such as read-only properties) appear according to the formal definition.

In UML, an entity class models information and behavior that is generally long-lived. It reflects a real-world entity or performs tasks internal to the application. Frequently, it lives independently of a single application. UML distinguishes between categories of classes by the use of a *stereotype*. A stereotype is a specifically formatted label for the class indicating the class's role in the application. In the sample application in chapter 4 (section 4.1.1), the Schedule-uleItem class acts in the role of an entity class in the application; it is shown in figure 12.3 tagged with the "entity" stereotype.

<<entity>>
ScheduleItem
+duration : int
+start : String
+eventType : int
+text : String
+ScheduleItem() : ScheduleItem
+validate() : java.util.List

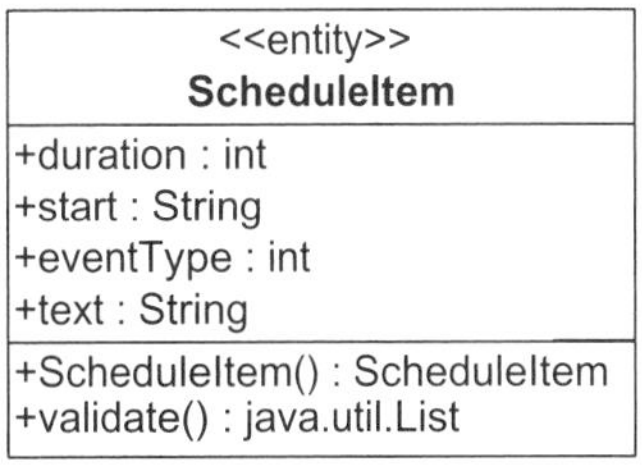

Figure 12.3   The ScheduleItem class represents an entity in the schedule application and should appear in diagrams with the entity stereotype.

Remember that the ScheduleItem class does not interact directly with the database. It represents a single row in a table from the database but does not have intrinsic knowledge of that fact. In other words, it contains no code for persisting or retrieving itself from the database. Boundary classes handle persistence and retrieval.

Aggregators (boundary classes)

The other type of model class appearing in the Model 2 application in chapter 4 (and all subsequent Model 2 applications) is an aggregator class. It interacts with the relational database and creates collections of entity objects. In UML terms, this represents a *boundary class*. A boundary class handles communication between the system surroundings and the inside of a system. Generally, it provides an interface to either a user or another subsystem (such as a database). Examples of boundary classes include databases, helper classes, and naming services. The boundary class represents any model object in the application that facilitates the use of but does not represent an entity. The UML stereotype for boundary classes is the label <<boundary>>.

In the schedule application in chapter 4 (section 4.1.1), the ScheduleBean class acts as a boundary class. It provides a list of ScheduleItem objects and the mappings between event types and their keys. The UML diagram for the ScheduleBean class is shown in figure 12.4.

Understanding the relationship between entity and boundary JavaBeans is important because the definition carries with it a predefined role. If you know that entities should never try to persist themselves in a database, you are much less likely to include database code in them by mistake. While ultimately they are all JavaBeans, each type has a role to play in Model 2 applications. The partitioning of functionality extends beyond the user interface and web APIs. It applies to the composition and use of the Java components as well.

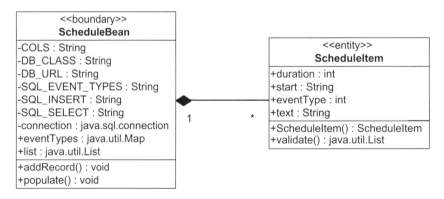

Figure 12.4 The ScheduleBean class is a boundary class that creates lists of the ScheduleItem entities, pulling them from a database table.

12.3 *Using Enterprise JavaBeans*

One of the scariest prospects of building web applications is the danger of their becoming too popular. The company eToys.com now exists only as a warning that the worst thing that can happen is success. This company launched itself with great fanfare, with Super Bowl advertisements and a huge campaign to convince shoppers to buy their toys from them. It worked magnificently. Shoppers arrived at their site in droves just as the Christmas shopping season kicked into full swing. It turns out that they spent too much money on the advertising and not enough on the application. Because they experienced more success than they had anticipated, the infrastructure of the web application couldn't support the number of simultaneous users. Connections dropped, orders were lost, and their customer service department couldn't staunch the flow of complaints. In other words, the application architecture didn't scale well enough to accommodate their users. They were so successful that they are no longer in business.

Scalability is a critical component of distributed applications and of web applications in particular. Applications that perform useful tasks have a tendency to not go away. Frequently, a small application moves to production as a stopgap measure or to solve a little problem. This application performs a useful service, so instead of the developer building new applications, functionality grows onto the existing one. Over time, the intended quick-and-dirty little application becomes the cornerstone of a large application infrastructure. It is difficult to grow client/server applications larger and larger if they suffer from poor design; it is almost impossible to do so with web applications because they are multitier distributed applications and thus have more components.

How do you build web applications that can start small and gracefully grow into very busy, scalable applications? The key lies in creating modular applications, whose parts interchange cleanly with the other parts of the application, making it easy to change one module for another. This clean separation of concerns forms the foundations of the Model-View-Controller and Model 2 design patterns. If you build your applications with scalability in mind from the outset, scaling them up becomes much easier.

Of course, you can design and build every web application to industrial-strength specifications. Obviously, if you build it to scale from the outset, it scales nicely. The problem lies in the fact that it is more difficult and time consuming to build highly scalable applications. If you need a small application quickly, you frequently don't have time to build the necessary infrastructure for scalability. This section discusses how to migrate Model 2 applications into more scalable web applications by utilizing Enterprise JavaBeans (EJBs).

12.3.1 *The EJB architecture*

If you are already familiar with the architecture of EJB, you can safely skip this section. It briefly introduces application servers and EJB. This topic has entire books devoted to it, and covering it in detail lies well beyond the scope of this book. However, it is an important topic for scalability because it represents the primary mechanism for super scalable web applications in the Java world. If you are unfamiliar with EJBs and need to build truly scalable web applications, I urge you to study this topic further (after you finish this book, of course!).

Even though their names are similar, a great many differences exist between JavaBeans and Enterprise JavaBeans. The rules that specify what makes a class a JavaBean appear in table 12.1. Creating JavaBeans is so easy that you can create a JavaBean by accident when you create a class. EJBs are much more complex. EJBs are componentized business logic and behavior. Like servlets, EJBs run inside the context of a container, an application server. The creation, destruction, and management of EJBs fall under the control of the application server. There are three fundamental types of EJBs, with subtypes within the main types (see table 12.2).

When using an application server, the web application runs alongside the EJBs, frequently in the same Java Virtual Machine (JVM). Stateless session beans handle single-call business logic methods. One of the scalability techniques employed by

Table 12.2   Types of Enterprise JavaBeans

EJB Type	Subtype	Description
Session	Stateless	Stateless components that perform single method invocations. These beans are used for business logic.
	Stateful	Stateful components that act as a proxy for client applications. These components keep their state between method invocations.
Message		Stateless components tied to the Java Message Service, allowing for asynchronous method invocations.
Entity	Component Managed (CMP)	Stateful component that encapsulates a database entity. The application server generates the code for connecting to a specified database.
	Bean Managed (BMP)	Stateful component that encapsulates a more complex database entity. The developer must write the database access code.

application servers utilizes pools of objects. Because new object instantiation is a process-intensive and memory-consuming task, the application server creates a large number of objects and associates them with a client request as the request appears. Rather than allowing the object to go out of scope and become garbage collected, the application server returns it to the pool so that it can be reused instead of being destroyed and later re-created. One of the secrets for creating scalable applications is to cache as much as possible. The application server performs this service automatically, freeing the developer to concentrate on the functionality of the application.

The relationship between the web part of the application (i.e., the servlets and JSPs) and the EJB part of the application is shown in figure 12.5.

The flow of an EJB web application has the user accessing either a servlet or a JSP. The servlet creates a link to a stateful session bean that in turn makes calls to stateless session beans (for behavior) and entity beans (for database access). Servlets can also directly access entity beans if the state of the application resides at the web layer rather than the EJB layer—that is the simplest way for web applications to utilize EJBs. However, the simplest way is not always best: accessing entity EJBs directly from the web tier is not the best choice in most cases. Servlets may access

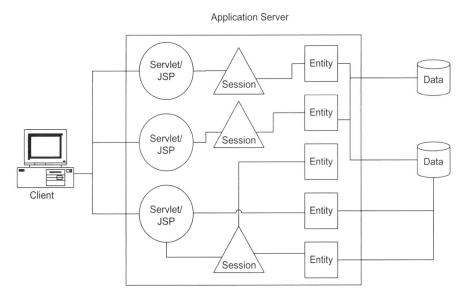

Figure 12.5 The relationship between servlets, JSP, and the various types of EJBs and databases show that the web components call into both session beans and entity beans, which in turn make calls into a relational database.

stateless session beans instead of stateful ones. Stateless session beans are light-weight objects and can accomplish tasks with little overhead. In this design, the stateless session bean acts as a façade proxy for the entity layer, simplifying the APIs exposed to the web tier. The stateless session beans coordinate entity EJBs to accomplish the requested tasks, isolating the business logic in the EJB tier and minimizing traffic between servlets and EJBs. Either architecture is acceptable, depending on the specific needs of the application.

Application servers work their magic by caching object instances, database connections, threads, and just about every other cacheable resource. The advantage of using the application server lies in the fact that you don't have to write code to do this yourself. For example, every web application benefits from database connection pooling. Application servers offer one-stop shopping for an entire range of such services. Application servers also contain code that allows them to cluster together so that multiple machines can load-balance requests for the application. This approach allows you to create clustered applications without having to modify the application code. The clustering is built into the application server.

Application servers represent complex code bases, much more complex than database servers. As with database servers, a wide range of prices and capabilities exist. For this book, we will be using the open-source JBoss application server. Like much open-source software, it is very capable and, of course, free of charge. Because our samples write to the Java 2 Enterprise Edition (J2EE) API, the code is interchangeable with other application servers.

12.3.2 *Porting from JavaBeans to Enterprise JavaBeans*

One of the key benefits of the Model 2 architecture is the ease with which you can port the application from a regular web application to one that uses EJBs. In this scenario, the model beans that used to contain the business logic become proxies for the EJBs, which handle both database connectivity and business logic. Figure 12.6 shows a Model 2 application utilizing EJBs.

The only parts of the application that must change are the boundary classes that connect the models to the database and the validation rules found in the entity classes. The database connectivity moves to entity EJB objects, and the business rules move to stateless session beans. The advantage of Model 2 shines through here: neither the controller classes nor the JSPs require any changes.

The EJB schedule application

The word has come down from management: the schedule application is so useful that thousands of users need access to it. Thus, you must scale it up to handle

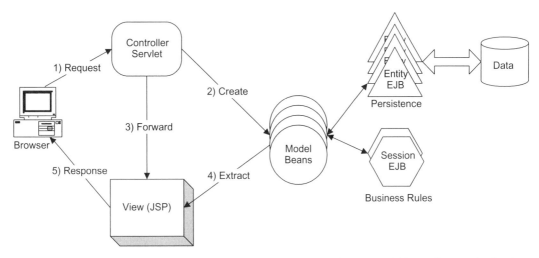

Figure 12.6 **Model 2 applications port to EJB applications by converting the model beans into proxies for the EJBs, which in turn handle both database connectivity and business rules.**

the newly acquired load. The first order of business requires that you create beans for the database connectivity. Even though entity beans represent entities from the database, you should really create them only when you need to insert, update, or delete a record. In other words, it is a waste of time to create all the entity objects if you are just going to display a list. Entity beans are designed to make permanent changes to database entities, not display them. To that end, the schedule application creates stateless session beans to provide lists of schedule items and entity beans to manipulate them further. This sample appears in the source code archive as art_sched_ejb.

The EventDBBean EJB

We create the first EJB, a stateless session bean, to access the list of schedule items appearing in the database. EJBs always come in at least three parts: the bean code, the remote interface, and the home interface. First, let's look at the bean code. Listing 12.1 shows the prelude and database-connectivity portions of EventDBBean.

Listing 12.1 The prelude to the EventDBBean stateless session bean

```
package com.nealford.art.ejbsched.ejb;

import java.rmi.*;
import javax.ejb.*;
import java.util.*;
import javax.naming.*;
```

```
import javax.sql.*;
import java.sql.*;
import com.nealford.art.ejbsched.model.ScheduleItem;
import javax.rmi.PortableRemoteObject;

public class EventDbBean implements SessionBean {
    private SessionContext sessionContext;
    private static final String SQL_SELECT = "SELECT * FROM event";
    private static final String COLS[] = {"EVENT_KEY", "START",
            "DURATION", "DESCRIPTION", "EVENT_TYPE"};

    public void ejbCreate() {
    }

    public void ejbRemove() {
    }

    public void ejbActivate() {
    }

    public void ejbPassivate() {
    }

    public void setSessionContext(SessionContext sessionContext) {
        this.sessionContext = sessionContext;
    }

    private DataSource getDataSource() throws RemoteException {
        DataSource ds = null;
        try {
            Context c = new InitialContext();
            Object o = c.lookup("java:/MySQLDS");
            ds = (DataSource) PortableRemoteObject.narrow(o,
                    DataSource.class);
        }
        catch (ClassCastException ex) {
            throw new RemoteException("Cast exception",
                    ex.getMessage());
        }catch (NamingException ex) {
            throw new RemoteException("Naming exception",
                    ex.getMessage());
        }
        return ds;
    }
```

The class EventDbBean implements SessionBean, which resides in the J2EE specification. Note that this is an interface, meaning that the EJB infrastructure relies on interfaces (as opposed to concrete classes) to ensure flexibility. The SessionBean interface defines a handful of methods, most of which are left blank for this bean. These methods represent callback hooks for the application server to manage the lifecycle of the bean. For example, the pair of methods for `ejbActivate()` and `ebjPassivate()` allow the developer to write code for a situation in which the application server needs to move the object out of memory temporarily. In this case, you can leave them blank but they must be present because of the interface. The next method accepts a `SessionContext` object. `SessionContext` is analogous to `ServletContext`—it is an object passed to this bean by the application server upon creation. It provides a connection to the application server's facilities.

The remaining method in this snippet returns a `DataSource` that allows the bean to connect to the database. The application server keeps the database connections in a pool. To access any resource of the application server, you create a Java Naming and Directory Interface (JNDI) context and ask for the resource by name. The `lookup()` method of `Context` returns an object reference to the requested resource (or null if the resource doesn't exist). This object is cast to the appropriate type via the `narrow()` method and returned.

The method for establishing the database connection pool within the application server is different with each application server. To create the named connection for JBoss, you edit the jboss.jcml configuration file and add the entries shown in listing 12.2.

Listing 12.2 Jboss.jcml entries that establish a named connection pool

```
<mbean code="org.jboss.jdbc.JdbcProvider"
      name="DefaultDomain:service=JdbcProvider">
   <attribute name="Drivers">
       org.hsqldb.jdbcDriver,org.gjt.mm.mysql.Driver
   </attribute>
</mbean>

<mbean code="org.jboss.jdbc.XADataSourceLoader"
  name="DefaultDomain:service=XADataSource,name=MySQLDS">
   <attribute name="PoolName">MySQLDS</attribute>
   <attribute name="DataSourceClass">
       org.jboss.pool.jdbc.xa.wrapper.XADataSourceImpl
   </attribute>
   <attribute name="URL">
       jdbc:mysql://localhost/schedule
   </attribute>
   <attribute name="JDBCUser">root</attribute>
   <attribute name="Password">marathon</attribute>
   <attribute name="MinSize">0</attribute>
   <attribute name="MaxSize">5</attribute>
</mbean>
```

The next order of business is to retrieve the schedule items from the connection delivered via the `DataSource` in the `getDataSource()` method. This code appears in listing 12.3.

Listing 12.3 Retrieving the schedule items and returning them as a List

```
    private ResultSet getResultSet() throws RemoteException,
            SQLException {
        return getDataSource().getConnection().createStatement().
                executeQuery(SQL_SELECT);
    }

    public List getScheduleItems() throws RemoteException {
        ResultSet rs = null;
        List list = new ArrayList(10);
        Map eventTypes = getEventTypes();
        try {
            rs = getResultSet();
            addItemsToList(rs, list, eventTypes);
        } catch (SQLException sqlx) {
            throw new RemoteException(sqlx.getMessage());
        } finally {
            try {
                rs.close();
                rs.getStatement().getConnection().close();
            } catch (SQLException ignored) {
            }
        }
        return list;
    }

    private void addItemsToList(ResultSet rs, List list,
            Map eventTypes) throws SQLException {
        while (rs.next()) {
            ScheduleItem si = new ScheduleItem();
            si.setStart(rs.getString(COLS[1]));
            si.setDuration(rs.getInt(COLS[2]));
            si.setText(rs.getString(COLS[3]));
            si.setEventTypeKey(rs.getInt(COLS[4]));
            si.setEventType((String) eventTypes.get(
                    new Integer(si.getEventTypeKey())));
            list.add(si);
        }
    }
```

The `getResultSet()` method simply returns a result set from the SQL query defined in a constant at the top of the class. This method is used by the `getScheduleItems()` method to execute the query. It creates the necessary data structures and in turn calls the addItemsToList() method to populate the individual ScheduleItems into the list. This code is similar to the non-EJB code that appears in chapter 4 (listing 4.2) in the original version of this application.

To use an EJB, you must first create it. To create a bean, you must look up the name of the home interface for the bean from JNDI. The home interface returns an object that implements the remote interface defined with the bean. In other words, the home interface is a factory for creating instances of EJBs. Listing 12.4 contains the code that creates an EventDb reference.

Listing 12.4 Creating an EventDb reference so that you can call its methods

```
Object o = context.lookup("EventDb");
EventDbHome home =
        (EventDbHome) PortableRemoteObject.narrow(o,
        EventDbHome.class);
EventDb eventDb = home.create();
```

One technique used by application servers for scalability involves *indirection*. The application server manages the actual objects and returns to the user a remote reference to the object. If the developer doesn't have a direct link to the object, the application server can manage the resources for the EJB much more effectively behind the scenes. When you get a reference to an EJB, you invoke the create() method on the home interface. The home interface returns a remote reference, which the application server attaches to a "real" object. In the code in listing 12.4, we look up the home interface for the EventDb bean, create an instance of the bean through its home interface, and return the EventDb reference. The home interface for EventDbBean is shown in listing 12.5.

Listing 12.5 The home interface for EventDbBean

```
package com.nealford.art.ejbsched.ejb;

import java.rmi.*;
import javax.ejb.*;

public interface EventDbHome extends EJBHome {
    public EventDb create() throws RemoteException, CreateException;
}
```

The home interface includes only a single method, which returns an EventDb reference. The EventDb reference is a Remote Method Invocation (RMI) interface that exposes the methods available through this object to the caller. It appears in listing 12.6.

```
package com.nealford.art.ejbsched.ejb;

import java.rmi.*;
import javax.ejb.*;
import java.util.List;

public interface EventDb extends EJBObject {
    public List getScheduleItems() throws RemoteException;
}
```

The public interface for `EventDbBean` exposes only one method, which returns a `List` of schedule items. Thus, this is the only method that is callable from the EJB. This remote reference represents the "outside world's" link to the code written inside the EJB. Once you have created a home reference and used it to create this remote reference, you call this method of the remote reference, which in turn calls the corresponding method of the bean:

```
scheduleItems = eventDb.getScheduleItems();
```

The EventTypeDbBean EJB

The other table whose items appear in the web application is the event_types table. The `EventTypeDbBean` stateless session bean encapsulates the application's access to this resource. The source for the `EventTypeDbBean` is shown in listing 12.7.

```
package com.nealford.art.ejbsched.ejb;

import java.rmi.*;
import java.sql.*;
import java.util.*;

import javax.ejb.*;
import javax.naming.*;
import javax.rmi.*;
import javax.sql.*;

public class EventTypeDBBean implements SessionBean {
    private SessionContext sessionContext;
    private static final String SQL_EVENT_TYPES =
            "SELECT event_type_key, event_text FROM event_types";

    public void ejbCreate() {
```

```java
}
public void ejbRemove() {
}
public void ejbActivate() {
}
public void ejbPassivate() {
}
public void setSessionContext(SessionContext sessionContext) {
    this.sessionContext = sessionContext;
}
public Map getEventTypes() throws RemoteException {
    Map eventTypes = new HashMap();
    Connection con = null;
    Statement s = null;
    ResultSet rs = null;
    try {
        con = getDataSource().getConnection();
        s = con.createStatement();
        rs = s.executeQuery(SQL_EVENT_TYPES);
        eventTypes = new HashMap();
        while (rs.next())
            eventTypes.put(rs.getObject("event_type_key"),
                            rs.getString("event_text"));
    } catch (SQLException sqlx) {
        throw new RemoteException(sqlx.getMessage());
    } finally {
        try {
            rs.close();
            s.close();
            con.close();
        } catch (Exception ignored) {
        }
    }
    return eventTypes;
}

private DataSource getDataSource() throws RemoteException {
    DataSource ds = null;
    try {
        Context c = new InitialContext();
        Object o = c.lookup("java:/MySQLDS");
        ds = (DataSource) PortableRemoteObject.narrow(o,
                DataSource.class);
    }
    catch (ClassCastException ex) {
        throw new RemoteException(ex.getMessage());
    }catch (NamingException ex) {
```

```
            throw new RemoteException(ex.getMessage());
        }
        return ds;
    }
}
```

The `EventTypeDbBean` class is similar to the `EventDbBean` class. The primary difference lies in the return type of the `getEventTypes()` method, which returns a `Map` instead of a `List`. The home and remote interfaces also resemble the ones from `EventDbBean` and don't appear here.

Both `EventDbBean` and `EventDbTypeBean` are stateless session beans that return collections of items from the database. These EJBs populate the views of the application but don't provide a way of modifying one of the items they encapsulate. Entity beans are used for that purpose.

The event entity EJB

The only updatable item in the application is a schedule item. To update records in a database in an EJB application, entity beans are used. Like session beans, entity beans implement a standard J2EE interface. Two types of entity beans exist: container-managed persistence (CMP) and bean-managed persistence (BMP). Container-managed entity beans use code generated by the application server to interact with the database. Each application server includes mapping tools that generate the appropriate JDBC code for creating, updating, deleting, and finding records. Container-managed beans offer ease of use—the developer doesn't have to write any JDBC code. However, these beans can work only in generic circumstances. For example, if the entity modeled spans multiple tables, most application servers cannot generate code to handle this contingency. In these cases, bean-managed persistence is the alternative.

In bean-managed persistence, the developer of the bean writes the necessary JDBC code to create, update, delete, and find objects inside the bean. While this approach involves much more work (and debugging), it offers infinite flexibility. In the case of the schedule application, it would seem that we could use container-managed persistence. After all, we're accessing a very simple table. However, the database server generates the keys for the records upon insert, which frees us from coming up with a scheme to ensure unique keys. Most database servers offer an auto-increment facility, and the MySQL database used in this application is no exception. Because the database server generates the key (and not the developer), we cannot use container-managed persistence and must rely on bean-managed persistence instead.

Another requirement for entity beans is a primary key class. Because they model database entities, each record must have a primary key. Generally, these key classes are simple encapsulated single values, but the infrastructure exists for complex compound keys. Listing 12.8 shows the primary key class for the event bean.

Listing 12.8 EventPk, the primary key class for EventBean

```
package com.nealford.art.ejbsched.ejb;

import java.io.*;

public class EventPk implements Serializable {

    public int key;

    public EventPk() {
    }

    public EventPk(int key) {
        this.key = key;
    }

    public boolean equals(Object obj) {
        if (this.getClass().equals(obj.getClass())) {
            EventPk that = (EventPk) obj;
            return this.key == that.key;
        }
        return false;
    }

    public int hashCode() {
        return key;
    }
}
```

The `EventPk` class is a serializable class with a single public member variable, which is typical for EJB primary key classes. It contains two constructors, including a parameterless one. It also contains overridden `equals()` and `hashCode()` methods. Including the `equals()` and `hashCode()` methods is a requirement for EJB and is critical to ensure that the application server can correctly compare two primary keys via the `equals()` method and can place them into hashtables via `hashCode()`. Listing 12.9 contains the prelude for `EventBean`.

Listing 12.9 The prelude for EventBean

```
package com.nealford.art.ejbsched.ejb;

import java.rmi.*;
import javax.ejb.*;
```

```
import javax.sql.DataSource;
import java.sql.*;
import javax.naming.Context;
import javax.naming.InitialContext;
import javax.rmi.PortableRemoteObject;
import javax.naming.NamingException;

public class EventBean implements EntityBean {
    private EntityContext entityContext;
    private static final String SQL_SELECT = "SELECT * FROM event" +
            " where event_key = ?";
    private static final String SQL_INSERT =
            "INSERT INTO event (start, duration, description, " +
            "event_type) VALUES(?, ?, ?, ?)";
    private static final String SQL_EVENT_TYPES =
            "SELECT event_type_key, event_text FROM event_types";
    private static final String SQL_UPDATE =
            "UPDATE event SET start = ?, duration = ?, " +
            "description = ?, event_type = ? WHERE event_key = ?";
    private static final String SQL_DELETE =
            "DELETE FROM event WHERE event_key = ?";
    private static final String SQL_LAST_INSERT_ID =
            "SELECT distinct last_insert_id() k from event";
    public String start;
    public int duration;
    public String text;
    public int eventType;
    public int eventKey;
```

The EventBean class implements the EntityBean interface from J2EE. It contains a large number of constants that handle the SQL needed to perform its work. It also includes public member variables for the fields of the entity. It is common in entity beans for the fields to be public, which seems like a violation of encapsulation. However, the application server code itself is the only code that has access to these public fields. Remember that the user always accesses the bean through the remote interface. The ejbCreate() method (listing 12.10) creates a new record in the database.

Listing 12.10 ejbCreate() creates a new Event entity.

```
public EventPk ejbCreate(String start, int duration,
                         String text, int eventType)
                         throws CreateException {
    this.start = start;
    this.duration = duration;
    this.text = text;
    this.eventType = eventType;
```

```
        Connection con = null;
        PreparedStatement ps = null;
        Statement s = null;
        ResultSet rs = null;
        int newKey = -1;
        try {
            con = getDataSource().getConnection();
            ps = con.prepareStatement(SQL_INSERT);
            ps.setString(1, start);
            ps.setInt(2, duration);
            ps.setString(3, text);
            ps.setInt(4, eventType);
            if (ps.executeUpdate() != 1) {
                throw new CreateException("Insert failed");
            }

            //-- get the generated id
            s = con.createStatement();
            rs = s.executeQuery(SQL_LAST_INSERT_ID);      Pulls the key from
            rs.next();                                     the database
            newKey = rs.getInt("k");

        } catch (SQLException sqlx) {
            throw new CreateException(sqlx.getMessage());
        } finally {
            try {
                if (rs != null)
                    rs.close();
                if (ps != null)
                    ps.close();
                if (s != null)
                    s.close();
                if (con != null)
                    con.close();
            } catch (Exception ignored) {
            }
        }
        EventPk eventPk = new EventPk();
        eventPk.key = newKey;
        return eventPk;
    }

    public void ejbPostCreate(String start, int duration,
                              String text, int eventType)
                              throws CreateException {
    }
```

The `ejbCreate()` method accepts parameters for all the fields except the key field, which comes from the database. The `getDataSource()` method of this bean is identical to the one in listing 12.1. This code performs a SQL INSERT command

and checks to ensure that the insert was successful. After the insert, the generated key is collected from the database. Each database has a proprietary way of generating and delivering keys, which explains why we must use bean-managed persistence for this entity bean. The EJB specification mandates that the `ejbCreate()` method returns the primary key of the inserted record, so we create a new `eventPk` instance and return it from the method.

The EJB specification also mandates that we include an `ejbPostCreate()` method with parameters matching each `ejbCreate()` method—there is a one-to-one relationship between them. In our case, we don't need to perform any postcreate tasks, so the `ejbPostCreate()` method is left blank. The next method of `EventBean` loads an entity from the database (see listing 12.11).

Listing 12.11 The ejbLoad() method loads an entity from the database.

```
public void ejbLoad() {
    EventPk eventPk = (EventPk) entityContext.getPrimaryKey();
    Connection con = null;
    PreparedStatement ps = null;
    ResultSet rs = null;
    try {
        con = getDataSource().getConnection();
        ps = con.prepareStatement(SQL_SELECT);
        ps.setInt(1, eventPk.key);
        rs = ps.executeQuery();
        start = rs.getString("start");
        duration = rs.getInt("duration");
        text = rs.getString("text");
        eventType = rs.getInt("event_type");

    } catch (SQLException sqlx) {
        throw new EJBException(sqlx.getMessage());
    } finally {
        try {
            if (rs != null)
                rs.close();
            if (ps != null)
                ps.close();
            if (con != null)
                con.close();
        } catch (Exception ignored) {
        }
    }
}
```

The `ejbLoad()` method is a relatively simple method that executes a SQL SELECT command to fill the fields of the entity. All the methods prepended with *ejb* represent methods called automatically by the application server. Note that the developer cannot call these methods—they do not appear in the remote interface for the bean. The application server decides when it is appropriate to call these methods and does so behind the scenes. The `ejbStore()` method, shown in listing 12.12, performs the opposite operation from `ejbLoad()`.

Listing 12.12 The ejbStore() method updates the entity to the database.

```
public void ejbStore() {
    EventPk eventPk = (EventPk) entityContext.getPrimaryKey();
    Connection con = null;
    PreparedStatement ps = null;
    ResultSet rs = null;
    try {
        con = getDataSource().getConnection();
        ps = con.prepareStatement(SQL_UPDATE);
        ps.setString(1, start);
        ps.setInt(2, duration);
        ps.setString(3, text);
        ps.setInt(4, eventType);
        ps.setInt(5, eventPk.key);
        int rowsAffected = ps.executeUpdate();
        if (rowsAffected != 1)
            throw new EJBException("Update failed");
    } catch (SQLException sqlx) {
        throw new EJBException(sqlx.getMessage());
    } finally {
        try {
            if (rs != null)
                rs.close();
            if (ps != null)
                ps.close();
            if (con != null)
                con.close();
        } catch (Exception ignored) {
        }
    }
}
```

The `ejbStore()` method takes the values from inside the fields and performs a SQL UPDATE in the database. Finally, the `ejbRemove()` method, which is shown in listing 12.13, deletes a record from the database.

Listing 12.13 The ejbRemove() method deletes records from the database.

```
public void ejbRemove() throws RemoveException {
    EventPk eventPk = (EventPk) entityContext.getPrimaryKey();
    Connection con = null;
    PreparedStatement ps = null;
    ResultSet rs = null;
    try {
        con = getDataSource().getConnection();
        ps = con.prepareStatement(SQL_DELETE);
        ps.setInt(1, eventPk.key);
        int rowsAffected = ps.executeUpdate();
        if (rowsAffected != 1)
            throw new EJBException("Delete failed");
    } catch (SQLException sqlx) {
        throw new EJBException(sqlx.getMessage());
    } finally {
        try {
            if (rs != null)
                rs.close();
            if (ps != null)
                ps.close();
            if (con != null)
                con.close();
        } catch (Exception ignored) {
        }
    }
}
```

The remainder of the EventBean class (omitted for brevity's sake) consists of public accessor and mutator methods for all the fields of this entity.

Just as with the session beans, the EventBean entity bean has both a home and a remote interface. As you can see in listing 12.14, the home interface is much like the ones for the session beans.

Listing 12.14 The home interface for the Event entity bean

```
package com.nealford.art.ejbsched.ejb;

import java.rmi.*;
import javax.ejb.*;

public interface EventHome extends EJBHome {
    public Event create(String start, int duration, String text,
                        int eventType) throws
                        RemoteException, CreateException;
    public Event findByPrimaryKey(EventPk primKey) throws
```

```
                ObjectNotFoundException, RemoteException,
                FinderException;
}
```

A key difference between EventBean's home interface and the previous ones lies in the presence of the findByPrimaryKey() method. Entity beans may include finder methods that return either a single reference or a collection of references. In this application, we never need to find an entity (the application currently doesn't allow editing for simplicity's sake). Otherwise, the home interface is functionally the same.

The remote interface for entity beans differs considerably from session beans. The remote interface for the EventBean is shown in listing 12.15.

Listing 12.15 The remote interface for the entity EJB EventBean

```
package com.nealford.art.ejbsched.ejb;

import java.rmi.*;
import javax.ejb.*;

public interface Event extends EJBObject {
    public void setStart(String start) throws RemoteException;
    public String getStart() throws RemoteException;
    public void setDuration(int duration) throws RemoteException;
    public int getDuration() throws RemoteException;
    public void setText(String text) throws RemoteException;
    public String getText() throws RemoteException;
    public void setEventType(int eventType) throws RemoteException;
    public int getEventType() throws RemoteException;
    public void setEventKey(int eventKey) throws RemoteException;
    public int getEventKey() throws RemoteException;
}
```

The Event remote interface includes the accessors and mutators for the fields of the entity. When the client accesses an entity EJB, it must do so through this remote interface. The client doesn't have access to the publicly created fields of the entity bean because the application server actually holds that object reference. Thus, the client's view of the entity must come entirely through this interface. Note the use by the application server of interfaces to hide implementation details.

Business rules in session beans

The last of the EJBs that contribute to this project are stateless session beans that encapsulate the business logic of the application. The primary business rules in this application validate the inserted data. Listing 12.16 shows ScheduleItemRules, the stateless session bean that handles this chore.

Listing 12.16 The ScheduleItemRules stateless session bean handles data validation.

```java
package com.nealford.art.ejbsched.ejb;

import java.rmi.*;
import javax.ejb.*;
import java.util.*;
import com.nealford.art.ejbsched.model.ScheduleItem;

public class ScheduleItemRulesBean implements SessionBean {
    private SessionContext sessionContext;
    static private final int MIN_DURATION = 0;
    static private final int MAX_DURATION = 31;

    public void ejbCreate() {
    }

    public void ejbRemove() {
    }

    public void ejbActivate() {
    }

    public void ejbPassivate() {
    }

    public void setSessionContext(SessionContext sessionContext) {
        this.sessionContext = sessionContext;
    }

    public List validate(ScheduleItem item) {
        List validationMessages = new ArrayList(0);
        if (item.getDuration() < MIN_DURATION ||
                item.getDuration() > MAX_DURATION)
            validationMessages.add("Invalid duration");
        if (item.getText() == null || item.getText().length() < 1)
            validationMessages.add("Event must have description");
        return validationMessages;
    }
}
```

The primary method of interest in ScheduleItemRulesBean is validate(). If you compare it to the validate() method appearing in the non-EJB version of this application (see chapter 4, listing 4.5), they are identical. The difference lies in the architecture. The application server maintains a pool of ScheduleItemRules objects and pulls one from the pool to perform validations. Contrast this with the normal behavior of a web application, which must create an instance of a class to perform the same function. In this case, the object is created by the application server and the invocation is much faster.

The home and remote interfaces to this class resemble the other stateless session beans and, in the interest of space, appear only in the chapter samples.

Changes to the models

The EJB infrastructure is now in place, and we've updated the web application to reflect the architectural change. The most radical change to the existing web application lies in the boundary class ScheduleBean. The populate() method formerly created a connection to the database, executed a query, and built a list of results to return as a list. The populate() method has now become a proxy for the real work, which occurs in the EJBs. The revised ScheduleBean populate() method is shown in listing 12.17.

Listing 12.17 The revised populate() method has become a proxy for an EJB.

```
public void populate() {
    try {
        Object o = context.lookup("EventDb");
        EventDbHome home =
                (EventDbHome) PortableRemoteObject.narrow(o,
                EventDbHome.class);
        EventDb eventDb = home.create();
        scheduleItems = eventDb.getScheduleItems();
    } catch (RemoteException ex) {
        ex.printStackTrace();
    } catch (ClassCastException ex) {
        ex.printStackTrace();
    } catch (NamingException ex) {
        ex.printStackTrace();
    } catch (CreateException ex) {
        ex.printStackTrace();
    }
}
```

ScheduleBean defers all work to the application server. The populate() method creates a remote reference and calls the getScheduleItems() method on it, which returns a list of ScheduleItem objects from the application server. Note that the ScheduleItems returned by this method are not remote references to anything—it is virtually the same ScheduleItem class used before in the application. The difference lies in the way the list is generated.

The addRecord() method has undergone a similar transformation, as shown in listing 12.18.

Listing 12.18 The addRecord() method has also become a proxy for an EJB.

```
public void addRecord(ScheduleItem item) throws
        ScheduleAddException {
    try {
        Context context = new InitialContext();
        Object o = context.lookup("Event");
        EventHome home =
                (EventHome) PortableRemoteObject.narrow(o,
                EventHome.class);
        home.create(item.getStart(),
                    item.getDuration(),
                    item.getText(),
                    item.getEventTypeKey());
    } catch (RemoteException ex) {
        ex.printStackTrace();
    } catch (ClassCastException ex) {
        ex.printStackTrace();
    } catch (NamingException ex) {
        ex.printStackTrace();
    } catch (CreateException ex) {
        ex.printStackTrace();
    }
}
```

To add a new record, the create() method of the home interface is called. The new item to be added passes into this method, and a new entity is created via the home interface to the EventBean. In this case, we never access a remote reference to the newly created item. If we need one, the create() method returns the newly generated primary key, so we can use the findByPrimaryKey() method of the home interface to return the reference.

The getEventTypes() method has also changed to accommodate the port to EJB. It creates a reference to the EventTypeDbBean to get the mappings between event type key and event type description. This method appears in listing 12.19.

Listing 12.19 The getEventTypes() method returns a mapping.

```
public Map getEventTypes() {
    try {
        if (eventTypes == null) {
            Context context = new InitialContext();
            Object o = context.lookup("EventTypeDB");
            EventTypeDBHome home =
```

```
                        (EventTypeDBHome)
                        PortableRemoteObject.narrow(o,
                        EventTypeDBHome.class);
                EventTypeDB eventTypeDB = home.create();
                eventTypes = eventTypeDB.getEventTypes();
            }
        } catch (RemoteException ex) {
            ex.printStackTrace();
        } catch (ClassCastException ex) {
            ex.printStackTrace();
        } catch (NamingException ex) {
            ex.printStackTrace();
        } catch (CreateException ex) {
            ex.printStackTrace();
        }
        return eventTypes;
    }
```

As before, the method shown in listing 12.19 caches the mappings. The eventType map is a class-level variable, and the method checks to see if it is already populated. This means that each instance of the ScheduleBean contains a cached copy of the mappings. This approach is safe because the mappings so rarely change.

The only change to the ScheduleItem local entity class is the deferment of the validation business rule to the stateless session bean. In both versions of the application, the ScheduleItem class consists of only accessors, mutators, and a single validate method. However, in the EJB version, the server handles the validation logic. Listing 12.20 shows the updated validate() method of the ScheduleItem class.

Listing 12.20 The validate() method is a proxy for business logic from a stateless session bean.

```
public List validate() {
    try {
        Object o = context.lookup("ScheduleItemRules");
        ScheduleItemRulesHome home = (ScheduleItemRulesHome)
                            PortableRemoteObject.narrow(o,
                            ScheduleItemRulesHome.class);
        ScheduleItemRules rules = home.create();
        return rules.validate(this);
    } catch (Exception ex) {
        List errors = new ArrayList();
        errors.add("EJB exception: " + ex);
        return errors;
    }
}
```

The session bean accepts a `ScheduleItem` object as the parameter, and this class passes itself. This illustrates the distinction between remote objects, accessible through their remote interfaces, and local objects. It is important to distinguish when it is appropriate to use a local object versus using a remote interface. In this case, the local object holds all the schedule item information and defers to the remote object to handle validations. When it comes time to create a new entry in the database, the local object is passed as a parameter to the `addRecord()` method of the `ScheduleBean`, which in turn creates a new entity.

In general, remote objects should be coarse grained, meaning that it is preferable to pass objects around as chunks of information rather than create remote interfaces with numerous small methods. Calling remote methods taxes the memory and resources of the application server more than simple objects—remote interfaces incur a significant overhead. It is better for local (non-remote) objects to encapsulate data and pass the local objects to bulk remote methods to handle persistence and highly scalable business rules.

Changes to the controllers and views

There are no changes to either the controller or the views—which illustrates the advantage of the clean separation of responsibilities in a Model 2 architecture. Because the original application used Model 2 to separate the parts of the application, it enabled us to change the infrastructure of one of the key parts (the model) without affecting the other parts. The model now acts as a proxy for the EJBs, which handle both persistence and business rules. The controller still creates local models and passes them to the views. The only difference lies in the encapsulated behavior of the model objects themselves.

12.3.3 Using EJBs in web frameworks

Most of the frameworks featured in part 2 of *Art of Java Web Development* adhere to the Model 2 architecture. As such, a similar transformation to EJB is possible. In fact, that is why we chose the generic Model 2 application as the base. The only framework we cover that prevents an easy porting to EJB is the sole Rapid Application Development (RAD) framework, InternetBeans Express. While it's certainly possible to incorporate EJBs into that framework, it would require a massive rewrite. InternetBeans Express relies heavily on its data-aware controls, which aren't designed to work with EJB.

Generally, web frameworks shouldn't care about the persistence layer of the application. When your application is built on Model 2, the clean separation of responsibilities mandates that you are free to implement the persistence layer in whatever manner you choose. Truly modular applications, with clean separation of concerns, make it easy to update (and replace) one module without breaking the others. Effective partitioning is an advantage of low coupling and high cohesion, both desirable characteristics in any framework.

12.3.4 *Managing JNDI context*

One of the services provided by application servers is a naming service. A *naming service* allows you to look up resources by name from a provider. The standard naming service in Java is the Java Naming and Directory Interface (JNDI). JNDI lets you find resources (such as database connections) by searching for them by name. The application server can deliver those resources within the same application or across machine boundaries. You can think of JNDI as a white pages phone book lookup for resources. If you know the resource name, JNDI can deliver it to you.

The JNDI context represents a single user's connection to the application server. The appropriate analogy is that of a connection to a database server. The JNDI context encapsulates the user's credentials (such as username and password) for the application server. In fact, you can consider this as a drop-in replacement for access control and security from the application server rather than the database. Notice that you can no longer use the access control features of the database server because the application server creates the database connections for you in a pool.

Just like database connections, the web application can create and destroy connections to the application server at will. However, also like database connections, establishing the connection is time consuming. Therefore, it is always a good idea to cache the JNDI context for the user in the user's session. The updated version of the schedule application does just that. The `ViewSchedule` controller creates a context for the user and places it in the user's session. Upon each subsequent request, it checks to see if the context is available. The pertinent methods from `ViewSchedule` appear in listing 12.21.

Listing 12.21 The controller caches the context object in the user's session.

```
private Context establishContext(HttpServletRequest request) {
    HttpSession session = request.getSession(true);
    Context c = (Context) session.getAttribute("context");
    if (c == null) {
        c = getInitialContext();
        session.setAttribute("context", getInitialContext());
    }
    return c;
}
```

```
private Context getInitialContext() {
    Context c = null;
    try {
        c = new InitialContext();
    }
    catch (NamingException ex) {
        ex.printStackTrace();
    }
    return c;
}
```

Of course, any time you store a link to an external resource in the user's session, you must anticipate the possibility of the user not cleaning up the session correctly. One of the annoying characteristics of web applications is that the user can just go away without telling you by closing the browser. You should add a session event listener to clean up the JNDI context if the user's session times out.

12.4 *Performing validations with model beans*

I'm sure you have figured out by now that I am a strong advocate of separating the concerns of the application by designing to the Model 2 architecture. Part of that philosophy states that the business rules in the application must reside in the model, whether locally or as an EJB in an application server. We've demonstrated how to perform server-side validations, both here and in chapter 4. However, there always exists a strong desire to make web applications act more like "traditional" client/server applications, which include immediate validations for user input errors. If you handle validations at the server, the user must wait for the round trip to the server.

12.4.1 *Client-side validations*

The way to avoid the wait on server-side validations is to create client-side validations using JavaScript or JScript. This scripting code runs in the browser, so the client gets immediate results, and this is its prime benefit. The disadvantages of client-side scripting are many. Scripting languages don't support modern software engineering practices like strong typing and extensible object systems, and they have a host of other deficiencies. Scripting languages work well for small, narrowly scoped tasks. However, developers who try to build too much behavior in scripting languages find that the code is hard to maintain.

If you must have application-like behavior, use scripting. Its usefulness outweighs the inconvenience in many situations. To that end, you should perform client-side validations in a way that has the least negative impact on the application.

Scheduling with client-side validation

The updated version of the Model 2 schedule application now incorporates Java-Script to perform input validation. Note that this section is not meant to be an introduction to JavaScript; many books are available that cover JavaScript thoroughly. This sample appears in the source code archive as art_sched_js.

A common practice when including JavaScript places the code in a separate file and includes it for the pages that need it. This file is a resource that must be addressable from the browser, so in this version of the application it appears in the same directory as the JSPs. The form validation JavaScript code is shown in listing 12.22.

Listing 12.22 JavaScript code included to assist in client-side data validation

```
<!--
function SubmitValidate(numberfield, datefield) {        ❶ Validates all the
    var StatusNum, StatusDate                              fields on the form

    StatusNum = CheckNum(numberfield);
    StatusDate = CheckDate(datefield);
    if (! StatusNum && ! StatusDate) {
        alert('Invalid number and/or date fields');
    } else {
        document.forms[0].submit();
    }
}

function CheckNum(numfield) {        ❷ Validates a
    var numstat, nval, snum             duration

    numstat = true;
    nval = numfield.value
    for (snum=0; snum < nval.length; snum++) {
        if (isNaN(parseInt(nval.charAt(snum)))) {
            numstat = false;
        }
    }
    if (numstat)
        nval = parseInt(numfield.value);
    return numstat && (nval > 0 && nval < 30);
    //return numstat;
}                                    ❸ Validates a date
function CheckDate(datefield) {  ⟵
    var dstat, dval, dformat, sp, ddel
```

```
        dstat = true;
        dval = datefield.value;
        ddel = "/";
        dformat = "mm" + ddel + "dd" + ddel + "yyyy";

        if (dval.length == dformat.length) {
            for (sp = 0; sp < dformat.length; sp++) {
                if (dformat.charAt(sp) == "m" ||
                        dformat.charAt(sp) == "d" ||
                        dformat.charAt(sp) == "y") {
                    if (isNaN(parseInt(dval.charAt(sp)))) {
                        dstat = false;
                    }
                } else if (dformat.charAt(sp) ==
                        ddel && dval.charAt(sp) != ddel) {
                    dstat = false;
                }
            }
        } else {
            dstat = false;
        }

        return dstat;
    }
    -->
```

❶ The SubmitValidate() method executes upon the HTML form's submit request.

❷ ❸ The other two methods, CheckNum() and CheckDate(), are helpers that are called from SubmitValidate() and are also called on the onBlur event of the pertinent HTML elements. This event corresponds to the focusLost() event for a Swing JTextField.

To use this JavaScript, you must include this file in any JSP that needs it, accomplished by a script element:

```
<script language="JavaScript" src="formval.js"></script>
```

Adding the script element with an src attribute is equivalent to including the JavaScript directly on the page.

To use the JavaScript methods, you attach them to the proper elements. For example, the form element in the ScheduleEntryView JSP changes to

```
<form action="saveentry" method="post"
    onsubmit="SubmitValidate(document.forms[0].duration,
    document.forms[0].start);return false;">
```

and both the duration and start elements feature a similar modification:

```
<input name="duration" size="16"
    value="<jsp:getProperty name="scheduleItem"
            property="duration"/>"
            onBlur="if (! CheckNum(this))
    alert('Duration must be a positive number > 0 and < 30');"/>
```

When this application runs and the user inputs invalid values, the browser catches the error immediately and displays a JavaScript alert dialog box, as shown in figure 12.7. As you can see, users receive instant feedback if they enter invalid data.

From a usability standpoint, the application is easier to use. However, from a design and architecture standpoint, it has degenerated badly. The business rules now exist in two locations: in the model beans and in the user interface. Changing the rules means that you now must find the code in more than one location. Once this slide begins, it accelerates and the application quickly degrades into an architectural mess. But there is a way to get the desirable client-side behavior without ruining the careful design; let's take a look.

12.4.2 Building client-side validations from the server

If you must have client-side validations and other business rules, it is a given that you have to use JavaScript—you have no other universally available options. But the previous flawed architecture is salvageable. Because the business rules should appear in the model, place them in the model as JavaScript. This technique places the JavaScript as constant strings in the proper model components with accessors to return the fully formed JavaScript to the user interface.

Server-generated client-side validation

This version of the schedule application uses client-side validation in JavaScript generated from the model objects. First, place the JavaScript in the model objects as constants with an accessor. This is demonstrated in listing 12.23.

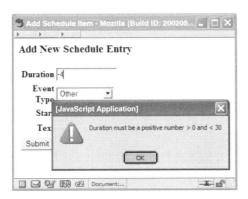

Figure 12.7
Using JavaScript allows the user to get instant feedback whenever invalid data is entered.

Listing 12.23 JavaScript validations in server models

```
    private static final String JS_ITEM_VALIDATION =
"   <script language='javascript'>\n" +
"       function SubmitValidate(numberfield, datefield) {\n"+
"           var StatusNum, StatusDate\n"+
"\n"+
"           StatusNum = CheckNum(numberfield);\n"+
"           StatusDate = CheckDate(datefield);\n"+
"           if (! StatusNum && ! StatusDate) {\n"+
"               alert('Invalid number and/or date fields');\n"+
"           } else {\n"+
"               document.forms[0].submit();\n"+
"           }\n"+
"       }\n"+
"\n"+
"       function CheckNum(numfield) {\n"+
"           var numstat, nval, snum\n"+
"\n"+
"           numstat = true;\n"+
"           nval = numfield.value\n"+
"           for (snum=0; snum < nval.length; snum++) {\n"+
"               if (isNaN(parseInt(nval.charAt(snum)))) {\n"+
"                   numstat = false;\n"+
"               }\n"+
"           }\n"+
"           if (numstat)\n"+
"               nval = parseInt(numfield.value);\n"+
"           return numstat && (nval > 0 && nval < 30);\n"+
"           //return numstat;\n"+
"       }\n"+
"\n"+
"       function CheckDate(datefield) {\n"+
"           var dstat, dval, dformat, sp, ddel\n"+
"           dstat = true;\n"+
"           dval = datefield.value;\n"+
"           ddel = \"/\";\n"+
"           dformat = \"mm\" + ddel + \"dd\" + ddel + \"yyyy\";\n"+
"\n"+
"           if (dval.length == dformat.length) {\n"+
"               for (sp = 0; sp < dformat.length; sp++) {\n"+
"                   if (dformat.charAt(sp) == \"m\" ||\n"+
"                           dformat.charAt(sp) == \"d\" ||\n"+
"                           dformat.charAt(sp) == \"y\") {\n"+
"                       if (isNaN(parseInt(dval.charAt(sp)))) {\n"+
"                           dstat = false;\n"+
"                       }\n"+
"                   } else if (dformat.charAt(sp) ==\n"+
"                           ddel && dval.charAt(sp) != ddel) {\n"+
"                       dstat = false;\n"+
```

```
"                        }\n"+
"                    }\n"+
"                } else {\n"+
"                    dstat = false;\n"+
"                }\n"+
"\n"+
"                return dstat;\n"+
"            }\n"+
"    </script>\n";
    private static final String JS_FORM_VALIDATION =
        "SubmitValidate(document.forms[0].duration," +
        "document.forms[0].start);return false;";
    private static final String JS_START_VALIDATION =
        "if (! CheckNum(this)) " +
        "alert('Duration must be a positive number > 0 and < 30');";
    private static final String JS_DATE_VALIDATION =
            "if (! CheckDate(this)) " +
            "alert('Invalid Date (MM/DD/YYYY');";

    public String getItemValidationJS() {
        return JS_ITEM_VALIDATION;
    }

    public String getFormValidationJS() {
        return JS_FORM_VALIDATION;
    }

    public String getStartValidationJS() {
        return JS_START_VALIDATION;
    }

    public String getDateValidationJS() {
        return JS_DATE_VALIDATION;
    }
```

The `JS_ITEM_VALIDATION` code is exactly the same as the code from listing 12.22, encoded as a long Java constant string. The public accessor methods return the constants. The JSP already has a reference to the `ScheduleItem` bean, so it is a simple matter to call the accessors in the appropriate places, as shown in listing 12.24.

Listing 12.24 The ScheduleEntryView JSP calls the model bean's accessors.

```
<jsp:getProperty name="scheduleItem" property="itemValidationJS" />

<form action="saveentry" method="post"
    onSubmit="<jsp:getProperty name="scheduleItem"
    property="formValidationJS"/>">

    <input name="duration" size="16"
        value="<jsp:getProperty name="scheduleItem"
```

```
                    property="duration"/>"
         onBlur="<jsp:getProperty name="scheduleItem"
                    property="startValidationJS"/>"/>
```

The end result for the user is exactly the same as embedding the JavaScript into the page. However, from an architectural standpoint, this version is much better. Now when the inevitable change of business rules occurs, the developer can go to a single location (the model objects) and make modifications with confidence, knowing that additional code isn't lurking somewhere in the user interface.

Placing JavaScript as a long constant string in the models is not very pretty. The code is written and debugged somewhere else and pasted into the model. However, the short-term inconvenience of placing the rules here outweighs the long-term disadvantage of compromising the architecture of the application. In general, use JavaScript as sparingly as possible. It is designed for small, single-purpose tasks (like validations, specialized navigation, etc.), and it is appropriate for these tasks.

Chapter 5 includes an example of the Jakarta Commons Validator, which allows for declarative validation rules in Struts (although it works outside of Struts as well). The Validator can also generate client-side JavaScript based on the declarative validation rules. If you need extensive client-side validation, you should use the Validator framework instead of writing your own.

12.5　Summary

Understanding where to put things is more than half the battle. The trend in software engineering decouples applications as much as possible. The use of design patterns is an example of this trend, as is the use of business component technologies like EJBs. It helps to see applications that successfully manage this separation. That is one of the goals of this chapter. Understanding the terminology and best practices is also important because only then can you communicate ideas effectively to other developers outside your team. Understanding at least parts of some core concepts makes communication easier. Design patterns, UML, and advanced Java language concepts (such as the way interfaces are used in enterprise systems) have become the lingua franca of Java web developers.

Changing fundamental infrastructure parts of your application is easy—if you have designed it to be extensible. Otherwise, doing so is a nightmare. This chapter provides the payoff of the groundwork laid in chapter 4. The Model 2 design pattern sprang into life to facilitate exactly the kind of transformation illustrated in section 12.3.1. The models changed significantly, new model pieces were constructed using EJBs, but neither the controller nor the view required a single change. The concerns of the application were separated enough to replace large pieces without breaking the whole.

In the next chapter, we look at handling the workflow and user interface of the application using Model 2.

Handling flow

In this chapter, we take a look at the usability and flow of a web application from a design standpoint. The greatest application in the world won't be used much if its flow doesn't meet the needs of its users, or if it doesn't handle exceptions gracefully and thus frustrates your users.

By studying flow, you can address both of these concerns. First, we look at how to reconcile often-requested usability elements (such as column sorting and page-at-a-time scrolling) with the design principles we've already discussed. We use the Model 2 version of the eMotherEarth e-commerce site introduced in chapter 4 as a base for this and future chapters.

You must also handle more infrastructural elements of flow, such as exception handling. Your application should be designed for robustness in the face of both user and application errors. In this chapter, you'll see how to build sortable columns, page-at-a-time scrolling, undo operations, and robust exception handling.

13.1 Application usability options

Users have an annoying habit of asking for features that seem easy and intuitive to use but that are difficult for the developer to implement. For example, two common features that users expect are sortable columns in tables and page-at-a-time scrolling. When adding bells and whistles to your application, you must avoid compromising its design and architecture. No matter how "pretty" it becomes, the developer who must maintain it later makes the final judgment on an application's quality.

13.1.1 Building the base: eMotherEarth.com

To illustrate these requests, an application must be in place. This and subsequent chapters use a simulated toy e-commerce site named eMotherEarth. The beginnings of this application appeared in chapter 2 to illustrate the evolution of web development from servlets and JSP. However, this version of the application is reorganized into a Model 2 application (see chapter 4). This section discusses the new architecture, and the following sections show how to incorporate usability options into a Model 2 application.

Packages

The application now appears in four major packages, shown in figure 13.1.

The boundary package contains two boundary classes, `ProductDb` and `OrderDb`, to persist the entities into the database. The application contains four entities: `Product`, `Order`, `Lineitem`, and `CartItem`. Only two boundary classes are required because `Order` and `Lineitem` are handled by the same boundary class; there is never a case in the application where you can add line items without adding an order, and the `CartItem` entity is never persisted. `CartItem` is a helper class that holds information until the time that an order is generated. The controller package contains the controller servlets for the application, and the util package contains miscellaneous utility classes, such as the database connection pool and the shopping cart.

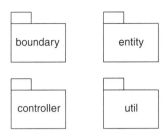

Figure 13.1   The Model 2 version of eMotherEarth.com is organized into four packages, each with different responsibilities.

For the sake of brevity, we show only the code that is unique to this application. The entire application is available with the source code archive as art_emotherearth_base. So, we won't show listings of classes that consist primarily of accessors and mutators and discuss only the interesting methods of the controller servlets.

Welcome

The first page of the application is a simple logon page, as shown in figure 13.2.

The welcome controller does more than just forward to a JSP with an entry field. It sets up global configuration items, like the database connection pool. Listing 13.1 shows the entire welcome controller.

Listing 13.1   The welcome controller

```
public class Welcome extends HttpServlet {

    public void init() throws ServletException {
        String driverClass =
                getServletContext().getInitParameter("driverClass");
        String password =
                getServletContext().getInitParameter("password");
        String dbUrl =
                getServletContext().getInitParameter("dbUrl");
        String user =
                getServletContext().getInitParameter("user");
        DBPool dbPool =
                createConnectionPool(driverClass, password, dbUrl,
                                     user);
        getServletContext().setAttribute("dbPool", dbPool);
    }

    private DBPool createConnectionPool(String driverClass,
                                        String password,
                                        String dbUrl,
                                        String user) {
```

```
        DBPool dbPool = null;
        try {
            dbPool = new DBPool(driverClass, dbUrl, user, password);
        } catch (SQLException sqlx) {
            getServletContext().log(new java.util.Date() +
                                 ":Connection pool error", sqlx);
        }
        return dbPool;
    }

    public void doGet(HttpServletRequest request,
                      HttpServletResponse response)
        throws ServletException, IOException {
        RequestDispatcher dispather =
                request.getRequestDispatcher("/WelcomeView.jsp");
        dispather.forward(request, response);
    }
}
```

The real action in the welcome controller occurs before the doGet() method is called. This method gets configuration parameters from the web.xml file and uses them to create the database connection pool that is utilized by the remainder of the application. Once the pool is created, it is added to the global collection. The doGet() method does nothing but forward directly to the view for the welcome.

Catalog

The next page of the application shows the user a catalog of all the items available for purchase. This page is shown in figure 13.3.

While the Welcome page strongly resembles the original version of the application from chapter 2, the Catalog page has some significant changes. First, it allows the user to click on the column heads to sort the items based on that column. Second, it offers multiple pages of items. Instead of showing all the items at the outset

Figure 13.2
This page allows the user to log on, while the servlet underneath sets up the web application.

Figure 13.3
The Catalog page shows users the first of several pages of items they can buy from the site.

(a potentially long list), it shows a subset with hyperlinks at the bottom that allow the user to choose the display page.

Catalog is the workhorse controller in the application because it must execute the code that makes all the display techniques possible. Ideally, the JSP should have as little logic as possible—all the "real" code should execute in the controller. Figure 13.4 shows a UML sequence diagram highlighting the classes and methods called by the catalog controller. The real work in the controller is split up among the methods that appear in the sequence diagram. The doPost() method, which is fired from the Welcome page, appears in listing 13.2.

Listing 13.2 The catalog controller's doPost() method breaks the work down into smaller chunks.

```
public void doPost(HttpServletRequest request,
                HttpServletResponse response) throws
      ServletException, IOException {

    HttpSession session = request.getSession(true);
    ensureThatUserIsInSession(request, session);
    ProductDb productDb = getProductBoundary(session);
    int start = getStartingPage(request);
    int recsPerPage = Integer.parseInt(getServletConfig().
                getInitParameter("recsPerPage"));
    int totalPagesToShow = calculateNumberOfPagesToShow(
            productDb.getProductList().size(), recsPerPage);
    String[] pageList =
            buildListOfPagesToShow(recsPerPage,
                                totalPagesToShow);
```

```
    List outputList = productDb.getProductListSlice(start,
            recsPerPage);
    sortPagesForDisplay(request, outputList);

    bundleInformationForView(request, start, pageList,
                            outputList);
    forwardToView(request, response);
}
```

The catalog controller makes sure the user is in the session. If the user isn't in the session (for example, upon the first invocation of the page), the `ensure-ThatUserIsInSession()` method adds the user to the session, pulling the name from the request collection. Either way, this method guarantees that the user is in the session.

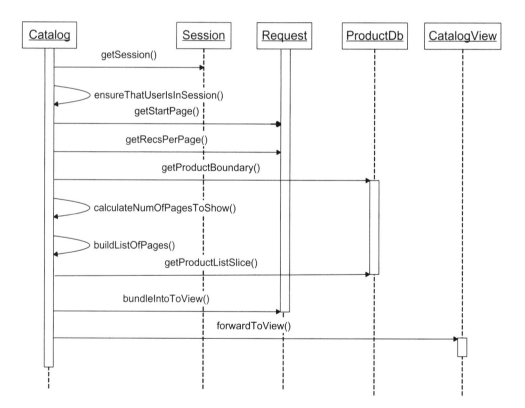

Figure 13.4   This sequence diagram shows the interactions and method calls from the catalog controller.

Next, the servlet starts to gather the components and information needed to build the display for the user. It calls the getProductBoundary() method to get the boundary class for product entities. This method is shown in listing 13.3.

Listing 13.3 The getProductBoundary() method either retrieves or creates a product boundary object.

```
private ProductDb getProductBoundary(HttpSession session) throws
        NumberFormatException {
    ProductDb products = (ProductDb) session.getAttribute(
            "productList");

    if (products == null) {
        products = new ProductDb();
        products.setDbPool(
                (DBPool) getServletContext().getAttribute(
                "dbPool"));
        session.setAttribute("productList", products);
    }
    return products;
}
```

The product boundary class encapsulates access to individual product entities, which it pulls from a database. All the data access code appears in the boundary class, leaving the product entities to include only product-specific domain information. The ProductDb class includes a property that is a java.util.List of Product entities. Figure 13.5 illustrates the relationship between these classes.

The application is designed so that every user gets a copy of this product boundary object. The controller's getProductBoundary() method is designed to place a copy of this object in the user's session upon first request. This behavior is a design decision whose goal is to ensure that every user has a copy of the object. The design represents a classic trade-off of memory versus speed. Although this strategy occupies more memory (a boundary object per user), the speed of access to the data is faster. If we wanted to create a more scalable application, we would handle the boundary differently. Chapters 14 and 15 include discussions of various caching and pooling mechanisms that are alternatives to this approach. The design decision to cache the boundary object in the user's

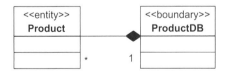

Figure 13.5 The ProductDb class includes an aggregation of Product objects and delivers them via a method that returns a java.util.List.

session highlights the fact that performance and scalability must illuminate every decision made in a web application.

13.1.2 *Page-at-a-time scrolling*

The page-at-a-time scrolling interface technique concerns the volume of information and the usability of the application. If you have a data-driven web application, you don't want to inundate the user with several thousand records on a single page. Most web sites handle this with page-at-a-time scrolling. When using this technique, the user sees only a single page worth of data and a list of pages. If users want to see more records, they can navigate to another page.

To implement this technique, the controller gathers some values from the request collection to help determine the number of pages to show at the bottom of the page. It calls the getStartPage() method, which appears in listing 13.4.

> **Listing 13.4 The getStartMethod() from the controller calculates the starting page number.**

```
private int getStartingPage(HttpServletRequest request) {
    String recStart = request.getParameter("start");
    int start = 0;

    if (recStart != null)
        start = Integer.parseInt(recStart);
    return start;
}
```

This method pulls the start parameter from the request, parses it, and returns it. This parameter is available because the view encodes it into self-posting requests back to the controller for this page. Note that this method is designed to work in cases where the start parameter is not available (such as the first invocation of the page).

Users must specify the page they want through the view, which is specified by the series of hyperlinks at the bottom of the page. The values of these hyperlinks (in other words, the generated HTML for them) are shown in listing 13.5.

> **Listing 13.5 The page links at the bottom allow the user to navigate between pages.**

```
<p> Pages:  
<a href='catalog?start=0'>1</a> 
<a href='catalog?start=6'>2</a> 
<a href='catalog?start=12'>3</a> 
<a href='catalog?start=18'>4</a> 
```

Each of the page links contains a reference to the controller (catalog) and the starting record for that page. You will notice in listing 13.5 that each page starts six records beyond the previous page. The `getStartPage()` method of the controller pulls the `start` parameter value from the request and uses it to calculate which records should appear on the page. The number of records per page is set through a servlet configuration parameter. In this case, it is set to six records per page. The next line of code in the controller is the retrieval of that value from the `servlet-Config` object.

The next method called by the controller is the `calculateNumberOfPages-ToShow()` method, which appears in listing 13.6.

Listing 13.6 This method calculates the number of pages it will take to show all the requested records.

```
private int calculateNumberOfPagesToShow(int numInList,
                                         int recsPerPage) {
    int totalToShow = numInList / recsPerPage;

    if (numInList % recsPerPage != 0)
        ++totalToShow;
    return totalToShow;
}
```

The `calculateNumberOfPagesToShow()` method accepts the total number of records available and the requested records per page, and then calculates the number of pages required. Note that the contingency of having a last page that isn't completely full is handled with the use of the modulus operator (`%`) to ensure that enough pages exist.

The next method called is `buildListOfPagesToShow()`, which builds up an array of strings containing the displayable hyperlinks. This method is shown in listing 13.7.

Listing 13.7 This method builds the list of hyperlinks embedded at the bottom of the page.

```
private String[] buildListOfPagesToShow(int recsPerPage,
                                        int totalPagesToShow) {
    String[] pageList = new String[totalPagesToShow];
    StringBuffer work = new StringBuffer(20);
    int currentPage = 0;

    for (int i = 0; i < totalPagesToShow; i++) {
        work.setLength(0);
        work.append("<a href='catalog?start=").append(
```

```
            currentPage).append("'>").append(i + 1).append(
            "</a> ");
        pageList[i] = work.toString();
        currentPage += recsPerPage;
    }
    return pageList;
}
```

The `buildListOfPagesToShow()` method builds up a list of hyperlinks with the appropriate page and start record information embedded in them. It iterates over a list up to the total number of pages to show, building a `StringBuffer` with the appropriate hyperlink and display data. Eventually, it returns the array of strings that includes the page list. This page list is passed to the view in a request parameter (it is one of the parameters to the `bundleInformationForView()` method).

The view extracts that information and places it on the bottom of the page. Listing 13.8 shows the snippet of code at the bottom of the page that builds this list of pages.

Listing 13.8 The CatalogView page uses the pageList to build the list of hyperlinks at the bottom.

```
<%-- show page links --%>
<p> Pages:  
<%
    String[] pageList = (String[]) request.getAttribute("pageList");
    if (pageList != null) {
        for (int i = 0; i < pageList.length; i++) {
            out.println(pageList[i]);
        }
    }
%>
```

The scriptlet in listing 13.8 walks over the `pageList` passed from the controller and outputs each of the links. The spacing is already built into the HTML in the `pageList`, simplifying the job of the scriptlet code.

Using JSTL

The kind of scriptlet code that appears in listing 13.8 is generally not required if you are using a modern JSP specification (and of course a servlet container that supports this specification). The JSP Standard Tag Library (JSTL) includes custom JSP tags that handle common chores like iteration. The JSTL version of this code is shown in listing 13.9

Listing 13.9 JSTL provides custom tags to help with iteration over a collection.

```
<% pageContext.setAttribute("pageList",
        (String[]) request.getAttribute("pageList")); %>
<p> Pages:  
<c:forEach var="page" items="${pageList}">
    <c:out value="${page}" escapeXml="false"/>
</c:forEach>
```

This code is much better than the scriptlet alternative because the custom JSTL tag handles conditions like null properties by just ignoring the tag. This is a case in which using JSTL does greatly improve the readability and maintainability of your code without compromising the clean separation of model, view, and controller.

JSTL is also used to show the rows of data on this view page. Listing 13.10 contains the code that displays the products available for purchase.

Listing 13.10 The Catalog page uses JSTL tags to help the readability of the JSP code.

```
<%
    Integer start = (Integer) request.getAttribute("start");
    int s = start.intValue();
%>
Catalog of Items
</h1>
<table border=1>
    <tr><th><a href="catalog?sort=id&start=<%= s %>">ID</a></th>
    <th><a href="catalog?sort=name&start=<%= s %>">NAME</a></th>
    <th><a href="catalog?sort=price&start=<%= s %>">PRICE</a></th>
    <th>Buy</th></tr>
    <c:forEach var="product" items="${outputList}">
    <tr>
        <td><c:out value="${product.id}"/></td>
        <td><c:out value="${product.name}"/></td>
        <td align='right'>
            <c:out value="${product.priceAsCurrency}"/>
        </td>
        <td>
            <form action="showcart" method="post">
                Qty: <input type="text" size="3" name="quantity">
                <input type="hidden" name="id"
                        value=<c:out value="${product.id}"/>>
                <input type="submit" value="Add to cart">
            </form>
        </td>
    </tr>
    </c:forEach>
</table>
```

You can contrast this code with the similar code in chapter 3 (section 3.5.2 and listing 3.16). This version is much better because the JSTL tag is used to output the values of the individual properties of the bean passed to this page by the controller. The version in listing 3.16 used a custom tag to output the HTML directly from Java code. In listing 13.10, a presentation expert has full access to the fields and can make changes to the look and feel of the application without touching any Java code.

Another powerful feature of JSTL is the ability to use dot notation to access embedded property values of objects. Consider the ShowCart JSP page for this Model 2 version of eMotherEarth. It appears in listing 13.11.

Listing 13.11 The ShowCart JSP uses JSTL to access the embedded product object in the CartItem class.

```
<%
    pageContext.setAttribute("cartItems", cart.getItemList());
%>
<table border=1>
    <tr>
        <c:forEach var="col" items="ID,NAME,PRICE,QUANTITY,TOTAL">
            <th><c:out value="${col}"/></th>
        </c:forEach>
    </tr>
    <c:forEach var="cartItem" items="${cartItems}">
    <tr>
        <td><c:out value="${cartItem.product.id}"/></td>
        <td><c:out value="${cartItem.product.name}"/></td>
        <td><c:out value="${cartItem.product.priceAsCurrency}"/></td>
        <td><c:out value="${cartItem.quantity}"/></td>
        <td><c:out value="${cartItem.extendedPriceAsCurrency}"/></td>
    </tr>
    </c:forEach>
    <tr>
        <td> </td>
        <td> </td>
        <td> </td>
        <td align='right'>Grand Total =</td>
        <td align='right'><%= cart.getTotalAsCurrency() %></td>
    </tr>
</table>
```

The `CartItem` and `Product` classes are related to each other. The `CartItem` class encapsulates a `Product` object so that it won't have to duplicate the information already encapsulated by `Product`. The `ShoppingCart` class composes the `CartItem` class because it includes a collection of `CartItems`. It is a composition relationship

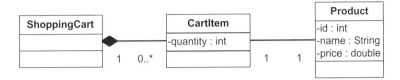

Figure 13.6 The ShoppingCart, CartItem, and Product classes are related.
ShoppingCart composes CartItem, which has a one-to-one association with a Product.

rather than an aggregation because the ShoppingCart class is responsible for the creation and destruction of the CartItem objects. The relationship between these classes is illustrated in figure 13.6.

Because of the relationship between CartItem and Product, you may find it difficult to cleanly access the encapsulated Product object. Using regular iteration scriptlets, you end up with code that looks like listing 13.12.

Listing 13.12 The embedded objects make iteration complex.

```
<table border=1>
<tr><th>ID</th><th>NAME</th><th>PRICE</th>
        <th>QUANTITY</th><th>TOTAL</th></tr>
<%
    Iterator iterator = cart.getItemList().iterator();
    while (iterator.hasNext()) {
        CartItem ci = (CartItem) iterator.next();
        pageContext.setAttribute("ci", ci);
        Product p = ci.getProduct();
        pageContext.setAttribute("p", p);
%>
<tr><td><jsp:getProperty name="p" property="id" /></td>
<td><jsp:getProperty name="p" property="name" /></td>
<td align='right'><jsp:getProperty name="p"
                        property="priceAsCurrency" /></td>
<td align='right'><jsp:getProperty name="ci"
                        property="quantity" /></td>
<td align='right'><jsp:getProperty name="ci"
                        property="extendedPriceAsCurrency" /></td>
</tr>
<%
    }
%>
<tr><td> </td><TD> </td><TD> </td>
<td align='right'>Grand Total =</td>
<td align='right'><%= cart.getTotalAsCurrency() %></td>
</tr>

</table>
```

In the iteration code, to be able to access both `CartItem` and `Product` through the standard JSP tags, you must add both to the `pageContext` collection as you iterate over the collection.

JSTL makes this job much easier. The syntax for embedded objects is much cleaner because you can directly access the embedded object using dot notation. The code in listing 13.11 performs the same task but is less cluttered by the use of the JSTL `forEach` tag instead of handcrafted iteration. Note that the chain of method calls follows the same standard Java guidelines. To get to the `Name` property of the product embedded inside `cartItem`, you write the following Java code:

```
cartItem.getProduct().getName()
```

This code is exactly equivalent to the JSTL code:

```
cartItem.product.name
```

In other words, the JSTL tag isn't looking for a public member variable when using the dot notation but rather a method that follows the standard Java naming convention for accessing methods.

13.1.3 *Sortable columns*

Users are accustomed to being able to manipulate data that they see on the screen. Most applications allow them to do so to one degree or another. Selective sorting is a facility that users are familiar with from such applications as spreadsheets and databases. When the user clicks on the title for a particular column, all the results are sorted based on that column.

As with much of the functionality users have come to expect in traditional applications, implementing this kind of dynamic behavior is more difficult in the HTTP/HTML-governed world of web applications. For a Model 2 application, the sorting is provided by the model, and the selection must be specified through the view. Like the page-at-a-time scrolling technique, sorting is handled through hyperlinks that post back to the Catalog page, passing a parameter indicating the desired sorting criteria.

Listing 13.2, the code for the catalog controller's `doPost()` method, includes the method call that handles sorting. Named `sortPagesForDisplay()`, this method appears in listing 13.13.

> **Listing 13.13 This method handles the sorting of the records for display.**

```
private void sortPagesForDisplay(HttpServletRequest request,
                                 ProductDb productDb,
                                 List outputList) {
```

```
        productDb.sortList(request.getParameter("sort"),
                           outputList);
}
```

The `sortPagesForDisplay()` method is called after the output list has already been generated. Note that it must appear after the code that decides what page's worth of records to show. The sorting must apply to the records that appear on the current page and not to the entire set of records from all pages. Thus, the sorting operation takes place on the list subset already generated by the previous methods.

The list for display is a `java.util.List` type, so the standard sorting mechanism built into Java is applicable. We need to be able to sort by a variety of criteria, so it is not sufficient to allow the `Product` class to implement the `Comparable` interface. The `Comparable` interface is used when you have a single sort criterion for a member of a collection. It allows you to specify the rules for how to sort the entities. The sort routines built into Java use these rules to determine how to sort the records. While it is possible to make the single `compareTo()` method of the `Comparable` interface handle more than one sort criterion, it is always a bad idea. This method becomes a long, brittle series of decision statements to determine how to sort based on some external criteria.

If you need to sort based on multiple criteria, you are much better off creating small `Comparator` subclasses. All the sort routines built into Java (for both the arrays and collections helpers) take an additional parameter of a class that implements the `Comparator` interface. This interface (minus the JavaDocs) appears in listing 13.14.

Listing 13.14 The Comparator interface allows the user to specify discrete sorting criteria.

```
package java.util;

public interface Comparator {

    int compare(Object o1, Object o2);
    boolean equals(Object obj);
}
```

For the `Product` sorting operation, you need the ability to sort on name, price, and ID. To that end, three `Comparator` implementers exist. Because of their similarity, only one of the three created for this application is shown (listing 13.15).

Listing 13.15 The PriceComparator class sorts Product objects based on price.

```
package com.nealford.art.emotherearth.util;

import java.util.Comparator;
import com.nealford.art.emotherearth.entity.Product;

public class PriceComparator implements Comparator {

    public int compare(Object o1, Object o2) {
        Product p1 = (Product) o1;
        Product p2 = (Product) o2;
        return (int) Math.round(p1.getPrice() - p2.getPrice());
    }

    public boolean equals(Object obj) {
        return this.equals(obj);
    }
}
```

The recipe for creating Comparator's compareTo() methods is always the same: cast the two objects passed to you by the sort routine into the type of objects you are comparing, and then return a negative, positive, or zero number indicating which object appears before the other when sorted.

Once Comparators exist, the sorting routines can use them to sort arrays or collections. The sortPagesForDisplay() method from listing 13.13 looks for a request parameter named sort. The actual sorting is done in the boundary class for products. The method called from the controller, sortList(), appears in listing 13.16.

Listing 13.16 The sortList() method is a helper method that sorts the list based on the column name passed to it.

```
public List sortList(String criteria, List theList) {
    if (criteria != null) {
        Comparator c = new IdComparator();
        if (criteria.equalsIgnoreCase("price"))
            c = new PriceComparator();
        else if (criteria.equalsIgnoreCase("name"))
            c = new NameComparator();

        Collections.sort(theList, c);
    }
    return theList;

}
```

If it is present, the appropriate Comparator class is applied to the output list. This output list is bundled in a request parameter and sent to the View page for display by the controller. The View page doesn't have to perform any additional work to display the sorted records—all the sorting is done in the boundary class, called by the controller.

The last piece of the sorting puzzle resides in the view portion, where the user specifies the sort criteria. Listing 13.10 shows the CatalogView JSP. The sorting portion of that page appears in listing 13.17.

Listing 13.17 The sorting criteria are embedded in hyperlinks at the top of the page.

```
<%
    Integer start = (Integer) request.getAttribute("start");
    int s = start.intValue();
%>
Catalog of Items
</h1>
<table border=1>
    <tr><th><a href="catalog?sort=id&start=<%= s %>">ID</a></th>
    <th><a href="catalog?sort=name&start=<%= s %>">NAME</a></th>
    <th><a href="catalog?sort=price&start=<%= s %>">PRICE</a></th>
    <th>Buy</th></tr>
```

The hyperlinks in listing 13.17 supply two values for reposting to the catalog controller. The first is the sort criteria to apply, and the second is the starting page. When the user clicks on one of these hyperlinks, the page reposts to the catalog controller, which uses these parameters to modify the contents of the page before redisplaying it.

Note that, as much as possible, the real workflow part of the application is performed in the controller. The data portions of the application are performed in the model classes. The view is very lightweight, handling display characteristics and supplying values, which allows the user to change the view via parameters sent to the controller.

Using factories

The sortList() method uses a simple set of if comparisons to determine which Comparator to apply to the list. This is sufficient for a small number of criteria but quickly becomes cumbersome if a large number of options are available. In that case, a factory class simplifies the code in the boundary class by handling the decision itself. An example of such a factory class appears in listing 13.18.

Listing 13.18 The ComparatorFactory class offloads the decision process to a singleton factory.

```
package com.nealford.art.emotherearth.util;

import java.util.Comparator;

public class ProductComparatorFactory {
    private static ProductComparatorFactory internalReference;

    private ProductComparatorFactory() {
    }

    public static ProductComparatorFactory getInstance() {
        if (internalReference == null)
            internalReference = new ProductComparatorFactory();
        return internalReference;
    }
    public synchronized final Comparator getProductComparator(
                String criteria) {
        String className = this.getClass().getPackage().getName() +
                '.' + toProperCase(criteria) + "Comparator";
        Comparator comparator = null;
        try {
            comparator = (Comparator) Class.forName(className).
                        newInstance().;
        } catch (Exception defaultsToIdComparator) {
            comparator = new IdComparator();
        }
        return comparator;
    }

    public String toProperCase(String theString) {
        return String.valueOf(theString.charAt(0)).toUpperCase() +
                theString.substring(1);
    }
}
```

Builds Comparator name from string parameter

Dynamically instantiates Comparator

Defaults to idComparator if an exception occurs

The ProductComparatorFactory class is implemented as a singleton object (so that only one of these objects will ever be created) via the static getInstance() method and the private constructor. This factory uses the name of the sort criteria to match the name of the Comparator it dynamically creates. When the developer sends a sort criterion (like name) to this factory, the factory builds up a class name in the current package with that criterion name plus "Comparator." If an object based on that class name is available in the classpath, an instance of that Comparator is returned. If not, the default IdComparator() is returned.

Using a factory in this way allows you to add new sorting criteria just by adding new classes to this package with the appropriate name. None of the surrounding code has to change. This is one of the advantages to deferring such decisions to a factory class, which can determine which instances to return.

This factory could be improved by removing the reliance on the name of the class. A superclass `Comparator` with a method indicating to what fields it is tied would remove the reliance on the name of the class matching the name of the criteria. In that case, the factory would iterate through all the potential `Comparators` and call the `getField()` method until it finds the appropriate `Comparator` object. This is easier if all the `Comparators` reside in the same package so that the factory could iterate over all the classes in that package.

13.1.4 *User interface techniques in frameworks*

Implementing page-at-a-time scrolling and sortable columns in the frameworks from part 2 is accomplished with varying degrees of difficulty. Some of the frameworks already include this behavior, whereas InternetBeans Express prevents it.

Struts

Using Struts to build the user interface elements that we've seen in the previous sections is easy. In fact, the code presented in this chapter works with few modifications. In Struts, you move the controller code to actions, but the model and view code remains the same. Of course, you can move the iteration and other display characteristics to Struts tags, but the fundamental code remains the same. Because Struts is close to a generic Model 2 application, the framework doesn't interfere with building code like this.

Tapestry

Tapestry already encapsulates the two user interface elements discussed in the previous sections. The built-in table component supports both page-at-a-time scrolling and sortable columns (see chapter 6, figure 6.6). The sortability in Tapestry is accomplished through interfaces that define the column headers. This behavior highlights one of the advantages of an all-encompassing framework like Tapestry. Chances are good that it already implements many of the common characteristics you would build by hand in other frameworks. The disadvantage appears when you want to build something that isn't already there. Because the framework is more complex, it takes longer to build additions.

WebWork

Like Tapestry, WebWork also includes a table component that features sortable columns and page-at-a-time scrolling (see chapter 7, figure 7.3). Although implemented differently from Tapestry, this behavior is still built into the framework. Even though WebWork generally isn't as complex as Tapestry, it still requires a fair amount of work to build something that isn't already supported.

InternetBeans Express

The architecture of InternetBeans Express effectively prevents this kind of customization without digging deeply into the components that make up the framework. While building applications quickly is this framework's forte, customizing the behavior of those applications is not. This is a shortcoming of overly restrictive frameworks and is common with Rapid Application Development (RAD).

Velocity

Our user interface code could easily be written using Velocity. Velocity's syntax would simplify the view portion of the code even more than JSTL. Generally, Velocity isn't complex enough to prevent adding features like the ones in this chapter. Because it is a simple framework, it tends to stay out of your way.

Cocoon

Using Extensible Server Pages (XSP), it shouldn't be difficult to build our user interface techniques in Cocoon. XSP generally follows similar rules to JSP, so the user interface portion isn't complicated. Because the web portion of Cocoon relies on Model 2, the architecture we presented in the previous sections falls right in line with a similar Cocoon application.

13.2 Building undo operations

Another common flow option in traditional applications is the ability to perform an undo operation. This feature is usually implemented as a conceptual stack, where each operation is pushed onto the stack and then popped off when the user wants to undo a series of operations. The stack usually has a finite size so that it doesn't negatively affect the operating system. After all, an infinite undo facility must either consume more memory or build a mechanism to offload the work to permanent storage of some kind.

Undo may also encompass traditional transaction processing. Ultimately, transactions that roll back can be thought of as sophisticated undo operations for a set of tables when the operation is unsuccessful. Either a database server or an application server working in conjunction with a database server normally handles transaction processing. You have two options when building undo operations for a web application: either using database transaction processing or building an in-memory undo.

13.2.1 *Leveraging transaction processing*

Most database servers handle transactions for you, at varying degrees of sophistication. The Java Database Connectivity (JDBC) API allows you to handle transactions via the `setAutoCommit()` method, which determines whether every atomic operation occurs within a transaction or if the developer decides the transaction boundaries. If the developer controls the transactions, then either a `commit()` or a `rollback()` method call is eventually issued. Modern JDBC drivers (those that support the JDBC 3 API) will also allow you to create save-points and roll back to a save-point within a larger transaction.

Transactions in Model 2 applications

In a Model 2 application, the transaction processing and other database-related activities occur in the boundary classes. In fact, if you ever find yourself importing `java.sql.*` classes into other parts of the application, you have almost certainly violated the clean separation of responsibilities.

In the eMotherEarth application, the transaction processing occurs within the `Order` boundary class. It must ensure that both order and line item records are completely written or not at all. The `addOrder()` method composes all the other methods of the class and appears in listing 13.19.

Listing 13.19 The OrderDb boundary class's addOrder() method

```java
public void addOrder(ShoppingCart cart, String userName,
                 Order order) throws SQLException {
    Connection c = null;
    PreparedStatement ps = null;
    Statement s = null;
    ResultSet rs = null;
    boolean transactionState = false;
    try {
        c = dbPool.getConnection();
        transactionState = c.getAutoCommit();
        int userKey = getUserKey(userName, c, ps, rs);
        c.setAutoCommit(false);
        addSingleOrder(order, c, ps, userKey);
        int orderKey = getOrderKey(s, rs);
```

```
            addLineItems(cart, c, orderKey);
            c.commit();
            order.setOrderKey(orderKey);
    } catch (SQLException sqlx) {
            s = c.createStatement();
            c.rollback();
            throw sqlx;
    } finally {
        try {
            c.setAutoCommit(transactionState);
            dbPool.release(c);
            if (s != null)
                s.close();
            if (ps != null)
                ps.close();
            if (rs != null)
                rs.close();
        } catch (SQLException ignored) {
        }
    }
}
```

The `addOrder()` method retrieves a connection from the connection pool and saves the transaction state for the connection. This behavior allows the transaction state to be restored before it is placed back into the pool. If you are creating your own connections every time you need one, you don't have to. If you are reusing connections from a pool or cache, you should also make sure that they go back into the pool with the same state they had when they came out.

The `addOrder()` method gets a connection, starts a transaction implicitly by calling `setAutoCommit(false)`, and calls the `addSingleOrder()` method. After obtaining the key of the new order, it adds the line items associated with this order and commits the transaction. If any operation fails, a `SQLException` is generated and the entire operation is rolled back.

None of the code in any of the called methods is in any way unusual—it is typical JDBC code for entering values into a table. Note that all database access, including the transaction processing, occurs in the boundary class. The boundary class accepts entity objects and handles persisting them into the database. It would be easy to change database servers (even to change to something radically different, like an object-oriented database server) and modify the code in this boundary class only. Chapter 12 describes the process of taking a Model 2 application and porting it to Enterprise JavaBeans by making changes to only the boundary classes.

Handling generated keys

One behavior that is not handled in a standard way across database servers is key generation. Most database servers have a facility for generating keys automatically. However, key generation is not part of the ANSI SQL standard, so each database server is free to implement it in any way it likes. In our sample, this detail is handled in the addOrder() method via the call to getOrderKey(), which uses the features specific to MySQL to retrieve the last-generated key. Listing 13.20 shows the getOrderKey() method.

Listing 13.20 The getOrderKey() method retrieves the last key generated for this connection to the database.

```
private int getOrderKey(Statement s, ResultSet rs) throws
        SQLException {
    rs = s.executeQuery("SELECT LAST_INSERT_ID()");
    int orderKey = -1;
    if (rs.next())
        orderKey = rs.getInt(1);
    else
        throw new SQLException(
                "Order.addOrder(): no generated key");
    return orderKey;
}
```

MySQL includes a built-in stored procedure that returns the last key generated for this connection to the database. This procedure protects against a large number of concurrent users inserting new records because it returns the key for the record associated with this connection. Notice that this forces our application to use the same connection across method calls because the key generation is tied to the database connection.

Because this procedure is not standardized across database servers, you should always be careful to isolate this behavior into its own method, decoupling it from the rest of the application. If you change database servers, you should be able to change this single method and not have to change the surrounding code. Separation of responsibilities and loose coupling works on both a micro and a macro level.

Transactions via JSTL

JSTL includes SQL-specific custom tags that allow transaction processing within the JSP. It works with the SQL-based tags also defined in JSTL. Listing 13.21 shows a couple of examples of using the transaction tag in JSTL.

Listing 13.21 JSTL includes a transaction tag that works with the SQL tags.

```
<h2>Creating table using a transaction</h2>

<sql:transaction dataSource="${example}">
  <sql:update var="newTable">
    CREATE TABLE PRODUCTS (
      ID INTEGER NOT NULL AUTO_INCREMENT,
      NAME VARCHAR(100),
      PRICE DOUBLE PRECISION,
      CONSTRAINT PK_ID PRIMARY KEY (ID)
      )
  </sql:update>
</sql:transaction>

<h2>Populating table in one transaction</h2>

<sql:transaction dataSource="${example}">
  <sql:update var="updateCount">
    INSERT INTO PRODUCTS (NAME, PRICE) values ("Snow", 2.45);
  </sql:update>
  <sql:update var="updateCount">
    INSERT INTO PRODUCTS (NAME, PRICE) values ("Dirt", 0.89);
  </sql:update>
  <sql:update var="updateCount">
    INSERT INTO PRODUCTS (NAME, PRICE) values ("Sand", 0.15);
  </sql:update>
</sql:transaction>
```

The ability to handle transactions directly within a JSP page is handy for small applications, but you should avoid using it in most applications. This facility was intended to make it easy for you to create web applications completely within JSP—without being forced to embed scriptlet code. One of its goals is to create RAD kinds of environments for JSP. The problem with this code is that it violates the tenets of Model 2 applications, namely the separation of responsibilities. While convenient, it introduces undesirable design flaws in your application. Therefore, I recommend that you don't use these tags, and use a cleaner Model 2 architecture instead.

13.2.2 *Using the Memento design pattern*

Transaction processing works nicely for information persisted in relational databases. It is the best kind of code to leverage—someone else wrote it, debugged it, and stands behind it! However, situations arise when you don't want to make use of transaction processing. For example, you may want to keep information in memory and not bother persisting it to permanent storage until a certain milestone is reached. The perfect example of this kind of information is the shopping cart in an e-commerce application. The shopper may never check out but instead abandon the shopping cart and wander away to another site without notifying your application. Beyond transaction-processing behavior, you might also want to make available undo behavior in your web application. This amounts to a kind of in-memory transaction processing, although the semantics are different.

Undo operations in traditional applications are typically handled via the Memento design pattern. The intent behind this pattern is to capture and externalize an object's internal state so that the object can be restored to the original state, all without violating encapsulation. Three participant classes exist for Memento, as shown in table 13.1.

Table 13.1   Participant classes of the Memento design pattern

Participant	Function
Memento	Stores the state of the original object and protects against access of that state by external objects.
Originator	Creates the Memento containing a snapshot of its state and uses the Memento to restore its state.
Caretaker	Holds onto the Memento without operating on it or spying on its internal state.

The relationship between these participants is illustrated in figure 13.7.

The Originator is the class whose state needs to be stored, and the Memento is where that state is stored. The Caretaker holds onto the Memento until the Originator needs it back. The Caretaker may encapsulate a collection of Mementos. When used for undo, the Caretaker usually keeps the Mementos in an undo stack.

Creating bookmarks in eMotherEarth

Using the Memento design pattern in a web application is slightly different than the implementation in traditional applications. This is a frequent side effect of applying design patterns to architectures beyond their original intent. For the

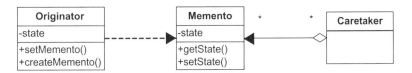

Figure 13.7   The participant classes in the Memento design pattern revolve around their relationship to the Memento class.

eMotherEarth application, we will allow the user to create bookmarks in their shopping cart. For example, the user can buy several related items, create a bookmark, and then later roll back to that bookmark. The bookmark facility uses a stack, which means users can create as many bookmarks as they like and unroll them in the reverse order from which they were created.

The first step is to create the Memento class. This class must access the private data of the ShoppingCart class without exposing it to the outside world. The best way to handle this in Java is with an *inner* class. Inner classes can access the private member variables of the outer class without exposing the encapsulated data to the rest of the world. The updated version of the ShoppingCart class is shown in listing 13.22.

Listing 13.22 The updated ShoppingCart class

```
package com.nealford.art.memento.emotherearth.util;

import java.io.Serializable;
import java.text.NumberFormat;
import java.util.ArrayList;
import java.util.Iterator;
import java.util.List;

import com.nealford.art.memento.emotherearth.entity.CartItem;

public class ShoppingCart implements Serializable {
    private List itemList;
    private static final NumberFormat formatter =
            NumberFormat.getCurrencyInstance();

    public ShoppingCart() {
        itemList = new ArrayList(5);
    }

    public void addItem(CartItem ci) {
        itemList.add(ci);
    }

    public double getCartTotal() {
        Iterator it = itemList.iterator();
        double sum = 0;
        while (it.hasNext())
            sum += ((CartItem) it.next()).getExtendedPrice();
        return sum;
    }

    public String getTotalAsCurrency() {
        return formatter.format(getCartTotal());
    }

    public java.util.List getItemList() {
```

```
        return itemList;
    }
    public ShoppingCartMemento setBookmark() {
        ShoppingCartMemento memento = new ShoppingCartMemento();
        memento.saveMemento();
        return memento;
    }
    public void restoreFromBookmark(ShoppingCartMemento memento) {
        this.itemList = memento.restoreMemento();
    }
    public class ShoppingCartMemento {
        private List itemList;

        public List restoreMemento() {
            return itemList;
        }

        public void saveMemento() {
            List mementoList = ShoppingCart.this.itemList;
            itemList = new ArrayList(mementoList.size());
            Iterator i = mementoList.iterator();
            while (i.hasNext())
                itemList.add(i.next());
        }
    }
}
```

Sets a bookmark

Restores a bookmark

Stores state information

The important change to the ShoppingCart class is the inclusion of the inner class ShoppingCartMemento. It includes a single private member variable of type List. This is the variable that will hold the current state of the shopping cart list when a bookmark is set. The restoreMemento() method simply returns the list. The save-Memento() method is responsible for taking a snapshot of the state of the shopping cart. To do this, it must access the private member variable from the outer shopping cart class. The syntax for this in Java uses the class name followed by this, followed by the member variable:

```
List mementoList = ShoppingCart.this.itemList;
```

Even though itemList is private in ShoppingCart, it is available to the inner class. This relationship is perfect for the Memento pattern, where the Memento needs access to the private member variables of the Originator without forcing the Originator to violate encapsulation.

The ShoppingCart class has two new methods: setBookmark() and restoreFrom-Bookmark(). The setBookmark() method creates a new Memento, saves the current state, and returns it. The `restoreFromBookmark()` method accepts a `Memento` and restores the state of the `itemList` back to the list kept by the `Memento`.

The Caretaker

For a web application, the session object is the perfect `Caretaker` for the `Memento`. It is tied to a particular user and contains arbitrary name-value pairs. However, saving a single `Memento` isn't very useful, and saving a stack of `Mementos` is just as easy as saving one. So, in the eMotherEarth application we allow the user to keep a stack of `Mementos`. This process is managed by the controller servlet. The updated `doPost()` method in the ShowCart controller servlet appears in listing 13.23.

Listing 13.23 The ShowCart controller acts as the Memento Caretaker.

```
public void doPost(HttpServletRequest request,
                   HttpServletResponse response) throws
      ServletException, IOException {
   RequestDispatcher dispatcher = null;
   HttpSession session = redirectIfSessionNotPresent(
         request, response, dispatcher);
   ShoppingCart cart = getOrCreateShoppingCart(session);
   Stack mementoStack = (Stack) session.getAttribute(
         MEMENTO_STACK_ID);
   if (request.getParameter("bookmark") != null)
      mementoStack = handleBookmark(cart, mementoStack);
   else if (request.getParameter("restore") != null)
      handleRestore(session, cart, mementoStack);
   else
      handleAddItemToCart(request, session, cart);
   if (mementoStack != null && !mementoStack.empty()) {
      request.setAttribute("bookmark", new Boolean(true));
      session.setAttribute(MEMENTO_STACK_ID, mementoStack);
   }
   dispatcher = request.getRequestDispatcher("/ShowCart.jsp");
   dispatcher.forward(request, response);
}
```

The ShowCart controller servlet now has three distinct paths of execution. The first path is the one from the previous version: adding an item to the shopping cart and forwarding to the show cart view. Two additional execution paths have been added. The first allows the user to set a bookmark, and the second allows the user to restore from a bookmark. The path of execution is determined by request parameters that are encoded if the show cart JSP reposts to this page. The body of the `doPost()` method checks for these request parameters and routes control appropriately.

The `handleBookmark()` method (listing 13.24) is invoked if the user has decided that he or she wants to bookmark the shopping cart.

Listing 13.24 This method handles generating a bookmark and saving it.

```
private Stack handleBookmark(ShoppingCart cart,
                            Stack mementoStack) {
    if (mementoStack == null) {
        mementoStack = new Stack();
    }
    mementoStack.push(cart.setBookmark());
    return mementoStack;
}
```

The `handleBookmark()` method checks to see if a stack already exists; if not, it creates one. In either case, it generates a new `Memento` from the `cart` object and pushes it onto the stack. The symmetrical `handleRestore()` method (listing 13.25) does the opposite—it pops the `Memento` off the stack and restores the `cart` contents.

Listing 13.25 The handleRestore() method restores the state back to the most recent bookmark.

```
private void handleRestore(HttpSession session,
                           ShoppingCart cart,
                           Stack mementoStack) {
    if (mementoStack == null)
        return;
    cart.restoreFromBookmark(
        (ShoppingCart.ShoppingCartMemento)
        mementoStack.pop());
    if (mementoStack.empty()) {
        session.removeAttribute(MEMENTO_STACK_ID);
    }
}
```

The `handleRestore()` method also removes the `Memento` stack from the session if the stack is empty, effectively relieving the session from its caretaker role.

The user interface for the shopping cart must change marginally to provide the user with a way to create and restore bookmarks. To that end, we've added a Create Bookmark button and, in case the `Memento` stack exists, we've added a Restore From Bookmark button as well. The updated user interface appears in figure 13.8.

The last portion of the controller servlet that manages bookmarks appears near the bottom of the `doPost()` method. It checks to see if a `Memento` stack exists

Figure 13.8
The user interface for the ShowCart page now incorporates buttons for managing bookmarks.

and, if it does, it adds a request parameter as a flag to the view to create the Restore button. It also updates the session with the current `Memento` stack.

The user interface JSP checks to see if the request parameter is available and shows the Restore button if it is. The updated portion of the ShowCart JSP appears in listing 13.26.

Listing 13.26 The ShowCart JSP must check to see if restoring from a bookmark should be presented as an option.

```
<form action="showcart" method="post">
<input type="submit" name="bookmark" value="Create bookmark">
<%
    if (request.getAttribute("bookmark") != null) {
%>
<input type="submit" name="restore" value="Restore from bookmark">
<%
    }
%>
</form>
```

The user interface currently does not provide any visual feedback indicating which records appear at each bookmark marker. It is certainly possible to color-code the records or provide some other indication of the bookmark boundaries.

As with other user interface techniques in Model 2 applications, most of the work appears in the model and controller, with supporting elements in the JSP. Undo using the Memento design pattern is fairly easy to implement in web applications because of the ready availability of the session, which is an ideal caretaker. The use of inner classes helps achieve the original intent of the pattern, exposing the inner workings of the `Originator` only enough to enable the snapshot and restoration through the `Memento`.

13.2.3 *Undo in frameworks*

Because most of the activity in building undo with transaction processing appears in the boundary classes, it is easy to add it to the Model 2 frameworks. Internet-Beans Express also facilitates this type of undo operation because the data-aware components are transaction aware. Thus, adding transaction processing to that framework is even simpler (it consists of setting a property).

Using Memento is also easy in Model 2 frameworks. For the lighter-weight ones, the same pattern of code that appears in the previous section works because they all support the standard web APIs, like `HttpSession`. The other medium-to-heavyweight frameworks also support using Memento, albeit with different mechanisms for the caretaker. In Tapestry, the caretaker moves to the `Visit` object, which is available to all the pages. In WebWork, it moves to WebWork's own session object, which is similar in intent but different in implementation to the standard `HttpSession`. Cocoon supports `HttpSession`, so no change is necessary.

13.3 *Using exception handling*

Java developers are familiar with exception handling and how exception-handling syntax works in the language, so I won't rehash that material here. However, many developers are reluctant to create their own exception classes. It is also important to distinguish between fundamental types of exceptions.

13.3.1 *The difference between technical and domain exceptions*

The Java libraries define a hierarchy of exception classes, starting with `Throwable` at the top of the tree. Most methods in libraries in Java throw exceptions tuned to the kinds of potential problems in that method. All these exceptions fall into the broad category of *technical exceptions*. A technical exception is one that is raised for some technical reason, generally indicating that something is broken from an infrastructure level. Technical exceptions are related to the area of how you are building the application, not why. Examples of technical exceptions are Class-NotFoundException, NullPointerException, SQLException, and a host of others. Technical exceptions come from the Java libraries or from libraries created by other developers. Frequently, if you use a framework developed by others, they have included technical exceptions in their methods to indicate that something is either broken or potentially broken.

Domain exceptions are exceptions that relate to the problem domain you are writing the application around. These exceptions have more to do with a business rule violation than something broken. Examples of domain exceptions include ValidationException, InvalidBalanceException, NoNullNameException, and any other exception you create to signify that some part of the application is violating its intended use. Domain exceptions are ones you create yourself and use within the application to help with the application flow.

13.3.2 *Creating custom exception classes*

Java makes it easy to create your own exception classes. At a minimum, you can subclass the Exception class and provide your own constructor that chains back to the superclass constructor. Listing 13.27 shows an example of such a lightweight exception class.

> **Listing 13.27 A custom exception that provides a new child of the Exception class**

```
public class InvalidCreditCardNumberException extends Exception {
    public InvalidCreditCardNumber(String msg) {
        super(msg);
    }
}
```

Instead of creating a lightweight class like this, it is possible to generate a new Exception object and pass the error message in it:

```
throw new Exception("Invalid Credit Card Number");
```

The problem with this approach is not the generation of the exception but the handling of it. If you throw a generic exception, the only way to catch it is with a catch block for the Exception class. It will catch your exception, but it will also catch every other exception that subclasses Exception, which encompasses most of the exceptions in Java. You are better off creating your own exception sub-classes to handle specific problems. There is no penalty for creating lots of classes in Java, so you shouldn't scrimp on exception classes.

If you extend `Exception`, you must provide a `throws` clause in any method where your exception might propagate. Checked exceptions and the mandated `throws` clause are actually one of the better safety features of the Java language because they prevent developers from delaying writing exception-handling code. This type of code isn't glamorous, so many developers like to put it off or avoid it. Other languages (such as C++) make it all too easy to do this. The checked exception mechanism in Java forces developers to handle exceptions where they occur and deal with them. Often, developers will say something like, "I know I should have some error-handling code here—I'll come back later and add it." But "later" never comes because one rarely has the luxury of extra time at the end of a project.

If you feel you must short-circuit the propagation mechanism in Java (and occasionally there are legitimate reasons for doing so), you can create your exception to subclass `RuntimeException` instead of `Exception`. `RuntimeException` is the parent class for all unchecked exceptions in Java, such as `NullPointerException`, `ArrayIndexOutOfBoundsException`, and many more. The semantic distinction between `Exception` and `RuntimeException` lies with their intended use. `Runtime-Exception` and its subclasses are bugs lying in the code, waiting for repair. They are unchecked because the developer should correct the code and the application cannot reasonably handle them. While it is possible to create domain exceptions based on `RuntimeException`, it is not recommended. `RuntimeExceptions` represent a flaw in the infrastructure code of the application and shouldn't mix with domain exceptions. Forcing developers to handle checked domain exceptions is not a burden but an opportunity afforded by the language to make your code more robust.

13.3.3 Where to catch and handle exceptions

It is impossible to generalize too much about where exceptions occur and are handled in Model 2 applications. Entities typically throw domain exceptions; boundary classes and other infrastructure classes tend to throw technical exceptions. In both cases, the controller is usually where the exception is handled. For example, in the eMotherEarth application, each boundary class must have a reference to the database connection pool. If they don't, they throw an exception. For this purpose, a `PoolNotSetException` class resides in the project (listing 13.28).

```
package com.nealford.art.emotherearth.util;

public class PoolNotSetException extends RuntimeException {
    private static final String STANDARD_EXCEPTION_MESSAGE =
            "Pool property not set";

    public PoolNotSetException(String msg) {
        super(STANDARD_EXCEPTION_MESSAGE + ":" + msg);
    }
}
```

The custom exception class in listing 13.28 extends `RuntimeException` to prevent it from cluttering up controller code by forcing an exception catch. It also contains a predefined message, to which the users of this exception can add as they generate the exception. This exception is used in the `ProductDb` boundary class:

```
if (dbPool == null) {
    throw new PoolNotSetException("ProductDB.getProductList()");
}
```

Rethrowing exceptions

Often, you are writing low-level library code that is called from many layers up by application code. For example, if you are writing a `Comparator` class to make it easy to sort within a boundary object, you have no idea what type of application (desktop, web, distributed, etc.) will ultimately use your code. You must handle an exception, but you don't really know the proper way to handle it within the method you are writing. In these cases, you can catch the checked exception and rethrow it as another kind, either as a `RuntimeException` or as a custom domain exception. An example of this technique appears in the `getProductList()` method (listing 13.29) of the `ProductDb` boundary class.

```
public List getProductList() {
    if (dbPool == null) {
        throw new PoolNotSetException(
                "ProductDB.getProductList()");
    }
    if (productList.isEmpty()) {
        Connection c = null;
        Statement s = null;
```

```
        ResultSet resultSet = null;
        try {
            c = dbPool.getConnection();
            s = c.createStatement();
            resultSet = s.executeQuery(SQL_ALL_PRODUCTS);
            while (resultSet.next()) {
                Product p = new Product();
                p.setId(resultSet.getInt("ID"));
                p.setName(resultSet.getString("NAME"));
                p.setPrice(resultSet.getDouble("PRICE"));
                productList.add(p);
            }
        } catch (SQLException sqlx) {                          ⟵─┐ Rethrows an
            throw new RuntimeException(sqlx.getMessage());   ⟵─┘ exception
        } finally {
            try {
                dbPool.release(c);
                resultSet.close();
                s.close();
            } catch (SQLException ignored) {
            }
        }
    }
    return productList;
}
```

Empty catch blocks

One of the frowned-upon tendencies in some Java developers is to create empty catch blocks to get code to compile. This is a bad thing because now the checked exception is raised and swallowed, and the application continues (or tries to continue) to run. Usually, the application will break in a totally unrelated place, making it difficult to track down the original error. For this reason, empty catch blocks are discouraged.

However, there is one situation where they make sense. If you look at the end of listing 13.29, the database code must close the statement and result set in the `finally` block. Both the `close()` methods throw checked `SQLException`s. In this case, as you are cleaning up, the worst thing that can happen is that the statement has already closed. In this case, it makes sense to include an empty catch block. To keep from having to write a comment to the effect of "I'm not lazy—this catch block intentionally left blank," name the instance variable in the catch block `ignored`. This is a self-documenting technique that keeps you from having to document it because it is documented by the variable name.

Redirecting to an error JSP

One of the nice automatic facilities in JSP is the ability to flag a page as the generic error page for the application. If any unhandled exceptions occur from other JSPs, the user is automatically redirected to the error page specified at the top of the source page. The error page has access to a special implicit exception object so that it can display a reasonable error message.

When you're building Model 2 applications, the controller won't automatically forward to an error page if something goes wrong. However, you can still forward to the error page yourself and take advantage of the implicit exception object. Before you forward to the error page, you can add the exception with a particular name that the error page is expecting. The CheckOut controller in eMotherEarth handles an insertion error by redirecting to the JSP error page. See this code in listing 13.30.

Listing 13.30 The CheckOut controller forwards to the JSP error page to inform the user that an exception occurred.

```
try {
    orderDb.addOrder(sc, user, order);
} catch (SQLException sqlx) {
    request.setAttribute(
        "javax.servlet.jsp.jspException", sqlx);
    dispatcher = request.getRequestDispatcher("/SQLErrorPage.jsp");
    dispatcher.forward(request, response);
    return;
}
```

The JSP error page looks for a request attribute named `javax.servlet.jsp.jspException` to populate the implicit exception object. The destination page has no idea if the JSP runtime or the developer added this attribute. This approach allows you to consolidate generic error handling across the application. If you want more control over the application-wide exception handling, you can write your own controller/view pair to handle exceptions generically.

13.3.4 Exceptions in frameworks

The Model 2 frameworks' exception-handling code generally follows the guidelines we stated earlier. Entities typically throw domain exceptions, and boundary classes and other infrastructure classes typically throw technical exceptions. In both cases, the controller is where the exception is handled. The frameworks themselves frequently throw exceptions, which fall under the category of technical exceptions. These exceptions are best handled in the controller or controller proxy classes (i.e., an `Action` class).

Handling exceptions in the two frameworks that try to mimic the event-driven nature of desktop applications is more difficult. An exception in a desktop application represents a state, and the propagation depends on the current call stack. It is much harder to emulate this call stack state in a web application, because the user always sees a fully unwound call stack. Tapestry has good mechanisms in place for both mimicking event-driven behaviors and handling exceptions. InternetBeans Express makes artificial exception state management more difficult because it uses a thinner veneer over the components it uses.

13.4 Summary

Users tend to request features in web applications that they have seen in desktop or other web applications. Many of these requests relate to the flow of information in the application. Building usable web applications in Model 2 applications generally touch all three moving parts: the controller, the model, and the view. These three pieces work together to provide an attractive application.

The flexibility of Model 2 applications makes it easy to implement even the most complex user requirements. Keeping the application well partitioned and the parts separate requires diligent effort, but it pays off in the long run with easy-to-maintain and scalable applications.

In the next chapter, we look at performance in web applications and how to measure and improve it.

Performance

This chapter covers

- Profiling
- Common performance pitfalls
- Pooling
- Designing for scalability

It is rare for users to complain that an application is simply "too fast to use." However, the opposite problem is common. Performance is a critical part of any web application. It is more important to consider performance early in the design and architecture phases of web projects than in traditional applications. Sometimes, traditional applications may be retrofitted to increase their performance. But because of the distributed nature of web applications, you may find it more difficult to improve performance after the fact. This is particularly true if the application is poorly designed.

In this chapter, we explore optimizing the performance of your web applications. We discuss memory management, including ways to measure memory (so that you'll know how much is being wasted) as well as optimization techniques. Several areas are candidates for optimization, and we examine each in turn. We also take a look at designing an application for scalability from the outset and discuss the ultimate scalability option in Java: Enterprise JavaBeans. Finally, we look at pooling options, one of the keys to building truly efficient, high-performance web applications.

14.1 Profiling

How can you tell how efficient an application is unless you have a way to measure that efficiency? Even though you may *think* that you know where a bottleneck exists in your application, until you have a technique of objective measurement you can't be certain. By measuring memory usage and other characteristics, you can get an objective look at your application and determine where you should spend your best efforts to improve it.

Using an objective measurement is also important if you are dealing with a variety of infrastructure elements. By definition, you are dealing with a distributed application when you build web applications, and frequently this involves external resources such as databases, web servers, and other elements out of your direct control. By creating accurate measurements, you can stop the acrimonious finger-pointing that occurs in some organizations ("It's the network … No, it's the database server … No, it's the application") and start to solve the real underlying problem.

14.1.1 Measuring memory

The first step in optimizing the memory of an application is to measure it. However, there is no simple way to determine the actual amount of memory your application is using, partly because of the technique used by the Java Virtual Machine (JVM) to measure memory.

The JVM manages its own memory and therefore maintains its own memory heap, separate from the underlying operating system. Most VMs are designed to allocate memory from the operating system as needed by the application, up to a maximum you specify as the VM starts up. You can specify the maximum memory that the VM is allowed to allocate by using the -Xmx flag:

```
java –Xmx128m <other options>
```

This command utilizes one of the -X command-line switches, which are VM extensions and therefore nonstandard (and subject to change in future versions of the VM). You can also tune the VM to start with a specific heap size by using the -Xms switch:

```
java –Xms64m <option options>
```

In any case, the VM manages its own memory once it has allocated that memory from the operating system.

This behavior complicates the process of measuring how much memory a given Java application is actually using. If you use the tools provided with the operating system, you see only how much memory is allocated to the VM, not how much memory your application is currently using. In other words, you only see the heap size, not the actual memory allocated on the heap. For example, the Windows Task Manager shows you how much is allocated for Tomcat but not how much your application is using, as shown in figure 14.1.

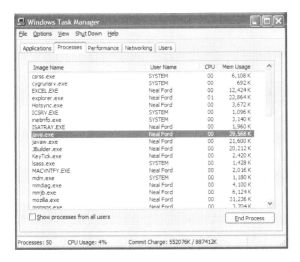

Figure 14.1
The Windows Task Manager shows you how much memory is allocated to the VM, but not how much of that memory is actually in use at the current time.

Even if you could determine how much memory is in use for the VM (rather than how much is allocated), you'd still have a problem. The amount of memory isn't independent of the container running your code. By definition, if you are running a web application, it must be running in a servlet engine. Thus, the memory measurements are of the servlet engine, not your code. The prospect of finding out how much your application is using is so daunting that it seems like it isn't even worth trying. However, there are techniques and tools that can help.

Using the Java Runtime class to determine memory

The VM can report to you how much memory it is using versus the amount allocated on the heap. The `Runtime` class has a few memory-related methods, shown in table 14.1.

Table 14.1   The Java Runtime class's memory-related methods

Method	Description
freeMemory()	Returns the amount of free memory in the VM
totalMemory()	Returns the total amount of memory in the VM
maxMemory()	Returns the maximum amount of memory the VM will attempt to use

To put these methods to work, you must write code in your application that periodically takes "snapshots" of the memory and generates statistics. This is time consuming but effective, because you can decide precisely where you want to measure memory statistics. One option is to output memory information to the console window via calls to `System.out.println()`. Another alternative is to use the logging facilities discussed in chapter 16.

14.1.2 Performance profiling

Memory isn't the only resource worth measuring. Frequently, a combination of memory use, CPU cycles consumed, network throughput, and other factors contribute to the performance of the application. Tools are available to help you measure these elements, including some that are built into the Software Development Kit (SDK).

Using the SDK profiler

The VM includes a memory profiler, activated by an `-X` command-line switch. Like the other extension switches, it is nonstandard and may go away in the future (although it has survived for a very long time):

```
java -Xrunhprof <other options>
```

This compiler switch has a variety of configuration options. To get a full list of the options, run it with the `help` option:

```
java -Xrunhprof:help
```

This command prints out a list of the available profiling options and parameters. A typical version of the command line is something like this:

```
java -Xrunhprof:cpu=samples,heap=sites,file=c:/temp/java.hprof.txt
```

This command line specifies that the memory heap information is organized by sites and that the output is sent to the specified file.

The built-in profiler uses the method-sampling technique of memory profiling, meaning that it takes a snapshot of the call stack at regular (frequent) intervals. The theory behind this type of profiler relies on the statistical fact that methods that appear more often at the top of the call stack are being called more often and/or are taking longer to execute. This common technique isn't code invasive, which means that you don't have to make changes to your source code to get it to work.

The profiler generates a large text file named java.hprof.txt (you can change the name via a command-line switch). The file is text by default, but a binary format is also available. The output may be streamed through a socket, which supports the creation of a remote profiling setup. The file is separated into multiple sections; each section covers a specific kind of information about the profile, as shown in table 14.2.

Table 14.2   Profiler output sections

Section	Description
THREAD START / END	Marks the beginning and ending of each thread's lifetime.
TRACE	A series-truncated Java stack trace (the number of entries is controlled by a command-line option). Each trace is numbered, and a profile file contains hundreds or thousands of traces.
HEAP DUMP	A complete snapshot of all the live objects currently allocated on the heap.
SITES	A sorted list of all the allocation sites and the trace that generated them.
CPU SAMPLES	A statistical profile of program execution. These are generated by the regular snapshots by the VM and consist of traces. The top-ranked traces are hotspots in the program.

continued on next page

Table 14.2   Profiler output sections *(continued)*

Section	Description
CPU TIME	Measures the time spent in a particular method, identified by its trace.
MONITOR TIME	A measure of thread contentions caused by the monitor thread waiting to enter a method.
MONITOR DUMP	A complete snapshot of all monitors and threads in the system.

The document created by the profiler is very large. For a sample two-page web application running under Tomcat, the profiler output consisted of 90,150 lines, weighing in at 5.21MB. The best way to make use of this document is to use one section to discover the information you need in another section. Here is a recipe for gleaning useful information from this profile output:

1   Use the CPU SAMPLES section to find out which methods are taking the most time.

2   Find the TRACE information about that entry.

3   Refer to the TRACE section to find out what method is being called and whether it can be optimized.

4   Repeat for a reasonable number of CPU SAMPLES.

To use the profiler with your servlet engine of choice, you need to modify the startup command for the servlet engine to include the profiler command line. Most servlet engines will allow you to get to their startup command. For this sample, we changed the batch file that starts Tomcat (called catalina.bat) to include the command-line switch to enable profiling. To avoid breaking anything (and to make it easy to switch back and forth), we created a new version of the startup file named catalina_prof.bat. Now, we can run Tomcat in the profiler—or not, depending on how it starts.

Here is a sample. For the profile generated from our simple site, let's look at the CPU SAMPLES section. The top part appears in listing 14.1.

Listing 14.1   The top portion of the CPU SAMPLES section generated by the VM profiler

```
CPU SAMPLES BEGIN (total = 2177) Mon Jan 27 09:52:53 2003
rank   self  accum   count trace method
  1 30.23% 30.23%     658 16000 java.net.PlainSocketImpl.socketAccept
  2  3.95% 34.18%      86   269 java.util.zip.ZipFile.read
```

```
3   2.02% 36.20%    44   5051 java.io.WinNTFileSystem.canonicalize
4   1.98% 38.17%    43    960 java.io.WinNTFileSystem.canonicalize
5   0.96% 39.14%    21   8274 java.lang.Object.clone
6   0.92% 40.06%    20    178 java.lang.StringBuffer.expandCapacity
```

By looking at the last entry for CPU_SAMPLES, you can see that the StringBuffer's expandCapacity() method is using less than 1 percent of the accumulated execution time and that it is tied to trace 178. By searching in the TRACE section, you can see the stack trace for trace 178, which appears in listing 14.2.

Listing 14.2 The TRACE section for the time-consuming operation found from the CPU SAMPLES

```
TRACE 178:
     java.lang.StringBuffer.expandCapacity(StringBuffer.java:202)
     java.lang.StringBuffer.append(StringBuffer.java:392)
     java.util.zip.ZipFile.getEntry(ZipFile.java:148)
     java.util.jar.JarFile.getEntry(JarFile.java:184)
```

Using the trace, we find that the ZipFile getEntry() method is the one calling the StringBuffer's expandCapacity() method, which is occupying a lot of time relative to the other methods in our application.

Analyzing the results

In this case, it isn't likely that we will replace the java.util.zip.ZipFile class with one of our own to speed it up (assuming that we *could* write a more efficient version). Working through this file frequently uncovers a lot of SDK classes and methods that aren't possibilities for replacement for optimization. We didn't choose one of the methods for our sample because the highest-ranking one came in at a measly 651 in the CPU SAMPLES section, and it was the Struts action we had written for the application. None of the boundary JavaBeans even made the list.

What this indicates is that you should apply logic and reasoning to the results. Why did the ZipFile class occupy so much processor time? When we ran the application, we started Tomcat, went to the two pages generated by our application, and halted the servlet engine. So, most of the time the application was running, Tomcat was managing web archive (WAR) file expansion. Thus, the ZipFile class spent a lot of time being sampled by the profiler, and it (mistakenly) looks like a hotspot.

To create realistic results, simulating a large number of concurrent users, we ran the same application with 110 simulated requests for both pages, spread out over a few minutes This time, one of our classes made it all the way up to 217, highlighting one of our database access methods. The TRACE entry appears in listing 14.3.

Listing 14.3 The profiler identified one of the database methods in our application as a potential hotspot.

```
TRACE 16541:
  com.nealford.art.strutssched.ScheduleBean.populate
                                   (ScheduleBean.java:38)
  com.nealford.art.strutssched.ViewScheduleAction.perform
                             (ViewScheduleAction.java:28)
  org.apache.struts.action.ActionServlet.processActionPerform
                                 (ActionServlet.java:1787)
  org.apache.struts.action.ActionServlet.process
                                 (ActionServlet.java:1586)
```

We *can* do something about this method! However, looking at the CPU SAMPLES, this method occupies only 0.06 percent of the CPU time. Even though it is the top of our methods, it still isn't a bottleneck in the application. Only a method that is occupying a significant amount of the CPU time is a candidate for optimization.

Keep in mind that your application doesn't execute in a vacuum. The measurements we've gathered here are hopelessly intertwined with the code from the servlet engine (Tomcat in this case). The results you obtain must be filtered to look at the code you can improve. For example, we would get completely different results if we ran this application through another servlet engine (although I would hope that the relative performance of our application elements would remain constant).

Using commercial profilers

The profile output generated by the SDK is useful, but analyzing this voluminous text file is time consuming. The results are in plain text (the binary version of the file contains the same information), so there is no easy way to view the results graphically. While the SDK profiler is useful, using it is labor intensive. The appropriate analogy here is a comparison to the debugger that ships with the SDK. While certainly functional, it is so complex and time consuming that most developers opt for an external tool to handle the job.

Numerous commercial profilers are available for Java, both for applications and web applications. These tools are relatively easy to set up, and most integrate nicely into commercial (and some open-source) integrated development environments (IDEs). Generally, these tools provide real-time analysis of memory allocation and CPU usage, and provide graphs and other niceties.

One example is Borland's Optimizeit profiler, which encompasses all the profiling capabilities from the SDK and more. In addition, it generates its output in real-time graphs to display the profiled characteristics of the application.

Figure 14.2 shows the Optimizeit graphs for a running application. The upper-left corner shows the VM heap, both graphically and numerically. The upper-right pane shows the garbage collector activity. The lower-left pane shows the number of threads running, and the lower right shows the number of classes currently loaded. As you can see, this provides a valuable snapshot of the running application's characteristics.

Another view provided by Optimizeit is the CPU profiling information (like that generated by the SDK profiler). Like the SDK profiler, it uses the CPU sampling technique of taking snapshots of the call stack at regular intervals. Figure 14.3 shows the CPU Samples window.

One of the shortcomings of the SDK profiler is that you can't filter the information it generates to find information you consider useful. Optimizeit's Filters text field allows you to eliminate all the classes except the ones you want to see.

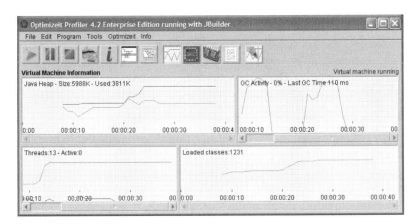

Figure 14.2 The commercial Optimizeit profiler shows a variety of VM metrics in real time, both graphically and numerically.

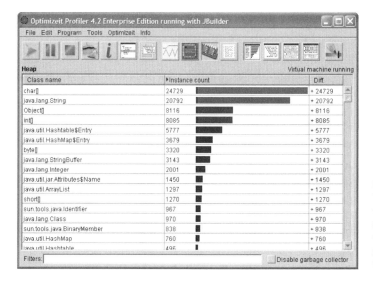

Figure 14.3
The CPU Samples window shows the same information as the SDK profiler, with graphical bars of relative time added.

Figure 14.4 shows the result of filtering our display to see the performance of the classes within our application's package (`com.nealford.*`).

This display allows you to quickly see exactly how your classes compare to the other code running in your application. That way, you can quickly pinpoint candidates for optimization in your code.

Of course, this tool also mixes your code in with the servlet engine. They are, after all, running in the same VM. However, Optimizeit provides views that let you

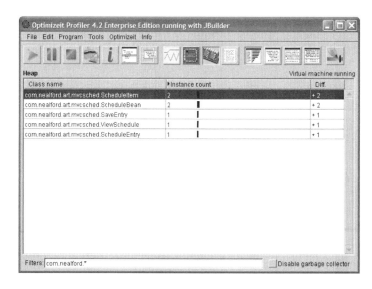

Figure 14.4
The CPU Samples page allows you to filter the display to look at certain categories of classes.

filter out the code that isn't *your* code (such as the servlet engine, database driver, and any third-party frameworks you are using). This feature is typical of the commercial profilers on the market. All of them allow you to focus quickly on particular hotspots in your application and identify candidates for improvement.

14.1.3 *Load testing*

Load-testing tools are a category of testing tools that goes hand in hand with performance profilers. These tools simulate a large number of users accessing pages in a web application to see how well it performs under load. To get a reasonable reading from any profiler on how your application will act in the real world, you need to stress-test it beyond the efforts of a single developer. One company I worked with used its intercom system to signal a large number of developers to hit the site at the same time. The only purpose this served was to annoy the receptionist (who quickly became wise to their ploy and refused further cooperation). It was not a reasonable test of the performance of the application. Load-testing tools aren't profilers, but they are symbiotic with profilers.

Numerous commercial products are available. Mercury Interactive's Load Runner is generally considered one of the best (http://www.mercuryinteractive.com). However, it is expensive, as are most tools geared toward enterprise development. An open-source load-balancing tool named JMeter offers some of the same facilities; let's take a look.

JMeter

JMeter is a Swing application designed to simulate a variety of requests made to an application, including web applications. It allows the developer to set up thread groups, each with a particular purpose. You can set up a thread group to simulate HTTP requests on a regular basis to a particular page and send specific request parameters. JMeter also allows you to establish FTP, JDBC, and a host of other load-testing requests.

JMeter includes graphs and tables that show the results of the load testing. You can set up test plans and customize them to include a variety of load tests. Figure 14.5 shows one of the graphs that display the throughput for an application being accessed randomly by a variety of simulated users.

In figure 14.5, the top line of the graph displays the throughput over time with 2000 individual samples; the bottom line shows the deviation from the average; the next-to-bottom line shows data throughput; and the second line from the top shows the average throughput. All this data is customizable and can be saved to a file. The test plan is kept in a specific file format and is reusable.

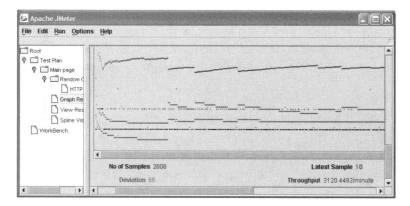

Figure 14.5   JMeter includes graphs that show throughput, deviation, and average response time for an HTTP request.

JMeter provides numerous listeners that can report on the results of the load testing under way. *Listeners* are reporting tools attached to a particular test. The graph in figure 14.5 is one example; another example is shown in figure 14.6, which displays the spline graph of average throughput over time. This graph can reveal how many users (threads) your application can handle before performance starts to degrade. JMeter doesn't require that you show the results of tests in any particular format. The listeners exist to allow you to attach the type of result you want to a given test.

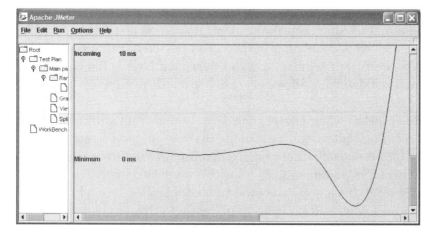

Figure 14.6   The spline graph is one of a variety of listeners that are attached to tests.

JMeter contains a large number of prebuilt test artifacts as well as the capability to build your own. It is highly customizable and provides a nonvisual mode that enables you to automate the testing. JMeter is open source, so the cost for using it consists of the time to learn how to use it. Once you have mastered it, you might consider moving to the more expensive and more capable commercial products if your needs warrant.

14.1.4 *Performance of profiling frameworks*

The performance characteristics of frameworks depend in large part on their relative size. Generally, the lighter-weight frameworks (like Struts) use less memory and other resources than the heavier-weight ones (like Tapestry or Cocoon). However, this measurement is deceiving. Even though it appears that Struts is more efficient, it isn't performing as much work as Tapestry. Tapestry already includes many of the performance-enhancing techniques covered here and in chapter 15. For example, it already pools many of the resources in the application. This fact makes it impossible to perform an "apples to apples" comparison between the two frameworks.

You can, however, perform reasonable load testing against two frameworks. After all, a load test more closely resembles the performance of the running application. In this case, the extra code in Tapestry should make it run better under high loads. After all, that is the reason for the extra code.

This strategy won't work on a framework like Cocoon, which is more than just a web framework. Cocoon also includes the publishing framework code, so it will generally run more slowly because it is performing more work. In the end, you have to decide why and how you want to use the framework and judge its performance accordingly.

14.2 *Common performance pitfalls*

Profiling is an important technique for finding and removing bottlenecks in your applications. However, the better practice is not to include bottlenecks in the first place! This way of thinking is similar to the philosophy that you wouldn't need debuggers if you just wouldn't include bugs in your code. However, it makes more sense to avoid obvious inefficiencies in your applications and let the profiler find the not-so-obvious problems.

14.2.1 *Object creation*

One of the most expensive operations in any object-oriented language is the construction of objects. It requires the VM to allocate memory and may entail many chained constructor calls before the object is available for use. One of the easiest ways to improve the performance of your application is to optimize the creation of objects as much as possible.

Stateless classes

One of the ways you can avoid creating new objects is to make all your classes *stateless*. Making a class stateless implies the following characteristics:

- No state information is kept in nonstatic member variables.

- The constructor can't set up any information (although static initializers are possible).

- All methods must be static.

- They can't be serialized (there is nothing there to serialize anyway!).

Generally, you make a class stateless by making all the methods static, which turns the class into a shell for related methods. Also, the constructor for the class should be made private so that no one will mistakenly attempt to create an instance of it. Notice that leaving a constructor off isn't sufficient, because Java will generate a parameterless constructor if no other constructor exists. Making it private prevents construction.

If the class is never constructed, then you don't have to worry about too many of them occupying memory. Conversely, you can't take any advantage of some of the object-oriented characteristics built into Java. You must decide on a case-by-case basis if the desire to manage the number of objects created entails going all the way to statelessness.

The type of class most suited for statelessness is boundary classes. These classes frequently have independent methods and don't need to keep state information internally. Frequently, boundary classes that act as a conduit to retrieve entities from a database avail themselves of statelessness because each method takes an entity as a parameter and does something with it. In this case, the only state information (the entity) is localized to the method and doesn't need to be shared with the other methods.

Statelessness is also a good strategy if you think that some of the business rules will end up in stateless session EJBs. If you think there is a good chance that the project will migrate to use EJBs, you might want to make an extra effort to create stateless methods in order to make the transition easier.

Many developers prefer singleton objects to stateless classes, which is considered a more object-oriented way to handle statelessness. Singletons also have advantages over stateless classes. First, because the singleton is an object instance, threading is easier because the singleton object can act as the synchronization point. Second, singletons can be built to create a finite number of object instances (rather than just one), which makes the singleton a factory as well. Third, some design patterns (like Strategy) rely on object instances that implement a particular interface and disallow stateless classes that are not object instances. For a good example of a singleton object, look at the factory example in chapter 13, section 13.1.3.

Object reuse

Another technique aimed at keeping the number of object constructions in check is to reuse the objects rather than create new ones. With this strategy, you don't allow objects to go out of scope when you have finished using them. Instead, you keep the object reference alive and reuse it by supplying new values for the properties.

Consider the class in listing 14.4, in particular the reset() method. Instead of allowing an object based on this class to go out of scope, you call the reset() method to return it to the same state that it had immediately after construction.

Listing 14.4 The ScheduleItem class has a reset() method to facilitate reuse.

```
package com.nealford.art.objects;

import java.io.Serializable;

public class ScheduleItem implements Serializable {
    private int duration;
    private String description;

    public ScheduleItem(int dureation, String description) {
        this.duration = duration;
        this.description = description;
    }

    public void setDuration(int duration) {
        this.duration = duration;
    }

    public int getDuration() {
        return duration;
    }
```

```
    public void setDescription(String description) {
        this.description = description;
    }

    public String getDescription() {
        return description;
    }                              Use reset() instead of
                                   allowing garbage collection
    public void reset() {  ←─┘
        this.duration = -1;
        this.description = "";
    }
}
```

Reusing existing object references is much more efficient than creating new ones. This approach works well for entity classes, which usually consist of lightweight classes with accessors, mutators, and a few business rules methods. In fact, the Struts `ActionForm` includes a `reset()` method for this very purpose so that Struts can reuse object references rather than re-create them.

One issue you face with reusing object references is where to put them. You can't let the objects go out of scope because they will be garbage-collected by the VM. The obvious choice is to place them in a pool, where they are retrieved just like database connections from a connection pool. In section 14.3, we investigate using pools to increase performance.

14.2.2 *Extraneous object references*

One performance pitfall that strikes many Java developers is keeping extraneous object references lying around. Java's garbage collection is designed to handle memory deallocation for you, but it can't do so if you keep "extra" references to objects. While every Java developer knows this, it is harder to guard against than it sounds. This is the source of apparent memory leaks in Java. A *memory leak* is an area of memory that is no longer accessible from a variable reference. Leaks are a serious problem in languages like C and C++, where the developer is responsible for memory allocation and deallocation. It is possible in these (and other languages) to allocate memory for a variable and allow it to go out of scope before the memory is reclaimed. Fortunately, it is impossible to leak memory in Java as in other languages because all memory that isn't referenced is automatically reclaimed. However, it is still possible to forget about object references.

Developers do not often create two independent variables that point to the same memory location and then forget to allow one of them to go out of scope. However, it is common to create references to variables in collections and forget

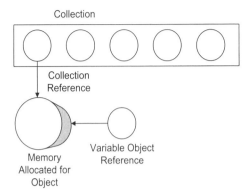

Figure 14.7
Collections hold on to memory references independently of the original object reference.

about the second reference held by the collection. This scenario is depicted in figure 14.7.

Once the variable object reference goes away, the memory allocated for the object is still alive because the collection reference still exists. Figure 14.8 illustrates this point.

The stray reference problem is acute in web development because so many collections are available and scoped for different lifetimes. For example, it is easy to place an object on the user's session and forget that it is there. Performance problems result if you have a large number of users, each with extraneous object references in their sessions. The session references will eventually go away when the session times out, but you have (by default) 30 minutes of wasted memory and performance waiting for that to happen.

As soon as an object is no longer needed in any collection, you should manually remove it. If the entire collection goes away (like the request collection), you don't have to worry about it because the collection will take the extra references

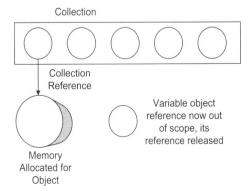

Figure 14.8
Variable object reference has been reclaimed, but the garbage collection cannot clean up the memory because the collection still holds a reference.

with it. However, for session and application collections, you must be diligent in cleaning them up; otherwise, you will inadvertently use extra memory and potentially harm the performance of your application.

It is a good rule of thumb to invalidate the user's session manually as soon as the user no longer needs it. This process is typically accomplished on a logout page (which is a good reason to have a logout page). However, users are finicky, so they don't always reliably log out. You hope that enough users cooperate to keep the session's memory from growing too rapidly. If they don't log out, the memory reclamation won't occur until the session times out.

14.2.3 String usage

This topic is well covered in almost any Java performance book, but it is worth reiterating here because using strings correctly makes an enormous difference in efficient memory usage. Web applications use strings extensively (after all, what the user eventually sees is a big long string formatted as HTML). Using strings wisely can speed up your application noticeably.

The immutability of the String class is well documented in Java, along with the implications of using the + operator to build strings. However well known a performance drag this is, many developers still use strings to build dynamic content instead of the more performance-friendly StringBuffer. The performance penalties of too much object creation is highlighted in section 14.2.2 and the + is one of the worst offenders.

Consider this line of code:

```
String s = "<BODY>" + someObj.someValue() + "</BODY>";
```

Depending on the intelligence of the compiler, you could get either of two translations. The first, using the concat() operator of String, is very inefficient:

```
String s = "<BODY>".concat(someObj.someValue()).concat("</BODY>");
```

This implementation creates two intermediate string objects that are discarded at the end of the line. The better implementation uses StringBuffer instead:

```
String s = (new StringBuffer()).append("<BODY>").
        append(someObj.someValue()).append("</BODY>").toString();
```

Creating only two objects (no matter how many concatenations are performed) is the optimal solution. The implementation details of how a compiler handles this are not mandated by Sun, so compiler writers are free to choose whatever implementation they like. It makes sense to avoid this whole issue by using a StringBuffer from the outset.

When using a `StringBuffer`, you should always specify an initial size. When Java collections and `StringBuffers` must grow, it is very time consuming because they have to allocate memory to do so. All the collections API classes handle this task by doubling by default when they need to grow. While not a collection in the strictest sense, a `StringBuffer` acts in the same way. If you give the `StringBuffer` a reasonable default size, you reduce the likelihood that it will need to grow multiple times. Even if you don't have the exact size, at least take your best guess. It is pretty certain that you can guess better than the compiler.

The `StringBuffer`'s `append()` method (along with other methods) returns the `StringBuffer` on which you are working. That means you can chain a number of append statements together:

```
StringBuffer sb = new StringBuffer(80);
sb.append("<body>").append(duration).append('\t').
        append(description).append('\n').append("</body>");
```

This is not more efficient than placing the code on separate lines, but it involves less typing. Whether you use the style of code with a `StringBuffer` is a matter of personal preference. Some developers think this is ugly, and others think it is the pinnacle of cool.

14.3 Pooling

If you have reusable object references, you have to place them somewhere. An *object pool* is a collection of memory, usually keyed, where object references can wait until they are needed to perform work. By creating a large number of objects up front and reusing them from the pool, you cut down on the constructor calls that take place while the application is running. Application servers use object pools to speed up object manipulation. In fact, application servers pool everything—database connections, threads, messages, objects, EJBs, and so forth. One of the secrets to high performance is to create resources in bunches rather than wait until they are needed.

14.3.1 Simple object pools

Object pools can range from very simple to very sophisticated. A simple object pool can consist of one of the collection classes from the SDK. For example, you can create a stack or queue to hold a collection of preconstructed entities. In a web application, this pool is initialized on application startup and placed in the application context, where it will be available to resources that need the objects.

Alternatively, you can use a lazy-loading technique to build the pool; in this scenario, objects are created as needed but instead of going out of scope, they are placed back in the pool for subsequent use. The first users of the site get the "normal" performance, whereas later users see improved performance because of cached resources.

If you implement your own pools, you do have to worry about keeping track of the objects and setting the attributes of your pool, such as minimum and maximum size. Some pools test the validity of the object as it is returned by calling a method that tests the "health" of the object. If a damaged object is returned, the pool automatically discards the object and retrieves another one.

Creating your own pool can be as simple as caching objects in the application context rather than re-creating them. However, simple object pools tend to grow in complexity over time as you realize that you need more facilities. In this case, you should move to one of the more sophisticated pools, such as the Commons pool discussed in section 14.3.3.

14.3.2 *Soft and weak references*

One problem with maintaining your own pools is the amount of memory they occupy. Ideally, you want the pool to enhance the application's performance by caching premade objects—and not hinder its performance by consuming all the memory. One way to mitigate this problem is to use *soft* or *weak* references. Both of these reference types resemble a regular object reference except that they interact more intelligently with the memory manager of the VM. If an object is held only by either a soft or a weak reference and the memory for the application becomes constrained, the VM has the option to reclaim the memory held by references. Note that this works only for object references held solely by either a soft or a weak reference.

The difference between a soft and a weak reference lies in how the VM treats them. The VM will attempt to keep soft references at the expense of weak ones. In other words, weak references are reclaimed before the soft ones. According to JavaDoc, weak references are intended for canonicalizing mappings. *Canonicalizing* objects refers to replacing multiple copies of an object with just a few objects. It is most efficient if you need a large number of reference objects. For example, if you require a large number of `Integer` objects from zero to five, it is more efficient to create six canonical objects and reuse them. This is shown in listing 14.5.

```
public class IntegerHelper {
    public static final Integer ZERO   = new Integer(0);
    public static final Integer ONE    = new Integer(1);
    public static final Integer TWO    = new Integer(2);
    public static final Integer THREE  = new Integer(3);
    public static final Integer FOUR   = new Integer(4);
    public static final Integer FIVE   = new Integer(5);
}

public class Tester {
    public void doIt(Integer i) {
        if (i == IntegerHelper.ONE) {
            doSomething();
        } else if (i == IntegerHelper.TWO) {
            doSomethingElse();
        } else . . .
```

You can create a class that stores a list of canonical integers as weak references, caching them unless the garbage collector needs to reclaim the memory. The class takes care of populating the list of references and either returning `Integer` objects from the list or re-creating them (see listing 14.6).

```
package com.nealford.art.references;

import java.lang.ref.WeakReference;
import java.util.ArrayList;
import java.util.List;

public class CanonicalInt {
    private static CanonicalInt internalReference = null;
    private static final int MAX = 100;
    private List intList;

    private CanonicalInt() {
        intList = new ArrayList(MAX);
        buildIntsToMax();
    }

    public static CanonicalInt getInstance() {
        if (internalReference == null)                    Gets the singleton
            internalReference = new CanonicalInt();        reference
        return internalReference;
    }

    private void buildIntsToMax() {
```

```
        for (int i = 0; i < MAX; i++ )
            intList.add(new WeakReference(new Integer(i)));
    }
    public synchronized Integer getCanonicalInteger(int i) {
        //-- only handle integers within range
        if (i > intList.size())
            return new Integer(i);
        Integer canonicalInt = null;
        WeakReference ref = (WeakReference) intList.get(i);
        if (ref == null ||
            ((canonicalInt = (Integer) ref.get()) == null)) {
            canonicalInt = new Integer(i);
            intList.set(i, new WeakReference(canonicalInt));
        }
        return canonicalInt;
    }
}
```

Checks the reference

Handles out-of-range requests

Gets the reference

Re-adds the reference

Pulls the object from the reference

Weak references are ideal for this type of optimization because the VM will reclaim the weak references first, meaning that you must go back to creating your own Integer objects but preserving memory. Soft references are designed for memory-intensive caches, which is the purpose of this discussion.

Soft references

Java includes a SoftReference class, which is designed to encapsulate a regular object reference and "soften" it. An example of using a SoftReference appears in listing 14.7.

Listing 14.7 An example of encapsulating an object reference inside a SoftReference

```
package com.nealford.art.references;

import java.lang.ref.SoftReference;
import java.util.ArrayList;
import java.util.List;

public class SoftReferenceTest {

    public SoftReferenceTest() {
        List softList = new ArrayList(5);

        StringBuffer s1 = new StringBuffer("Now is the time");

        softList.add(new SoftReference(s1));
        softList.add(new SoftReference(
                new StringBuffer("for all good men")));
        softList.add(new SoftReference(
                new StringBuffer("to come to the aid")));
```

StringBuffers are wrapped in SoftReferences

```
        s1 = null;

        for (int i = 0; i < softList.size(); i++) {
            StringBuffer s = (StringBuffer)
                    ((SoftReference) softList.get(i)).get();
            System.out.print("List item # " + i + '\t');
            if (s == null)
                System.out.println(" has been reclaimed");
            else
                System.out.println(s);
        }
    }

    public static void main(String[] args) {
        new SoftReferenceTest();
    }
}
```

The list item must be cast twice upon retrieval

In the `SoftReferenceTest` example, an `ArrayList` of soft references (serving as a cache) is created. The first `StringBuffer` is explicitly created, placed in the list as a soft reference, and then dereferenced. The other objects are directly added as soft references. The code is equivalent, and no advantage exists for either version. The `SoftReference` class contains a `get()` method that returns the object to which the reference points. When an item is pulled from the cache, it must be cast twice. The object returned from the list is a `SoftReference`, whose `get()` method is called to get the underlying object.

It is important if you use `SoftReferences` to implement a cache that no hard references exist to the objects in the collection. Any hard references prevent the garbage collector from reclaiming the objects. Any time you pull a soft reference from a collection, you must check to see whether the object still exists. Because `SoftReferences` are reclaimable at any time, you must always perform a null check on the returned object. If the object has been reclaimed, you have no way to get it back. It must be re-created. That means that this mechanism is not suitable for objects whose states must be persistent. This use of `SoftReference` is best for objects that have been reset to their original state and are ready to be pulled from a pool.

Weak references

The same issues exist for weak references. However, the SDK includes a collection specifically designed to make it easy to use weak references. The `WeakHashMap` class is semantically like a regular `HashMap`. The difference is that all the references in the WeakHashMap are weak references. Listing 14.8 illustrates the use of a WeakHashMap.

Listing 14.8 The WeakHashMap is a Map that holds all references as weak references.

```java
package com.nealford.art.references;

import java.util.Iterator;
import java.util.Map;
import java.util.Set;
import java.util.WeakHashMap;

public class WeakReferenceTest {

    public WeakReferenceTest() {
        StringBuffer s1 = new StringBuffer("Now is the time");

        Map weakMap = new WeakHashMap(5);
        weakMap.put("No. 1", s1);
        weakMap.put("No. 2", new StringBuffer("for all good men"));
        weakMap.put("No. 3", new StringBuffer("to come to the aid"));

        s1 = null;

        Set keySet = weakMap.keySet();
        Iterator keys =  keySet.iterator();
        while (keys.hasNext()) {
            String key = (String) keys.next();
            System.out.print("Key = " + key + '\t');
            Object o = weakMap.get(key);
            if (o == null)
                System.out.println("object has been reclaimed");
            else
                System.out.println(o);
        }
    }

    public static void main(String[] args) {
        new WeakReferenceTest();
    }
}
```

As with SoftReferences, you must always check the object you get back to ensure that it still points to a real object. Also, like SoftReferences, weak references may disappear at any time. A WeakHashMap is not thread-safe (although it can be wrapped in Collections.synchronizedMap() like any standard Map). However, even if it is synchronized, this collection acts as if another thread is removing objects if the garbage collector needs to reclaim memory.

As with a collection backed with soft references, you should not store any objects in a `WeakReference` or `WeakHashMap` that you must keep. Both these collections are suitable for pools of objects in an expendable state.

14.3.3 *Commons pools*

Pooling is such a common requirement for web applications that the Jakarta project has provided a generic solution. As stated in section 14.3.1, simple pools have a habit of growing in complexity as the needs of the application grow. Before long, what started as a simple caching mechanism grows into a full-blown object-pooling solution, with bells and whistles galore.

The Pooling component of the larger Commons project includes classes that make it relative easy to add sophisticated object pools to your application. The starting point to creating your own pools it to implement the `KeyedPoolable-ObjectFactory` interface, which appears in listing 14.9.

Listing 14.9 The Commons KeyedPoolableObjectFactory interface

```
public abstract interface KeyedPoolableObjectFactory {
    Object makeObject(Object object)
            throws Exception;

    void destroyObject(Object object, Object object1)
            throws Exception;

    boolean validateObject(Object object, Object object1);

    void activateObject(Object object, Object object1)
            throws Exception;

    void passivateObject(Object object, Object object1)
            throws Exception;
}
```

The `KeyedPoolableObjectFactory` interface includes callback methods used by the pool to manage the lifecycle events for the pool. The `makeObject()` method is called whenever the pool needs to create a new instance of one of your pooled objects. The `destroyObject()` method does the opposite and handles any cleanup required by your object (for example, returning resources such as database connections). The `validateObject()` method provides a callback that allows you to determine whether the object is a valid instance and should be returned. Finally, the `activateObject()` and `passivateObject()` methods enable you to write code in case the pool needs to move your objects out of memory. An example of a task performed in these methods is dropping a database connection upon passivation

and restore it upon activation. An instance of your class that implements this
interface is passed to the `GenericKeyedObjectPool` constructor, which creates a
keyed pool of any object you wish.

eMotherEarth with pooled boundary classes

To show how to implement the `GenericKeyedObjectPool` pool, we've modified
the eMotherEarth e-commerce site to store the boundary classes in a pool. This
version of the application features a customized view for each user (allowing
the user to sort records and utilize page-at-a-time scrolling for the catalog).
Therefore, each user needs his or her own boundary objects. This version
issues boundary objects from a pool, which are restored when the user leaves
the site. Because it is a large application, only the portions pertinent to pooling appear here. The complete sample appears in the source code archive as
art_emotherearth_cachingpool.

The first order of business is to create a class that implements the `KeyedPool-
ableObjectFactory` interface. This class is shown in listing 14.10.

Listing 14.10 The KeyedBoundaryPoolFactory class

```
package com.nealford.art.cachingpool.emotherearth.util;

import org.apache.commons.pool.KeyedPoolableObjectFactory;
import com.nealford.art.cachingpool.emotherearth.boundary.ProductDb;
import com.nealford.art.cachingpool.emotherearth.boundary.OrderDb;

public class KeyedBoundaryPoolFactory
        implements KeyedPoolableObjectFactory {

    public Object makeObject(Object key) {
        if (key.equals(com.nealford.art.cachingpool.
                    emotherearth.boundary.ProductDb.class)) {
            return new ProductDb();
        } else if (key.equals(com.nealford.art.
                cachingpool.emotherearth.boundary.OrderDb.class)) {
            return new OrderDb();
        } else
            return null;
    }

    public void destroyObject(Object key, Object obj) {
    }

    public boolean validateObject(Object key, Object obj) {
        return true;
    }

    public void activateObject(Object key, Object obj)  {
```

```
        }
    public void passivateObject(Object key, Object obj)  {
        }
    }
```

The KeyedBoundaryPoolFactory class contains the callback methods for the generic pool class. So, in the makeObject() method of this class, we must determine how to store the keyed values in the pool and how to create new ones. Because we are storing boundary objects, it makes sense to differentiate them by their class. The object passed in as the key to makeObject() is the instance of the class itself, which is available via the .class member of any class. Using the class reference will absolutely ensure that we only get an instance of the type of class that we need. Two boundary classes exist in the application (ProductDb and OrderDb), so makeObject() has the facilities to make either type.

We have no special need in this application for cleanup, so let's leave the destroyObject() method empty. Similarly, we don't bother to validate the objects, so we return true from validate. In addition, we have no need for special code to activate or passivate the objects.

Now that we have the class, we can create the generic pool. This code has been moved into a servlet named StartupConfiguration. This is a GenericServlet subclass that handles creating both the database connection pool and the boundary object pool and adds both pools to the application collection. Listing 14.11 shows this servlet.

Listing 14.11 The StartupConfiguration servlet

```
package com.nealford.art.cachingpool.emotherearth.servlet;

import javax.servlet.*;
import javax.servlet.http.*;
import java.io.*;
import java.util.*;
import com.nealford.art.cachingpool.emotherearth.util.DBPool;
import java.sql.SQLException;
import org.apache.commons.pool.impl.GenericKeyedObjectPool;
import org.apache.commons.pool.KeyedObjectPoolFactory;
import org.apache.commons.pool.KeyedPoolableObjectFactory;
import com.nealford.art.cachingpool.emotherearth.util.
        KeyedBoundaryPoolFactory;

public class StartupConfiguration extends GenericServlet {
    private static final String DRIVER_CLASS = "driverClass";
```

```
private static final String PASSWORD = "password";
private static final String DB_URL = "dbUrl";
private static final String USER = "user";
private static final String CONNECTION_POOL = "dbPool";
private static final String BOUNDARY_POOL = "boundaryPool";
private static final String POOL_MAX_ACTIVE = "poolMaxActive";
private static final String POOL_WHEN_EXHAUSTED =
        "poolWhenExhausted";

public void init() throws javax.servlet.ServletException {
    String driverClass =
            getServletContext().getInitParameter(DRIVER_CLASS);
    String password =
            getServletContext().getInitParameter(PASSWORD);
    String dbUrl =
            getServletContext().getInitParameter(DB_URL);
    String user =
            getServletContext().getInitParameter(USER);
    DBPool dbPool =
            createConnectionPool(driverClass, password, dbUrl,
            user);
    getServletContext().setAttribute(CONNECTION_POOL, dbPool);

    GenericKeyedObjectPool boundaryPool = createBoundaryPool();
    getServletContext().setAttribute(BOUNDARY_POOL,
            boundaryPool);
}

private GenericKeyedObjectPool.Config getPoolConfiguration() {
    GenericKeyedObjectPool.Config conf =
            new GenericKeyedObjectPool.Config();
    conf.maxActive = Integer.parseInt(getServletContext().
            getInitParameter(POOL_MAX_ACTIVE));
    conf.whenExhaustedAction = Byte.parseByte(
            getServletContext().getInitParameter(
            POOL_WHEN_EXHAUSTED)) ;
    return conf;
}

private GenericKeyedObjectPool createBoundaryPool() {
    GenericKeyedObjectPool pool = null;
    try {
        pool = new GenericKeyedObjectPool(
                new KeyedBoundaryPoolFactory());
        pool.setConfig(getPoolConfiguration());
    }
    catch (Throwable x) {
        System.out.println("Pool creation exception: " +
                            x.getMessage());
        x.printStackTrace();
    }
    return pool;
```

1 Initializes the servlet, creating pools and caches

2 Returns pool configuration parameters

3 Creates the boundary object pool

```
        }
        private DBPool createConnectionPool(String driverClass,        ◁─┐ Creates the
                                           String password,              │ database
                                           String dbUrl,                 │ connection
                                           String user) {               │ pool
            DBPool dbPool = null;
            try {
                dbPool = new DBPool(driverClass, dbUrl, user, password);
            } catch (SQLException sqlx) {
                getServletContext().log(new java.util.Date() +
                                    ":Connection pool error", sqlx);
            }
            return dbPool;
        }
                                                    ┌─ Contains an empty
                                                    │  (but required)
                                                    │  service() method
        public void service(ServletRequest req,  ◁─┘
                            ServletResponse res)
                throws javax.servlet.ServletException,
                       java.io.IOException {
            //-- This method must be present because of the base class.
            //-- It is intentionally left blank in this servlet.
        }
    }
```

❶ The StartupConfiguration servlet sets up the pools and other infrastructure used by the rest of the application. It never services an HTTP request, so we subclass it from GenericServlet instead of HTTPServlet. In fact, the service() method is blank—all the behavior we need occurs in the init() method. The load on startup flag in the web.xml file ensures that this servlet executes on startup. The first part of the init() method handles setting up the database connection pool, and there is nothing worth noting about that code.

❷ The GenericKeyedObjectPool has so many configuration options that the designers of the class created an inner class to hold all the options. To make it easy to tweak the configuration options, we created a separate method that returns a GenericKeyedObjectPool.Config object. In our case, we set two configuration options in the web.xml file. These options are extracted and set to members of the Config object. All the options take on default values, so we only have to override the ones we want to differ from the defaults.

❸ The createBoundaryPool() method sets up the GenericKeyedObjectPool. The constructor for this class is an instance of our class that implements the KeyedPoolableObjectFactory interface (which appears in listing 14.10).

After the pool is created, the servlet adds it to the application collection, which makes it available to all subsequent servlets. Note that this servlet will stay in memory for the duration of the application, which means that it occupies a bit of memory. Ideally, the setup code could move to the welcome servlet, but in this case, the memory impact is so small that we preferred to have it in its own class.

Now that the pool is available, the catalog servlet can make use of it to get a `ProductDb` boundary class. The catalog servlet is extensive, so listing 14.12 shows only the `getProductBoundary()` method.

Listing 14.12 The getProductBoundary() method, which retrieves a boundary class from the pool

```
private ProductDb getProductBoundary(HttpSession session) {
    ProductDb products = (ProductDb)session.getAttribute(
                              "productBoundary");

    if (products == null) {
        GenericKeyedObjectPool boundaryPool =
                (GenericKeyedObjectPool) getServletContext().
                getAttribute("boundaryPool");
        try {
            products = (ProductDb)
                    boundaryPool.borrowObject(ProductDb.class);
        }
        catch (Throwable x) {
            System.out.println("Pool exception");
            getServletContext().log("Object pool exception", x);
        }
        products.setDbPool(
                (DBPool)getServletContext().getAttribute(
                        "dbPool"));

        session.setAttribute("productList", products);

        int recsPerPage = Integer.parseInt(getServletConfig().
                getInitParameter("recsPerPage"));
        products.setRecordsPerPage(recsPerPage);
    }
    return products;
}
```

In this application, each user must have an instance of the boundary class, because it holds the cached view of data that this user sees (including customizations). To keep from having to build the result set multiple times, we place this boundary class in the user's session upon first creation. This method checks to see if the boundary object already resides in the session and returns it if it does. If not, it must retrieve an instance from the boundary pool. That process entails getting the boundary pool from the application context and calling the `borrowObject()` method, passing the class type of the type of object requested from the keyed collection. Once the object has been returned, it is associated with a database connection pool and added to the session.

The same code exists to retrieve an `OrderDb` boundary in the checkout servlet. Once the user has finished with these boundary classes, they should be returned to the pool, which makes them available for other users. This cleanup occurs in two methods, called from the `doPost()` method of the checkout servlet. These methods appear in listing 14.13.

Listing 14.13 The pooled objects must return to the pool once the user has finished with them.

```
private void cleanUpUserResources(HttpSession session,
        GenericKeyedObjectPool boundaryPool, OrderDb orderDb) {
    returnBoundaryObjectsToPool(session, boundaryPool, orderDb);
    session.invalidate();
}

private void returnBoundaryObjectsToPool(HttpSession session,
        GenericKeyedObjectPool boundaryPool, OrderDb orderDb) {
    ProductDb productDb =
            (ProductDb) session.getAttribute("productList");
    try {
        if (productDb != null)
            boundaryPool.returnObject(ProductDb.class,
                    productDb);
        if (orderDb != null)
            boundaryPool.returnObject(OrderDb.class, orderDb);
    }
    catch (Exception x) {
        getServletContext().log("Pool exception", x);
    }
}
```

The first of the controller methods returns the boundary objects, and then invalidates the user's session, cleaning up any leftover memory associated with this user. The `returnBoundaryObjectsToPool()` method is passed the instance of the `OrderDb` boundary class and must retrieve the `ProductDb` class from the application collection. Each object is returned to the pool via the `returnObject()` method, passing both the key (which is the class type) and the actual object that was borrowed.

The setup for the `GenericKeyedObjectPool` is fairly extensive, although minor compared to the facilities it provides. The Commons project has done a good job of writing most of the elaborate code necessary to implement a robust object pool. The only requirement for the user to make use of this pool is to implement a single simple interface to tell the pool how to manage a particular type of object.

If your needs are not extensive, implementing your own pool, especially using `SoftReferences` (which the `GenericKeyedObjectPool` doesn't support), should suffice. But if you need robust object pooling, the Commons pool is a good choice.

14.3.4 *Pooling in frameworks*

The pooling code in the previous section should work without modification in all the Model 2 frameworks because it involves boundary classes. The setup code could move to the native setup code for the framework. For example, when using Struts, you may find it better to subclass its `Action` servlet and perform the setup code for the pool in it, and then pass control to the parent servlet. The code in the controllers moves to the `Action` classes in Struts and to the corresponding controller proxies in the other frameworks.

This level of pooling generally isn't necessary in Tapestry because that framework implements its own pooling code. You can add your own objects to Tapestry's pools through its API. InternetBeans Express doesn't support the previous code because it doesn't use boundary classes.

14.4 *Designing for scalability*

Web applications are unique because you may not always be able to judge how many peak concurrent users you will have—especially if you have a public site. You must be diligent in your design to ensure that your site can scale gracefully. The servlet API already handles a large part of the scalability for web applications; it allows a single instance of a servlet to handle many simultaneous requests—that is, unless you are implementing the `SingleThreadModel` interface in your servlets. This interface is the answer to the question "How can I cripple the scalability of my web application?" Do yourself a favor and learn to deal with the threading issues and avoid this interface.

14.4.1 *When to scale up to EJB*

Fortunately, when you are building web applications in Java, you have a ready-made scalability option in Enterprise JavaBeans (EJBs). The benefits of EJBs can easily fill entire books. EJBs achieve scalability by creating as much as possible in advance: object pools, database connection pools, thread pools, and so forth. We're interested in using them for building scalable web applications. The mechanics of using EJBs in web applications are discussed in chapter 12. The question to be answered here is when you should start using EJBs.

Why not use them for every project?

You can use EJBs for every web application and never worry about scalability. However, a cost is involved with using them, both in money and time. When building a web application, you may use any number of servlet engines, some of which are freely available. However, to use EJBs you must have a full-blown application server. While open-source application servers exist, they are rare indeed. Commercial application servers are very expensive, on the scale of enterprise database servers.

A greater concern is the complexity of writing EJBs. As the specification has matured, it has gotten easier to write them (especially entity beans). However, it is never an easy undertaking. Including distributed components adds a great deal of work throughout the application. A well-partitioned application insulates you from this to a degree, but the setup and debugging time will not be trivial.

14.4.2 *Molding your architecture for the future*

The good news is that you don't have to make the decision to move to EJB right away. If you follow the design guidelines highlighted throughout this book, you should be able to port your project to EJB without too much work. As long as you have been diligent about the separation of user interface, database logic, and business logic, you can port to EJB by replacing a single layer of your application.

The key to being able to support EJBs (or another persistence mechanism for that matter) is a clean separation between boundary classes and entities. The boundary classes should handle all persistence details in the non-EJB application. When it is time to move to EJB, the boundary layer becomes a proxy layer to the EJBs running in the application server. Chapter 12 walks through a complete example of taking a well-partitioned Model 2 application and moving it to EJB. Partitioning is the key.

14.5 *When to optimize*

> Rules of Optimization:
>   Rule 1: Don't do it.
>   Rule 2 (for experts only): Don't do it yet.
>
> *—M.A. Jackson*

> More computing sins are committed in the name of efficiency (without necessarily achieving it) than for any other single reason—including blind stupidity.
>
> *—W.A. Wulf*

> We should forget about small efficiencies, say about 97% of the time: premature optimization is the root of all evil.
>
> *—Donald Knuth*

> The best is the enemy of the good.
>
> *—Voltaire*

The gist of these quotes is pretty clear: you should not optimize prematurely. Make sure there is a need to change architecture, design, and code before you launch into an optimization effort that gains almost nothing in performance but that takes a great deal of time and obfuscates your code. It is a classic blunder to assume that some part of the application will be a bottleneck. After you take a great deal of time to fix it before the fact, it turns out that the months of work have yielded a performance gain of a few microseconds, while an unexpected part of the application takes minutes to run.

It is important to get the architecture right from the outset. For every project, you should write proof-of-concept projects (called "Architectural Spikes" in agile programming methodologies). That way, you ensure that no major problems crop up in the overall design and architecture. Then, as the project progresses, it is fine to performance-test subsystems as they become available. When you have identified a genuine hotspot, spend the time to fix it, then test some more. Note the quote that admonishes "Don't do it yet." Make sure that you get a reasonable bang for the buck out of your optimizations.

You should rely on tools to help you identify the problems in your application. If you guess (no matter how educated your guess might be), you are probably wrong. Even if you just use the profiler that ships with the SDK, at least you have an objective tool to tell you facts, not speculation, about the performance of your application.

14.6 Summary

To determine the performance of an application, you must measure it objectively. Measuring memory in web applications is difficult because of the way the Java Virtual Machine interacts with the operating system and because of the presence of the servlet engine. Profiling the "hotspots" in your code is possible via the built-in profiler in the VM, invoked via command-line options. You can analyze the very large profile document generated by the profiler to determine application performance bottlenecks. Commercial profilers also exist that make it much easier to measure memory.

Another category of performance monitoring is load testing, where you simulate large numbers of users. The open-source JMeter project allows you to set up tests and reports on the results in a variety of formats. Commercial load testers are also available but are typically quite costly.

Web development offers a variety of performance pitfalls. The expense of object creation can be mitigated by creating stateless classes or by building an object reuse infrastructure. You must also watch for extraneous object references, especially from collection classes. StringBuffers should always be used instead of Strings for dynamic string manipulation.

Object pooling allows you to create a large number of preconstructed objects and retrieve them rather than create new objects as needed. Pools can be created using either SoftReferences or WeakReferences, which both hold object references unless the application runs short of memory. The WeakHashMap class is a collection class that uses WeakReferences to make it easy to create a loosely held cache. If you have more elaborate pooling needs, the Commons pool from the Jakarta project provides sophisticated object-pooling facilities. The eMotherEarth application incorporates the Commons pool to handle customized boundary classes for users.

The ultimate scalability option lies with Enterprise JavaBeans. However, there is overhead involved in creating and using them, so you should decide whether the cost outweighs the benefits. If the application is well architected, it is easy to port to EJB.

Make sure that you are performing useful work when optimizing your application. Many times developers assume that parts of the application will be slow and spend a great deal of time optimizing them, only to discover that other parts are slower. You must also measure performance objectively and optimize where you get the largest return on investment.

In the next chapter, we look at how to manage the resources in your applications.

Resource management

This chapter covers
- Caching strategies
- Managing non-memory resources
- Using design patterns

The previous chapter covered various aspects of performance in Java web applications. However, if the resources in your application are poorly handled, it doesn't matter how much effort you expend toward performance tuning. In other words, you must have a good base design to enable many of the optimization techniques covered in chapter 14. This is the realm of resource management—the topic of this chapter.

Web applications have a variety of resources, some that the developer can control and others that are maintained by the application server or servlet engine. Examples of resources that the developer cannot control are threads, file handles, and other low-level characteristics of the application server and underlying operating system. The only solution to problems with such resources is to either upgrade/replace your application server or upgrade/replace your hardware. We will not try to help you manage that process here!

Instead, we focus on resources that you *can* control, either explicitly or implicitly. One example is memory. Although you can't control the way your application server allocates memory, you certainly can control how much your application uses and, more important, how it uses that memory. We discuss several strategies for managing the resources in your application. We first look at a couple of variations on caching implementations. We introduce two design patterns, Flyweight and Façade, which are well adapted for saving and sharing resources. We also discuss optimizing Java Naming and Directory Interface (JNDI) usage and resource issues that arise when you're using standard collections in Java. We also examine the topic of when to use lazy instantiations, and how their use can improve resource usage but might hurt performance.

15.1 *Caching strategies*

Memory is a constant bottleneck for large, busy applications. It is also the area in web development where the most abuse occurs and where the most benefit may be gained. In some cases, effective caching strategies can both lower the memory footprint and speed up the application. Caching is a well-known optimization technique because it keeps in memory items that have been recently used, anticipating that they will be needed again. Caching can be implemented in numerous ways, including the judicious use of design patterns.

15.1.1 Caching with the Flyweight design pattern

The first caching scheme uses the Flyweight design pattern. This pattern appears in the Gang of Four book, which is the seminal work on patterns in software development. The pattern uses sharing to support a large number of fine-grained object references. With the Flyweight strategy, you keep a pool of objects available and create references to the pool of objects for particular views. This pattern uses the idea of *canonical* objects. A canonical object is a single representative object that represents all other objects of that type. For example, if you have a particular product, it represents all products of that type. In an application, instead of creating a list of products for each user, you create one list of canonical products and each user has a list of references to that list.

The default eMotherEarth application is designed to hold a list of products for each user. However, that design is a waste of memory. The products are the same for all users, and the characteristics of the products change infrequently. Figure 15.1 shows the current architectural relationship between users and the list of products in the catalog.

The memory required to keep a unique list for each user is wasted. Even though each user has his or her own view of the products, only one list of products exists. Each user can change the sort order and the catalog page of products he or she sees, but the fundamental characteristics of the product remain the same for each user.

A better design is to create a canonical list of products and hold references to that list for each user. Figure 15.2 illustrates this user/product relationship.

In this scenario, each user still has a reference to a particular set of products (to maintain paging and sorting), but the references point back to the canonical list of products. This main list is the only actual product object present in the application. It is stored in a central location, accessible by all the users of the application.

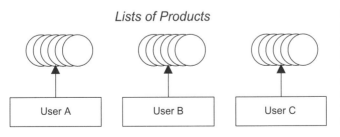

Lists of Products

User A   User B   User C

Figure 15.1
In the eMotherEarth application, each user has his or her own list of products when viewing the catalog. However, even though users have different views of the products, they are still looking at the same list of products.

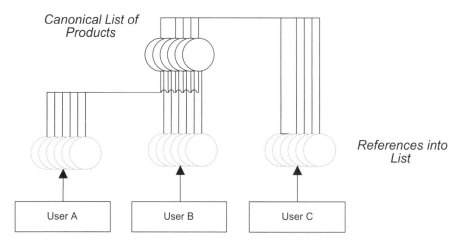

Canonical List of Products

References into List

User A

User B

User C

Figure 15.2   A single list of product objects saves memory, and each user can keep a reference to that list for the particular products he or she is viewing at any given time.

Implementing Flyweight

Because the eMotherEarth application is already modular, it is easy to change it to use the Flyweight design pattern. This version of the eMotherEarth application appears in the source code archive with the name art_emotherearth_flyweight.

The first step is to build the canonical list of products and place it in a globally accessible place. The obvious choice is the application context. Therefore, we've changed the welcome controller in eMotherEarth to build the list of products and place them in the application context. The revised `init()` and new `buildFly-weightReferences()` methods of the welcome controller are shown in listing 15.1.

Listing 15.1   The welcome controller builds the list of flyweight references and stores it in the application context.

```
public void init() throws ServletException {
    String driverClass =
            getServletContext().getInitParameter("driverClass");
    String password =
            getServletContext().getInitParameter("password");
    String dbUrl =
            getServletContext().getInitParameter("dbUrl");
    String user =
            getServletContext().getInitParameter("user");
    DBPool dbPool =
            createConnectionPool(driverClass, password, dbUrl,
                                    user);
```

```
    getServletContext().setAttribute("dbPool", dbPool);
    buildFlyweightReferences(dbPool);
}

private void buildFlyweightReferences(DBPool dbPool) {
    ProductDb productDb = (ProductDb) getServletContext().
                        getAttribute("products");
    if (productDb == null) {
        productDb = new ProductDb();
        productDb.setDbPool(dbPool);
        List productList = productDb.getProductList();
        Collections.sort(productList, new IdComparator());
        getServletContext().setAttribute("products",
                productList);
    }
}
```

The `buildFlyweightReferences()` method first checks to verify that it hasn't been built by another user's invocation of the welcome servlet. We are probably being more cautious than necessary because the `init()` method is called only once for the servlet, as it is loaded into memory. However, if we moved this code into `doGet()` or `doPost()`, it would be called multiple times. This is an easy enough test to perform, and it doesn't hurt anything in the current implementation.

If the canonical list doesn't exist yet, it is built, populated, and placed in the global context. Now, when an individual user needs to view products from the catalog, the user is pulling from the global list. We've changed the catalog controller to pull the products for display from the global cache instead of creating a new one. The `doPost()` method of the catalog controller is shown in listing 15.2.

Listing 15.2 The Catalog controller pulls products from the global cache rather than building a new list of products for each user.

```
public void doPost(HttpServletRequest request,
                   HttpServletResponse response) throws
    ServletException, IOException {

    HttpSession session = request.getSession(true);
    ensureThatUserIsInSession(request, session);
    List productReferences =
            (List) getServletContext().getAttribute("products");

    int start = getStartingPage(request);
    int recsPerPage = Integer.parseInt(getServletConfig().
            getInitParameter("recsPerPage"));
    int totalPagesToShow = calculateNumberOfPagesToShow(
            productReferences.size(), recsPerPage);
    String[] pageList =
```

```
            buildListOfPagesToShow(recsPerPage,
                            totalPagesToShow);
     List outputList = getProductListSlice(productReferences,
          start, recsPerPage);
     sortPagesForDisplay(request, outputList);

     bundleInformationForView(request, start, pageList,
                         outputList);
     forwardToView(request, response);
 }
```

The previous version of the catalog controller called a method that created and populated a ProductDb boundary class. However, we simplified this version; it can safely assume that the product records already exist in memory. Thus, the entire getProductBoundary() method is no longer present in this version of the application. This is a rare case of less code, faster performance, and less memory!

However, one other minor change was required to accommodate the caching. Previously, the sortPagesForDisplay() method did nothing if no sorting criteria were present in the request parameter—it simply returned the records without sorting them. The controller is now designed to return a slice of the canonical list in the getProductListSlice() method. This method appears in listing 15.3.

Listing 15.3 The getProductListSlice() method returns a subset of the entire canonical list.

```
private List getProductListSlice(List productReferences,
                            int start, int recsPerPage) {
    if (start + recsPerPage > productReferences.size()) {
        return productReferences.subList(start,
                productReferences.size());
    } else {
        return productReferences.subList(start,
                start + recsPerPage);
    }
}
```

Previously, the lack of a sort criterion didn't cause any problems because every user had his or her own copy of the "master" list. This method returned a subset of that user's list. But now all users are sharing the same list. The subList() method from the collections API does not clone the items in the list; it returns references to them. This is a desirable characteristic because if it cloned the list items as it returned them, caching the product list would be pointless.

However, because there is now only one actual list, the members of the list are sorting in page-sized chunks as the user gets a reference to some of the records in the list and applies the `sortPagesForDisplay()` method. Listing 15.4 shows this method.

```
private void sortPagesForDisplay(HttpServletRequest request,
                                 List outputList) {
    String sortField = request.getParameter("sort");

    Comparator c = new IdComparator();
    if (sortField != null) {
        if (sortField.equalsIgnoreCase("price"))
            c = new PriceComparator();
        else if (sortField.equalsIgnoreCase("name"))
            c = new NameComparator();
    }
    Collections.sort(outputList, c);
}
```

The previous version of `sortPagesForDisplay()` called the sort method only if the user had specified a `Comparator` in the request parameter (which is generated when the user clicks on one of the column headers in the view). However, if that implementation remained, then a new user logging into the application would get the same sorted list as the last user to sort the page-sized chunks of records. This is because a new user hasn't specified a sort criterion (in other words, no one has had a chance yet to click on a column header and generate the sorting flag). To prevent this behavior, we moved the `IdComparator` out of the `if` statement and applied that sorting characteristic if no others are present. The side effect of this caching technique is that every user is sorting the list of products in page-sized chunks. Even though that involves changing the position of records for a given page-sized chunk, each user applies his or her own sorting criteria to the list before seeing the records. This implementation could be improved to prevent this side effect, but with a small number of records, it doesn't hurt the performance.

One characteristic of this controller makes it easy to retrofit to use this design pattern. The user chooses his or her page of records before sorting them. If the sorting occurred before the user specified a subset of records, this controller would have to be changed. However, it is unlikely that users would make such a request—they would have to guess on which page their sorted record ended up.

Flyweight considerations

The effectiveness of the Flyweight pattern as a caching mechanism depends heavily on certain characteristics of the data you are caching:

- The application uses a large number of objects.
- Storage (memory) cost is high to replicate this large number for multiple users.
- Either the objects are immutable or their state can be made external.
- Relatively few shared objects may replace many groups of objects.
- The application doesn't depend on object identity. While users may think they are getting a unique object, they actually have a reference from the cache.

One of the key characteristics enabling this style of caching is the state information in the objects. In the previous example, the product objects are immutable as far as the user is concerned. If the user is allowed to make changes to the object, then this caching scenario wouldn't work. It depends on the object stored in the cache being read-only. It is possible to store non-immutable objects using the Flyweight design pattern, but some of their state information must reside externally to the object, as shown in figure 15.3.

It is possible to store the mutable information needed by the reference in a small class that is associated to the link between the flyweight reference and the flyweight object. A good example of this type of external state information in eMotherEarth is the preferred quantity for particular items. This is information particular to the user, so it should not be stored in the cache. However, there is a discrete chunk of information for each product. This preference (and others) would be stored in an association class, tied to the relationship between the

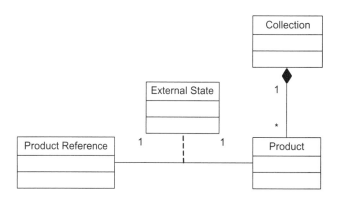

Figure 15.3
The Flyweight design pattern supports mutable objects in the cache by adding additional externalizable information to the link between product and reference.

reference and the product. When you use this option, the information must take very little memory in comparison to the flyweight reference itself. Otherwise, you don't save any resources by using the flyweight.

The Flyweight design pattern is not recommended when the objects in the cache change rapidly or unexpectedly. It would not be a suitable caching strategy for the eMotherEarth application if the products changed several times a day. However, with our application's inventory, that scenario seems unlikely. This solution works best when you have an immutable set of objects shared between most or all of your users. The memory savings are dramatic and become more pronounced the more concurrent users you have.

15.1.2 *Caching with the Façade design pattern*

Another approach to caching makes use of the Façade design pattern. This design pattern helps hide complex interactions between objects by creating a unified interface to them. It is designed to make it easy to use a complex subsystem by providing a friendly interface to that subsystem so that the user doesn't have to understand the complexities of the interactions between the objects. Consider figure 15.4.

In this diagram, the outer objects must understand too much about the relationship of the subsystem objects to easily use the subsystem. Façade solves this problem by creating a class (or classes) that hides the complexities of the subsystem by providing an easy-to-use interface to access the subsystem. The Façade solution appears in figure 15.5.

Unlike Flyweight, which is a caching strategy in its own right, Façade is more useful for hiding the details of a complex caching subsystem from the everyday

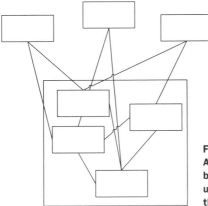

Figure 15.4
A complex subsystem (represented by the enclosed box) is difficult for other systems to use without understanding the complex interactions between the subsystem objects.

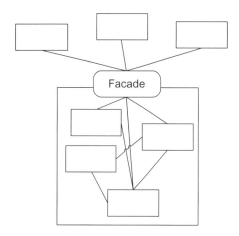

Figure 15.5
Façade defines a higher-level interface that makes a complex subsystem easier to use.

developer. Façade is broadly useful in many places in your applications. Frequently, you may need to call code that exists in a reusable library that has complex interactions between the classes of that library. You can use this design pattern to wrap that complex API into one that is easy to use for the developers of the current application.

We're going to apply Façade to a complex subsystem that already exists in one of the iterations of the eMotherEarth application. In chapter 14, we created a Commons pool for boundary objects. The interface that we must use for the Commons GenericKeyedObjectPool is detailed, with multiple objects and factories that interact. The developers of the application shouldn't have to know the relationship between those objects. In fact, developers shouldn't know or care that the ones they are using actually come from a cache. In that way, a façade may act as a kind of factory object, delivering objects without forcing the developers to understand how it was obtained.

Automating façade creation

The version of eMotherEarth used as the starting point of this example is from chapter 14 (section 14.3.3), which uses the Jakarta Commons pool facility to pool the boundary objects in the application. Along the way, we'll change a few other aspects of the application to update it to the latest web APIs. This version of the eMotherEarth application appears in the source code archive under the name art_emotherearth_facade.

The first change in the application involves the creation of the pools. In the previous example, we introduced a GenericServlet subclass with a startup configuration parameter designed to automatically launch it. The startup servlet ensured that its `init()` method would be called during the startup of the application. When you're using older servlet specifications, this is the best way to ensure that code will execute upon application startup. Now, an alternative technique exists, and we will implement it here. Instead of creating a servlet that initializes the pools, we create a `ServletContextListener` (which became available with the servlet 2.3 API). A `ServletContextListener` allows the developer to tie an event to the application object (the `ServletContext`). The listener class is an interface with two method signatures, which appears (without comments) in listing 15.5.

Listing 15.5 The ServletContextListener interface defines callback methods called by the application upon initialization.

```
package javax.servlet;

import java.util.EventListener;

public interface ServletContextListener extends EventListener {

    public void contextInitialized ( ServletContextEvent sce );
    public void contextDestroyed ( ServletContextEvent sce );
}
```

The `ServletContextListener` interface allows the developer to execute code as the application object (i.e., the `ServletContext`) is initialized and destroyed. To use this interface, the developer creates an implementing class and registers that class in the web configuration file. For our example, we have created a class named `StartupConfigurationListener` that implements this interface. To associate this listener with the application, add the code in listing 15.6 to web.xml.

Listing 15.6 Web application listeners are registered in web.xml.

```
<listener>
  <listener-class>
  com.nealford.art.emotherearth.util.StartupConfigurationListener
  </listener-class>
</listener>
```

The `StartupConfigurationListener` class initializes both the database connection pool and the boundary class pool. It appears in listing 15.7.

Listing 15.7   The contextInitialized() method executes as the web application is launching.

```
package com.nealford.art.facade.emotherearth.util;

import javax.servlet.ServletContextEvent;
import javax.servlet.ServletContextListener;
import javax.servlet.ServletContext;
import org.apache.commons.pool.impl.GenericKeyedObjectPool;
import java.sql.SQLException;

public class StartupConfigurationListener implements
        ServletContextListener, AttributeConstants {
    public void contextInitialized(ServletContextEvent sce) {
        initializeDatabaseConnectionPool(sce.getServletContext());
        BoundaryFacade.initializeBoundaryPool(
                sce.getServletContext());
    }
    public void contextDestroyed(ServletContextEvent sce) {
    }

    private void initializeDatabaseConnectionPool(
            ServletContext sc) {
        DBPool dbPool = null;
        try {
            dbPool = createConnectionPool(sc);
        } catch (SQLException sqlx) {
            sc.log(new java.util.Date() + ":Connection pool error",
                    sqlx);
        }
        sc.setAttribute(DB_POOL, dbPool);
    }

    private DBPool createConnectionPool(ServletContext sc)
            throws SQLException {
        String driverClass = sc.getInitParameter(DRIVER_CLASS);
        String password = sc.getInitParameter(PASSWORD);
        String dbUrl = sc.getInitParameter(DB_URL);
        String user = sc.getInitParameter(USER);
        DBPool dbPool = null;
        dbPool = new DBPool(driverClass, dbUrl, user, password);
        return dbPool;
    }
}
```

Because we don't have any particular cleanup to perform as the application exits, we left the contextDestroyed() method in StartupConfigurationListener empty, although it must be present because it is part of the interface. The real action in this class is in the contextInitialized() method, which creates all the global resources the web application will need. The actual details of the `GenericKeyedOb-jectPool` and supporting classes are hidden in the façade class.

Establishing the façade class

The façade class is responsible for hiding the details of how objects are obtained and returned to the pool, along with the setup information for the pool. The pooling subsystem details are complex enough to warrant hiding them from the body of the application, leaving the façade class as the only code that needs to understand anything about how the object pools work.

The `BoundaryFacade` class is a singleton class, meaning that all other classes that need to use it share a single instance. The declaration and the initialization methods are shown in listing 15.8.

> **Listing 15.8 The BoundaryFacade class hides the details of creating object pools from the application.**

```
public class BoundaryFacade implements AttributeConstants {
    private static BoundaryFacade singleton;          ◁——— Contains the internal singleton reference
    private  BoundaryFacade() {        ◁—— Contains the private singleton constructor
    }
    public static BoundaryFacade getInstance() {       ◁—— Contains the singleton access
        if (singleton == null)
            singleton = new BoundaryFacade();
        return singleton;                              Initializes and persists boundary pool
    }

    public void initializeBoundaryPool(ServletContext context) {   ◁———
        GenericKeyedObjectPool boundaryPool =
                createBoundaryPool(context);
        context.setAttribute(BOUNDARY_POOL, boundaryPool);    Returns object pool configuration
    }
    private GenericKeyedObjectPool.Config getPoolConfiguration(   ◁——
            ServletContext context) {
        GenericKeyedObjectPool.Config conf =
                new GenericKeyedObjectPool.Config();
        conf.maxActive = Integer.parseInt(context.getInitParameter(
            POOL_MAX_ACTIVE));
        conf.whenExhaustedAction = Byte.parseByte(context.
            getInitParameter(POOL_WHEN_EXHAUSTED));
        return conf;
    }
    private GenericKeyedObjectPool createBoundaryPool(   ◁—— Creates the boundary pool
            ServletContext context) {
        GenericKeyedObjectPool pool = null;
        try {
```

```
            pool = new GenericKeyedObjectPool(
                    new KeyedBoundaryPoolFactory());
            pool.setConfig(getPoolConfiguration(context));
        } catch (Throwable x) {
            System.out.println("Pool creation exception: " +
                                x.getMessage());
            x.printStackTrace();
        }
        return pool;
    }
```

The code that initializes GenericKeyedObjectPool is the exact same as the code in chapter 14, listing 14.10, which first describes the use of this class and its supporting classes. The only difference in this code is the location—it moved from the startup servlet or listener to this façade class. Note that this class is a classic singleton. It contains a static reference to itself, a private constructor, and a static getInstance() method to allow access.

Using façade to borrow objects

The next method in the façade class is the borrowOrderBoundary() method, which returns a boundary object for the Order entity from the pool. This method is shown in listing 15.9.

Listing 15.9 This method returns an instance of a boundary class that delivers Order objects.

```
public OrderDb borrowOrderBoundary(HttpSession session) {
    ServletContext sc = session.getServletContext();
    OrderDb orderDb = null;
    try {
        GenericKeyedObjectPool boundaryPool =
                (GenericKeyedObjectPool) sc.getAttribute(
                BOUNDARY_POOL);

        orderDb = (OrderDb) boundaryPool.borrowObject(OrderDb.class);
    } catch (Exception x) {
        session.getServletContext().log("Pool exception", x);
    }
    orderDb.setDBPool((DBPool) sc.getAttribute(DB_POOL));
    return orderDb;
}
```

The semantics of the `borrowOrderBoundary()` method are also similar to listing 14.11 in chapter 14. This method retrieves the boundary pool from the servlet context and borrows an `OrderBoundary` class based on the class type of the entity that it returns. After the façade retrieves the object, it associates the boundary with an instance of the database connection pool and returns it.

The other boundary class in the application is the `ProductDb` class. Pulling this object from the pool works the same as for the `OrderDb` boundary. However, for efficiency's sake, we are allowing caching the `Product` boundary in the user's session. The reasoning here is that users will need to access product information a number of times during their access to the catalog page of the application. This is the primary page and we can assume that users will spend most of their time there. As you may recall, this boundary keeps the list of products and returns a page-at-a-time slice of products to the user. Thus, it makes sense to associate this boundary with the user. In addition, this solution illustrates the flexibility of selectively caching objects that come from the pool.

Because this boundary has different behavior, it has its own method for returning an instance of it, either from the user's session or from the pool. The `getProductBoundary()` method appears in listing 15.10.

Listing 15.10 This method returns a Product boundary from either the pool or the user's session.

```
public ProductDb getProductBoundary(HttpSession session) {
    ServletContext sc = session.getServletContext();

    boolean cacheInBoundaryInSession =
            Boolean.valueOf(sc.getInitParameter(
            CACHE_BOUNDARY_IN_SESSION)).
            booleanValue();
    ProductDb productDb = null;
    if (cacheInBoundaryInSession)
        productDb = (ProductDb) session.getAttribute(
                PRODUCT_BOUNDARY);

    if (productDb == null) {
        GenericKeyedObjectPool boundaryPool =
                (GenericKeyedObjectPool) sc.getAttribute(
                BOUNDARY_POOL);
        try {
            productDb = (ProductDb)
                        boundaryPool.borrowObject(ProductDb.class);
        } catch (Throwable x) {
            sc.log("Object pool exception", x);
        }
```

```
        productDb.setDBPool((DBPool) sc.getAttribute(DB_POOL));
        if (cacheInBoundaryInSession)
            session.setAttribute(PRODUCT_BOUNDARY, productDb);
    }
    return productDb;
}
```

The getProductBoundary() method first checks a flag set as an init parameter to see whether the application is configured to cache the boundary in the session. By placing the flag in the configuration file, you can easily change the caching strategy just by editing the configuration and avoiding recompiling the application. Doing so also means that a nonprogrammer can change the setting.

If caching is turned on, the façade tries to get the boundary from the session. If that is unsuccessful, it goes to the object pool and borrows a boundary from the pool. At the end of the method, it stores the retrieved boundary object in the session for the next access if caching is turned on.

Using the façade to return objects

Objects borrowed from the pool must be returned to the pool. When returning the Product boundary, we have to check for the presence of the caching flag and return the boundary object accordingly. This job is split between two methods: one to conditionally return the object to the pool, based on the caching flag in the session, and the other to always return the object. The code for both these façade methods appears in listing 15.11.

Listing 15.11 Returning the Product boundary must take caching into account.

```
public void returnProductBoundary(ProductDb productDb) {
    try {
        boundaryPool.returnObject(ProductDb.class,
                productDb);
    } catch (Throwable x) {
        session.getServletContext().log(
                "Pool return exception: " +
                x.getMessage());
    }
}

public void conditionallyReturnProductBoundary(
        ProductDb productDb) {
    ServletContext sc = session.getServletContext();
    boolean cacheInBoundaryInSession =
            Boolean.valueOf(sc.getInitParameter(
            CACHE_BOUNDARY_IN_SESSION)).
            booleanValue();
```

```
        if (! cacheInBoundaryInSession && productDb != null) {
            GenericKeyedObjectPool boundaryPool =
                    (GenericKeyedObjectPool)
                    session.getServletContext().getAttribute(
                    BOUNDARY_POOL);
            returnProductBoundary(productDb);
        }
    }
```

The code in `returnProductBoundary()` is typical code for returning a borrowed object to the pool. The `conditionallyReturnProductBoundary()` method returns the object only if it isn't cached in the session.

This work is split between two methods, in case the user wanders away from the application without finishing the order. As web developers are well aware, users of a web application can lose interest at any time and never notify the application that they are leaving. The session's timeout will eventually fire, removing the session. However, removing the session only nullifies the reference to the `Product` boundary held by the session—it does not return the boundary to the pool. To solve this problem, we've added another listener to the application for handling the event in which the user doesn't complete the interaction with the application normally, but instead leaves the session to time out. The `HttpSessionAttributeListener` interface was introduced with the servlet 2.3 specification. It allows the developer to attach event handlers to session attribute events. In this case, we've attached code to the `attributeRemoved()` method to handle this special case. When the session times out, it removes all its attributes and fires the code that removes the cached `Product` boundary. Listing 15.12 shows the `SessionScrubber` listener.

Listing 15.12 The SessionScrubber handles the case in which the user never logs out.

```
package com.nealford.art.facade.emotherearth.util;

import javax.servlet.ServletContext;
import javax.servlet.http.HttpSessionAttributeListener;
import javax.servlet.http.HttpSessionBindingEvent;

import com.nealford.art.facade.emotherearth.boundary.ProductDb;

public class SessionScrubber implements
        HttpSessionAttributeListener, AttributeConstants {

    public void attributeAdded(HttpSessionBindingEvent se) {
    }

    public void attributeRemoved(HttpSessionBindingEvent se) {
        ServletContext sc = se.getSession().getServletContext();
```

```
            if (se.getName().equals(PRODUCT_BOUNDARY))
                BoundaryFacade.getInstance().
                        returnProductBoundary((ProductDb) se.getValue());
        }
        public void attributeReplaced(HttpSessionBindingEvent se) {
        }
    }
```

While returning an Order boundary would seem to be less complicated (because it doesn't have any caching options), the solution is not as simple as just returning the Order boundary. The Order boundary is used at the end of the user's interaction with the web application. Generally, when the user has placed an order, he or she has finished using the web site and is preparing to leave. Thus, it is very unlikely that the user will use the product catalog again for this session. Taking the use of the web application into consideration, we return the Product boundary class if it is cached in the session at the same time we return the Order boundary. The code for returnBoundaries() appears in listing 15.13.

Listing 15.13 The returnBoundaries() method returns both Order and Product boundaries.

```
public  void returnBoundaries(HttpSession session,
                                     OrderDb orderDb) {
    ServletContext sc = session.getServletContext();
    boolean cacheInBoundaryInSession =
            Boolean.valueOf(sc.getInitParameter(
            CACHE_BOUNDARY_IN_SESSION)).
            booleanValue();

    ProductDb productDb =
            (ProductDb) session.getAttribute(PRODUCT_BOUNDARY);
    GenericKeyedObjectPool boundaryPool =
            (GenericKeyedObjectPool) sc.getAttribute(
            BOUNDARY_POOL);

    try {
        if (productDb != null && !cacheInBoundaryInSession)
            boundaryPool.returnObject(ProductDb.class,
                    productDb);
        if (orderDb != null)
            boundaryPool.returnObject(OrderDb.class,
                    orderDb);
    } catch (Exception x) {
        sc.log("Pool exception", x);
    }
}
```

The returnBoundaries() method pulls the Product boundary from the session if it exists and returns it at the same time the Order boundary is returned. If the user decides to return to the Catalog page and place an additional order, the Product boundary will no longer exist in the user's session, but the façade handles this invisibly by borrowing another Product boundary from the object pool.

Façade benefits

Our goal in choosing the Façade design pattern to implement caching was to hide the details of the object cache and the caching layer in the user's session. We have been successful in meeting this goal. Both the catalog and checkout controllers have been greatly simplified. As an illustration, listing 15.14 contains the doPost() method of the simplified checkout controller. The use of the Façade pattern reduced the code from the previous version by more than 30 lines. And, more important, the new version of the controller doesn't import any of the classes from the Commons library that implements object pools. You will also note that the SessionScrubber listener also uses the façade to hide the details of interacting with the pool code. All the code in the entire application that understands how the Commons pools work resides in the façade.

Listing 15.14 The CheckOut controller's doPost() method is greatly simplified by the use of the façade.

```
public void doPost(HttpServletRequest request,
                   HttpServletResponse response) throws
       ServletException, IOException {
    RequestDispatcher dispatcher = null;
    HttpSession session = redirectIfSessionNotPresent(
            request, response);
    String user = (String) session.getAttribute(USER);
    ShoppingCart sc =
            (ShoppingCart) session.getAttribute(CART);
    BoundaryFacade facade = BoundaryFacade.getInstance();
    OrderDb orderDb =
        (OrderDb) facade.borrowBoundary(session, OrderDb.class);
    Order order = createOrderFrom(request);
    validateOrder(request, response, order);
    addOrder(request, response, user, sc, orderDb,
            order);
    cleanUpUserResources(session);
    buildConfirmationViewProperties(request, user, order);
    forwardToConfirmation(request, response);
}
```

Making the façade more generic

The façade we've created is effective because it isolates the caching code in a single location. However, the way it is implemented doesn't make it easy to add more boundary classes to the application. If the façade must be modified every time another boundary is added, it will soon collapse under the weight of maintaining it. Therefore, we created a more generic version of the boundary façade that takes advantage of the reflection API in Java.

The first way to generalize the creation of the boundaries is to make sure they all extend the same base. Fortunately, we already have a `BoundaryBase` class, which encapsulates the association of the database connection pool with a boundary subclass. Listing 15.15 shows the `BoundaryBase` class.

Listing 15.15 The BoundaryBase class serves as the parent of all boundary classes.

```
package com.nealford.art.facade.emotherearth.boundary;

import com.nealford.art.facade.emotherearth.util.DBPool;

public class BoundaryBase {
    private DBPool dBPool;

    public BoundaryBase() {
    }

    public DBPool getDBPool() {
        return dBPool;
    }

    public void setDBPool(DBPool dBPool) {
        this.dBPool = dBPool;
    }
}
```

Once we know that all boundary classes are really specialized versions of the base class, we can write a method in the façade that returns boundaries in terms of the base class. The façade becomes a factory for returning boundaries keyed to a particular entity. Thus, we can write a generic `borrowBoundary()` method in the façade that can return any type of boundary object. This improved method appears in listing 15.16.

Listing 15.16 The borrowBoundary() method is generic for all kinds of boundary objects.

```
public BoundaryBase borrowBoundary(HttpSession session,
        Class boundaryClass) {
    ServletContext sc = session.getServletContext();
```

```
boolean cacheInBoundaryInSession =
        Boolean.valueOf(sc.getInitParameter(
        CACHE_BOUNDARY_IN_SESSION)).
        booleanValue();

BoundaryBase boundary = null;
if (cacheInBoundaryInSession)
    boundary = (BoundaryBase) session.getAttribute(
            boundaryClass.getName());
if (boundary == null) {
    try {
        GenericKeyedObjectPool boundaryPool =
                (GenericKeyedObjectPool) sc.getAttribute(
                BOUNDARY_POOL);
        boundary = (BoundaryBase) boundaryPool.
                borrowObject(boundaryClass);
        if (cacheInBoundaryInSession &&
                boundary instanceof Cacheable)
            session.setAttribute(boundaryClass.getName(),
                    boundary);
    } catch (Exception x) {
        session.getServletContext().log("Pool error", x);
    }
    boundary.setDBPool((DBPool) sc.getAttribute(DB_POOL));
    borrowedObjects.add(boundary);
}
return boundary;
}
```

The borrowBoundary() method takes advantage of the reflection API in Java to supply a parameter that is actually a class (i.e., it is an instance of the Class class). The second parameter is the class of the boundary that this method returns. An example of its invocation comes from the catalog controller:

```
BoundaryFacade facade = BoundaryFacade.getInstance();
ProductDb products = (ProductDb) facade.borrowBoundary(session,
        ProductDb.class);
```

Every class in Java has a property named class, so invoking the class name with a .class modifier returns the Class object for this class. This object has methods and properties that pertain to the class itself, not to instances of the class. By passing the class as a parameter to the borrowBoundary() method, we can use the class information to determine what kind of boundary object we eventually return.

The borrowBoundary() method begins by gathering state information from the servlet context to determine how to handle caching boundaries. If caching is turned on, it attempts first to retrieve the boundary from the user's session. The boundaries are stored in both the pool and the session by their class names, which are unique because they include the package name. Because of the way packages in Java must correspond to physical locations, it is impossible to have two classes with the same fully qualified name (because you can't have two files with the same name in a directory). If the method can't retrieve a boundary from the session, it goes to the object pool to get the boundary.

As you know from the discussion in chapter 14, section 14.3.3 (particularly listing 14.10), the Commons pool relies on a class that implements the Keyed-PoolableObjectFactory interface to return the appropriate object from the pool. The pool uses this class to construct and name the objects that it pools. To pool and store the boundaries by their class names, we use the KeyedBoundaryPoolFactory class shown in listing 15.17.

Listing 15.17 The KeyedBoundaryPoolFactory populates the object pool.

```
package com.nealford.art.facade.emotherearth.util;

import org.apache.commons.pool.KeyedPoolableObjectFactory;
import com.nealford.art.facade.emotherearth.boundary.ProductDb;
import com.nealford.art.facade.emotherearth.boundary.OrderDb;

public class KeyedBoundaryPoolFactory
        implements KeyedPoolableObjectFactory {

    public Object makeObject(Object key) {
        if (key.equals(com.nealford.art.facade.emotherearth.
                    boundary.ProductDb.class)) {
            return new ProductDb();
        } else if (key.equals(com.nealford.art.facade.emotherearth.
                            boundary.OrderDb.class)) {
            return new OrderDb();
        } else
            return null;
    }

    public void destroyObject(Object key, Object obj) {
    }

    public boolean validateObject(Object key, Object obj) {
        return true;
    }

    public void activateObject(Object key, Object obj)  {
    }

    public void passivateObject(Object key, Object obj)  {
    }
}
```

You must exercise caution when caching objects in both an object pool and the user's session. If you have 60 objects in the pool with session caching enabled, and you have 60 concurrent users, each user will have an instance from the pool checked out, residing in his or her session cache, which means no objects are left in the pool. You can solve this problem by turning off session caching (which slows down each user's interaction slightly because the boundary is no longer cached in the user's session) but lowering the memory requirements for the entire application and supporting more concurrent users. You can also solve this problem by creating pools that automatically grow so that you never run out of boundary objects from the pool. Design decisions pitting users' response time against scalability frequently arise in web applications.

The Cacheable interface

One other item of note in the borrowBoundary() method is the use of an interface named Cacheable. This is a tagging interface, built as part of the application, that serves as a flag to indicate which boundary classes we want to cache in the application. This interface appears in listing 15.18.

Listing 15.18 Cacheable allows a boundary to specify that it should be cached.

```
package com.nealford.art.facade.emotherearth.util;

public interface Cacheable {
}
```

The Cacheable interface allows a developer to flag a particular boundary class as one that should be cached. Because it contains no methods, its use is restricted to acting as a discriminator via the instanceof operator. To specify that a class is cached, the definition of the class should implement this interface:

```
public class ProductDb extends BoundaryBase implements Cacheable {
```

The borrowBoundary() method tests both the deployment flag from the servlet context and the presence of this interface via instanceof to determine if a boundary is placed in the session when it is borrowed from the pool.

Generically returning boundaries

We've also modified the returnBoundaries() method to accommodate the generic boundary façade. The new method appears in listing 15.19.

Listing 15.19 The returnBoundaries() method

```
public void returnBoundaries(HttpSession session,
                            boolean preserveCachedBoundaries) {
    GenericKeyedObjectPool boundaryPool =
        (GenericKeyedObjectPool) session.getServletContext().
        getAttribute(BOUNDARY_POOL);
    boolean cacheInBoundaryInSession =
        Boolean.valueOf(session.getServletContext().
        getInitParameter(CACHE_BOUNDARY_IN_SESSION)).
        booleanValue();
    Iterator borrowedObject = borrowedObjects.iterator();
    while (borrowedObject.hasNext()) {
        Object o = borrowedObject.next();
        if (o instanceof BoundaryBase)
            if (cacheInBoundaryInSession &&
                    preserveCachedBoundaries &&
                    o instanceof Cacheable)
                break;
            else {
                try {
                    boundaryPool.returnObject(o.getClass(), o);
                } catch (Exception x) {
                    session.getServletContext().log(
                            "Pool return exception: " +
                            x.getMessage());
                } finally {
                    borrowedObject.remove();
                }
            }
    }
}
```

One of the changes required in the generic façade class is the class-level member variable that keeps track of all the objects referenced by the façade so that it can gracefully remove them. The returnBoundaries() method receives two parameters: the user's session and a Boolean flag indicating whether the cached boundary objects should be preserved. The method uses the session to gather session- and context-level variables, and then iterates over the list of borrowed objects, conditionally returning them based on the cache settings, whether the caller wants the caches preserved, and the cacheability of the object. Once the objects are returned to the pool, they are removed from the list.

The list of borrowed objects is not necessary if the objects are cached in the session. However, not all boundaries will be cached in the session, so an additional reference is kept within the façade to ensure the successful return of the pooled objects.

The other change to the application for the generic façade appears in the `SessionAttributeListener`, which is also simplified. The `attributeRemoved()` method shrinks to a mere two lines:

```
public void attributeRemoved(HttpSessionBindingEvent se) {
    BoundaryFacade facade = BoundaryFacade.getInstance();
    facade.returnBoundaries(se.getSession(), false);
}
```

You never want the boundaries preserved in the cache, so the Boolean parameter is passed as false to ensure that all the objects are returned. This method serves as insurance in case the user abandons the application and allows the session to time out.

The result for all the classes that use the façade is even greater simplification. For example, each controller that needs a boundary can call the façade with the appropriate class and call `returnBoundaries()` when their work is completed. All the intelligence about caching, pooling, and other management issues is strictly encapsulated inside the façade.

15.1.3 *Resource management in frameworks*

Both design patterns introduced in this chapter work well with the Model 2 frameworks in part 2. As in the last chapter, these strategies pertain mostly to the boundary and entity classes, leaving the infrastructure to the framework. The only framework that might not benefit from these patterns is Tapestry, simply because much of the object pooling and caching is built into that framework.

Notice the trend in the best practices chapters thus far. Once you have a clean Model 2 application, either with or without a framework in place, the main coding focus for resource management and optimization moves to the boundary and entity layer. Frameworks are built to manage plumbing for you, freeing you to focus your coding efforts on the parts of the application where you can have the most impact. This is not an accident, but the result of using a well-thought-out architecture like Model 2. You will also notice that the framework where most of these optimizations aren't possible is the non-Model 2 framework, InternetBeans Express. While quicker to build in the initial case, the RAD framework imposes so many restrictions that it ends up not being flexible enough.

15.2 *Other resources you need to manage*

The chapter has so far concentrated on memory usage; we've discussed several design patterns that support caching strategies. Memory is perhaps the most important resource you must manage. However, it isn't the only one. You must also be aware of other external resources, such as the JNDI lookup context for application servers, as well as internal resources, such as the various collections.

15.2.1 *Effectively using JNDI*

If you use JNDI to handle database connection pooling or Enterprise JavaBeans, you must manage the connection maintained on behalf of the user. The JNDI connection to the application server is similar to a connection to a database for a client/server application. Both handle authentication, and each takes a relatively long time to establish.

It is important to establish the connection to JNDI on behalf of the user and hold that connection. Because it holds the login to the application server, the connection is unique to a particular user. Thus, a connection cannot be pooled like other objects. The typical strategy when using JNDI is to establish the connection for the user at logon and place the context in the user's session. This is illustrated in the sample application from chapter 12, section 12.3.1 (the Model 2 schedule application rewritten to use EJBs). This sample appears in the source code archive under the name art_sched_ejb. The `ViewSchedule` controller servlet is a good example of the effective use of JNDI; it appears in listing 15.20.

Listing 15.20 This controller establishes and holds the JNDI context for this user.

```
package com.nealford.art.ejbsched.controller;

import java.io.IOException;
import javax.naming.Context;
import javax.naming.InitialContext;
import javax.naming.NamingException;
import javax.servlet.RequestDispatcher;
import javax.servlet.ServletException;
import javax.servlet.http.HttpServlet;
import javax.servlet.http.HttpServletRequest;
import javax.servlet.http.HttpServletResponse;
import javax.servlet.http.HttpSession;
import com.nealford.art.ejbsched.model.ScheduleBean;

public class ViewSchedule extends HttpServlet {

    public void doGet(HttpServletRequest request,
                      HttpServletResponse response) throws
            ServletException, IOException {
```

```
        Context c = establishContext(request);
        forwardToView(request, response, populateModel(c));
    }

    public void doPost(HttpServletRequest request,
                       HttpServletResponse response) throws
            ServletException, IOException {
        doGet(request, response);
    }

    private void forwardToView(HttpServletRequest request,
                               HttpServletResponse response,
                               ScheduleBean scheduleBean) throws
            ServletException, IOException {
        request.setAttribute("scheduleBean", scheduleBean);
        RequestDispatcher rd = request.getRequestDispatcher(
                "/ScheduleView.jsp");
        rd.forward(request, response);
    }

    private ScheduleBean populateModel(Context c) {
        ScheduleBean scheduleBean = new ScheduleBean();
        scheduleBean.setContext(c);
        try {
            scheduleBean.populate();
        } catch (Exception x) {
            getServletContext().log(
                    "Error: ScheduleBean.populate()");
        }
        return scheduleBean;
    }

    private Context establishContext(HttpServletRequest request) {
        HttpSession session = request.getSession(true);
        Context c = (Context) session.getAttribute("context");
        if (c == null) {
            c = getInitialContext();
            session.setAttribute("context", getInitialContext());
        }                                         Creates and saves the
        return c;                                         JNDI context
    }

    private Context getInitialContext() {
        Context c = null;
        try {
            c = new InitialContext();
        } catch (NamingException ex) {
            ex.printStackTrace();
        }
        return c;
    }
}
```

The `establishContext()` method checks to see if the context has already been added to this user's session. If not, it executes the relatively time-expensive operation of establishing the context and places it in the session for future use.

Generally, in applications with a resource like JNDI, the developer provides both a logon and a logout page to handle the resources. Of course, users aren't forced to visit the logout page, so it is also a good idea to create a `SessionAttributeListener` to take care of cleaning up resources when the user's session times out. You still waste those resources for exactly the amount of time you have set as the session timeout, but at least you are sure that the resources are eventually reclaimed properly.

15.2.2 *Using lazy instantiation*

Lazy instantiation is a resource-allocation strategy that lets you put off creating resources until they are absolutely needed. This approach works best for relatively heavyweight resources that may or may not be required for a user. For example, suppose you have an administration part of your web application that must connect to a variety of databases, gather a lot of records, and make web service calls, in addition to other time-consuming stuff. Because it is used only by a handful of users, you should put off building resources for it until they are necessary.

This strategy runs counter to the way that most servlet engines and application servers work. One of the keys to performance is pre-creation, pooling, and caching. Application servers can afford to do this because all the resources they allocate are generally infrastructural in nature. It is a safe bet that all web applications will need database connections, threads, and other boundary kinds of resources. Lazy instantiation is a more useful strategy for domain-level artifacts, such as administration modules or other resource-intensive items. This strategy presents you with the classic trade-off of saving resources at the expense of taking more time to deliver the resource when it is needed.

15.2.3 *Working with web collections*

Any Java developer who has gotten this far in our book has a good understanding of the attribute collections available through the Java web APIs. The collections are well documented in numerous books. However, it seems that developers are fixated on the session collection as a magical repository when sometimes other collections are better suited. In particular, most of the code I end up seeing makes too little use of the request collection in favor of session. I bring this up because misuse of the standard collections is a classic resource waster. You should always pick the attribute collection that has the narrowest scope that will get the job done.

Session cops

It is a good idea to establish the position of "session cop" on the development team for resource-intensive web applications. This person's duty is to monitor all the items developers are placing in collections to ensure that the application isn't going to be overwhelmed when it comes time to deploy it. Specifically, the session cop should verify that:

- The correct collection is being used.
- Collection attributes are cleaned up as quickly as possible.
- Developers aren't placing large data structures in memory that will harm the scalability of the application.
- Developers have a good justification for placing an object in the collection.

The session cop should warn the technical leader of the project when cross-developer contentions over collections usage arise (for example, two groups of developers absolutely *must* cache large chunks in the session, but the infrastructure can't handle both).

15.3 *Summary*

The Java web APIs provide a wealth of opportunities for managing resources. Caching is an effective way to manage resources, and two design patterns offer good alternatives for creating caches. The Flyweight design pattern creates a collection of canonical objects, which are representatives of all objects of that type. The Façade design pattern creates a simple interface to a large number of complex, interrelated classes. While Façade isn't a caching strategy per se, it is effective for hiding the details of elaborate caching scenarios behind an easy-to-use façade of classes.

You must manage other resources as well, such as JNDI connections and the standard collections. You should always save the JNDI context for the user rather than establishing it when needed. To handle collections correctly, choose the most suitable collection for the job at hand. Careless use of these collections can needlessly harm the scalability of the application. The establishment of a "session cop" to act as an application-wide overseer helps complex applications manage resources gracefully and lets you spot problems quickly.

In chapter 16, we look at debugging and logging in web applications.

16 *Debugging*

I don't have to tell you that debugging is a necessary evil of software development. If by some chance you write perfect code that never requires debugging, you can safely skip this chapter.

Debugging web applications creates unique difficulties. The problems are not easy to reproduce and generally don't show up until you have a number of people accessing the application (which typically doesn't happen until it moves to production). This chapter covers several avenues for debugging. First, we look at debugging with no tools except what is provided with the Software Development Kit (SDK). While primitive, that strategy works. Next, we look at debugging in two different integrated development environments (IDEs): the free, open-source NetBeans and the commercial IDE JBuilder.

Creating application logs is the "poor man's debugger." Although some negative connotations surround the use of logging as a low-tech solution to chasing bugs, it can be quite effective, particularly for distributed applications such as web applications. It is difficult to debug an application in-place after deployment on a server, and logging can solve this problem by providing a debugging hook no matter where the application is running. The other benefit of logging is that the code can stay in the application after deployment and provide a constant roadmap of problems that pop up.

This chapter concludes with a discussion of logging techniques and how they can provide benefits related to debugging. We cover both the logging support built into the SDK starting with version 1.4 and the open-source log4j project.

16.1 Debugging web applications

Debugging is the bane of many a programmer's existence and is often viewed as an onerous chore. However, until you can write perfect code the first time, you must debug your applications. Debugging web applications is especially difficult for five reasons. First, a web application is distributed, which means that it will eventually run on multiple machines. Even if you aren't debugging it on multiple physical machines, you are still dealing with logical machines, or boundaries between the application and what is running the application (the browser). Second, web applications are multithreaded. Even though the web APIs in Java effectively hide almost all the threaded nature of the servlet engine from you at development time, you must deal with it as you are debugging the application. Local variables in Java exist in terms of the thread that owns them. Thus, you cannot avoid threads if you need to look at the values of local variables. Some debuggers in IDEs simplify this task for you.

Third, you don't control the execution context of your application. By their nature, web applications run inside the context of the servlet engine, which does most of the method invocations for you. If you are accustomed to having complete control over the code that executes your code, this detail results in some frustration.

Fourth, if you are dealing with JSPs, you don't even have direct access to the source code that is running. The JSP is compiled into a servlet, which is executed by the servlet engine. You can have the servlet engine save the source code for you, but you must perform the mapping from the generated source back to the page where the code executes.

Fifth, the debugger might modify the behavior of the code, making bugs disappear when you're debugging but reappear when the code is running outside the debugger. This scenario is less common in Java than in other languages but is still possible.

Consider the very simple JSP in listing 16.1. Then, consider the excerpt from the generated servlet source shown in listing 16.2.

Listing 16.1 The source for a simple Hello JSP

```
<html>
<head>
<title>
Hello
</title>
</head>
<body bgcolor="#ffffff">
<h3>Hello!</h3>
<p>
<%  for (int i = 1; i < 6; i++) { %>
        Hello for the <%=i%><%= i == 1 ? "st" : i == 2 ? "nd" :
            i == 3 ? "rd" : "th" %>  time<br>
<%  } %>
</P>
</body>
</html>
```

Listing 16.2 A portion of the servlet engine's generated source for the Hello page

```
// HTML // begin [file="/Hello.jsp";from=(0,0);to=(9,0)]
    out.write("<html>\r\n<head>\r\n<title>\r\nHello\r\n</title>"+
    "\r\n</head>\r\n<body bgcolor=\"#ffffff\">\r\n<h3>Hello!"+
    "</h3>\r\n<p>\r\n");

// end
// begin [file="/Hello.jsp";from=(9,2);to=(9,34)]
    for (int i = 1; i < 6; i++) {
```

```
// end
// HTML // begin [file="/Hello.jsp";from=(9,36);to=(10,22)]
    out.write("\r\n        Hello for the ");
// end
// begin [file="/Hello.jsp";from=(10,25);to=(10,26)]
    out.print(i);
// end
// begin [file="/Hello.jsp";from=(10,31);to=(11,33)]
    out.print( i == 1 ? "st" : i == 2 ? "nd" :
i == 3 ? "rd" : "th" );
// end
// HTML // begin [file="/Hello.jsp";from=(11,35);to=(12,0)]
    out.write("  time<br>\r\n");
// end
// begin [file="/Hello.jsp";from=(12,2);to=(12,6)]
    }
// end
// HTML // begin [file="/Hello.jsp";from=(12,8);to=(16,0)]
    out.write("\r\n</P>\r\n</body>\r\n</html>\r\n");
// end
```

As you can see, the generated code is an ugly mess. At least the servlet engine is "kind enough" to include comments that indicate the column and row where the source originates. Debugging through a JSP by matching line numbers in the servlet's source back to the JSP page is very labor intensive.

This situation becomes even worse if you use a custom tag library, like the JSP Standard Tag Library (JSTL). Consider listing 16.3, the revised example in which we use JSTL to simplify the coding of the page.

Listing 16.3   JSTL simplifies writing the code by removing the scriptlet tags.

```
<%@ taglib prefix="c" uri="http://java.sun.com/jstl/core" %>
<html>
<head>
<title>
Hello
</title>
</head>
<body bgcolor="#ffffff">
<h3>Hello!</h3>
<p>
<c:forEach var="i" begin="1" end="5">
Hello for the <c:out value="${i}" />
  <c:choose>
```

```
      <c:when test="${i == 1}">
        <c:out value="st" />
      </c:when>
      <c:when test="${i == 2}">
        <c:out value="nd" />
      </c:when>
      <c:when test="${i == 3}">
        <c:out value="rd" />
      </c:when>
      <c:otherwise>
        <c:out value="th" />
      </c:otherwise>
    </c:choose>
  <br>
  </c:forEach>
  </P>
  </body>
  </html>
```

This code is a little more verbose but doesn't suffer from mixed HTML and scriptlet code. Generally, JSPs made with JSTL are easier to read and much easier for non-Java programmers to understand. However, this code creates a debugging nightmare. Consider listing 16.4, which includes only the beginning of the forEach tag and one of the choose tags.

Listing 16.4 The generated servlet source for a JSTL page is very convoluted.

```
// begin [file="/HelloSTL.jsp";from=(10,0);to=(10,37)]
/* ---- c:forEach ---- */
org.apache.taglibs.standard.tag.el.core.
  ForEachTag _jspx_th_c_forEach_0 = new org.apache.taglibs.standard.
  tag.el.core.ForEachTag();
_jspx_th_c_forEach_0.setPageContext(pageContext);
_jspx_th_c_forEach_0.setParent(null);
_jspx_th_c_forEach_0.setVar("i");
_jspx_th_c_forEach_0.setBegin("1");
_jspx_th_c_forEach_0.setEnd("5");
try {
    int _jspx_eval_c_forEach_0 = _jspx_th_c_forEach_0.doStartTag();
    if (_jspx_eval_c_forEach_0 ==
            javax.servlet.jsp.tagext.BodyTag.EVAL_BODY_BUFFERED)
        throw new JspTagException(
        "Since tag handler class org.apache.taglibs.standard.tag."+
        "el.core.ForEachTag does not implement BodyTag, it can't "+
        "return BodyTag.EVAL_BODY_TAG");
    if (_jspx_eval_c_forEach_0 !=
            javax.servlet.jsp.tagext.Tag.SKIP_BODY) {
```

```
        do {
        // end
        // HTML // begin [file="/HelloSTL.jsp";
        // from=(10,37);to=(11,14)]
          out.write("\r\nHello for the ");
        // end
        // begin [file="/HelloSTL.jsp";from=(11,14);to=(11,36)]
          /* ----   c:out ---- */
          org.apache.taglibs.standard.tag.el.core.
              OutTag _jspx_th_c_out_0 = new org.apache.taglibs.
              standard.tag.el.core.OutTag();
          _jspx_th_c_out_0.setPageContext(pageContext);
          _jspx_th_c_out_0.setParent(_jspx_th_c_forEach_0);
          _jspx_th_c_out_0.setValue("${i}");
          try {
            int _jspx_eval_c_out_0 =_jspx_th_c_out_0.doStartTag();
            if (_jspx_eval_c_out_0 !=
                  javax.servlet.jsp.tagext.Tag.SKIP_BODY) {
            try {
            if (_jspx_eval_c_out_0 !=
                javax.servlet.jsp.tagext.Tag.EVAL_BODY_INCLUDE) {
            out = pageContext.pushBody();
            _jspx_th_c_out_0.setBodyContent(
                  (javax.servlet.jsp.tagext.BodyContent) out);
            _jspx_th_c_out_0.doInitBody();
          }
          do {
          // end
          // begin [file="/HelloSTL.jsp";from=(11,14);to=(11,36)]
          } while (_jspx_th_c_out_0.doAfterBody() ==
                javax.servlet.jsp.tagext.BodyTag.EVAL_BODY_AGAIN);
        } finally {
            if (_jspx_eval_c_out_0 !=
                javax.servlet.jsp.tagext.Tag.EVAL_BODY_INCLUDE)
            out = pageContext.popBody();
        }
      }
  if (_jspx_th_c_out_0.doEndTag() ==
        javax.servlet.jsp.tagext.Tag.SKIP_PAGE)
      return;
} finally {
  _jspx_th_c_out_0.release();
}
// end
// HTML // begin [file="/HelloSTL.jsp";from=(11,36);to=(12,2)]
out.write("\r\n  ");
// end
// begin [file="/HelloSTL.jsp";from=(12,2);to=(12,12)]
/* ----   c:choose ---- */
org.apache.taglibs.standard.tag.common.core.
```

```
      ChooseTag _jspx_th_c_choose_0 =
        new org.apache.taglibs.standard.tag.common.core.ChooseTag();
_jspx_th_c_choose_0.setPageContext(pageContext);
_jspx_th_c_choose_0.setParent(_jspx_th_c_forEach_0);
try {
  int _jspx_eval_c_choose_0 = _jspx_th_c_choose_0.doStartTag();
  if (_jspx_eval_c_choose_0 ==
        javax.servlet.jsp.tagext.BodyTag.EVAL_BODY_BUFFERED)
      throw new JspTagException("Since tag handler class org."+
      "apache.taglibs.standard.tag.common.core.ChooseTag does not"+
      "implement BodyTag, it can't return BodyTag.EVAL_BODY_TAG");
  if (_jspx_eval_c_choose_0 !=
        javax.servlet.jsp.tagext.Tag.SKIP_BODY) {
      do {
      // end
      // HTML // begin [file="/HelloSTL.jsp";from=(12,12);to=(13,4)]
        out.write("\r\n      ");
      // end
      // begin [file="/HelloSTL.jsp";from=(13,4);to=(13,29)]
          /* ----  c:when ---- */
          org.apache.taglibs.standard.tag.el.core.
              WhenTag _jspx_th_c_when_0 = new org.apache.taglibs.
              standard.tag.el.core.WhenTag();
          _jspx_th_c_when_0.setPageContext(pageContext);
          _jspx_th_c_when_0.setParent(_jspx_th_c_choose_0);
          _jspx_th_c_when_0.setTest("${i == 1}");
          try {
              int _jspx_eval_c_when_0 =
                  _jspx_th_c_when_0.doStartTag();
              if (_jspx_eval_c_when_0 ==
              javax.servlet.jsp.tagext.BodyTag.EVAL_BODY_BUFFERED)
              throw new JspTagException("Since tag handler class"+
              "org.apache.taglibs.standard.tag.el.core.WhenTag "+
              "does not implement BodyTag, it can't return "+
              "BodyTag.EVAL_BODY_TAG");
          if (_jspx_eval_c_when_0 !=
              javax.servlet.jsp.tagext.Tag.SKIP_BODY) {
              do {
          // end
          // HTML // begin [file="/HelloSTL.jsp";
          // from=(13,29);to=(14,6)]
              out.write("\r\n        ");
          // end
          // begin [file="/HelloSTL.jsp";from=(14,6);to=(14,26)]
              /* ----  c:out ---- */
              org.apache.taglibs.standard.tag.el.core.
                OutTag _jspx_th_c_out_1 = new org.apache.taglibs.
                standard.tag.el.core.OutTag();
              _jspx_th_c_out_1.setPageContext(pageContext);
              _jspx_th_c_out_1.setParent(_jspx_th_c_when_0);
```

```
            _jspx_th_c_out_1.setValue("st");
            try {
            int _jspx_eval_c_out_1= _jspx_th_c_out_1.doStartTag();
            if (_jspx_eval_c_out_1 !=
                    javax.servlet.jsp.tagext.Tag.SKIP_BODY) {
                try {
                if (_jspx_eval_c_out_1 != javax.servlet.jsp.tagext.
                    Tag.EVAL_BODY_INCLUDE) {
                out = pageContext.pushBody();
                _jspx_th_c_out_1.setBodyContent(
                        (javax.servlet.jsp.tagext.BodyContent) out);
                _jspx_th_c_out_1.doInitBody();
            }
            do {
            // end
            // begin [file="/HelloSTL.jsp";from=(14,6);to=(14,26)]
            } while (_jspx_th_c_out_1.doAfterBody() ==
                    javax.servlet.jsp.tagext.BodyTag.EVAL_BODY_AGAIN);
        } finally {
            if (_jspx_eval_c_out_1 !=
                javax.servlet.jsp.tagext.Tag.EVAL_BODY_INCLUDE)
            out = pageContext.popBody();
        }
    }
    if (_jspx_th_c_out_1.doEndTag() ==
            javax.servlet.jsp.tagext.Tag.SKIP_PAGE)
            return;
    } finally {
    _jspx_th_c_out_1.release();
    }
    // end
```

Debugging this code is so difficult that it generally isn't done. The generated servlet for the original JSP consists of 91 lines of code. The generated servlet for the exact same page using JSTL consists of 419 lines! Of course, one of the benefits of using custom tags is the lack of debugging required for code that is already debugged. What about the developer who writes the custom tag and must debug it during development?

Now that we've painted an impossibly bleak picture of debugging web applications, let's discuss some strategies for handling this chore. First, we'll look at debugging with just the tools supplied by the SDK, namely the jdb debugger. Then, we'll cover two debuggers in IDEs.

16.2 Debugging with the SDK

The SDK comes with a command-line based debugger named jdb. Using a command-line debugger to debug a distributed web application may seem like a less-than-optimal way to spend your time. However, once you learn to use this debugger, you can glean important information from it. Given the choice, any developer would use a graphical debugger, such as the ones found in IDEs. However, this is exactly the reason you should at least become familiar with the SDK debugger. Situations will arise when you don't have access to anything but the SDK. For example, it is unlikely that the production application server running your application will have an IDE installed alongside your application. If you need a quick-and-dirty look at the internals of the application, you can use the SDK debugger. Also, if you work as a consultant, you generally don't have a choice of the tools that are available. Because it is part of the SDK, the jdb debugger is always there for you.

16.2.1 Starting the debugger

The jdb debugger documentation is provided in the JavaDocs for the SDK and reveals the basic details of how to start it and the available command-line options. Two startup options exist for the `jdb` debugger. The `jdb` command can act as a replacement for the `java` command to start the application. The debugger launches a debug virtual machine (VM). The other option allows you to attach to an existing VM that is already running, either on a local or remote machine.

If you connect to a VM running on a remote server, that VM must have started with certain command-line options. In other words, you must have determined that you want the remote machine to be debugged. Otherwise, anyone could attach to any VM and start snooping around at the values of its variables. Table 16.1 shows the two options you must use to invoke the VM to enable debugging.

Table 16.1 Attachment command-line options

Option	Purpose
-Xdebug	Enables debugging support in the VM
-Xrunjdwp:transport=dt_shmem,server=y,suspend=n	Loads the in-process debugging libraries and selects the transport mechanism for communication

The second option in the table specifies the default values for loading the libraries. This option uses the shared memory model to exchange information, which is
available only on Windows because it uses Windows shared memory primitives to
communicate information between debugger applications and the target VM. To
launch the VM in debug mode, use a command line like this (on a single line):

```
java -Xdebug -Xrunjdwp:transport=dt_shmem,address=jdbcon,server=y,
        suspend=n MyClass
```

Once the application is running, you can start the debugger and attach to it with
the following command line:

```
jdb -attach jdbcon
```

where `jdbcon` is the address specified with the VM that was invoked.

Using shared memory isn't possible when the VM runs on a remote machine.
The other transport mechanism, `dt_socket`, is available for all platforms and for
cross-machine communication. It allows the debugger and VM to communicate
via a socket. This mechanism takes advantage of the Java Platform Debugger
Architecture (JPDA) and command-line options. To launch a debug session using
socket transport, use a similar syntax to the one shown earlier but with `dt_socket`
as the transport parameter. A large number of tuning options exist for the second
parameter passed to the VM; they are summarized in table 16.2.

Table 16.2   jdwp options

Name	Required?	Default Value	Description
help	No	none	Prints a brief help message and exits the VM.
transport	Yes	none	Contains the name of the transport you want to use when connecting to the debugger.
server	No	n	If `y`, listens for a debugger application to attach; otherwise, attaches to the debugger application at the specified address. If `y` and no address is speci-fied, chooses a transport address at which to listen for a debugger application, and prints the address to the standard output stream.
address	Yes, if `server=n`; no, otherwise		Contains the transport address for the connection. If `server=n`, attempts to attach to debugger appli-cation at this address. If `server=y`, listens for a connection at this address.

continued on next page

Table 16.2 jdwp options *(continued)*

Name	Required?	Default Value	Description
launch	No	none	At completion of Java Debugging Wire Protocol (JDWP) initialization, launches the process given in this string. This option is used in combination with `onthrow` and/or `onuncaught` to provide just-in-time debugging, in which a debugger process is launched when a particular event occurs in this VM.
onthrow	No	none	Delays initialization of the JDWP library until an exception of the given class is thrown in this VM. The exception class name must be package-qualified. Connection establishment is included in JDWP initialization, so it will not begin until the exception is thrown.
onuncaught	No	n	If `y`, delays initialization of the JDWP library until an uncaught exception is thrown in this VM. Connection establishment is included in JDWP initialization, so it will not begin until the exception is thrown.
stdalloc	No	n	By default, the JDWP reference implementation uses an alternate allocator for its memory allocation. If `y`, the standard C runtime library allocator will be used. This option is mainly for testing; use it with care. Deadlocks can occur in this VM if the alternative allocator is disabled.
strict	No	n	If `y`, assumes strict Java Virtual Machine Debugging Interface (JVMDI) conformance. This will disable all workarounds to known bugs in JVMDI implementations. This option is mainly for testing and should be used with care.
suspend	No	y	If `y`, `VMStartEvent` has a `suspendPolicy` of `SUSPEND_ALL`. If n, `VMStartEvent` has a `suspendPolicy` of `SUSPEND_NONE`.

As an example, this command line (invoked on a single line) enables debugging with socket transport on a server using socket 8000:

```
java -Xdebug -Xrunjdwp:transport=dt_socket,
     server=y,address=8000 MyClass
```

The options listed in table 16.2 apply to the starting of the VM that hosts your application. In a web application, the servlet engine governs that VM. Different servlet engines have different startup semantics, but most allow you to modify the startup parameters (and frequently the complete command line). In that case,

Figure 16.1
Starting Tomcat with the
debug option prints
configuration information and
pauses at a command prompt
for the debugger.

you can either substitute the command options listed in the table or change the invocation of the servlet engine from java to jdb.

The servlet engine used for most of the examples in this book is Tomcat, currently at version 4. The developers of Tomcat anticipated the need to use jdb to debug web applications, so the startup batch file (named Catalina.bat) includes a debug command-line option. If you invoke Tomcat with this switch, you'll see the results shown in figure 16.1.

16.2.2 *Running the debugger*

Once you start the debugger, it pauses, waiting for the next command. It does not actually invoke the servlet engine yet. There is a possibility that you'll want to investigate some options (like classpath) or set a breakpoint before the application starts. To see a list of all the commands available for the debugger, enter a question mark at this prompt. A small portion of this list of commands appears in figure 16.2.

The first command runs the application. Invoking the run command starts the servlet engine, and you will see the normal startup logging information for the servlet engine. At that point, you can invoke one of the applications through a browser. Table 16.3 summarizes some important debugger options.

Notice that the first few commands (thread, threads, resume, suspend) pertain to threads. Because the servlet engine is multithreaded, you must discover the

```
 cCmd - catalina.bat debug                                  _ □ ×
Initializing jdb ...
> ?
** command list **
run [class [args]]        -- start execution of application's main class

threads [threadgroup]     -- list threads
thread <thread id>        -- set default thread
suspend [thread id(s)]    -- suspend threads (default: all)
resume [thread id(s)]     -- resume threads (default: all)
where [thread id] | all   -- dump a thread's stack
wherei [thread id] | all  -- dump a thread's stack, with pc info
up [n frames]             -- move up a thread's stack
down [n frames]           -- move down a thread's stack
kill <thread> <expr>      -- kill a thread with the given exception object
interrupt <thread>        -- interrupt a thread

print <expr>              -- print value of expression
dump <expr>               -- print all object information
eval <expr>               -- evaluate expression (same as print)
set <lvalue> = <expr>     -- assign new value to field/variable/array element
locals                    -- print all local variables in current stack frame
```

Figure 16.2
The help command (a
question mark) lists all the
commands available for
the debugger.

Table 16.3   Useful debugger commands

Command	Description
run [class [args]]	Starts execution of the application's main class.
threads [threadgroup]	Lists all the threads in the application, both running and suspended.
thread <thread id>	Sets the default thread.
suspend <thread id>	Suspends threads (the default suspends all threads).
resume [thread id(s)]	Resumes threads (the default resumes all threads).
where [thread id] | all	Dumps a thread's stack.
up [n frames]	Moves up a thread's stack.
down [n frames]	Moves down a thread's stack.
kill <thread> <expr>	Kills a thread with the given exception object.
print <expr>	Prints the value of an expression.
dump <expr>	Prints the information for an entire object.
set <lvalue> = <expr>	Assigns a new value to a field/variable/array element.
locals	Prints all local variable information.
fields <class id>	Lists a class's fields.
stop in <class id>.<method>[(argument type, ...)]	Sets a breakpoint in a method (if the method is overloaded, you must supply the parameter signature).
stop at <class id>:<line>	Sets a breakpoint at a particular source line.
clear <class id>.<method>[(argument type, ...)]	Clears a method breakpoint.
clear <class id>:<line>	Clears a line number breakpoint.
catch [uncaught|caught|all] <exception class id>	Breaks when an exception occurs.
watch [access|all] <class id>.<field name>	Sets a watch for access/modification to a field.
unwatch [access|all] <class id>.<field name>	Cancels the watch previously set.
trace methods [thread]	Traces method entry and exit.
step	Executes the current line.
step up	Executes until the current method returns.
next	Steps one line (steps over method calls).
cont	Continues execution from a breakpoint.

continued on next page

Table 16.3   Useful debugger commands *(continued)*

Command	Description
list [line number|method]	Prints the source code.
use (or sourcepath) [source file path]	Makes the source code accessible for listing.
classpath	Prints the current classpath information.
pop	Pops the stack through and includes the current frame.
redefine <class id> <class file name>	Redefines the code for a class.
!!	Repeats the last command.
<n> <command>	Repeats the command *n* times.
help (or ?)	Lists all commands.
exit (or quit)	Exits the debugger.

thread ID that your application is using. Issuing the `threads` command shows you all of the currently running threads in the servlet engine. A sample invocation of this command appears in figure 16.3.

A hexadecimal number appearing on the left-hand side of the output identifies the threads. To find the one for your application, look for the name on the right and match it with the thread ID on the left. Matching the rows exactly is difficult if you have a large number of entries. In Windows, you can enable the *mark*

Figure 16.3   The `threads` command shows all currently running threads in the servlet engine.

feature of the console window to highlight the row, which makes it easy to match the web application name to the thread. The thread ID for your application is important because most of the other commands are thread-centric, meaning that you must specify a thread ID along with the command. Another useful command is thread, which allows you to set a thread as the default thread for this debugging session.

One of the important options in the debugger lets you list portions of your source code while the application is running. To enable this option, you must set a path to your source files. You set the source path on the command line using the sourcepath command-line option. However, if you don't have direct access to the command line (which is often the case for servlet engines), the sourcepath debugger command allows you to set this option after the debugger has started.

16.2.3 *Breakpoints and steps*

Breakpoints are set at the method level, on a line number, or for an uncaught exception. To set a breakpoint, you issue the stop in, stop at, or catch command. In figure 16.4, we've set a line number breakpoint before the execution of the application.

After you run the servlet engine (via the run command), you can access your web application from a browser and interact with it until you reach the class containing the breakpoint. At that point, the application will stop and allow you to analyze it. For information purposes, you can issue a list command to see the context in which the breakpoint occurred. Figure 16.5 shows a breakpoint hit, followed by a list command that reveals the context.

Now that the application is stopped, you can step through it to investigate variable values and other characteristics. The step command moves you to the next line of code and enters methods if the current line features a method call. If you don't want to trace into a method, use the next command instead. The thread command is important here. If you haven't set a default thread for the application, then step and next will take you to the next line of code to be executed by the servlet engine, which is likely to be in another web application (or

Figure 16.4
Breakpoints are best set before the beginning of the application's execution.

```
cCmd - catalina.bat debug                                           _ □ ×
Breakpoint hit: "thread=Thread-9", com.nealford.art.emotherearth.controller.Catalog.doPost(), line=45 bci=72
45              List outputList = productDb.getProductListSlice(start,
>
Thread-9[1] list
41                      productDb.getProductList().size(), recsPerPage);
42              String[] pageList =
43                      buildListOfPagesToShow(recsPerPage,
44                                      totalPagesToShow);
45 =>           List outputList = productDb.getProductListSlice(start,
46                      recsPerPage);
47              sortPagesForDisplay(request, productDb, outputList);
48
49              bundleInformationForView(request, start, pageList,
50                                      outputList);
Thread-9[1]
```

Figure 16.5   The breakpoint halts the application and the `list` command shows the current execution context.

in the servlet engine code itself). Using the `thread` command keeps the execution context within the current thread (although the other threads continue to run—you just don't step or trace through them).

Once you have stepped through the code, you can issue the `cont` command to continue execution at full speed. The servlet engine will execute code until it hits another breakpoint. You must keep an eye on the browser as you are running the debugger. If you execute enough code to complete the request, the debugger is no longer stopped in a thread. It waits on the user of the application to do something that it can debug again.

16.2.4 *Accessing variables*

When the debugger stops at a breakpoint, you need to access the values of variables to understand what your application is doing. Several commands are available for printing out the values of variables and expressions. The `locals` command prints out the values of the local variables in scope for the current thread. The results of this command are shown in figure 16.6.

The `locals` command shows the values of the primitives and the class type of the object references. If you want to further investigate the object references, use the `dump` command. It allows you to access more details on variables and fields. Figure 16.7 shows an invocation of the `dump` command.

**Figure 16.6
The `locals` command prints a list of all the local variables in scope for the current thread context.**

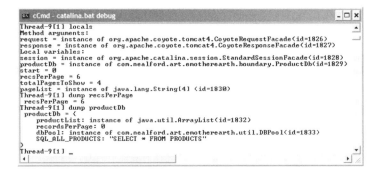

Figure 16.7 The `dump` command allows you to investigate the contents of object references. In this case, it shows all the fields of the `ProductDb` class, including the values of the primitives and strings.

When viewing the "dump" of the `ProductDb` instance, you can see the values of all the fields. The primitives and strings display their values, and the object references show their class type and reference ID. Using the `dump` command, you can further drill into the fields of the object. For example, you can investigate the properties of the `productList` variable inside the `productDb` instance. This debugger (like all debuggers in Java) allows you to see the values of private member variables, which are normally inaccessible.

The syntax for `dump` (as well as some of the other investigative commands) also accepts an expression. You can use any legal Java expression that eventually returns a value represented as a string. Even if you return object references, the debugger can call the `toString()` method on them. Figure 16.8 shows the results of two such invocations of the `dump` command. The first dumps the contents of the `outputList` variable. The second invocation evaluates an expression for the contents of the first element of the list. Notice that type casts, method calls, and other legal Java syntax is permitted with this command.

```
cx cCmd - catalina.bat debug                                        _ □ ×
Thread-9[1] dump outputList
 outputList = (
     java.util.SubList.l: instance of java.util.ArrayList(id=1832)
     java.util.SubList.offset: 0
     java.util.SubList.size: 6
     java.util.SubList.expectedModCount: 19
     java.util.AbstractList.modCount: 0
 )
Thread-9[1] dump ((ArrayList) outputList).get(0)
 ((ArrayList) outputList).get(0) = (
     name: "Ocean"
     price: 1.3934562E9
     formatter: instance of java.text.DecimalFormat(id=1838)
     id: 1
 )
Thread-9[1] _
```

Figure 16.8
The `dump` command in conjunction with expressions is a powerful way to determine the contents of variables, including values that require method calls to retrieve.

16.2.5 *Effectively using jdb*

The previous sections provided numerous details about the commands in jdb. However, discussing the commands doesn't provide a roadmap for effective use. The following section walks through a debug session with jdb and provides a recipe for interactions with this debugger.

First, start the servlet engine using the debug flag. This step may be as easy as running Tomcat with the debug command-line option or as difficult as editing a startup configuration file to replace java with jdb. In any case, you should get to the point where the debugger is running in a console window. Once it has completed initializing, use the sourcepath or use command to point to the source code for your project. This is a reference to the source root path for your code. Next, set one or more breakpoints at methods, line numbers, or exceptions. Then, run the servlet engine with the run command.

Once the servlet engine is running, you can determine the thread ID for your application via the threads command. Once you have the thread ID, use it to set the default thread via the thread command. Next, invoke your application through a browser and interact with it until you reach code that will trigger a breakpoint. The browser will "hang," waiting for the servlet engine to complete the request. Go to the debug window and use the commands for determining values and stepping through code to determine what the bug is and how to fix it. If you need to make a change to one of the source files, you can change it, recompile it, and use redefine to load the new class into memory. Continue this process until your application is bug free.

Here is a quick summary of the process we've outlined in this section:

1 Start the servlet engine in debug mode.

2 Attach to the source path for your code.

3 Set one or more breakpoints, either on line numbers or contingent on method invocations.

4 Run the application.

5 Find the thread ID for your application.

6 Set it as the default thread.

7 Invoke your application in a browser and interact with it until you hit a breakpoint.

8 Use step and/or next to walk through your code.

9 Use dump, locals, and eval to analyze your variables.

10   If you need to make a small change to a file and test it, use `redefine` to load the new class file.

11   Use `cont` to resume execution of the application until the next breakpoint.

12   Iterate until done.

Of course, `jdb` would not be most people's first choice as a debugger for Java applications. Using it is labor intensive and time consuming. While it does provide most of the information that more sophisticated debuggers give you, it is harder to access because of the command-line nature of the tool. However, being familiar with its use may be a lifesaver because it is the only debugger that you *know* for sure will always be present.

16.3   Debugging with IDEs

A lot of Java development, especially web development, may be done without elaborate IDEs. With a good text editor and Ant, developers can build an effective development environment. This process is more labor intensive because the developer must configure everything by hand, but it also provides the ultimate amount of control. However, one area where you need an IDE is for debugging.

16.3.1 Debugging with NetBeans

NetBeans is an open-source Java IDE available from www.netbeans.org. Its code base originated with Forte for Java, although it has been heavily modified since those roots and is now called SunONE Studio. It is owned by Sun Microsystems and serves as the basis for its commercial IDE. However, the core IDE is open source and freely available.

NetBeans is modular, with a variety of add-ons that you may install. Some of these plug-ins enhance the web development and debugging support in Net-Beans, including adding support for such tasks as debugging in JSPs. NetBeans supports all the same operations as the jdb debugger, but in a much friendlier and intuitive environment. The examples shown in this section assume that you've installed the latest web development plug-ins.

Starting the debugger
To start debugging a web project in NetBeans, you have to import the application into the NetBeans IDE. This is a straightforward and well-documented process, so I won't cover it here. Once you've imported the project, create a web module that

points to the document root of your project's web application. The base eMother-Earth project is the subject of debugging for this example; the NetBeans Explorer view of this project is shown in figure 16.9.

When you choose to debug a web project, NetBeans will automatically launch Tomcat for you from within the environment. Once the application is running, NetBeans switches over to the debug view, which appears in figure 16.10.

The NetBeans debug environment is customizable. The left-hand side features properties sheets for a variety of views. The buttons at the top of the view act as toggles to turn properties sheets on and off. From left to right, this tool allows you to see data on sessions (an instance of the servlet engine running), threads, the call stack, local variables, "all in one" (a view of multiple pieces of information in one page), watches, loaded classes, breakpoints, and properties. The view in figure 16.10 has local variables, watches, and breakpoints toggled on. The right-hand side of the environment shows the source code. In figure 16.10, the editor is stopped on a breakpoint on line 36. The bottom right-hand side shows the output from Tomcat that you would normally see at the command prompt. The toolbar buttons at the top right allow you to control execution, with Step Over, Step Into, Step Out, and Continue Execution. Buttons also appear here for adding new breakpoints and watches.

Watches

NetBeans allows you to set *watches* for variables and expressions. The watches appear in the left-hand side pane when the Watches button is toggled on. The watches show the name, type, and value of the variable. For primitives and strings, the value displays the actual values, and for objects an identifier is shown that corresponds to the object instance. There is no intrinsic meaning to this value, but it

Figure 16.9
The web module in NetBeans points to the document root of your web application and also includes a link to the project source for compilation purposes.

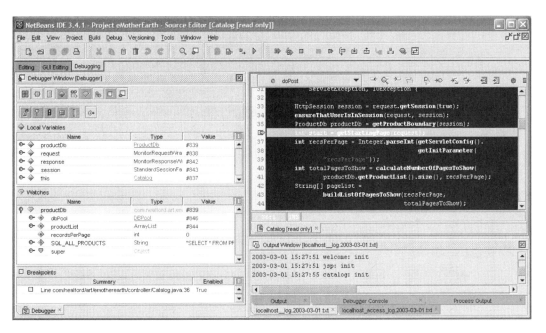

Figure 16.10 The NetBeans debug view features status sheets along the left, and code and command-line output along the right. The tool buttons at the top allow for code execution.

can be used to determine whether two objects point to the same memory location. The Watches pane is shown in figure 16.11.

The toolbar buttons on the left, under the view toggles, allow you to specify which aspects of variables you'll see. For example, notice in figure 16.11 that the

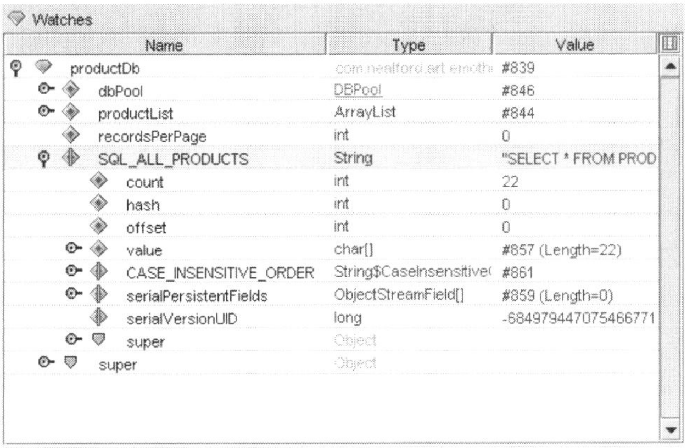

Figure 16.11
The Watches pane shows the variable (both primitives and objects), the type, and the current value.

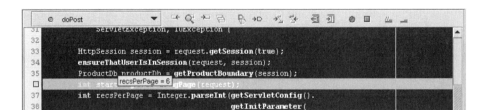

Figure 16.12   To see the value of a variable in the editor, you can position your mouse cursor over it and pause, and the value will appear.

super class appears, along with all fields of the object, both private and public. You can set toggles to only display variables of a certain scope and restrict the view of the super class reference.

Local variables

Watches are fine for values that you want to watch change over time. However, suppose you only care about the current value of a variable or field. NetBeans allows you to see the values of variables by moving the cursor over them in the editor and pausing. Figure 16.12 shows this effect in the source editor.

The other way to learn the values of local variables is to check the pane dedicated to them on the left. Figure 16.13 shows the Local Variables pane.

Breakpoints

You set breakpoints in NetBeans by clicking in the editor's gutter next to the line of code. The breakpoints show up as highlighted lines. Figure 16.10 shows a breakpoint set on a line in a servlet. NetBeans also allows you to set breakpoints in JSP pages. Figure 16.14 shows two breakpoints set in a JSP, followed by the execution line. NetBeans allows you to set breakpoints and single-step through code in

Name	Type	Value	
productDb	ProductDb	#839	
recsPerPage	int	6	
request	MonitorRequestWrapp	#838	
response	MonitorResponseWrap	#842	
session	StandardSessionFaca	#843	
start	int	0	
this	Catalog	#837	

Figure 16.13
The Local Variables pane shows the values and types of all variables currently in scope.

JSPs. It also lets you see the corresponding line of code in the generated servlet. If you expand the breakpoint view, it shows the line number in the generated servlet, and you can double-click on it to go to the code.

Other tools

NetBeans also includes a tool named `HttpMonitor`, shown in figure 16.15. It shows you information about the HTTP aspects of your running application, such as the cookies, the values of variables maintained by the servlet engine, and other data. This tool launches automatically when you debug a web application, or you can select it from the Tools menu.

Debugging with NetBeans

Debugging an application in NetBeans is obviously easier than the command-line `jdb` debugger. The tool consolidates information and places it at your fingertips instead of forcing you to wrestle with a command line. With plug-ins available that support web development, NetBeans makes a nice environment for developing

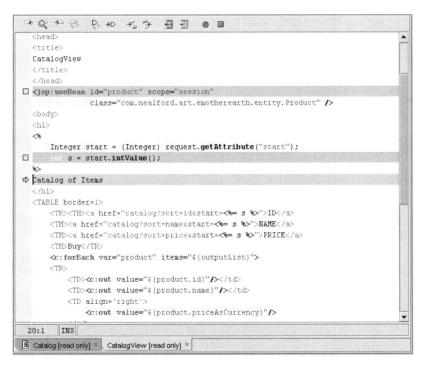

Figure 16.14   NetBeans allows the developer to set breakpoints on code in a JSP.

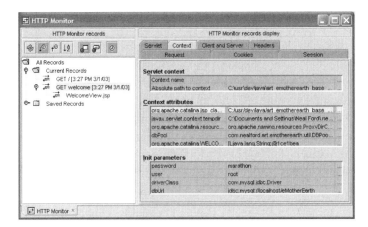

Figure 16.15
The `HTTPMonitor` tool
shows numerous web
aspects of your running
application, including
attributes and parameters.

and debugging web applications. It is one of the better open-source IDEs for debugging tasks.

16.3.2 Debugging with JBuilder

Having looked at the open-source world of web application debugging, let's now turn to the commercial world. Borland's JBuilder is widely regarded as the best overall Java development environment, and it is one of the finest developer IDEs on the market for any language. From a cost standpoint (over two thousand dollars for the Enterprise Edition), it lies on the other end of the spectrum from the open-source NetBeans IDE. JBuilder does have a free Community Edition, but it doesn't support web development or debugging, so we're using the Enterprise version for this section.

Projects

As with other IDEs, you must first establish a context for your application. In JBuilder, this is done with a project, which encapsulates such information as the paths (source path, classpath, etc.) used for the application. The project also specifies the target VM (any VM can be targeted from JBuilder). In addition, a project lets you establish what JBuilder calls "libraries." Libraries are root directories or JAR files containing classes that you can add to a project in order to utilize their code. JBuilder takes the libraries for the project and places the corresponding classes on the classpath for the compiler and VM when it runs the project.

JBuilder supports a variety of application servers and servlet engines. You can specify the server you want to use in the Project Properties dialog box, shown in figure 16.16. JBuilder allows you to run projects under different application servers so that they don't interfere with one another. Once you have established an application server for a project, JBuilder runs the project within the IDE using that application server. This means that you can set breakpoints and otherwise debug your application regardless of which server the project uses. Testing (and debugging) the application under a different application server is as simple as changing a project setting. JBuilder makes it easy to move from one application server to another.

Even if you are using a servlet engine or application not natively supported by JBuilder, you can still set up JBuilder to run the application server within the environment (which in turn allows you to debug your application within that environment). You specify the run context for a project in the project's properties, which in turn encapsulates the run configurations for that project. Each project can have an unlimited number of runtime configurations, allowing you to specify main classes, parameters, and other execution information. To enable JBuilder to run an application server that it doesn't natively support, you must know the startup class name and the required parameters to start the server. If you already know how to start the server from a command line, you probably already know enough to incorporate it into JBuilder.

For example, as of this writing Macromedia's JRun server is not natively supported by JBuilder. To set up a web application for debugging using JRun, you need the JRun libraries, the name of the main JRun class, and the application's

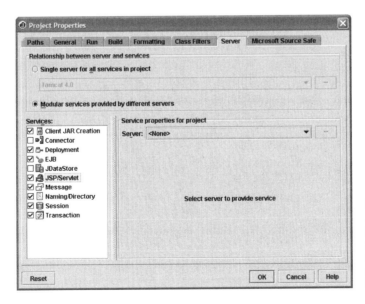

**Figure 16.16
JBuilder's Project
Properties dialog box lets
you assign the application
server and its
characteristics on a project-
by-project basis.**

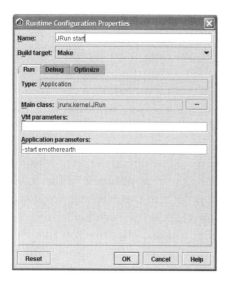

Figure 16.17
Setting up alternate servers requires setting the main class name and the required parameters.

startup parameters. Include the JRun libraries in the properties for the project, and then open the Runtime Configuration Properties dialog box. Figure 16.17 shows this dialog box after we added JRun's information. The configuration information for JRun is summarized in table 16.4.

Since JBuilder isn't built with prior knowledge of JRun, you must also create a runtime configuration to stop the server. The only difference between the start and stop runtime configuration is that you include the stop flag instead of start. Figure 16.18 shows the eMotherEarth application running in debug mode inside JBuilder, which launched the JRun server from within the environment.

This flexibility is an important feature. JBuilder is designed to support capabilities beyond those built in by the JBuilder development team. It is a hallmark of a well-designed application when you can extend it gracefully, using the framework that is already in place.

Table 16.4   The JRun configuration information

Configuration Item	Value
JRun libs directory (used to create a JBuilder library)	{jrun.home}\lib
Main class	jrunx.kernel.JRun
Application parameters: to start and specify the server	-start emotherearth

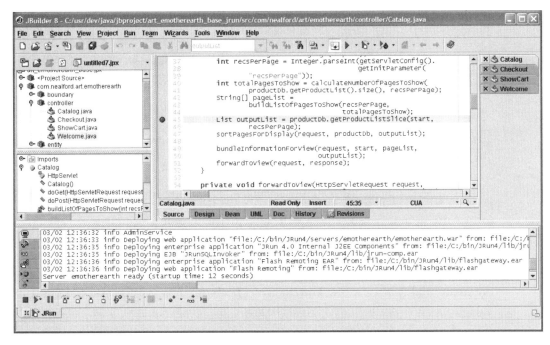

Figure 16.18 Here JBuilder debugs the eMotherEarth application running in JRun (launched from JBuilder).

Starting the debugger

JBuilder's `debug` command launches the VM with the debugging information you specified, automatically supplied on the command line. When you run the application in the debugger, JBuilder's message pane at the bottom of the screen adds new tabs along the left-hand side. You can see the new tabs in figure 16.18. The content of these tabs is summarized in table 16.5.

Table 16.5   The debug view tabs in JBuilder

Tab	Description
Console Output	Shows the console window output from the application server. If another tab is selected when new output appears, this tab glows green.
Threads	Shows the running threads and all local variables in scope for that thread.

continued on next page

Table 16.5   The debug view tabs in JBuilder *(continued)*

Tab	Description
Watches	Shows the values of the watches that have been set.
Loaded Classes	Shows a list of all classes that have been loaded by the application.
Breakpoints	Shows details of all breakpoints that the user has set.
Classes With Tracing Disabled	Shows a list of classes flagged to disable tracing. This tab allows you to flag some classes (like the ones from the SDK) that you don't want to accidentally step into.

JBuilder supports all the common behaviors of IDE-based debuggers. It allows you to view the output console, set watches, create breakpoints using a variety of criteria (five different ways in all), and view threads. These are all features that JBuilder has in common with NetBeans, so we won't bother to highlight them here. The user interface you use to get to these elements is slightly different, but the functionality is the same. For example, both debuggers allow you to float your cursor over a variable to see its current value.

16.3.3   *Differences between debuggers*

Let's now focus on the ways that JBuilder significantly differs from NetBeans. Each of the tabs in the JBuilder message pane is detachable. Simply right-click on any of the tabs (except the `Console` tab) and detach it via the pop-up menu into a floating window. This feature comes in handy when you want to see two pieces of information maintained by debugger tabs simultaneously. For example, if you want to see the watch values and the console at the same time, float and dock each of these tabs independently.

Investigating values

The thread view in JBuilder contains a vast amount of information about the running application. Local variables in Java are kept in the thread's stack frame, so looking at the characteristics of a thread also reveals information about the variables the thread owns. Figure 16.19 shows the thread view in JBuilder.

The threads appear in the left-hand pane, and the variables referenced by each thread appear on the right. The object references on the right are in outline form and you can expand a reference to display the values of the variables. Unlike NetBeans, JBuilder shows you the drilled-into values of the objects right from this thread view in addition to the internal ID of the object reference. This view is useful because it consolidates so much information into a small place.

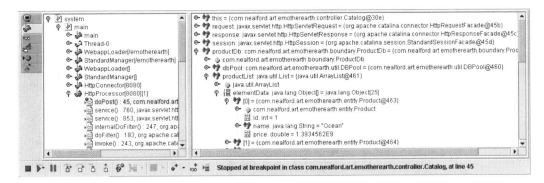

Figure 16.19 The thread view in JBuilder shows both the stack frame and values of all variables referenced by that thread. You can expand each of the object references to show its contents.

Another useful view in JBuilder is the loaded classes view, shown in figure 16.20. This view consists of an outline of all the classes loaded by the application, categorized by package. Each class view in turn displays the values of the class-level variables defined in that class. This view is handy for debugging dynamic class loading, particularly when you're using a factory class to load other classes.

Evaluate and modify

Perhaps the most powerful of JBuilder's debugging views is the Evaluate/Modify dialog box, which you open by selecting Evaluate/Modify from the Run menu. This dialog box allows you to evaluate variables and expressions while the debugger is stopped on a breakpoint. As you can see in figure 16.21, the dialog box

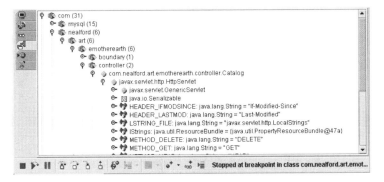

Figure 16.20 The loaded classes view shows you a summary of all the classes used by the application in addition to class-level values of variables.

Figure 16.21
The Evaluate/Modify dialog box allows you to view the contents of any field or local variable.

shows the typical JBuilder view of an outline of the fields of an object reference. In figure 16.21, we are evaluating a List object. The Evaluate/Modify dialog box lets you drill all the way to the contents of the list.

The ability to view the list contents is useful in its own right. However, this dialog box goes even further. One of the compelling reasons to use IDEs for Java development is the help they provide while you're coding. Every environment has its own copyrighted name for this feature; JBuilder calls it *Code Insight*. You enter a

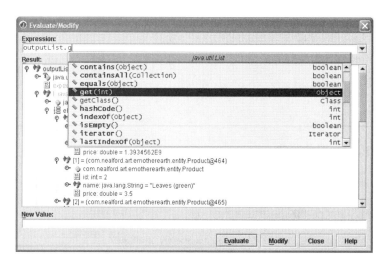

Figure 16.22   Code Insight in JBuilder extends all the way into the expression field of the Evaluate/Modify dialog box.

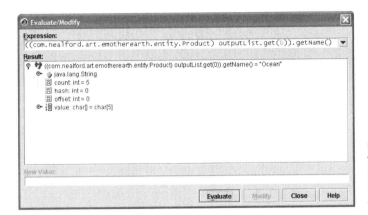

Figure 16.23
The Expression field of the Evaluate/Modify dialog box can include complex Java expressions.

variable name, followed by a period, and you can view a list of all the fields' methods available for that object. Once you get used to this feature, you'll find it hard to work without it.

JBuilder goes even further with Code Insight, extending it into the debug dialog box. The Evaluate/Modify dialog box supports Code Insight in the Expression text box at the top. As you are typing in expressions to evaluate, it provides a list of the available methods, as shown in figure 16.22.

One more feature of this dialog box is worth mentioning. The Expression text box takes an expression, which can be an arbitrarily complex Java expression. With the help of Code Insight, you can build complex expressions for evaluation during your debug session. This feature lets you dynamically investigate the context of your application, as illustrated in figure 16.23.

16.4 *Evaluating debuggers*

Debugging is one aspect of development—particularly in the area of web applications—where proficiency is critical to the success of the project. Which debugger should you use, given the spectrum of choices? Several factors should influence your decision.

If you are interested in a no-cost debugger, you can choose between the SDK debugger or one of the open-source offerings. The SDK debugger is for hard-core command-line junkies. While you can use it to glean useful information, it is much more labor intensive than the IDE-based alternatives. However, proficiency using the SDK debugger is important. It is the only debugger that you know will always be available. And, it may be your only choice when you need quick-and-dirty debugging of a deployed application that's running on servers far away from your IDE of choice.

If you are considering either the open-source or free world, I think that open source is better. Getting the project set up to run in the IDE takes a little effort, but it is a one-time operation and you more than make up for it in the time you save using the debugger. Debugging is a task that requires a wide variety of disparate information, and an environment that organizes information that makes it easier to see saves time and effort. We've discussed NetBeans, but of course it is not the only open-source debugger. In fact, the debuggers in Java generally have improved significantly of late, so it is rare to find a truly deficient one.

For the ultimate in productivity and flexibility, you can't beat commercial IDEs. These products are more polished and generally easier to set up and run than the open-source or free offerings. The great ones are well designed enough to offer extreme flexibility. Almost every commercial IDE extends beyond the open-source alternatives in the niceties associated with debugging. In other words, all the modern debuggers support watches, breakpoints, and the other tasks common to all debuggers. The commercial products generally go beyond the base capabilities; for example, JBuilder (which I personally like the best) offers views that consolidate a valuable combination of information. A variety of commercial products are available (some based on open-source IDEs) that offer similar advantages.

The real question is whether it's worth the extra money to get an IDE for debugging. I would have to say yes. The answer to this question lies in the value of developer time. Paying developers is expensive. If you can provide a tool to make them more productive—even 10 percent more productive—it will always pay off in the end. The initial cost of a commercial IDE pales in comparison to the months and years spent paying the salaries of developers.

16.5 Debugging in frameworks

In part 2, we discussed the debugging aspects of each framework in turn. However, this seems like a good place to summarize that information. Ease of debugging is one of the evaluation criteria for choosing a framework.

16.5.1 Struts

Debugging in Struts is essentially the same as debugging any other Model 2 application because the framework is so relatively lightweight. Struts includes no additional debugging support (like Tapestry's Inspector) but doesn't really need it.

One shortcoming that Struts shares with all JSP custom tag–based frameworks is the inability by debuggers to evaluate the custom tags within the JSP. You can single-step through the code in the generated servlet, but that code is so convoluted that rarely will anything of value will emerge.

16.5.2 *Tapestry*

Tapestry has good support for debugging, including specialized tools. The stack traces delivered to the browser are very informative; they contain both Tapestry internal messages and the full Java stack trace, so you can track down bugs. The Inspector tool included with Tapestry makes it easy to discover information about the interaction of the framework and the web API it encapsulates. The exception pages in Tapestry are state of the art, unwinding nested exceptions automatically. When you're using Tapestry and you get an exception, you may find the volume of information generated overwhelming. However, more information is always better than less. Some developers are moving to Tapestry just because the debugging support is so good. The next version of Tapestry (version 3) includes even better debugging support.

It is easy to debug JSPs in Tapestry because it doesn't use them! All the code in Tapestry is embedded in the framework itself, so there is never a need to try to debug a custom tag.

16.5.3 *WebWork*

WebWork includes no specific special support for debugging. In particular, it would be useful if it provided some mechanism (like Tapestry's Inspector) for looking at the value stack because so much of WebWork's behavior revolves around it. WebWork makes extensive use of custom JSP tags, which causes a problem for debuggers because it is difficult to debug custom tags. This difficulty is particularly acute in WebWork because the custom tags interact so much with the built-in data structures.

16.5.4 *InternetBeans Express*

Debugging InternetBeans Express typically involves using JBuilder's debugger (because InternetBeans Express is only available with JBuilder). The stack traces and other information provided by this framework are detailed and to the point. The event-driven nature and reliance on postback servlets makes debugging a little tricky because you must fight with the framework's use of event handlers. However, this is more a characteristic of the framework itself, not of debugging per se.

16.5.5 *Velocity*

The worst part of debugging Velocity is the lack of an interactive debugger for the Velocity Template Language. It forces you into an iterative "hunt and destroy" method of debugging. It is possible to set breakpoints in the Velocity servlet, but doing that doesn't give you access to the template language.

In Velocity's defense, it is not a complex framework, so there really isn't much to debug. I can't remember struggling with Velocity trying to get things to work and needing more extensive debugger support. Simplicity is its redeeming feature.

16.5.6 *Cocoon*

Debugging Cocoon is difficult because it is a dual-purpose framework: part publishing engine and part web framework. The error messages are particularly non-intuitive, and it is frequently difficult to determine if the message relates to the publishing side or the framework side. Cocoon relies on the complex sitemap configuration document, which is unforgiving of errors. The messages generated when errors occur are not very intuitive.

16.6 Logging

Logging is in some ways related to debugging. Before there were IDEs (when all development was done with code editors), logging was one of the key weapons against bugs. One of the better quotes advocating logging as a debugging technique comes from the book *The Practice of Programming*, by Brian Kernighan (one of the fathers of the C language) and Rob Pike:

> As personal choice, we tend not to use debuggers beyond getting a stack trace or the value of a variable or two. One reason is that it is easy to get lost in details of complicated data structures and control flow; we find stepping through a program less productive than thinking harder and adding output statements and self-checking code at critical places. Clicking over statements takes longer than scanning the output of judiciously placed displays. It takes less time to decide where to put print statements than to single-step to the critical section of code, even assuming we know where that is. More important, debugging statements stay with the program; debugging sessions are transient.

Logging first came to prominence in Java with the open-source log4j package, hosted on the Jakarta web site. However, with the release of the 1.4 SDK, logging is now part of the core Java Runtime Environment (JRE). Let's look at logging with both these APIs and see how to use this tried and true technique to improve your applications.

16.6.1 *General logging concepts*

Developers have written log packages for decades and have learned some best practices and patterns that make their packages more powerful and easier to configure. Both of the packages covered in this chapter take advantage of these best practices.

Hierarchies

When working with logging packages, you should understand the concept of a *hierarchy* of loggers. Frequently, several logging jobs exist in your application. It would be nice if you could create various loggers, each focused on a particular job. Creating logger hierarchies allows you to do this. Both logging packages that we discuss here use the Factory design pattern to deliver a logger object to you. The creation of the logger associates a name with the logger instance. For example, you could create a logger named `com.nealford.art.db` that deals strictly with database methods. At the same time, you could create another logger named `com.nealford.art.web` that deals with the web aspects of your application. Neither of these loggers will interfere with each other, even if they appear in the same class.

This approach results in a flat hierarchy of logger objects. However, Java already features a well-defined hierarchy for its classes. Rather than tie the loggers to a particular task, you can instead use the names of classes, including the package names, to define your hierarchy of loggers. It is likely that your database classes exist in common packages, so using the package structure would automatically create loggers for database access.

The other enabling factor that makes it popular to use the fully qualified name of a class (i.e., the package name and class name) is the behavior of loggers created for higher-level classes. Each logger keeps track of its "parent" logger, which is the logger one level higher in the namespace hierarchy. Loggers in Java "know" about package name hierarchies. In other words, it is assumed that the loggers themselves will be named with the dot notation common in Java packages.

For example, if you have a logger named `com.nealford.art.emotherearth.logging.boundary`, its parent logger would be `com.nealford.art.emotherearth.logging`. Changes to the parent logger will flow down the hierarchy to the child loggers. If we set the logging level of the parent logger to a value (for example, `Level.SEVERE`), the child logger will automatically take that setting if it doesn't have its own setting. This hierarchy exists for all sorts of configuration elements of loggers. It allows the developer to make broad changes to the characteristics of a large number of loggers just by changing properties of loggers higher in the hierarchy. Regardless, any child logger can override a setting inherited by a parent by setting its own value for that property. You may decide that there are some events that must have log entries that occur in classes deep in the package hierarchy. You can set properties for such classes and not affect the other classes at the same level that inherit their logging characteristics.

Both the SDK logging and log4j use the same kind of hierarchy of loggers. Once you understand how the logger hierarchy works, you'll find it to be a powerful mechanism because it lets you control large sections of your logging behavior with a few changes.

Levels

While you are debugging an application, you want to have as much information as possible about the objects and events in the application. However, once it is debugged and in production, you only want to be notified when critical errors and situations arise. It is too cumbersome to add logging code for debugging and later strip it out for production—you may need that code again to investigate problems.

Modern loggers handle this by defining levels of logging. Logging activation is encapsulated into a `Level` class in both logging packages. Differences exist in the `Level` class implementations, but the semantics are basically the same. The levels defined by the SDK appear in table 16.6.

Table 16.6 Logger levels defined by the SDK

Level	Description
ALL	Indicates that all messages should be logged.
CONFIG	Provides a message level for static configuration messages.
FINE	Provides tracking information.
FINER	Provides fairly detailed tracking information.
FINEST	Provides highly detailed tracking information.
INFO	Contains informational messages.
OFF	Turns off all logging levels.
SEVERE	Indicates serious failure.
WARNING	Indicates a potential problem.

The level is set as one of the properties of the logger instance. If a logger lower in the hierarchy doesn't have a level setting, it takes on the level of the parent logger using the rules specified earlier.

Testing

If the logging code is going to stay in the application, it should have as little impact on performance as possible. Both of the logging APIs discussed in this chapter have made the initial test very fast to determine if logging is enabled. The test for whether logging is turned on and the test to see if a particular logging event should occur (for example, based on logging level) are designed to have as little impact as possible on your application.

Formatting

The format of the resulting log is configurable in both logging APIs. They handle this behavior with different classes, but the results are the same. Both support typical formats like plain text files, but they both also output logs as XML documents. The default output format for the SDK logger is an XML document, whereas the default is a text file for log4j. Each API has a variety of format classes, creating a hierarchy that may be extended by developers.

Of the two APIs, log4j has more formatting options. The list of formatters, their API, and a brief description appear in table 16.7.

Table 16.7 Formatters for both platforms

Formatter	API	Description
SimpleFormatter	SDK	Prints a brief summary of the LogRecord in a human-readable format. The summary will typically be one or two lines.
XMLFormatter	SDK	Formats a LogRecord into a standard XML format. The DTD specification is provided in the Java Logging APIs specification.
DateLayout	log4j	Takes care of all the date-related options and formatting work.
HTMLLayout	log4j	Outputs events in an HTML table.
PatternLayout	log4j	Allows you to completely customize every aspect of the log display.
SimpleLayout	log4j	Consists of the level of the log statement, followed by " - " and then the log message itself.
XMLLayout	log4j	Outputs a portion of an XML document, based on a DTD supplied with log4j.

Both APIs support a wide variety of output destinations. For example, you can log records to the console, to a file, or to a socket. These output classes are called *appenders* in log4j and *handlers* in the SDK. The APIs treat these output objects as multicast, meaning that you can register as many as you want to a particular logger. For example, you may want logging messages to go to both the console and to a file. You can register handlers for both types of output, and the API will take care of the rest.

16.6.2 SDK logging

Beginning with the SDK 1.4, Sun included a logging class and other supporting classes in the SDK. This class is based on best logging practices, many of them from the log4j package itself. The main logging class is `java.util.Logging`. It defines the basic characteristics of the logger and provides hooks for plugging in formatters, output handlers, and the other behaviors discussed earlier. The example art_emotherearth_logging in the source code archive shows a version of the eMotherEarth application that features logging in some of the methods. This example takes advantage of handlers, levels, and the hierarchical nature of loggers.

Logging eMotherEarth with the SDK

The first order of business in the eMotherEarth application is to establish the logging characteristics. For this application, we'll create two logging hierarchies. The package hierarchy for this application is shown in figure 16.24.

The first logger applies to the entire application and is tied to the top-level package name `com.neal-ford.art.logging.emotherearth`. This is the base package for all other packages. It will capture all the logging messages for the entire application. The second logger is tied just to the boundary classes. We want to separately log all database access, including information about the number of records returned and the order added. The second logger is tied to the package `com.nealford.art.logging.emotherearth.boundary`.

Figure 16.24   The package hierarchy for the project also becomes the logging hierarchy.

The welcome controller is the first one executed in the application, so we set up the first logger here. Listing 16.5 shows the class declaration, which includes the logger declaration, and the setupLogger() method.

Listing 16.5 The Welcome controller declares and sets up the logging keyed to the package for the entire application.

```
public class Welcome extends HttpServlet {
    private static Logger logger = Logger.getLogger(
        Welcome.class.getPackage().getName().substring(0,
        Welcome.class.getPackage().getName().lastIndexOf('.')));

    private void setupLogger() {
        Handler outputHandler = null;
        try {
            outputHandler = new FileHandler("/tmp/basic_log.xml");
        } catch (Exception x) {
            logger.severe("Create handler: "+ x.getMessage());
        }
        if (outputHandler != null)
            logger.addHandler(outputHandler);
        String logLevel = getServletContext().
                        getInitParameter("logLevel");
        if (logLevel != null)
            logger.setLevel(Level.parse(logLevel.toUpperCase()));
        else
            logger.setLevel(Level.SEVERE);
    }
```

The declaration of the logger is pretty elaborate, but it serves to capture the package name above the current package. The declaration is static and makes the logger available throughout the class. Loggers are retrieved through the getLogger() method, and a string identifying the name of the logger is the parameter. In this case, we take the name of the current package and snip off the last term, leaving the top-level package name as the logger name. As we create other loggers in this application, they will inherit the characteristics (such as the level and handler) created in the setupLogger() method.

The setupLogger() method creates an output handler tied to a file. It also sets the logging level based on a setting in the web configuration file. That way, you can set the logging level without recompiling the application. Listing 16.6 shows code that utilizes the logger to output messages.

Listing 16.6 Using the logger

```java
public void init() throws ServletException {
    setupLogger();
    logger.entering(this.getClass().getName(), "init()");
    String driverClass =
            getServletContext().getInitParameter("driverClass");
    String password =
            getServletContext().getInitParameter("password");
    String dbUrl =
            getServletContext().getInitParameter("dbUrl");
    String user =
            getServletContext().getInitParameter("user");
    DBPool dbPool =
            createConnectionPool(driverClass, password, dbUrl,
                                 user);
    getServletContext().setAttribute("dbPool", dbPool);
    logger.exiting(this.getClass().getName(), "init()");
}
```

The SDK logger has convenience methods for entering and exiting a method, which is a common logging chore. These methods map to the Level.FINER logging level.

Setting up additional loggers for classes that inherit these characteristics is easy. The catalog controller has a single declaration that creates a logger with inherited properties:

```java
public class Catalog extends HttpServlet {
    static Logger logger =Logger.getLogger(Catalog.class.getName());
```

The output from these loggers appears in the XML document specified by the handler in the welcome servlet. A portion of that document is shown in listing 16.7.

Listing 16.7 The SDK logger automatically uses the XMLFormatter.

```xml
<record>
  <date>2003-03-03T13:13:03</date>
  <millis>1046715183560</millis>
  <sequence>1</sequence>
  <logger>com.nealford.art.logging.emotherearth</logger>
  <level>FINER</level>
  <class>
    com.nealford.art.logging.emotherearth.controller.Welcome
  </class>
  <method>init()</method>
  <thread>10</thread>
  <message>RETURN</message>
```

```
</record>
<record>
  <date>2003-03-03T13:13:06</date>
  <millis>1046715186564</millis>
  <sequence>2</sequence>
  <logger>
    com.nealford.art.logging.emotherearth.controller.Catalog
  </logger>
  <level>FINER</level>
  <class>
    com.nealford.art.logging.emotherearth.controller.Catalog
  </class>
  <method>doPost()</method>
  <thread>10</thread>
  <message>ENTRY</message>
</record>
```

The other logger established for this application is tied to the boundary classes. We want to log database access information in its own log file. For this purpose, let's create a new named logger in the ProductDb class, which is the first of the boundary classes accessed. This declaration uses the package name of the boundary classes as the logger:

```
public class ProductDb {
    private static Logger logger = Logger.getLogger(
        ProductDb.class.getPackage().getName());
```

As before, we assign the properties for this logger in the first accessed class and each child class inherits those properties from the logger hierarchy. The unique property for this set of boundary loggers is a logging file with a different name that contains only database information.

Entry and exit are not the only activities that can be logged. Listing 16.8 shows the getProduct() method of the boundary class, which logs entry, exit, and information of interest to the reader of this log file.

Listing 16.8 The getProduct() method logs entry, exit, and the product found by the user.

```
public Product getProduct(int id) {
    logger.entering(this.getClass().getName(), "getProduct");
    Iterator it = getProductList().iterator();
    while (it.hasNext()) {
        Product p = (Product) it.next();
        if (p.getId() == id) {
            logger.info("Found product: " + p);
            return p;
```

```
        }
    }
    logger.info("Product for id[" + id + "] not found");
    return null;
}
```

The logging method `logger.log()`, which includes an overloaded version that accepts a logging level, string, and object, is the default method for logging. So, typical logging code might look like this:

```
logger.log(Level.INFO, "This is a log message");
```

To help eliminate extra typing, the `Logger` class also includes methods that already set the level for you—you need only supply the description. The call to `logger.info()` here is an example of a convenience method that logs a message at the `INFO` level.

16.6.3 *log4j logging*

What's the worst part of the logging API included with the SDK? The fact that it appeared so late (in the 1.4 SDK). If you are using an earlier version of the SDK (for example, because your application server hasn't updated to the newest version yet), you cannot use it. You can, however, use log4j. It is an open-source project that has been around for a long time. The code base is refined and well established. In fact, it was influential in the design of the logging API in the SDK. log4j supports all the features highlighted in section 16.6.1. While the class names are different, it features the same functionality (and in some cases more) than the SDK logger.

Logging eMotherEarth with log4j

The primary distinction between the two logging APIs is the difference in class and method names. log4j has a larger variety of output formats than the SDK, including a pattern formatter that allows developers to handcraft exactly the format they want. The sample that uses log4j appears in the source code archive under the name art_emotherearth_log4j.

The loggers are set up the same way, using the same hierarchy as before. The code for creating the top-level logger appears in the welcome controller, which is shown in listing 16.9.

Listing 16.9 The welcome controller creates and configures the log4j logger instance.

```
public class Welcome extends HttpServlet {
    static Logger logger = Logger.getLogger(
        Welcome.class.getPackage().getName().substring(0,
        Welcome.class.getPackage().getName().lastIndexOf('.')));

    private void setupLogger() {
        Appender outputAppender = null;
        try {
            outputAppender = new FileAppender(new XMLLayout(),
                    "/temp/log4j_basic.xml");
        } catch (IOException x) {
            logger.error("Appender error", x);
        }
        logger.addAppender(outputAppender);

        String logLevel = getServletContext().
                        getInitParameter("logLevel");
        if (logLevel != null)
                    logger.setLevel(Level.toLevel(logLevel));
        else
            logger.setLevel(Level.FATAL);
    }
```

The primary differences between listing 16.9 and listing 16.5 are the layered syntax used to create the appender and the technique for converting a string representation of a level to the Level representation. The SDK uses a static `parse()` method to perform the conversion whereas log4j uses a static `toLevel()` method. One is not preferred over the other; they merely represent two ways to achieve the same results.

Another difference between the logger in the SDK and log4j is the presence in the SDK of the `entering()` and `exiting()` methods. In log4j, you must invoke `info()` methods as a substitute. Listing 16.10 shows an example of logging entry and exit using log4j.

Listing 16.10 Using the `info()` method to mimic the SDK's `entering()` method

```
private void forwardToView(HttpServletRequest request,
                    HttpServletResponse response) throws
        ServletException, IOException {
    logger.info(this.getClass().getName()+"fowardToView enter");
    RequestDispatcher dispatcher = request.getRequestDispatcher(
```

```
                "/CatalogView.jsp");
        dispatcher.forward(request, response);
        logger.info(this.getClass().getName()+"forwardToView exit");
}
```

The XML format produced by the two APIs differs as well. log4j doesn't try to generate a fully formed XML document. It produces XML fragments, suitable for embedding into a larger XML document. A portion of the log file created for our sample application appears in listing 16.11.

Listing 16.11 The XML produced by log4j is designed for encapsulation within a larger XML document.

```
<log4j:event
    logger="com.nealford.art.logging.emotherearth"
    timestamp="1046666191595"
    level="INFO"
    thread="HttpProcessor[8080][0]">

    <log4j:message><![CDATA[
        com.nealford.art.logging.emotherearth.controller.Welcome:
        init() entry]]></log4j:message>
</log4j:event>
<log4j:event
    logger="com.nealford.art.logging.emotherearth"
    timestamp="1046666191635"
    level="INFO"
    thread="HttpProcessor[8080][0]">
    <log4j:message><![CDATA[
        com.nealford.art.logging.emotherearth.controller.Welcome:
        init() exit]]></log4j:message>
</log4j:event>
```

This XML is a "rawer" format than the one provided by the SDK. However, log4j includes numerous customization features for formatters. Developers could easily subclass the built-in XMLFormatter and generate whatever format XML they like.

log4j has extensive configuration options. One of the important areas of interest is the ease with which it installs into a web application. The documentation for log4j includes considerable information on how best to configure it for web applications, including where to place resource files and how to control the output and other properties through configuration documents. In this area, log4j surpasses the SDK.

16.6.4 *Choosing a logging framework*

Both frameworks provide the important aspects of logging and are state-of-the-art logging packages. They have many similarities. Some of the classes are named differently, but the same basic functionality exists for both. Here is a list of the criteria you should use to determine which framework best suits you:

Choose the SDK logging framework if:

- You don't want to use a third-party framework.

- You are using SDK 1.4 or later.

- You don't have a need for sophisticated configuration information to set properties.

log4j is better when:

- You can't use the latest SDK.

- You need more control over the format of the log entries.

- You need a great deal of control over the configuration information.

If you must use an earlier version of the SDK, log4j is the obvious choice. log4j has the benefit of a long product cycle compared with the SDK logging facilities, which are a recent addition. However, logging is so well understood that the stability of either package shouldn't be in question. In fact, it is likely that the SDK logging package is heavily based on log4j, which explains many of the similarities. If you need logging in your application, you can't go wrong with either choice.

16.6.5 *Logging in frameworks*

Logging is generally orthogonal to frameworks, meaning that it has no impact on the design or implementation of the application. None of the frameworks are hostile to logging—logging generally falls outside the scope of what the framework manages.

Several of the frameworks already include log4j, which is almost universally used in the Java world. Both Tapestry and WebWork already include log4j and have specific configuration parameters that allow you to set it up. See chapters 6 and 7 for examples of log4j integration into Tapestry and WebWork.

16.7 Summary

Debugging and logging are necessary chores when you're building applications. Debugging web applications is difficult because of the presence of the multithreaded servlet engine that hosts the application code. Learning to use the SDK debugger is a good idea because it is always available. The debugger provides numerous commands that allow you to interact with the running application. It lets you set breakpoints, step through code, and print out values from both primitives and objects.

Integrated development environments feature richer, more interactive debuggers. NetBeans is an open-source IDE that provides the same information from the SDK in a more attractive, easier-to-use interface. It also allows you to debug JSPs.

Commercial IDEs tend to have even richer feature sets, and Borland's JBuilder is a good example. It includes all the features of NetBeans as well as very powerful dialog boxes that provide detailed information on the running application. In particular, the Evaluate/Modify dialog box offers impressive flexibility when evaluating variables.

Logging is an adjunct to debugging that supplies some of the same information but in a more permanent form. Starting in version1.4, the SDK includes a logging framework similar to the popular log4j open-source framework. Both loggers feature the concept of logging hierarchies, and they support levels, differing output formats, and efficient logging tests.

In the next chapter, we look at unit testing web applications.

Unit testing

This chapter covers

- The motivation for unit testing
- The JUnit testing framework
- The JWebUnit testing framework

521

One of the key best practices that has risen to prominence recently is the task of unit testing. *Unit testing* refers to the testing of atomic functionality for the methods of a class. It differs from functional testing in its scope. The ideal unit test examines one small aspect of the behavior of a method. Unit tests are typically small and cohesive. It is not unusual for a single method to generate several test methods, each testing one piece of behavior.

Developers have long known that they should test their code. However, testing was viewed as something that consumed valuable time while development was under way and that didn't yield equivalent time savings at the end of the project. This is not the case; a good testing strategy repays effort several times. This chapter discusses testing in general and covers the most well-known testing framework, JUnit.

17.1 *The case for testing*

Why talk about unit testing in a book about web development? First, it falls under the heading of a best practice. It is a well-known fact that code that is tested as it is developed is higher quality. Like regular physical exercise, it is an activity that we all know we should do but that we still have a difficulty getting around to doing. Second, it supports aggressive development schedules. Development has sped up to the point that the special term "Internet time" was coined for it. Ten years ago, the development schedule for a typical client/server application was positively pastoral compared to the typical schedule for web applications today. Managers have discovered that time to market is an important characteristic, sometimes outweighing all others. Thus, time schedules have compressed over the last few years.

17.1.1 *Agile development*

Project time compression, among other factors, has led to the development of more agile development methodologies. Over the last decade, developers have researched traditional heavyweight methodologies and found them deficient for "Internet time" projects. Many of the past methodologies focused heavily on documentation and up-front design (and are now referred to as "BDUF" projects—"Big Design Up Front"). While it is true that some projects are healthier if much of the design occurs up front than later in the process, the time required to do so is a luxury.

Another problem facing traditional development is the rapidity at which changes to the requirements occur. It is a rare project indeed where the requirements remain stable and well known for the entire lifecycle of the project. This has led to agile development methodologies like Extreme Programming, Scrum (named after a rugby scrum as a model for an informal meeting), and the Crystal methodologies, among others. Each of these methodologies are well documented online and in other books. What they have in common is a style of development that relishes change rather than avoids it. It is typical in each of these methodologies to put off much of the design and requirements gathering for an iteration of the project until it is time to actually code it. This strategy allows the project to grow with the requirements and has the side effect of producing high-quality code very early in the development cycle, which helps to mitigate the time-to-market pressure. You can find out more about agile programming by referring to www.extremeprogramming.org (for information on Extreme Programming) or http://collaboration.csc.ncsu.edu/agile/Bibliography.htm (for links to a variety of agile methodologies).

If you are using an agile methodology, you must be able to respond quickly to design changes in production code that were not anticipated when the code was written. In other words, you must refactor existing code mercilessly, without fear of breaking working code. Unit testing is a tool that gives you the confidence to change working code without accidentally breaking something. Once you have a suite of unit tests for a body of code, you can run them as regression tests. *Regression testing* refers to running older tests again that have passed against the body of code to ensure that nothing has accidentally broken because of subsequent development. The typical agile project runs the entire suite of tests every night, making sure that code hasn't been broken by changes made that day. In many agile methodologies, the unit tests are written before the code they are testing is written (called *test-first coding* or *test-driven development*). The unit tests become the final step of requirements gathering. If you know how to test something, you must understand how it works, and you are therefore more prepared to write code for it.

Many managers and developers think that taking the time to build tests slows the project's progress. When testing is done properly, the opposite is true. If you haphazardly write tests just when you feel like it, you don't have a body of tests that reasonably covers the scope of the project. If you have been writing tests all along, you have the freedom to make major changes in the design and implementation of code without worrying that you have caused an unfortunate side effect. But even if you have, the regression test run that night will expose it and allow you to fix it before it affects the rest of the system.

17.1.2 *Unit testing in web applications*

In properly designed Model 2 applications, the code is partitioned enough to allow easy access to the individual modules so that you can test them. One of the problems with code that isn't very cohesive is that it is difficult to write tests for it. If the code you are touching with the test affects every other part of the application, you end up writing one massive test, which takes more time than it is worth.

Within well-designed modules, creating very granular methods also assists in unit testing. If the methods are in fact a single unit of work, it is easy to create a unit test that examines that unit of work. On the other hand, if the methods are huge and perform dozens of tasks, you'll find it much more difficult to write tests because the tests themselves must be so comprehensive. Here is another argument for writing small, cohesive methods that combine to form the public methods of the application.

In Model 2 web applications that access a database or other external resource, the code in the boundary classes is generally the most complex. This makes sense—the boundaries between the application and the rest of the world tend to be complicated. The boundary classes are the ones that most benefit from unit tests. For example, you need to be sure that the entities in the application update the database correctly.

Entities are easy to test if they are properly limited in functionality. Accessors and mutators generally don't have to be tested unless they have some side effect that occurs along with the assignment or access. The business rules methods of entities must be checked thoroughly. It is a good idea to let a developer who hasn't written the code create some of the tests. Programmers tend not to be comprehensive testers for code they have written. If you write code, you make certain assumptions. When you write tests for that code, you make the same assumptions you made when you wrote it. This is also why unit testing alone isn't enough in an application. You also need domain experts to test the application to make sure it solves the targeted problem and performs in the expected manner.

Controller servlets are among the most difficult to test. Because they are servlets, they must run in the context of the servlet engine. They don't lend themselves well to the atomic level of testing provided by unit tests. Later in this chapter, we'll look at a testing framework built on top of JUnit and HttpUnit that makes it easier to test entire pages in the application, which includes the controllers.

17.2 *Unit testing and JUnit*

JUnit is an open-source testing framework, written originally for Java. However, it has become so popular that it has been ported to a variety of other languages and platforms. It provides a simple but powerful framework against which you can write unit tests. It features just the right level of abstraction for usefulness without placing unnecessary constraints on developers. This project is credited with finally making unit tests acceptable for a large body of developers.

You can download the JUnit binaries and documentation from www.junit.org. This web site contains links to the entire xUnit family of tools, which encompasses the ports to other languages as well as ancillary tools that make unit testing easier.

17.2.1 *Test cases*

The core unit of work in JUnit is the `TestCase`, a class designed to serve as the base class for your tests. It includes some helper methods for creating and running your tests. When you execute a `TestCase`, it automatically runs every method in the class that begins with `test`. This means that you don't have to register your test methods anywhere or do anything special to add new test methods. If you need to add a new test method, simply define it (be sure to include `test` at the beginning of the method name), and JUnit will automatically include it in the test run. JUnit uses reflection to determine which tests to run, making it easy for you to add new test methods to existing test cases.

`TestCase` also includes methods for implementing fixtures. A *fixture* is a constant artifact against which you run tests. It is not something you are testing but a resource that is required for the test to run. For example, if you are testing database access, you need a `Connection` object to access database tables. You aren't interested in testing the connection itself, but the connection is required before you can write the rest of the test. The test case will include a `Connection` as a fixture.

Two methods that are overridden in a `TestCase` facilitate fixtures. The `setUp()` method is automatically called by the framework before each test is run. Similarly, the `tearDown()` method is called after each test is run. For example, in a database connection fixture, `setUp()` establishes the connection to the database and `tearDown()` closes it.

17.2.2 *Testing entities*

To begin, we'll look at a unit test for the shopping cart class, which is part of the eMotherEarth application. The source for this project appears in the source code archive under the name art_emotherearth_junit. The primary code in the shopping cart for testing is the getCartTotal() method, which returns the sum of the extended prices for all items in the shopping cart. Listing 17.1 shows the TestShoppingCart test case.

Listing 17.1 The TestShoppingCart test case tests the getCartTotal() method.

```
package com.nealford.art.emotherearth.util.test;

import com.nealford.art.emotherearth.entity.CartItem;
import com.nealford.art.emotherearth.entity.Product;
import com.nealford.art.emotherearth.util.ShoppingCart;
import junit.framework.TestCase;                        ← Extends
                                                           TestCase
public class TestShoppingCart extends TestCase {
    protected ShoppingCart shoppingCart = null;
    static int productNum = 0;
    protected CartItem[] items;
                                                ← Required
    public TestShoppingCart(String name) {         by JUnit
        super(name);
    }
                                                     ← Fires before
    protected void setUp() throws Exception {          each test
        super.setUp();
        shoppingCart = new ShoppingCart();
        items = new CartItem[4];
        for (int i = 0; i < items.length; i++) {
            items[i] = generateRandomCartItem();
            shoppingCart.addItem(items[i]);
        }
    }
                                                      ← Fires after
    protected void tearDown() throws Exception {        each test
        shoppingCart = null;
        items = null;
        super.tearDown();
    }
                                              ← Tests validity of
    public void testGetCartTotal() {             getCartTotal()
        double expectedReturn = 0.0;
        for (int i = 0; i < items.length; i++) {
            expectedReturn += items[i].getExtendedPrice();
        }
        double actualReturn = shoppingCart.getCartTotal();
        assertEquals("cart total", expectedReturn, actualReturn,
                    0.01);
    }
                                              ← Generates a
    private CartItem generateRandomCartItem() {  random cart item
        CartItem c = new CartItem();
        c.setProduct(getProduct());
```

```
        c.setQuantity((int) Math.round(Math.random() * 100));
        return c;
    }

    private Product getProduct() {
        Product p = new Product();
        p.setName("Test Product " + ++productNum);
        p.setPrice(Math.random() * 1000);
        return p;
    }
```

Generates a product

The `TestShoppingCart` class extends JUnit's `TestCase`, inheriting the framework's methods for running tests. The `setUp()` method, which runs before each test, creates the fixture against which we will run the tests. For the `getCartTotal()` method to work, the shopping cart must have items. To generate items, you must have products. Thus, several methods exist for generating the necessary supporting objects to create a nontrivial test of the `getCartTotal()` method. The `setUp()` method calls the superclass `setUp()` method to handle any initialization needed in the parent class. Then, it creates a new `ShoppingCart` object and an array of `CartItems`. It iterates over the array, calling the `generateRandomCartItem()` method to fill in the items array. The `generateRandomCartItem()` method works by calling `getProduct()`, which generates a nonsense product object with a random price, and setting a random quantity for the cart item. We don't need to go to the database and get a real product for this test. The only characteristic of a product we care about is the price, for which a random number suffices. And the only characteristic we care about for the cart item is the quantity, which also accommodates a random number. These two values drive the shopping cart's total.

The items array is used in two places. The test code we ultimately write must check to ensure that the shopping cart is adding items correctly. To perform this check, we must manually calculate the total of all the items in the cart. This is the main unit of work in the `testGetCartTotal()` method. It manually iterates through the array and calculates the expected total of the items. Then, the shopping cart's actual method is called. The comparison is performed by the `assertEquals()` method, which is part of the JUnit framework. The framework contains a number of methods for testing values against one another. A long list of `assertEquals()` methods exists, along with `assertSame()`, `assertTrue()`, `assertNotNull()`, and others. These methods form the main evaluation aspect of JUnit. The goal of tests is to generate the expected value and the actual value, and then compare them. If the expected and actual values equal, the test passes. Each of these methods includes a descriptive string that identifies the test. The assertEquals() method is heavily overloaded, with versions that take all Java primitives and objects. The versions of the method that check floats and doubles include an additional parameter for an error factor. Comparing two floating-point numbers for equality almost never yields the same result. The last parameter is the delta, indicating the maximum tolerance for inequality.

17.2.3 *Running tests*

JUnit features a couple of ways to run the tests. The framework includes text-based and Swing-based test runners. The test runners point to an individual test case or a package containing test cases and runs everything that begins with test. When pointed at a package, it loads every class starting with Test that implements TestCase and tries to run the methods starting with test. In this way, JUnit allows you to create new tests that are automatically picked up and run. The results of running the AllTests suite (which includes TestShoppingCart) in the Swing-based test runner are shown in figure 17.1.

The test runner displays the test class name at the top, along with a Run button. When invoked, the test runner performs the tests. The bar in the center turns either green or red, with obvious connotations. If a single test fails to run, the bar turns red and the test was a failure. The results window under the progress bar shows the tests that were run, along with the results. The successful tests show up with green checkmarks, and the failures show up in red. The Failures tab shows a stack trace for the failed test runs.

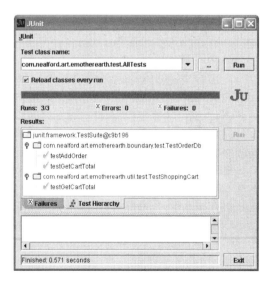

Figure 17.1
The Swing-based test runner automatically runs the test cases found in a particular package.

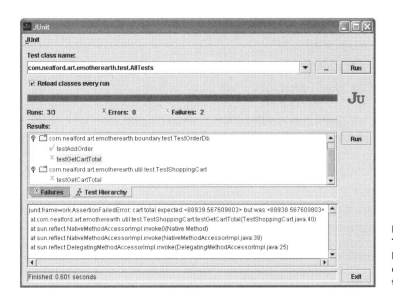

**Figure 17.2
The results progress
bar glows red when
even a single test fails
to run.**

Figure 17.2 shows the results when one of the tests in the suite fails to run.

In this case, the `testGetCartTotal()` test failed, dooming the entire test run to failure.

17.2.4 *Test suites*

Figures 17.1 and 17.2 show a collection of tests running. JUnit allows you to bundle a group of tests together into a test suite. The *test suite* is a collection of individual test cases that run as a group. Our project includes two test cases that are related and thus should be run in the same suite. The AllTests suite appears in listing 17.2.

Listing 17.2   The AllTests suite registers tests that run as a group.

```
package com.nealford.art.emotherearth.test;

import junit.framework.*;

public class AllTests extends TestCase {
    public AllTests(String s) {
        super(s);
    }

    public static Test suite() {
        TestSuite suite = new TestSuite();
        suite.addTestSuite(com.nealford.art.emotherearth.
                boundary.test.TestOrderDb.class);
```

```
        suite.addTestSuite(com.nealford.art.emotherearth.
                util.test.TestShoppingCart.class);
        return suite;
    }
}
```

The `AllTests` test suite is very simple. It is itself a `TestCase` child that includes a static `suite()` method. Inside this method, a new `TestSuite` is created, and each test case class is added to it. The parameter for `addTestSuite()` is a `Class` class, so the passed values are the class objects for the test case classes. When the framework encounters a test suite, it executes the test cases inside it in order. JUnit is designed to automatically pick up test cases in a particular package. The test suite lets the developer control which tests are run together.

17.2.5 Testing boundaries

Testing boundary classes is difficult because of the elaborate fixtures that must exist to support the tests. In the case of the eMotherEarth application, the most complex (and therefore most critical to test) boundary is the one that adds new orders to the database. Because it uses so many classes and must interact with the database, this boundary class is more complex than the test case shown earlier. The first portion of the class is shown in listing 17.3.

Listing 17.3 The declaration section of TestOrderDb

```java
public class TestOrderDb extends TestShoppingCart {
    private OrderDb orderDb = null;
    private int addedOrderKey;
    private DBPool dbPool;
    private Connection connection;
    private static final String SQL_DELETE_ORDER =
            "delete from orders where order_key = ?";
    private static final String SQL_SELECT_ORDER =
            "select * from orders where order_key = ?";
    private static final String DB_URL =
            "jdbc:mysql://localhost/eMotherEarth";
    private static final String DRIVER_CLASS =
            "com.mysql.jdbc.Driver";
    private static final String USER = "root";
    private static final String PASSWORD = "marathon";
    private static final String TEST_CC_EXP = "11/1111";
    private static final String TEST_CC_NUM = "1111111111111111";
    private static final String TEST_CC_TYPE = "Visa";
    private static final String TEST_NAME = "Homer";
    private static final int TEST_USER_KEY = 1;
```

```
public TestOrderDb(String name) {
    super(name);
}
```

The first item of note in the `TestOrderDb` class is the parent class, which is the `Test-ShoppingCart` unit test created earlier. We subclass it because one of the fixture items we need is a populated shopping cart. The `TestShoppingCart` test case needs the same fixture, so we inherit from it to cut down on the duplicate code we would need otherwise. The top of this class consists primarily of constants that define the characteristics of SQL statements and test data. The constants for connecting to the database reside in this class because we cannot easily get them from the web application deployment descriptor. This test case is not part of the web application and does not have access to the services provided by the servlet engine.

The next two methods of the `TestOrderDb` test case are the inherited `setUp()` and `tearDown()` methods, shown in listing 17.4.

Listing 17.4 The setUp() and tearDown() methods of the TestOrderDb test case

```
protected void setUp() throws Exception {
    super.setUp();
    orderDb = new OrderDb();
    dbPool = new DBPool(DRIVER_CLASS, DB_URL, USER, PASSWORD);
    orderDb.setDbPool(dbPool);
    connection = dbPool.getConnection();
}

protected void tearDown() throws Exception {
    deleteOrder(addedOrderKey);
    dbPool.release(connection);
    orderDb = null;
    super.tearDown();
}
```

The `setup()` and `teardown()` methods are typically protected so that other test cases may inherit from them just as we have done. It is important to remember to invoke the superclass's `setUp()` as the first line of the `setUp()` method and invoke the superclass's `tearDown()` as the last line of that method. The `setUp()` method creates the necessary fixtures for an `Order` object and gets a connection for use by the non-order code in the test case. The `tearDown()` method releases resources and deletes the order added by the test case. For perfectly encapsulated tests, you should make sure that the test cleans up after itself. Depending on the database in use, you might not have to do this. For example, if you know that the application is always tested with a test database where partial and meaningless records are tolerated, you don't have to make sure that the test cases clean up after themselves. However, if there is any chance that the test runs against production data, you should make sure that the test is well encapsulated.

The next two methods (listing 17.5) are part of the fixture of the test. They get an inserted order from the database (to compare against the one that was added) and delete the new order upon tear-down.

Listing 17.5 These two methods are part of the database fixture of the test case.

```
private Order getOrderFromDatabase() {
    Order o = new Order();
    PreparedStatement ps = null;
    ResultSet rs = null;
    try {
        ps = connection.prepareStatement(SQL_SELECT_ORDER);
        ps.setInt(1, addedOrderKey);
        rs = ps.executeQuery();
        rs.next();
        o.setOrderKey(rs.getInt("order_key"));
        o.setUserKey(1);
        o.setCcExp(rs.getString("CC_EXP"));
        o.setCcNum(rs.getString("CC_NUM"));
        o.setCcType(rs.getString("CC_TYPE"));
    } catch (Exception ex) {
        throw new RuntimeException(ex.getMessage());
    } finally {
        try {
            if (ps != null)
                ps.close();
        } catch (SQLException ignored) {
        }
    }
    return o;
}

private void deleteOrder(int addedOrderKey) {
    Connection c = null;
    PreparedStatement ps = null;
    int rowsAffected = 0;
    try {
        ps = connection.prepareStatement(SQL_DELETE_ORDER);
        ps.setInt(1, addedOrderKey);
        rowsAffected = ps.executeUpdate();
        if (rowsAffected != 1)
            throw new Exception("Delete failed");
```

```
        } catch (Exception ex) {
            throw new RuntimeException(ex.getMessage());
        } finally {
            try {
                if (ps != null)
                    ps.close();
                if (c != null)
                    c.close();
            } catch (SQLException ignored) {
            }
        }
    }
```

The last method of the test case is the actual test method. It creates a simulated order, uses the Order object to add it to the database, and then compares the results by querying the database to retrieve the record. Listing 17.6 shows this method.

Listing 17.6 The lone test method in the boundary test case

```
public void testAddOrder() throws SQLException {
    Order actualOrder = new Order();
    actualOrder.setCcExp(TEST_CC_EXP);
    actualOrder.setCcNum(TEST_CC_NUM);
    actualOrder.setCcType(TEST_CC_TYPE);
    actualOrder.setUserKey(TEST_USER_KEY);
    orderDb.addOrder(shoppingCart, TEST_NAME, actualOrder);
    addedOrderKey = orderDb.getLastOrderKey();
    Order dbOrder = getOrderFromDatabase();
    assertEquals("cc num", actualOrder.getCcNum(),
                dbOrder.getCcNum());
    assertEquals("cc exp", actualOrder.getCcExp(),
                dbOrder.getCcExp());
    assertEquals("cc type", actualOrder.getCcType(),
                dbOrder.getCcType());
    assertEquals("user key", actualOrder.getUserKey(),
                dbOrder.getUserKey());
    deleteOrder(addedOrderKey);
}
```

Unlike the test case in listing 17.1, the test case in listing 17.6 has numerous assert methods for checking the various characteristics of the order. This method generates an order using the shopping cart generated by the inherited setUp() method and the constants defined at the top of the class. Next, it adds the order by using the addOrder() method. Once the order has been added, the record is retrieved from the database to ensure that the values are correct.

If you refer back to figure 17.1, you will notice that when this test case runs, it also runs the test case from its parent class, testGetCartTotal(). Because the order test case inherits from the shopping cart test case, both tests are run via the framework.

Building test cases for boundaries is complex because of the amount of hand-generated SQL required. Here is a case where using helper classes eliminates the redundant nature of this kind of code. For example, it is quite common to build a JDBCFixture class that encapsulates most of the generic details of interacting with the database. Alternatively, you can use components normally reserved for client/server development to ease generating test code. For example, many IDEs include components that wrap much of the complexity of JDBC. While you might be reluctant to use the components in your web applications because of the overhead, the speed of development is more important in unit tests, and scalability and overhead are secondary concerns.

One of the utilities available on the JUnit web site is a set of helper classes called DbUnit, which automates much of the testing of boundary classes. If you don't want to write the database access code yourself, DbUnit makes it easy to generate test code against relational databases.

17.2.6 *Tool support*

Many IDEs, both commercial and open source, now support JUnit. Like the Ant build tool, it has become ubiquitous in Java development circles. IDE support ranges from predefined test case templates for building the main infrastructure to test runners that run tests inside the IDE.

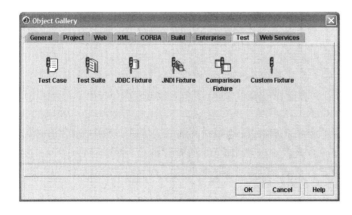

**Figure 17.3
JBuilder includes prebuilt fixtures and other support classes for JUnit.**

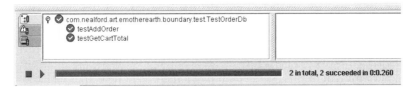

Figure 17.4   The JBuilder test runner runs tests inside the IDE with its own test runner interface.

JBuilder's JUnit support

Figure 17.3 shows the JBuilder New gallery, which features an entire page of pre-built JUnit test classes.

Figure 17.4 shows the `TestOrderDb` test running inside the JBuilder IDE, which supplies its own graphical test runner.

NetBean's JUnit support

The NetBeans IDE also includes support for JUnit, both in test generation and test running. For any class, you can right-click, choose Tools, and let NetBeans generate JUnit tests for you. Figure 17.5 shows the dialog box that lets you specify what JUnit characteristics you want to implement in your test case.

NetBeans also has a custom test runner, based on the JUnit text test runner.

Automating regression testing

You must run unit tests as regression tests to receive the full benefit of unit testing. However, no one wants to sit at a computer and run regression tests all day. One of the aspects of testing that make it useful is the invisibility of needless details.

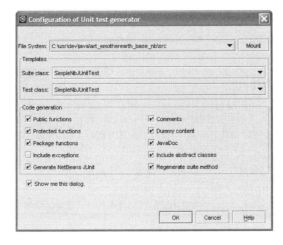

Figure 17.5
NetBeans assists in creating JUnit tests for any class.

Another open-source tool you are probably already using facilitates running regression tests. The Ant build tool includes a JUnit task in its optional tasks. Using Ant, you can set up a build file that runs the unit tests for multiple suites overnight. Depending on how much you want to automate the process, you can run the tests with Ant and have it email you a list of the tests that failed so that you can address them the next morning. Listing 17.7 shows a sample Ant invocation of the JUnit task.

> **Listing 17.7 The Ant JUnit task simplifies the setup and execution of JUnit tests.**

```
<junit printsummary="withOutAndErr" haltonfailure="yes" fork="true">
  <classpath>
    <pathelement location="${build.tests}" />
    <pathelement path="${java.class.path}" />
  </classpath>

  <formatter type="plain" />

  <test name="my.test.TestCase" haltonfailure="no"
        outfile="result" >
    <formatter type="xml" />
  </test>

  <batchtest fork="yes" todir="${reports.tests}">
    <fileset dir="${src.tests}">
      <include name="*Test.java" />
      <exclude name="**/AllTests.java" />
    </fileset>
  </batchtest>
</junit>
```

Ant is an extraordinarily popular build tool, used by virtually every Java project under the sun. You can find out much more about Ant from the excellent *Java Development with Ant*, by Erik Hatcher and Steve Loughran.

17.3 Web testing with JWebUnit

One of the most difficult kinds of applications to unit test are web applications. Web applications rely on a deployment platform, the browser, which is completely out of the control of the developers of the application. Web applications also have a strong visual component, for which it is also difficult to automate testing. Commercial products are available to test web applications; they generally allow a user to interact with the application while recording keystrokes and mouse gestures.

These records are then played back to simulate a user's interaction. These tools are specialized and very expensive. The open-source world hasn't produced a tool exactly like the commercial ones yet.

However, the open-source world hasn't totally ignored this problem. One of the adjuncts to the JUnit project was a project named HttpUnit. It features extensions to JUnit for building a framework that tests applications running over HTTP. It is an effective tool for verifying that the actual output is what you expected. Other open-source tools are aimed at testing atomic behavior of web applications. For example, tools exist that test the JavaScript on a web page.

Recently, another project popped up on the JUnit site that combines many of the existing open-source web testing frameworks, including HTTPUnit. Like its precursors, JWebUnit is an open-source testing framework. It encapsulates many of the existing open-source tools to create a more comprehensive package. It also provides new classes that encapsulate many of the existing HTTPUnit classes to reduce the amount of code a developer must write. You can download JWebUnit from the JUnit web site. You should also download HTTPUnit while you are there because JWebUnit relies on some classes that come from HTTPUnit.

17.3.1 *JWebUnit TestCases*

Because JWebUnit is based on JUnit, the concepts of test cases, suites, and fixtures are the same. Let's create tests for a couple of the pages of the eMotherEarth application as an example. One of the setup items common to all the test cases in JWebUnit is the BaseURL. All the other URLs in the test case are based on this URL. Instead of replicating the same setup code across multiple test cases, let's create a base test case that handles this setup chore. The BaseWebTestCase appears in listing 17.8.

> **Listing 17.8 The BaseWebTestCase handles setting the base URL for all test cases that inherit from it.**

```
package com.nealford.art.emotherearth.test;

import net.sourceforge.jwebunit.WebTestCase;

public class BaseWebTestCase extends WebTestCase {

    public BaseWebTestCase(String name) {
        super(name);
    }

    public void setUp() throws java.lang.Exception {
        super.setUp();
```

```
    getTestContext().setBaseUrl(
            "http://localhost:8080/emotherearth");
    }
}
```

Once the base test case is established, we can subclass it to create tests for pages in the web application. The first test is for the logon page. We want to ensure that the proper elements appear on the page and that it forwards successfully to the catalog page. The `TestLogonPage` test case is shown in listing 17.9.

Listing 17.9 This test case tests the elements on the logon page.

```
package com.nealford.art.emotherearth.test;

public class TestLogonPage extends BaseWebTestCase {

    public TestLogonPage(String name) {
        super(name);
    }

    public void testIntro() {
        beginAt("/welcome");
    }

    public void testLogonElements() {
        beginAt("/welcome");
        assertFormPresent("welcomeform");
        assertFormElementPresent("user");
        assertFormElementPresent("gotocatalog");
    }

    public void testForwardToCatalog() {
        beginAt("/welcome");
        setFormElement("user", "Homer");
        submit();
    }
}
```

HttpUnit has extended the standard assert methods in JUnit to include web-specific assertions. The `testLogonElements()` method checks to see if the required elements are on the page. The framework also includes methods that allow the developer to programmatically interact with the application. The `testForwardToCatalog()` method lets the developer fill in form values, "click" buttons, and otherwise interact with the web application.

The test runners defined for JUnit also work for JWebUnit. The primary difference is that the web application must be running before you can conduct the tests.

In other words, the test runner will not automatically spawn the web application. The results appear just as in other JUnit tests, with green and red bars. You do not see any interaction with the web application. All the code is directly accessing the application via HTTP.

17.3.2 *Testing complex elements*

JWebUnit contains methods for testing sophisticated HTML elements such as tables. Listing 17.10 shows a test case that tests some of the table properties of the catalog page.

Listing 17.10 This test case tests for the presence and validity of table elements.

```
package com.nealford.art.emotherearth.test;

import java.io.File;
import java.io.FileNotFoundException;
import java.io.FileOutputStream;
import java.io.PrintStream;

public class TestCatalogPage extends BaseWebTestCase {
    private static String LOG_DIR = "c:/temp/emotherearth/";

    public TestCatalogPage(String name) {
        super(name);
    }

    public void setUp() throws java.lang.Exception {
        super.setUp();
        File outputDir = new File(LOG_DIR);
        if (!outputDir.exists())
            outputDir.mkdir();
    }

    public void testCatalog() {
        beginAt("/welcome");
        beginAt("/catalog?user=Homer");
        assertTablePresent("catalogTable");
        assertTextInTable("catalogTable",
                new String[] {"ID", "NAME", "PRICE", "Buy"});
        PrintStream ps = null;
        try {
            ps = new PrintStream(new FileOutputStream(
                    "c:/temp/emotherearth/catalogText.txt"));
        } catch (FileNotFoundException ex) {
            ex.printStackTrace();
        }
        dumpTable("catalogTable", ps);
    }
}
```

The testCatalog() method of the test case in listing 17.10 first issues two beginAt() method invocations. We cannot create a test case that goes directly to the catalog page because the welcome page executes code that establishes connection pools and other global resources. To solve this problem, we issue a beginAt() command that invokes the welcome page and then immediately moves to the catalog page, passing the parameter normally supplied by the welcome page. JWebUnit includes methods that ensure the presence of a table and that check the contents of individual rows. The assertTextInTable() method verifies that the header row contains the correct elements.

One of the more powerful table tests is the ability to dump the entire contents of the table to a file. The dumpTable() method accepts a table name and a Print-Stream and outputs the entire contents of the table to the file. The contents of the catalogText file appear in listing 17.11.

Listing 17.11 The dumpTable() method outputs the table into a formatted text file.

```
catalogTable:
    [ID] [NAME] [PRICE] [Buy]
    [1] [Ocean] [$1,393,456,200.00] [Qty:]
    [2] [Leaves (green)] [$3.50]Qty:]
    [3] [Leaves (brown)]$0.0]Qty:]
    [4] [Mountain]$2,694,381.3]Qty:]
    [5] [Lake]$34,563.1]Qty:]
    [6] [Snow]$2.4]Qty:]
```

Even the simple tests defined in this chapter begin to show the power of automating tests against web applications. Although the generated output doesn't look like the original table, it does contain the same data. If you run this test as a regression test, you can compare the contents from one run to another using a diff utility. Without ever looking at the table, you can determine that something has changed in the output and investigate further. Testing visual output by looking at it is a poor way to test. Eyes miss details, and it is labor intensive to force someone to look at the page whenever you fear something might have broken. However, dumping the contents to a file where the comparison can be automated ensures consistent appearance and notifies you of unexpected changes.

JWebUnit, like many open-source projects, is short on flash but long on functionality. It provides a powerful framework for automating the consistency and validity of the visual part of your web application, which is the hardest to test by hand.

17.4 Summary

Unit testing is not the most glamorous job in a development project, but it is a critical piece of the development lifecycle. It took agile methodologies and Internet time projects to get developers and managers to see the benefits of unit testing. Like design, writing unit tests seems to take an inordinate amount of time away from development. However, the time you spend on either of those activities saves countless hours on the back end of a project.

Given that you should do unit testing, the choice is easy in the Java world. JUnit is an open-source project that is so convenient that it is used almost universally. This chapter focused on the highlights of how JUnit is structured and showed you how to write test cases, fixtures, and test suites. One of the benefits of JUnit is that it isn't complex. Most developers can use it with very little research.

This chapter also discussed the relative ease of testing entities and the corresponding difficulties involved in testing boundaries. We also highlighted some strategies, such as inheritance of test cases, that can ease the complexity and volume of code.

JUnit has made it relatively easy to write unit tests for everything but servlets and web user interfaces. JWebUnit, based on JUnit, includes methods that help automate the testing of the visual aspect of web pages. By constructing tests to check for the presence of elements and dumping the contents of complex data structures to files, JWebUnit enables you to test the visual portion of your web application—the most difficult part to test.

In the next chapter, we cover web services and how to incorporate them into web applications.

Web services and Axis

18

This chapter covers

- Defining web services concepts
- Using Axis
- Retrofitting web applications to expose web services

Over the last few years, web services have been the industry-specific buzzword *du jour.* You cannot read a technical journal or product announcement without the phrase popping up. It is a very simple mechanism for doing something that has been done since the 1960s—and that is the point. It is a new way to do something for which there is a need. The difference this time is that it is based on open standards upon which the entire industry agrees (for the time being). As web developers, you cannot avoid this topic. In the near future, you will work on a web application that must support web services (if you aren't already).

This chapter provides a brief overview of web services and, more important, the issues you face retrofitting an existing web application to take advantage of this new paradigm. It covers the essentials of web services concepts. (There are plenty of full books written on this topic.) We cover web services from a pragmatic approach. For example, as you read all the specifications, you'll find that a lot of emphasis is placed on the open nature of the technology. You can transmit Simple Object Access Protocol (SOAP) over any number of protocols. From a practical standpoint, everyone uses HTTP. I assume you're using web protocols and web application design principles because that is the most common case.

18.1 *Key concepts*

Web services represent a new paradigm for executing remote procedure calls (RPC) and stateless messaging. RPCs have existed for many years—since administrators started having to split the processing load across machine boundaries. Many protocols have emerged to do this: Component Object Model (COM)/Distributed COM (DCOM), Common Object Request Broker Architecture (CORBA), Remote Method Invocation (RMI). Each has advantages and disadvantages. However, the biggest hurdle to widespread adoption is the fact that no one can agree on which one to use. Even though CORBA is administered by an open standards organization (the Object Management Group, or OMG), it has never received ubiquitous support.

Even if everyone could agree on the technology, a common technical problem hampers each one. All these technologies use a binary protocol for transmitting information over a network. Each has its own protocol, and some of them can interact. For example, RMI and CORBA can talk to each other over via RMI over IIOP protocol (the Remote Method Invocation over Internet Inter-operable Orb Protocol from CORBA). However, they are still binary protocols. This isn't a problem for applications over internal networks, but it is a huge problem for Internet applications. To enable one of these protocols to work across firewalls, you have to open ports on the firewall for binary data. Anyone who has tried to convince a network administrator that this is a good idea knows what kind of response to expect. Opening binary communication to the outside world opens up the network to attacks of various kinds.

To address this problem, a consortium of companies defined the web services API. This API is based partially on existing technologies such as XML, HTTP, and other well-established open standards. Microsoft, DevelopMentor, and Userland Software created an XML-based protocol for passing procedure call information over HTTP, then submitted the protocol to the Internet Engineering Task Force (IETF) for recommendation. It was quickly adopted by the World Wide Web Consortium (W3C), and web services were born. When version 1.1 appeared, many large corporations joined the project, making it a de facto standard.

Web services is an umbrella term for making RPCs over HTTP using SOAP as the data-marshalling mechanism. The web services standard also includes a technology for metadata information about the methods and parameters for a remote method called Web Services Description Language (WSDL). It also includes the Universal Description, Discovery, and Integration (UDDI) standard for finding web services, which acts as a web services phone book format.

Web services are based on existing standard protocols like HTTP. This means that web services are stateless in nature. As with web applications, you cannot rely on the state of the object between invocations. Statelessness is a good characteristic for scalability and is one of the reasons that HTTP is such a scalable protocol. However, this characteristic limits some of the types of code you can write as a web service. Some frameworks allow you to create stateful web service calls, but this approach creates problems because you have to include state management and define who is responsible for maintaining state. Generally, web service methods must be comprehensive and perform all the required work in a single invocation. It is not unusual to create web service methods that internally call many other methods to perform a task. For example, if you have transactional method calls, they must all execute within the same web service method call.

18.2 Axis

A variety of frameworks are available for using web services in Java. The one we'll use is the open-source Axis (Apache Extensible Interaction System) framework from Apache. You can download it at http://ws.apache.org/axis. It is the successor to Apache's SOAP version 2. The developers of that package realized that it had some shortcomings that were irreparable; the ground-up rewrite is Axis. Axis includes:

- A simple stand-alone server (primarily for testing)
- A server that plugs into servlet engines such as Tomcat
- Extensive support for WSDL
- An emitter tool that generates Java classes from WSDL
- Some sample programs
- A tool for monitoring TCP/IP packets

18.2.1 *Architecture of Axis*

The general architecture of Axis appears in figure 18.1. The *requestor* is any client that makes a request over any of the protocols supported by Axis. Generally, HTTP is used. The requestor may be a desktop application, another web application, or another web service. The Axis engine acts as a facilitator between the client and the web service method, managing the translation to and from web services standards.

Axis allows the developer to define a series of *handlers*, tied to either the request or the response. These handlers are similar to filter servlets; each handler performs a specific task and forwards to the next handler in line. Handlers fit together into a *chain*, which is a specific set of handlers that a web service request or a response traverses. This process is shown in figure 18.2.

Examples of handlers are security components, logging systems, and transformations. One special handler, known as the *pivot point handler*, exists for every web service. This handler performs the actual invocation of the web service method. It is the point at which the request becomes the response. In other words, this is where the content defined by the method called as a web service is sent back to the requesting client.

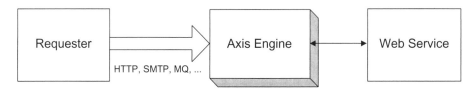

Figure 18.1   Axis acts as a facilitator between the client request and the code that executes as a web service.

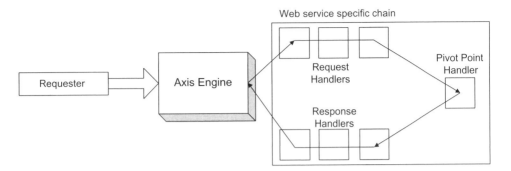

Figure 18.2 Axis allows the developer to define a series of handlers to partition the work performed on a web service request or response.

Handler chains are defined in a configuration document used by the Axis engine named (by default) server.config. This file is an XML document that defines configuration parameters for how Axis behaves. An example of a handler definition appears in section 18.4.2.

18.2.2 *Axis tools*

Axis comes with tools that make it easy to develop web services in Java. The first is a facility for creating simple web services; Axis creates the entire infrastructure for you. The other tools are transformation tools that take WSDL definitions and convert them to Java classes, and vice versa.

Simple web services

To create a simple web service, you can develop a web application that includes Axis and a publicly accessible file (available from the web application's root directory) with a .jws extension. Note that this isn't a standard extension—both Axis and WebLogic use this extension to define simple web services, but they aren't compatible. Listing 18.1 shows a simple Java source file that Axis will convert into a web service.

Listing 18.1 A simple Java source file with a .jws extension that Axis will convert into a web service

```
public class Simple {
    public String sayHello(String name) {
        return "Hello, " + name;
    }
}
```

Figure 18.3
Accessing the web service via an HTTP GET displays a message indicating that a web service is running at that URI.

When someone invokes the simple service via HTTP, Axis automatically builds the necessary infrastructure to make it accessible as a web service. Like a JSP, Axis generates a Java source file for the web service, compiles it, and redirects the request to it automatically. If you access this file through a browser (executing a GET instead of a POST, which calls the method), you see the message shown in figure 18.3.

Another facility offered by Axis is the automatic generation of a WSDL file for any web service (not just the ones created with a JWS file). To access the WSDL for the simple web service defined above, simply invoke it with ?WSDL tagged onto the end of the URI. A portion of the resulting WSDL is shown in figure 18.4.

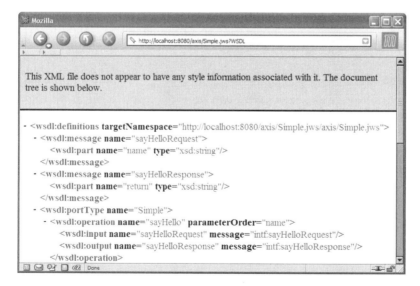

Figure 18.4   Axis automatically generates the WSDL for web services when you add the flag ?WSDL to the HTTP GET request of the web service.

WSDL2Java

To call a web service that already exists, you must generate Java interfaces and helper classes. Axis includes a tool called WSDL2Java that takes a WSDL file and generates all the necessary Java classes to call the web service. If you are familiar with RMI or CORBA, this process is exactly like running the rmic or idl2java compilers used for those distributed platforms. This similarity is not just skin deep. Every distributed architecture must supply a tool that allows you to translate back and forth between the native language representation of classes and objects and the distributed format for the same constructs.

Let's look at an example of what WSDL2Java produces. Consider the WSDL file generated from the simple web service defined in listing 18.1. Running WSDL2Java on that document produces four Java source files, summarized in table 18.1.

Table 18.1 WSDL2Java output

Java Source File	Description
Simple.java	The remotable interface that describes the method available through this web service (see listing 18.2).
SimpleService.java	The Java interface that defines methods that return an instance of a class implementing the Simple interface defined in Simple.java.
SimpleServiceLocator.java	A utility class for locating, binding, and returning a class that implements `SimpleService.java`. This is the class you call to bind to the web service.
SimpleSoapBindingStub.java	A class that implements all the details of actually calling the web service from the client.

As you can see, WSDL2Java performs a lot of work on your behalf. Fortunately, you don't have to understand anything about the internal structure of those generated classes. The only ones you care about are the interface and the `ServiceLocator`. The interface (`Simple.java`) appears in listing 18.2.

Listing 18.2 The Java class generated from the WSDL for the web service

```
/**
 * Simple.java
 *
 * This file was auto-generated from WSDL
 * by the Apache Axis WSDL2Java emitter.
 */

package localhost;
```

```
public interface Simple extends java.rmi.Remote {
    public java.lang.String sayHello(java.lang.String name)
            throws java.rmi.RemoteException;
}
```

The ServiceLocator class implements the methods you call to retrieve a class that implements the interface defined in listing 18.2. The SimpleServiceLocator class appears in listing 18.3.

Listing 18.3   The ServiceLocator helper class returns a class that calls the web service for you.

```
package localhost;

public class SimpleServiceLocator
    extends org.apache.axis.client.Service
    implements localhost.SimpleService {
    // Use to get a proxy class for Simple
    private final java.lang.String Simple_address =
            "http://localhost:8080/axis/Simple.jws";

    public String getSimpleAddress() {
        return Simple_address;
    }

    public localhost.Simple getSimple()
            throws javax.xml.rpc.ServiceException {
        java.net.URL endpoint;
        try {
            endpoint = new java.net.URL(Simple_address);
        } catch (java.net.MalformedURLException e) {
            return null;
        }

        return getSimple(endpoint);
    }

    public localhost.Simple getSimple(java.net.URL portAddress)
            throws javax.xml.rpc.ServiceException {
        try {
            return new localhost.SimpleSoapBindingStub(
                    portAddress, this);
        } catch (org.apache.axis.AxisFault e) {
            return null; // ???
        }
    }

    public java.rmi.Remote getPort(Class serviceEndpointInterface)
            throws javax.xml.rpc.ServiceException {
        try {
```

```
            if (localhost.Simple.class.isAssignableFrom(
                    serviceEndpointInterface))
                return new localhost.SimpleSoapBindingStub(
                        new java.net.URL(Simple_address), this);
        } catch (Throwable t) {
            throw new javax.xml.rpc.ServiceException(t);
        }

        throw new javax.xml.rpc.ServiceException(
                "There is no stub implementation:  " +
                ((serviceEndpointInterface == null)
                 ? "null"
                 : serviceEndpointInterface.getName()));
    }
}
```

You'll read about an example of using the WSDL2Java tool to call a web service not defined locally in section 18.3.

Java2WSDL

Axis also includes the Java2WSDL utility, which takes a Java interface and generates the necessary WSDL to implement it as a web service. Using this utility is certainly more complex than letting the Axis framework automatically generate the WSDL for you. Use it in cases where you need to customize the WSDL or the deployment options for your web service.

18.3 Calling web services

Calling web services using Axis is almost trivial. The hardest part is locating a web service you want to call. Numerous sites publish a list of web services. One of the very good ones is www.xmethods.com. All you nned to know to call the web service is the WSDL—Axis generates everything else you need.

For example, say you have a need in your application to be able to look up quotes from Shakespearean plays and get information about the plays. Fortunately, a web service exists to handle this job (you'll find it on the xmethods web site). The WSDL in question is www.xmlme.com/WSShakespeare.asmx?WSDL.

The first step is to run WSDL2Java on this WSDL file, which generates four files. Next, you can implement your class that needs to call the web service. This class is shown in listing 18.4.

Listing 18.4 This simple class calls the web service defined by the WSDL.

```
package com.nealford.art.ws.clientcall;

import java.rmi.RemoteException;
import javax.xml.rpc.ServiceException;
import com.xmlme.ShakespeareLocator;
import com.xmlme.ShakespeareSoap;

public class ShakespeareQuotes {
    public ShakespeareQuotes() {
        ShakespeareSoap bard = null;
        try {
            bard = new ShakespeareLocator().          ❶ Uses ServiceLocator
                            getShakespeareSoap();          to get web service
        } catch (ServiceException ex) {
            ex.printStackTrace();
        }
        String speech = "To be, or not to be";
        System.out.println("The quote:'" + speech + "'");
        try {
            System.out.println(bard.getSpeech(speech));  ❷ Calls the
        } catch (RemoteException ex1) {                      web service
        }
    }

    public static void main(String[] args) {
        new ShakespeareQuotes();
    }
}
```

❶ The `ServiceLocator` returns an instance of a class that implements the `Shakes-peareSoap` interface. This interface defines the lone method `getSpeech()`. Once you have the interface reference, you can treat the object as a local object.

❷ The call to `bard.getSpeech()` executes the web service and returns the matching speaker, play, and speech. The results of running this application are shown in figure 18.5.

As you can see, Axis makes it easy to consume web services in Java. One of the nice characteristics of web services as a distributed execution protocol is the irrelevance of what language or platform implements the web service method. The Shakespeare quote service happens to be implemented using the Microsoft .NET Framework, but I have no idea what language it uses. The only reason I know the implementation platform is that xmethods lists the technology. Consumers of web services don't have to care about details like data types, languages,

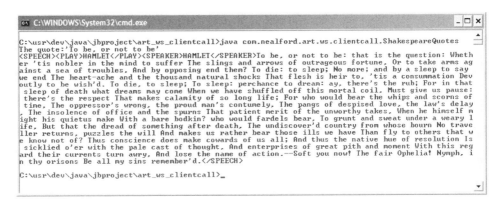

Figure 18.5   Running the ShakespeareQuotes application uses the web service to print out the play, the speaker, and the entire speech.

platforms, or operating systems. Web services act as a homogenizing layer for distributed computing.

18.4   eMotherEarth web services

Now that we've shown you how to create simple web services as well as how to consume them, let's add a couple of web services calls to the eMotherEarth application. As you know, this is an existing application, based on the chapter 13 example. Here, let's add two web service methods for orders: one to return the order status and another to return the shipping status. This sample appears in the source code archive as art_emotherearth_ws.

18.4.1   Configuration

Three configuration changes are required to retrofit the existing application to use a web service. Two are web service specific; the other is a change in the way we create database connections.

Changes to web.xml

The first step in adding a web service is to add the Axis JAR files to the existing project. The Axis JAR files include a servlet that acts as the Axis engine when embedded in a larger web application. To enable this servlet, add a reference to the web.xml configuration file along with a URL mapping that uses prefix mapping to send anything identified as "service" to the `AxisServlet`. Listing 18.5 shows these two entries.

Listing 18.5 Adding Axis support to web.xml

```
<servlet>
  <servlet-name>AxisServlet</servlet-name>
  <display-name>Apache-Axis Servlet</display-name>
  <servlet-class>
      org.apache.axis.transport.http.AxisServlet
  </servlet-class>
</servlet>

<!-- items omitted here -->

<servlet-mapping>
  <servlet-name>AxisServlet</servlet-name>
  <url-pattern>/services/*</url-pattern>
</servlet-mapping>
```

Database connections

The welcome servlet creates the database connection pool when the user first accesses it. Creating the connection pool in the welcome servlet is a given when it is solely a web application. However, we can no longer assume that a user will hit the application first. It is now a service called programmatically. To solve this problem, we must ensure that the database connection pool is established as soon as the application starts. Several ways exist to handle this, including using database connection pooling built into the servlet engine. However, we don't want to rely on that because it isn't standard across servlet engines.

The web service isn't implemented as a servlet—it is a simple Java class. Therefore, it will not have access to the standard web collections. Even when the welcome servlet loads on startup, that still doesn't make it any easier to deliver a database connection from the pool to the web service.

The easiest solution is to create a class that has characteristics of both a singleton object and a servlet. It isn't possible to create a singleton servlet (they are already a kind of singleton), but it is possible to borrow the singleton concept of allowing a class to hold on to a reference. The servlet engine creates and maintains the servlet objects for you. However, it never reveals the name of the object. Listing 18.6 shows the implementation of a ConnectionPoolProxy class.

Listing 18.6 The ConnectionPoolProxy is a servlet that maintains an internal reference to itself.

```
package com.nealford.art.emotherearth.util;

import javax.servlet.GenericServlet;
```

```
import javax.servlet.ServletException;
import javax.servlet.ServletRequest;                         Extends
import javax.servlet.ServletResponse;                        GenericServlet

public class ConnectionPoolProxy extends GenericServlet {    ❶
    static private ConnectionPoolProxy cpp;          ❷              Holds a private
                                                                    instance of
    public void init() throws ServletException {     ❸              itself
        cpp = this;           Saves a reference to the object
    }                          created by servlet engine

    public void service(ServletRequest req, ServletResponse res)  ❹
            throws javax.servlet.ServletException,
            java.io.IOException {                          Contains a required
        //-- intentionally left blank                       (but empty)
    }                                                       service() method

    public static ConnectionPoolProxy getInstance() {  ❺   Returns an
        return cpp;                                         instance of
    }                                                       the servlet
                                           Returns the
    public DBPool getDbPool() {     ❻      connection
        return (DBPool) getServletContext().getAttribute("dbPool");
    }
}
```

❶ The ConnectionPoolProxy class extends GenericServlet so that the servlet engine
can automatically create it.

❷ Like a singleton, the servlet class holds a private static reference to itself.

❸ In the init() method (after the servlet engine has created the servlet object), the
servlet class stores the object reference in the static variable.

❹ The service() method is required but not used in this class.

❺ The getInstance() method is also similar to a singleton—it returns the internal
reference to the object held by the servlet engine.

❻ The getDbPool() method has full access to the servlet context collection, where
the welcome servlet placed the connection pool upon startup.

The web.xml file has both the welcome and ConnectionPoolProxy servlets load
on startup. The web service can use the ConnectionPoolProxy class name to get an
instance of the object owned by the servlet engine.

Server.config

Implementing web services using the JWS file is simple. However, Axis builds a
web service call for every public method in the class. Obviously, there are

situations where that would be undesirable. Because we aren't going to implement our web service as a JWS file, we must configure Axis to publish it. We can accomplish that via an XML document named server-config.wsdd, which resides in the WEB-INF directory. It defines all the handlers for Axis and contains numerous entries for the built-in handlers for Axis. Listing 18.7 shows the excerpt for our web service methods.

Listing 18.7 The server-config.wsdd entries for the new web services

```
<!-- service registration for Order Status -->
<service name="OrderStatus" provider="java:RPC">
  <parameter name="className"
             value="com.nealford.art.emotherearth.ws.OrderInfo"/>
  <parameter name="allowedMethods"
    value="getWsDescription, getOrderStatus, getShippingStatus"/>
</service>
```

The configuration entry in listing 18.7 creates an OrderStatus web service name, using the RPC semantics to call it. The class that implements the web service is OrderInfo, which publishes three methods: getWsDescription(), getOrderStatus(), and getShippingStatus(). This entry exposes the methods of the class as calls that will be available to clients. None of the other methods of the class are affected.

18.4.2 Orders

The existing application handles orders in the typical Model 2 fashion. An Order boundary class returns instances of order entity objects. For the purposes of this web service, we don't need an entire order object. All we need is the status for a particular order whose key is passed. While we could have the boundary class return an entire order entity for this purpose, it is a waste of resources to do so.

One of the key characteristics of web services is that the method calls are generally stateless. This is a requirement imposed by the protocol used to call them (HTTP). As with web pages, the calls to web service methods are stateless. Therefore, it is always a good idea to make the web services methods as cohesive as possible so that they don't perform needless work. Notice that this paradigm fits nicely with the idea of a stateless session EJB. It is easy to place a web services layer over an existing stateless session bean method call.

Order boundary

To add the web services layer, we don't need the state implied by creating an entire entity object just to access one field. This is a case wherein a few stateless methods added to the boundary class supplies all the information we need. For the web service, we add three new methods to the boundary, and the entity incurs no changes. Listing 18.8 shows the added methods.

Listing 18.8   Methods added to the OrdersDb boundary

```
private String getStatusFor(String sql, int orderKey) throws
        SQLException {
    Connection c = null;
    PreparedStatement ps = null;
    ResultSet rs = null;
    String result = "Error: Order not found";
    try {
        c = dbPool.getConnection();
        ps = c.prepareStatement(sql);
        ps.setInt(1, orderKey);
        rs = ps.executeQuery();
        if (rs.next())
            result = rs.getString(1);
    } finally {
        ps.close();
        dbPool.release(c);
    }
    return result;
}

public String getShippingStatus(int orderKey)
        throws SQLException {
    return getStatusFor(SQL_GET_SHIPPING_STATUS, orderKey);
}

public String getOrderStatus(int orderKey) throws SQLException {
    return getStatusFor(SQL_GET_ORDER_STATUS, orderKey);
}
```

The primary method we added to OrderDb is a helper method that gets the status for either an order or shipping. Because the infrastructure of both calls is identical, the single getStatusFor() method handles the details of querying the database. The two methods used by the web service call the helper method with the appropriate SQL (defined in a constant) and the order key.

The orders web service

The web service itself is also simple. As we mentioned earlier, Axis handles the details of creating the web services infrastructure. The developer of the web service need only worry about delivering the information. The OrderInfo class that defines the web service methods appears in listing 18.9.

Listing 18.9 The OrderInfo class defines the web service methods.

```
package com.nealford.art.emotherearth.ws;

import java.sql.SQLException;
import com.nealford.art.emotherearth.boundary.OrderDb;
import com.nealford.art.emotherearth.util.ConnectionPoolProxy;
import com.nealford.art.emotherearth.util.DBPool;

public class OrderInfo {

    public String getWsDescription() {
        return "eMotherEarth order information";
    }

    public String getOrderStatus(int orderKey) {
        OrderDb orderDb = new OrderDb();
        orderDb.setDbPool(getConnectionPool());
        try {
            return orderDb.getOrderStatus(orderKey);
        } catch (SQLException ex) {
            return "error accessing status: " + ex.getMessage();
        }
    }

    public String getShippingStatus(int orderKey) {
        OrderDb orderDb = new OrderDb();
        orderDb.setDbPool(getConnectionPool());
        try {
            return orderDb.getShippingStatus(orderKey);
        } catch (SQLException ex) {
            return "error accessing status: " + ex.getMessage();
        }
    }

    private DBPool getConnectionPool() {
        return ConnectionPoolProxy.getInstance().getDbPool();
    }

}
```

The OrderInfo class implements a stateless call to the OrderDb boundary class that gets the status information and a call that returns a simple description.

The `OrderInfo` class accesses the connection pool through the `ConnectionPool-Proxy` defined in listing 18.6. That class acts as a bridge between the web API world (which contains the collections that owns the connection pool) and this simple class.

The class is itself a proxy for the `OrderDb` boundary. While you could add these methods directly to the boundary class, we don't recommend that. Classes should be as cohesive as possible. Adding web service methods to a boundary class dilutes its purpose. No class should perform two distinct jobs. You are much better off keeping the classes as simple and cohesive as possible. This class utilizes the order boundary, but it does so by asking the boundary to perform its single job: accessing information from the persistence layer.

Axis automatically maps Java types to the appropriate WSDL types so that the developer of the implementing class doesn't have to worry about them. The Java2WSDL utility will even generate the necessary code for user-defined classes, making them legal WSDL types. As you are writing classes targeted as web services like the one shown here, you don't have to be concerned about typing and other details of the distributed protocol.

18.4.3 *Calling the web service*

For testing purposes, JUnit makes a great test client. It contains code external to the web application with very little infrastructure. It also lets you implement your web services one feature at a time and apply immediate testing to make sure it works.

To utilize the web service that now exists in eMotherEarth, we created a desktop application that can check on the status of an order. This application allows the user to enter an order key and get back the corresponding status information. This application is shown in figure 18.6.

To call the web service, we must first call WSDL2Java on the WSDL returned from the web service. Executing WSDL2Java yields several source files, only two of which are directly used by the desktop application. The first is the Java interface that defines the methods. This interface appears in listing 18.10.

Figure 18.6 This desktop application calls the eMotherEarth status web service to find out the status of an order.

Listing 18.10 The OrderInfo interface, generated by WSDL2Java

```
/**
 * OrderInfo.java
 *
 * This file was auto-generated from WSDL
 * by the Apache Axis WSDL2Java emitter.
 */

package localhost;

public interface OrderInfo extends java.rmi.Remote {
    public java.lang.String getWsDescription()
            throws java.rmi.RemoteException;

    public java.lang.String getOrderStatus(int orderKey)
            throws java.rmi.RemoteException;

    public java.lang.String getShippingStatus(int orderKey)
            throws java.rmi.RemoteException;
}
```

The `OrderInfo` interface defines how the client application will make the calls to the web service. The other file generated by WSDL2Java is the service locator class, which returns a concrete class that implements the interface.

Most of the code in the application is Swing user interface code that has no bearing on the web services aspect of this application, so it won't be shown. The only code of interest is the code in the event handler for the button that invokes the web service. This event handler appears in listing 18.11.

Listing 18.11 The event handler code that calls the web service

```
void btnInvokeWs_actionPerformed(ActionEvent e) {
    localhost.OrderInfo ws;
    try {
        ws = new localhost.OrderInfoServiceLocator().
                getOrderStatus();
    } catch (javax.xml.rpc.ServiceException jre) {
        if (jre.getLinkedCause() != null) {
            jre.getLinkedCause().printStackTrace();
        }
        throw new RuntimeException(
                "JAX-RPC ServiceException caught: " + jre);
    }

    try {
        int orderNo =
                Integer.parseInt(jTextField1.getText());
        ws.getShippingStatus(orderNo);
```

```
        lblOrderStatus.setText(ws.getOrderStatus(orderNo));
        lblShippingStatus.setText(
                ws.getShippingStatus(orderNo));
    } catch (java.rmi.RemoteException re) {
        throw new RuntimeException("Web service call failed");
    }
}
```

The event handler uses the service locator class to get the instance of the web service and then calls the methods defined in the interface based on the information supplied by the user.

Calling the web service from other languages

One of the benefits of using web services is cross-language and cross-platform support. To illustrate this, we created a simple console application in C# that calls the eMotherEarth status web service. The C# class appears in listing 18.12.

Listing 18.12 This C# class calls the eMotherEarth status web services.

```
using System;

namespace art_emotherearth_ws {
    class Class1 {
        [STAThread]
        static void Main() {
            com.nealford.art.emotherearth.OrderInfoService
                orderInfo = new com.nealford.art.emotherearth.
                        OrderInfoService();
            Console.WriteLine("Order status for order # 1 is " +
                orderInfo.getOrderStatus(1));
            Console.WriteLine("Shipping status for order # 1 is " +
                orderInfo.getShippingStatus(1));
        }
    }
}
```

This level of cross-platform and -language support is one of the key factors in making web services the dominant distributed computing platform, especially for stateless information exchange.

18.5 *Summary*

Web services is the umbrella term defining RPCs over HTTP using SOAP. The open standard defines the semantics of the calls, a description service (WSDL), and a directory mechanism (UDDI). The standard includes capabilities for numerous protocols, but from a practical standpoint, HTTP is the primary protocol of interest.

The Axis project is a complete rewrite of the previous open-source project that enabled SOAP messaging from Java. It includes a framework and tools to make it easy to add support for web services to Java applications, especially web applications. Axis includes tools that generate Java classes from WSDL documents and that generate WSDL documents from Java classes. It also provides a facility similar to the JSP mechanism that automatically generates the appropriate infrastructure for a Java class (named with a .jws extension) for making SOAP calls against it. For any web service defined using Axis, the WSDL for that web service is available by performing an HTTP GET operation and adding the parameter ?WSDL to the URL.

Creating a web service in a Model 2 application requires creating stateless methods that will be called via HTTP. Some infrastructure changes are necessary, as demonstrated in the eMotherEarth application. Most of the changes dealt with the logistics of connection pooling and startup code execution because of the stateless nature of the web services call. The actual methods we added to the OrderDb boundary class and the web service class itself were minimal.

Once the web service exists, client applications (written in any language that supports web services) can call it. The client applications need only access the WSDL for the web service, which defines all the semantics of how to call the web service.

Axis lets you easily add web service support to web applications. If the application is architected using Model 2, which promotes the separation of responsibilities, the changes required to implement stateless web service methods calls are simple.

In the final chapter, we talk about what isn't covered in this book.

What won't fit in this book

This chapter covers

- Persistence options
- HTML and the user interface
- JavaScript

In lieu of trying to cram all the topics involved in building web applications into a single volume, we've included in this chapter the important items that are beyond the scope of this book. We chose this arrangement because these topics are too large to fit into a single chapter (or in some cases, a single book).

The topics covered here (persistence, the user interface, and JavaScript) are critical parts of a web developer's arsenal. You should be familiar with all three even if you don't address them daily.

19.1 Persistence

Persistence in this context refers to storing information externally, typically in a relational database. Although that sounds like a simple chore, a vast amount of research and code has been written for managing this process. Consequently, several options are available to help you achieve data persistence. They range from simple Java objects to entire complex APIs managed by Sun.

19.1.1 Plain old Java objects

The strategy we've adopted throughout most of this book involves using plain old Java objects (POJOs). This approach entails creating boundary objects in the application that are "normal" classes and that don't implement any special persistence API. You can find many examples of this type of database access in virtually every chapter, including the evolution, framework, and best practices parts of the book (see chapters 2, 4, and 13). For detailed coverage of the POJOs in use, consult chapter 4, section 4.1.1, which discusses the POJO implementation used for the generic Model 2 applications as well as the POJOs used for all the frameworks (except InternetBeans Express).

The developer attitude has come full circle on the use of POJOs. They were once ridiculed as too simple to be effective, and numerous other approaches have been developed (some of which we discuss in the sections that follow). However, building an effective persistence layer is difficult and requires generating complex APIs. Many developers, especially of small and medium-sized applications, have come back to POJO as a simple, effective persistence mechanism.

19.1.2 Enterprise JavaBeans

One of the most popular topics in the Java universe is Enterprise JavaBeans (EJBs). Many books are available that cover this subject in detail. *Art of Java Web*

Development covers EJBs in chapter 12, which discusses how well-designed Model 2 applications port easily to EJBs by making the boundary classes proxies for the corresponding EJBs.

The EJB standard is quite complex, with various specifications and versions. Like most of the solutions from Sun, it is a well-thought-out specification that successfully manages to handle the intricate problem of efficient persistence between Java objects and traditional databases. It has proved its worth in complex, scalable deployments.

Developers' primary complaint against EJBs is the shear complexity of the API and the code that underpins it. No one denies that a generic persistence layer is a complicated undertaking, but some wonder if there might be an easier way that doesn't mean sacrificing the power and scalability of EJB. In any case, EJB is currently the gold standard for scalable applications.

19.1.3 *Java data objects (JDO)*

The Java data object (JDO) provides a persistence mechanism that doesn't force the developer to know how to map Java classes to any type of foreign model. For example, to use POJO and JDBC, you must understand and build the relationship between your Java objects and the set-based nature of SQL. To use container-managed EJBs, you must define the relationships between the class and the relational world. JDO allows the developer to create classes with no extraneous code in them for persistence. The metadata relating to the class resides in an XML document, and JDO takes care of persistence, transaction management, and similar services.

Java serialization provides much of the same transparency. However, it is not suitable for a robust persistence layer because it does not support transaction processing and other necessary features. JDO is designed as an alternative to container-managed entity beans because it is much simpler for the developer to implement while providing some of the same benefits. JDO utilizes an API for generating the necessary code to handle persistence, which frequently operates on the byte code of the classes that are to be persisted.

JDO is an official extension to Java, sanctioned by Sun, and provides a reasonable alternative to other persistence schemes. Using JDO, the boundary classes found in *Art of Java Web Development* would essentially vanish, while JDO would manage the services provided by the boundaries. JDO is a powerful way to create a persistence layer that is robust yet simple. Time will tell if it scales well enough to become the de facto standard for data access.

19.1.4   *Hibernate*

Hibernate, an open-source alternative to JDO and EJB, is an object/relational persistence and query service. It allows you to create "normal" Java classes and utilizes all the features of Java's object-oriented nature. For example, you can use composition, inheritance, polymorphism, and the collections framework to create your object hierarchy. Hibernate uses the reflection API in Java to handle persistence. One of the common rumors in Java is that the reflection API is not efficient. While that may have been true in the first versions of the SDK, it is no longer the case. Reflection in Java is efficient and fast in modern SDKs. Hibernate takes advantage of this language feature by building a persistence mechanism around it. It does not require any code generation (like EJB) or byte-code processing (like JDO) to work. Instead, SQL generation occurs at system startup.

Hibernate handles mappings to all major database vendors. It has defined a mechanism that maps Java objects to relational databases and leaves the intrinsic relationships intact. Because it uses its own mapping mechanism, you may find it difficult to use the tables generated by Hibernate in other, non-Java applications because you must understand how Hibernate performs its mappings.

Hibernate is a popular open-source project, with many loyal followers. The Hibernate developers have taken yet another approach to the object/relational mapping problem. It combines the desirable characteristics of being lightweight and providing high performance and is an excellent alternative for applications that are primarily Java based.

19.2   *HTML and the user interface*

Not many developers have the ability to create an effective and attractive user interface (UI). It is a specialized part of software development, best handled by experts in usability. Developers who write low-level code have produced some truly hideous UIs.

One of the benefits of the Model 2 architecture espoused in *Art of Java Web Development* is the clean separation of behavior from the UI. Once you achieve that goal, you can leave the design of the UI to an expert. However, all developers should know some of the details of building HTML UIs. As you can tell by looking at the UI of all the samples in this book, I am not, nor do I pretend to be, a user interface designer. The UI of each sample is left as simple as possible.

19.2.1 *HTML/XHTML*

You can find all kinds of books that cover HTML syntax and programming, as well as many sophisticated tools. The non-UI developer's job is twofold: to ensure that any HTML generated by custom tags or other programming elements adheres to the HTML standards, and to stay out of the way of the UI designer as much as possible.

An emerging standard for HTML is Extensible HTML (XHTML), which applies the stricter rules of XML to HTML. The use of XHTML is an encouraging trend because it removes the long list of exceptions that browsers must support for standard HTML. As a developer, you should make the effort to move your HTML to XHTML for two reasons. First, XHTML will eventually supplant HTML, so building your artifacts in XHTML anticipates future needs. This includes not only the explicit UI pieces but also any code generated by custom tags or Java code.

Second, because XHTML is a variant of XML, you can both check your syntax and validate the document. That way, you can rest assured that you're creating UIs that you know are both syntactically and semantically correct (and render correctly in different browsers). While HTML can also be validated, the rules and infrastructure for XML validation are much stronger.

19.2.2 *Cascading Style Sheets*

The other UI technology with which you should be familiar is Cascading Style Sheets (CSS). CSS allows you to create templates to achieve a particular look and feel for output in your HTML document. A CSS can include colors, fonts, and a host of other UI-related items.

CSS is the preferred technique for handling as much of the look and feel of the UI as possible. It is important not to generate any code that conflicts with CSS's ability to perform this task. For example, it is a bad idea to hard-code colors, fonts, and other visual elements in Java code, JSP, servlets, or custom tags. You should always make your code CSS-friendly, which gives the UI designer full latitude in creating (and changing) the look and feel of the application.

This book doesn't include any HTML that utilizes CSS, but that omission should not be viewed as a dislike or underappreciation of the power of this facility. Our goal was to keep the focus strictly on the code and architecture. It is up to a UI designer to take what we have created and make it suitable for public consumption.

19.3 *JavaScript*

The topic of JavaScript appears in chapter 12, during our discussion of client-side validation. That chapter also explained the rationale for using JavaScript to handle client-side chores. JavaScript is a perfectly good language for handling the problems for which it was designed. Developers get into trouble with it (and other scripting languages) when they try to build too much in the scripting language.

Scripting languages are designed for ease of use and quick implementation. Characteristics of higher-level languages, like strong typing, improved scoping, and object-oriented features, don't appear in JavaScript. The emphasis lies with quick implementation and using the prebuilt object model to manipulate elements in the HTML document or provide validations.

In chapter 12, you learned how to avoid placing your business rules solely in the view part of the application, which violates the tenants of Model 2 architecture. Instead, the JavaScript is generated as a field of the model bean and inserted using a standard JSP tag:

```
<input name="duration" size="16"
    value="<jsp:getProperty name="scheduleItem"
          property="duration"/>"
    onBlur="<jsp:getProperty name="scheduleItem"
          property="startValidationJS"/>"/>
```

Many developers think that this is a radical idea, and that I'm going too far in keeping the business rules so adamantly in the server. The reason I feel so strongly is simple: I've had to maintain too many web applications that suffered from poor separation of concerns. While extreme, using this technique ensures that all the business rules reside in a single location.

I have nothing against JavaScript. In fact, it is one of my favorite scripting languages. I'm not even opposed to using scripting languages to handle the jobs for which they were designed. I just want to warn you against the practice of trying to do too much in the scripting language and thus compromising the overall architecture, design, and performance of your application.

JavaScript is necessary for building web applications. As such, it is an important weapon in the arsenal of web developers. However, it is a weapon whose use can damage the wielder as much as the target. Some frameworks (like the Struts Validator) automatically generate JavaScript for you—which is the best of both worlds because you get the capabilities of JavaScript in the client without having to maintain the generated code. Someone else has already implemented common JavaScript functionality, freeing the developer to focus on the web application's server-side implementation.

19.4 Summary

No single book can cover the entire breadth and depth of a topic as large and varied as web development. This book examines the critically important areas of architecture, design, and effective best practices. However, some topics are simply too large or too peripheral to provide adequate coverage in one volume.

Persistence is a pervasive problem in all software development, aggravated by the impedance mismatch between object-oriented language and relational databases. A couple of alternatives exist for persistence. The first, Java data objects, is an official Java extension. It manages persistence by modifying byte codes based on metadata about your classes, stored in an XML configuration document. Another persistence mechanism is the open-source project Hibernate, which uses the native Java facilities for reflection to handle automatic persistence of entities.

Web applications ultimately generate UIs in either HTML or XHTML. Although UI design is best left to experts, web developers should understand some aspects of HTML. In particular, web developers must be careful not to generate code within servlets or custom tags that undermine the work of the visual designers. Cascading Style Sheets are the preferred way to handle visual elements on web pages, and the web designer must take care not to interfere with that mechanism, either.

JavaScript is the best of the client-side scripting languages for browsers (and the only one universally supported, albeit with slight differences among browser vendors). The use of JavaScript for validations and other simple tasks is a key element in effective web applications. However, it offers a double-edged sword, because too much scripting code compromises the maintainability of the application.

bibliography

Beck, Kent. *Smalltalk Best Practice Patterns.* Upper Saddle River, N.J.: Prentice Hall PTR, 1996.

Gamma, Erich, Richard Helm, Ralph Johnson, and John Vlissides. *Design Patterns: Elements of Reusable Object-Oriented Software.* Reading, Mass.: Addison-Wesley, 1994.

Hatcher, Erik, and Steve Loughran. *Java Development with Ant.* Greenwich, Conn.: Manning Publications, 2002.

Husted, Ted, Cedric Dumoulin, George Franciscus, and David Winterfeldt. *Struts in Action: Building Web Applications with the Leading Java Framework.* Greenwich, Conn.: Manning Publications, 2002.

Kernighan, Brian, and Rob Pike. *The Practice of Programming.* Reading, Mass.: Addison-Wesley, 1999.

Lewis Ship, Howard. *Tapestry in Action.* Greenwich, Conn.: Manning Publications, 2003.

Massol, Vincent and Ted Husted. *JUnit in Action.* Greenwich, Conn.: Manning Publications, 2003.

Shachor, Gal, Adam Chace, and Magnus Rydin. *JSP Tag Libraries.* Greenwich, Conn.: Manning Publications, 2001.

index

571